CHILTON BOOK COMPANY

REPAIR & TUNE-UP GUIDE

TOYOTA CORONA / CROWN CRESSIDA / MARK II VAN 1970-86

All U.S. and Canadian models

Vice President and General Manager JOHN P. KUSHNERICK
Editor-in-Chief KERRY A. FREEMAN, S.A.E.
Managing Editor DEAN F. MORGANTINI, S.A.E.
Senior Editor RICHARD J. RIVELE, S.A.E.
Senior Editor W. CALVIN SETTLE, JR., S.A.E.
Editor JOHN BAXTER

CHILTON BOOK COMPANY
Radnor, Pennsylvania
19089

SAFETY NOTICE

Proper service and repair procedures are vital to the safe, reliable operation of all motor vehicles, as well as the personal safety of those performing repairs. This book outlines procedures for servicing and repairing vehicles using safe, effective methods. The procedures contain many NOTES, CAUTIONS and WARNINGS which should be followed along with standard safety procedures to eliminate the possibility of personal injury or improper service which could damage the vehicle or compromise its safety.

It is important to note that repair procedures and techniques, tools and parts for servicing motor vehicles, as well as the skill and experience of the individual performing the work vary widely. It is not possible to anticipate all of the conceivable ways or conditions under which vehicles may be serviced, or to provide cautions as to all of the possible hazards that may result. Standard and accepted safety precautions and equipment should be used when handling toxic or flammable fluids, and safety goggles or other protection should be used during cutting, grinding, chiseling, prying, or any other process that can cause material removal or projectiles.

Some procedures require the use of tools specially designed for a specific purpose. Before substituting another tool or procedure, you must be completely satisfied that neither your personal safety, nor the performance of the vehicle will be endangered.

Although information in this guide is based on industry sources and is as complete as possible at the time of publication, the possibility exists that the manufacturer made later changes which could not be included here. While striving for total accuracy, Chilton Book Company cannot assume responsibility for any errors, changes, or omissions that may occur in the compilation of this data.

PART NUMBERS

Part numbers listed in this reference are not recommendations by Chilton for any product by brand name. They are references that can be used with interchange manuals and aftermarket supplier catalogs to locate each brand supplier's discrete part number.

SPECIAL TOOLS

Special tools are recommended by the vehicle manufacturer to perform their specific job. Use has been kept to a minimum, but where absolutely necessary, they are referred to in the text by the part number of the tool manufacturer. These tools can be purchased, under the appropriate part number, from Toyota dealers or Toyota Motor Sales, U.S.A. (address below) or an equivalent tool can be purchased locally from a tool supplier or parts outlet. Before substituting any tool for the one recommended, read the SAFETY NOTICE at the top of this page.

ACKNOWLEDGEMENTS

The Chilton Book Company expresses appreciation to Toyota Motor Sales, U.S.A., Inc. 2055 W. 190th Street, Torrance, California 90504, Biscotte Toyota, 2062 W. Main Street, Norristown, Pennsylvania 19401 and Speedcraft Enterprises, Inc., Devon, Pennsylvania 19333 for their generous assistance.

Manufactured in the United States of America
    4567890   65432109

Chilton's Repair & Tune-Up Guide: Toyota Corona/Crown/Cressida/Mark II/Van 1970–86
ISBN 0-8019-7674-X pbk.
Library of Congress Catalog Card No. 85-47976

CONTENTS

Quick Reference
Specifications For Your Vehicle

Fill in this chart with the most commonly used specifications for your vehicle. Specifications can be found in Chapters 1 through 3 or on the tune-up decal under the hood of the vehicle.

Tune-Up

Firing Order_____

Spark Plugs:

    Type_____

    Gap (in.)_____

Torque (ft. lbs.)_____

Idle Speed (rpm)_____

Ignition Timing (°)_____

    Vacuum or Electronic Advance (Connected/Disconnected)_____

Valve Clearance (in.)

    Intake_____   Exhaust_____

Capacities

Engine Oil Type (API Rating)_____

    With Filter Change (qts)_____

    Without Filter Change (qts)_____

Cooling System (qts)_____

Manual Transmission (pts)_____

    Type_____

Automatic Transmission (pts)_____

    Type_____

Front Differential (pts)_____

    Type_____

Rear Differential (pts)_____

    Type_____

Transfer Case (pts)_____

    Type_____

FREQUENTLY REPLACED PARTS
Use these spaces to record the part numbers of frequently replaced parts.

PCV VALVE	OIL FILTER	AIR FILTER	FUEL FILTER
Type_____	Type_____	Type_____	Type_____
Part No._____	Part No._____	Part No._____	Part No._____

General Information and Maintenance

HOW TO USE THIS BOOK

Chilton's Repair and Tune-Up Guide for the Toyota Corona, Cressida, Crown, Mark II and Van is designed for the car owner who wishes to do some of the service on his/her own car. Included are step-by-step instructions for maintenance, troubleshooting and repair or replacement of many of the components on your car.

Corona, Cressida, Crown, Mark II, and Van models, from 1970 through 1986 are covered by this guide. Separate Chilton Repair and Tune-Up Guides are available for other Toyota cars and trucks.

This book is organized so that the most often used portions appear at the front, the least used portions at the rear. The first chapter covers all the information that may be required at a moment's notice, information like the locations of the various serial numbers, and proper towing instructions. Chapter 1 will probably be the most often used part of the book because of the need to carefully follow the maintenance schedule which it includes to ensure good performance and long component life. Chapter 2 covers tune-up and will be used regularly to keep the engine running at peak performance and to restore operation in case of failure of any of the more delicate components. Chapters 3 through 10 cover repairs (rather than maintenance) for various portions of the car, with each chapter covering either one system or two related systems. The appendix then lists general information which may be used in rebuilding the engine or performing some other operation on any car.

In using the Table of Contents, refer to the bold listings for the beginning of the chapter. See the smaller listings or the index for information on a particular component or specifications.

In general, there are three things a profi-cient mechanic has which must be allowed for when a nonprofessional does work on his car. These are:

1. A sound knowledge of the construction of the parts he is working with, their order of assembly, etc.

2. A knowledge of potentially hazardous situations.

3. Manual dexterity, which includes the ability to put the right amount of torque on a part to ensure that it will not be damaged or warped.

This book provides step-by-step instructions and illustrations wherever possible. Use them carefully and wisely. Do not just jump head-long into disassembly. Where you are not sure about being able to readily reassemble something, make a careful drawing of it before beginning to take it apart. Assembly always looks simple when everything is still assembled.

Cautions and notes will be provided where appropriate to help keep you from injuring yourself or damaging the car. Therefore, you should read through the entire procedure before beginning work, and make sure that you are aware of the warnings. Since no number of warnings could cover every possible situation, you should work slowly and try to envision what is going to happen in each operation ahead of time.

When it comes to tightening things, there is generally a slim area between too loose to properly seal or resist vibration and so tight as to risk damage or warping. When dealing with major engine parts, or with any aluminum component, it pays to procure a torque wrench and go by the recommended figures.

When reference is made in this book to the right side or left side of the car, it should be understood that these positions are to be viewed from the front seat. Thus, the left side of the car is always the driver's side, even when one is facing the car, as when working on the engine.

We have attempted to eliminate the use of special tools wherever possible, substituting more readily available hand tools. However, in some cases, the special tools are necessary. These can be purchased from your Toyota dealer, or from an automotive parts store.

Safety is an important factor when performing any service operation. Areas of special hazard are noted in the text; but common sense should always prevail.

Here are some general safety rules:

1. When working around gasoline or its vapors, don't smoke, and remember to be careful about sparks which could ignite it.

2. Always support the car securely with jackstands (not milk crates!) if it is necessary to raise it. Don't rely on a tire changing jack as the only means of support. Be sure that the jackstands have a rated load capacity adequate for your car.

3. Block the wheels of the car which remain on the ground, if only one end is being raised. If the front end is being raised, set the parking brake as well.

4. If a car equipped with an automatic transmission must be operated with the engine running and the transmission in gear, always set the parking brake and block the front wheels.

5. If the engine is running, watch out for the cooling fan blades. Be sure that clothing, hair, tools, etc., can't get caught in them.

6. If you are using metal tools around or if you are working near the battery terminals, it is a good idea to disconnect it.

7. If you want to crank the engine, but don't want it to start, remove the high tension lead which runs from the coil to the distributor.

8. Most importantly, try to be patient, even in the midst of an argument with a particularly stubborn bolt; reaching for the largest hammer in the garage is usually a cause for later regret and more extensive repair. As you gain confidence and experience, working on your car will become a source of pride and satisfaction.

TOOLS AND EQUIPMENT

The service procedures in this book presuppose a familiarity with hand tools and their proper use. However, it is possible that you may have a limited amount of experience with the sort of equipment needed to work on an automobile. This section is designed to help you assemble a basic set of tools that will handle most of the jobs you may undertake.

In addition to the normal assortment of screwdrivers and pliers, automotive service work requires an investment in wrenches, sockets and the handles needed to drive them, and various measuring tools such as torque wrenches and feeler gauges.

You will find that virtually every nut and bolt on your Toyota is metric. Therefore, despite a few close size similarities, standard inch-size tools will not fit and must not be used. You will need a set of metric wrenches as your most basic tool kit, ranging from about 6mm to 17mm in size. High quality forged wrenches are available in three styles: open end, box end, and combination open/box end. The combination tools are generally the most desirable as a starter set; the wrenches shown in the illustration are of the combination type.

The other set of tools inevitably required is a ratchet handle and socket set. This set should have the same size range as your wrench set. The ratchet, extension, and flex drives for the sockets are available in many sizes; it is advisable to choose a $\frac{3}{8}''$ drive set initially. One break in the inch/metric sizing war is that metric-sized sockets sold in the U.S. have inch-sized drive ($\frac{1}{4}$, $\frac{3}{8}$, $\frac{1}{2}$, etc.). Thus, if you already have an inch-sized socket set, you need only buy new metric sockets in the sizes needed. Sockets are available in six and twelve point versions; six point types are stronger and are a good choice for a first set. The choice of a drive handle for the sockets should be made with some care. If this is your first set, take the plunge and invest in a flex-head ratchet; it will get into many places otherwise accessible only through a long chain of universal joints, extensions, and adapters. An alternative is a flex handle, which lacks the ratcheting feature but has a head which pivots 180°; such a tool is shown below the ratchet handle in the illustration. In addition to the range of sockets mentioned, a rubber-lined spark plug socket should be purchased. The correct size for the plugs in your Toyota's engine is $\frac{13}{16}''$.

The most important thing to consider when purchasing hand tools is quality. Don't be misled by the low cost of bargain tools. Forged wrenches, tempered screwdriver blades, and fine tooth ratchets are much better investments than their less expensive counterparts. The skinned knuckles and frustration inflicted by poor quality tools make any job an unhappy chore. Another consideration is that quality tools come with an unbeatable replacement guarantee, if the tool breaks, you get a new one, no questions asked.

Most jobs can be accomplished using the tools on the accompanying lists. There will be an occasional need for a special tool, such as

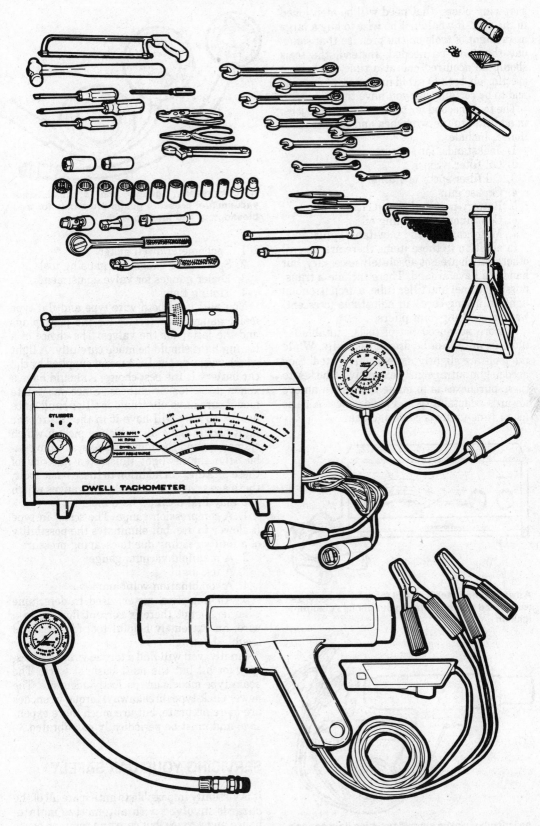

A basic collection of hand tools is necessary for automotive services

snap ring pliers; that need will be mentioned in the text. It would not be wise to buy a large assortment of tools on the premise that some-day they will be needed. Instead, the tools should be acquired one at a time, each for a specific job, both to avoid unnecessary expense and to be certain that you have the right tool.

The tools needed for basic maintenance jobs, in addition to the wrenches and sockets mentioned, include:

1. Jackstands, for support
2. Oil filter wrench
3. Oil filter spout or funnel
4. Grease gun
5. Battery post and clamp cleaner
6. Container for draining oil
7. Many rags for the inevitable spills

In addition to these items there are several others which are not absolutely necessary, but handy to have around. These include a trans-mission funnel and filler tube, a drop (trouble) light on a long cord, an adjustable (crescent) wrench, and slip joint pliers.

A more advanced list of tools, suitable for tune-up work, can be drawn up easily. While the tools are slightly more sophisticated, they need not be outrageously expensive. The key to these purchases is to make them with an eye towards adaptability and wide range. A basic list of tune-up tools could include:

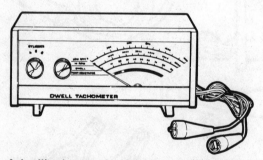

A dwell/tachometer is useful for tune-up work; you won't need a dwell meter if your car has electronic ignition

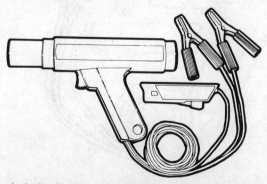

An inductive pickup simplifies timing light connection to the spark plug wire

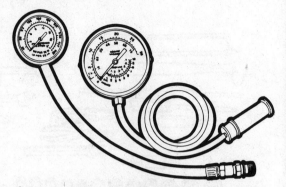

A compression gauge and a combination vacuum/fuel pressure gauge are handy for trou-bleshooting and tune-up work

1. Tachometer/dwell meter
2. Spark plug gauge and gapping tool
3. Feeler gauges for valve adjustment
4. Timing light

You will need both wire-type and flat-type feeler gauges, the former for the park plugs and the latter for the valves. The choice of a timing light should be made carefully. A light which works on the DC current supplied by the car battery is the best choice; it should have a xenon tube for brightness. Since most late model cars have electronic ignition, and since nearly all cars will have it in the future, the light should have an inductive pickup which clamps around the number one spark plug ca-ble (the timing light illustrated has one of these pickups). In addition to these basic tools, there are several other tools and gauges which you may find useful. These include:

1. A compression gauge. The screw-in type is slower to use, but eliminates the possibility of a faulty reading due to escaping pressure
2. A manifold vacuum gauge
3. A test light
4. A combination volt/ohmmeter
5. An induction meter, used to determine whether or not there is current flowing in a wire, an extremely helpful tool for electrical troubleshooting.

Finally, you will find a torque wrench neces-sary for all but the most basic of work. The beam-type models are perfectly adequate. The newer click-type (breakaway) torque wrenches are more accurate, but are much more expen-sive, and must be periodically recalibrated.

SERVICING YOUR CAR SAFELY

It is virtually impossible to anticipate all of the hazards involved with automotive mainte-nance and service, but care and common sense will prevent most accidents. The rules of safety for mechanics range from, don't smoke around gasoline, to, use the proper tool for the job. The trick to avoiding injuries is to develop safe work habits and take every possible precaution.

Dos

• Do keep a fire extinguisher and first aid kit within easy reach.

• Do wear safety glasses or goggles when cutting, drilling, grinding or prying. If you wear glasses for the sake of vision, they should be made of hardened glass that can serve also as safety glasses, or wear safety goggles over your regular glasses.

• Do shield your eyes whenever you work around the battery. Batteries contain sulphuric acid. In case of contact with the eyes or skin, flush the area with water or a mixture of water and baking soda and get medical attention immediately.

• Do use safety stands for any undercar service. Jacks are for raising vehicles; safety stands are for making sure the vehicle stays raised until you want it to come down. Whenever the car is raised, block the wheels remaining on the ground and set the parking brake.

• Do use adequate ventilation when working with any chemicals or hazardous materials. Like carbon monoxide, the asbestos dust resulting from brake lining wear can be poisonous in sufficient quantities.

• Do disconnect the negative battery cable when working on the electrical system. The secondary ignition system can contain up to 40,000 volts.

• Do follow manufacturer's directions whenever working with potentially hazardous materials. Both brake fluid and antifreeze are poisonous if taken internally.

• Do properly maintain your tools. Loose hammerheads, mushroomed punches and chisels, frayed or poorly grounded electrical cords, excessively worn screwdrivers, spread

open end wrenches, cracked sockets, slipping ratchets, or faulty droplight sockets can cause accidents.

• Do use the proper size and type of tool for the job being done.

• Do when possible, pull on a wrench handle rather than push on it, and adjust your stance to prevent a fall.

• Do be sure that adjustable wrenches are tightly closed on the nut or bolt and pulled so that the face is on the side of the fixed jaw.

• Do select a wrench or socket that fits the nut or bolt. The wrench or socket should sit straight, not cocked.

• Do strike squarely with a hammer; avoid glancing blows.

• Do set the parking brake and block the drive wheels if the work requires the engine running.

Don'ts

• Don't run an engine in a garage or anywhere else without proper ventilation – EVER! Carbon monoxide is poisonous; it takes a long time to leave the human body and you can build up a deadly supply of it in your system by simply breathing in a little every day. You may not realize you are slowly poisoning yourself. Always use power vents, windows, fans or open the garage doors.

• Don't work around moving parts while wearing a necktie or other loose clothing. Short sleeves are much safer than long, loose sleeves; hard-toed shoes with neoprene soles protect your toes and give a better grip on slippery surfaces. Jewelry such as watches, fancy belt buckles, beads or body adornment of any kind is not safe working around a car. Long hair should be hidden under a hat or cap.

• Don't use pockets for toolboxes. A fall or bump can drive a screwdriver deep into your body. Even a wiping cloth hanging form the back pocket can wrap around a spinning shaft or fan.

• Don't smoke when working around gasoline, cleaning solvent or other flammable material.

• Don't smoke when working around the battery. When the battery is being charged, it gives off explosive hydrogen gas.

• Don't use gasoline to wash your hands; there are excellent soaps available. Gasoline may contain lead, and lead can enter the body through a cut, accumulating in the body until you are very ill. Gasoline also removes all the natural oils from the skin so that bone dry hands will suck up oil and grease.

• Don't service the air conditioning system unless you are equipped with the necessary tools and training. The refrigerant, R-12, is ex-

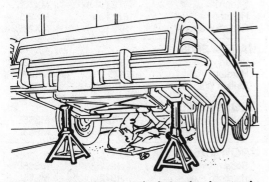

Always support the car on jackstands when working under it

tremely cold when compressed, and when released into the air will instantly freeze any surface it contacts, including your eyes. Although the refrigerant is normally non-toxic, R-12 becomes a deadly poisonous gas in the presence of an open flame. One good whiff of the vapors from burning refrigerant can be fatal.

HISTORY

In 1933, the Toyota Automatic Loom Works started an automobile division. Several models, mostly experimental, were produced between 1935 and 1937. Automobile production started on a large scale in 1937 when the Toyota Motor Co. Ltd. was founded. The name for the automobile company was changed from the family name, Toyoda, to Toyota, because a numerologist suggested that this would be a more auspicious name to use for this endeavor. It must have been; by 1947, Toyota had produced 100,000 vehicles. Today Toyota is Japan's largest producer of motor vehicles and ranks among the largest in world production.

It was not until the late 1950s, that Toyota began exporting cars to the United States. Public reception of the Toyopet was rather cool. The car was heavy and under-powered by U.S. standards. Several other models were exported, including the almost indestructible Land Cruiser. It was not until 1965, however, with the introduction of the Corona sedan, that Toyota enjoyed a real success on the U.S. market.

SERIAL NUMBER IDENTIFICATION

Vehicle

All models have the vehicle identification number (VIN) stamped on a plate which is attached to the left side of the instrument panel.

VIN plate on the firewall

This plate is visible through the windshield.

The VIN is also stamped on a plate in the engine compartment which is usually located on the firewall.

Through 1980 the serial number consists of a series identification number (see the chart below) followed by a six-digit production number.

Vehicle Identification

Model Type	Year	Series Identification Number*
CORONA 1900		
Sedan	1970 (late)–71	RT83L
Hardtop	1971	RT93L
CORONA 2000		
Sedan	1972–73	RT85L
Hardtop	1972–73	RT95L
Station Wagon	1973	RT89L
CORONA 2000		
Sedan	1974	RT104L
Hardtop	1974	RT114L
Station Wagon	1974	RT118L
CORONA 2200		
Sedan	1975–77	RT105L
Hardtop	1975–77	RT115L
Station Wagon	1975–77	RT119L
CORONA 2200		
Sedan	1978–80	RT134L
Liftback		
Station Wagon	1978–80	RT134LG
CORONA 2400	1981–82	RT135L
MARK II 1900		
Sedan	1970–71	RT62L
Hardtop	1970–71	RT72L
Station Wagon	1970–71	RT78L
MARK II 2000		
Sedan	1972 (early)	RT63L
Hardtop	1972 (early)	RT73L
Station Wagon	1972 (early)	RT79L
MARK II 2300		
Sedan	1972 (late)	MX12L
Hardtop	1972 (late)	MX22L
Station Wagon	1972 (late)	MX28L
MARK II 2600		
Sedan	1973–76	MX13L
Hardtop	1973–76	MX23L
Station Wagon	1973–76	MX29L
CROWN 2300		
Sedan	1970–71	MS55L
Station Wagon	1970–71	MS53L
CROWN 2600		
Sedan	1972	MS65L
Hardtop	1972	MS75L
Station Wagon	1972	MS63L

Vehicle Identification (cont.)

Model Type	Year	Series Identification Number*
CRESSIDA 2600		
Sedan	1978–80	MX32L
Station Wagon	1978–80	MX36L
CRESSIDA 2800	1981–84	MX-62L
Sedan	1985–86	MX-72
Wagon	1985–86	MX-73
VAN	1984	YR
Wagon	1985–86	YR-22
Van	1985–86	YR-29

*The suffixes, L, V, KA, etc., may not appear in the serial number; a typical Toyota serial number would look like this: MS55-132246

Beginning with 1981 models the serial number consists of seventeen symbols (letters and numbers).

Engine

The engine serial number consists of an engine series identification number, followed by a six-digit production number.

The location of this serial number varies from one engine type to another. Serial numbers may be found in the following locations:

1900cc (8R-C)

The serial number for this engine is embossed beside the fuel pump on the right side of the engine.

2000cc (18R-C)

The serial number is stamped on the left side of the engine, behind the dipstick.

2200 AND 2400cc (20R AND 22R)

The serial number is stamped on the left side of the engine, behind the alternator.

2300, 2600 AND 2800cc (2M, 4M, 4ME, 5ME, 5M-GE)

The serial numbers on these engines are stamped on the right side of the cylinder block, below the oil filter.

2000, 2200cc (3Y-EC, 4Y-EC)

The serial number is stamped on the left side of the engine, behind the alternator.

Engine Idenfication

Model	Year	Displacement (cc/cu in.)	Number of Cylinders	Type	Engine Series Identification
CORONA					
1900	1970–71	1858/113.4	4	OHC	8R-C
2000	1972–74	1908/120.0	4	OHC	18R-C
2200	1975–80	2189/133.0	4	OHC	20R
2400	1981–82	2367/144.4	4	OHC	22R
MARK II					
1900	1970–71	1858/113.4	4	OHC	8R-C
2000	1972	1980/120.0	4	OHC	18R-C
2300	1972 (late)	2258/137.5	6	OHC	2M
2600	1973–76	2563/156.4	6	OHC	4M
CROWN					
2300	1970–71	2258/137.5	6	OHC	2M
2600	1972	2563/156.4	6	OHC	4M
CRESSIDA					
2600	1978–79	2563/156.4	6	OHC	4M
2600	1980	2563/156.4	6	OHC	4M-E
2800	1981–84	2759/168.4	6	OHC	5M-E, 5M-GE
2800	1985–86	2759/168.4	6	OHC	5M-GE
VAN	1984–86	1998/122	4	OHV	3Y-EC

ROUTINE MAINTENANCE

Air Cleaner

The air cleaners used on Toyota vehicles are of the dry element, disposable type. They should never be washed or oiled.

Clean the element every 3,000 miles, or more often under dry, dusty conditions, by using low pressure compressed air. Blow from the inside toward the outside.

CAUTION: *Never use high air pressure to clean the element, as this will probably damage it.*

Replace the element every 18,000 miles, (1970–72); every 24,000 miles (1973–74); 25,000 miles (1975–77); 30,000 miles (1978–86); or more often under dry, dusty conditions. Be sure to use the correct one; all Toyota elements are of the same type but they come in a variety of sizes.

To remove the air cleaner element, unfasten the wing nut(s) and clips (if so equipped) on top of the housing and lift off the top section. Set it aside carefully since the emission system hoses are attached to it on some models. Unfasten these hoses first (if so equipped), to remove it entirely from the car. Lift the air cleaner element out for service or replacement.

Installation is the reverse of removal.

PCV Valve

The positive crankcase ventilation (PCV) valve should be replaced every 12 months/12,000 miles on models made prior to 1972. On 1972–74 models, check the PCV valve every 12 months/12,000 miles and replace it every 24 months/24,000 miles (whichever occurs first). On 1975–77 models, replace the PCV valve every 25,000 miles. On 1978 and later models, replace the PCV valve every 30,000 miles or 24 months. (California models, 1980 and later, every 60,000 miles).

NOTE: *For PCV valve removal and installation, See Chapter 4.*

Charcoal Canister

Toyota used the charcoal canister storage system for fuel vapor for the first time in 1972. Prior to this, Toyota used a case system which had no charcoal canister.

The charcoal canister vacuum lines, fittings, and connections should be checked every 6,000 miles for clogging, pinching, looseness, etc. Clean or replace components as necessary. If the canister is clogged, it may be cleaned using low pressure compressed air, as shown.

The entire canister should be replaced every five years/50,000 miles (60,000 miles on 1978 and later cars).

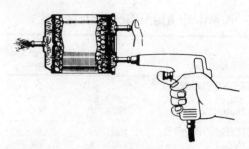

Using compressed air to clean the charcoal canister

Battery

FLUID LEVEL (EXCEPT MAINTENANCE FREE BATTERIES)

Check the battery electrolyte level at least once a month, or more often in hot weather or during periods of extended car operation. The level can be checked through the case on translucent polypropylene batteries; the cell caps must be removed on other models. The electrolyte level in each cell should be kept filled to the split ring inside, or the line marked on the outside of the case.

If the level is low, add only distilled water, or colorless, odorless drinking water, through the opening until the level is correct. Each cell is

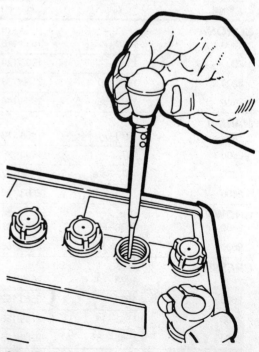

Specific gravity can be checked with an hydrometer

completely separate from the others, so each must be checked and filled individually.

If water is added in freezing weather, the car should be driven several miles to allow the water to mix with the electrolyte. Otherwise, the battery could freeze.

SPECIFIC GRAVITY (EXCEPT MAINTENANCE FREE BATTERIES)

At least once a year, check the specific gravity of the battery. It should be between 1.20 and 1.26 at room temperature.

The specific gravity can be checked with the use of an hydrometer, an inexpensive instrument available from many sources, including auto parts stores. The hydrometer has a squeeze bulb at one end and a nozzle at the other. Battery electrolyte is sucked into the hydrometer until the float is lifted from its seat. The specific gravity is then read by noting the position of the float. Generally, if after charging, the specific gravity between any two cells varies more than 50 points (.050), the battery is bad and should be replaced.

It is not possible to check the specific gravity in this manner on sealed (maintenance free) batteries. Instead, the indicator built into the top of the case must be relied on to display any signs of battery deterioration. If the indicator is dark, the battery can be assumed to be OK. If the indicator is light, the specific gravity is low, and the battery should be charged or replaced.

CABLES AND CLAMPS

Once a year, the battery terminals and the cable clamps should be cleaned. Loosen the clamps and remove the cables, negative cable first. On batteries with posts on top, the use of a puller specially made for the purpose is recommended. These are inexpensive, and available in auto parts stores. Side terminal battery cables are secured with a bolt.

Clean the cable clamps and the battery terminal with a wire brush, until all corrosion, grease, etc. is removed and the metal is shiny. It is especially important to clean the inside of the clamp thoroughly, since a small deposit of foreign material or oxidation there will prevent a sound electrical connection and inhibit either starting or charging. Special tools are available for cleaning these parts, one type for conventional batteries and another type for side terminal batteries.

Before installing the cables, loosen the battery holddown clamp or strap, remove the battery and check the battery tray. Clear it of any debris, and check it for soundness. Rust should be wire brushed away, and the metal given a coat of anti-rust paint. Replace the battery and tighten the holddown clamp or strap securely, but be careful not to over-tighten, which will crack the battery case.

After the clamps and terminals are clean, reinstall the cables, negative cable last; do not hammer on the clamps to install. Tighten the clamps securely, but do not distort them. Give

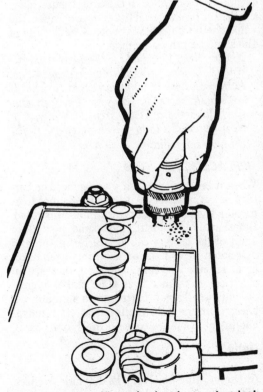

Clean the posts with a wire brush, or a terminal cleaner made for the purpose (shown)

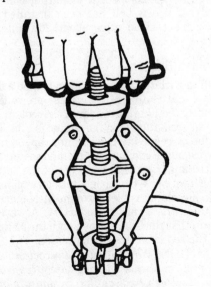

Pullers make clamp removal easier

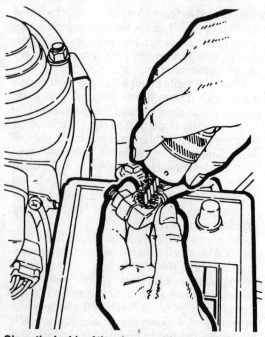

Clean the inside of the clamps with a wire brush, or the special tool

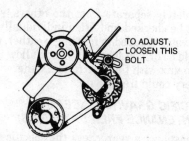

Fan belt adjustment

the clamps and terminals a thin external coat of grease after installation, to retard corrosion.

Check the cables at the same time that the terminals are cleaned. If the cable insulation is cracked or broken, or if the ends are frayed, the cable should be replaced with a new cable of the same length and gauge.

NOTE: *Keep flame or sparks away from the battery; it gives off explosive hydrogen gas. Battery electrolyte contains sulphuric acid. If you should splash any on your skin or in your eyes, flush the affected area with plenty of clear water; if it lands in your eyes, get medical help immediately.*

REPLACEMENT

When it becomes necessary to replace the battery, select a battery with a rating equal to or greater than the battery originally installed. Deterioration, embrittlement and just plain aging of the battery cables, starter motor, and associated wires makes the battery's job harder in successive years. The slow increase in electrical resistance over time makes it prudent to install a new battery with a greater capacity than the old. Details on battery removal and installation are covered in Chapter 3.

Belts

At engine tune-up (every 12,000 miles), check the condition of the drive belts and check and adjust belt tension as below:

1. Inspect belts for signs of glazing or cracking. A glazed belt will be perfectly smooth from slippage, while a good belt will have a slight texture of fabric visible. Cracks will usually start at the inner edge of the belt and run outward. Replace the belt at the first sign of cracking or if glazing is severe.

2. Belt tension does not refer to play or droop. By placing your thumb midway between two pulleys, it should be possible to depress each belt about 3/8 to 1/2" with 22–24 lbs. of pressure. If the belt can be depressed more than this, or cannot be depressed this much, adjust the tension. Inadequate tension will result in slippage and wear, while excessive tension will damage bearings and cause belts to fray and crack.

To adjust the tension; loosen the pivot and mounting bolts or idler pulley of the component which the belt is driving. Use a soft wooden hammer handle, a broomstick, or the like to pry the component toward or away from the engine until the proper tension is achieved.

CAUTION: *Do not use a screwdriver or other metal device, such as a prybar, as a lever.*

Tighten the component mounting bolts securely. If a new belt has been installed, recheck the tension after about 200 miles of driving.

Cooling System

Dealing with the cooling system can be a dangerous matter unless the proper precautions are observed. It is best to check the coolant level in the radiator when the engine is cold. This is done by removing the radiator cap, on models without an expansion tank, and seeing that the coolant is within two inches of the bottom of the filler neck. On models with an expansion tank, if coolant visible above the MIN mark on the tank, the level is satisfactory. Always be certain that the filler caps on both the radiator and the reservoir are tightly closed.

CAUTION: *When draining the coolant, keep in mind that cats and dogs are attracted by the ethylene glycol antifreeze, and are quite likely to drink any that is left in an uncovered*

How to Spot Worn V-Belts

V-Belts are vital to efficient engine operation—they drive the fan, water pump and other accessories. They require little maintenance (occasional tightening) but they will not last forever. Slipping or failure of the V-belt will lead to overheating. If your V-belt looks like any of these, it should be replaced.

Cracking or weathering

This belt has deep cracks, which cause it to flex. Too much flexing leads to heat build-up and premature failure. These cracks can be caused by using the belt on a pulley that is too small. Notched belts are available for small diameter pulleys.

Softening (grease and oil)

Oil and grease on a belt can cause the belt's rubber compounds to soften and separate from the reinforcing cords that hold the belt together. The belt will first slip, then finally fail altogether.

Glazing

Glazing is caused by a belt that is slipping. A slipping belt can cause a run-down battery, erratic power steering, overheating or poor accessory performance. The more the belt slips, the more glazing will be built up on the surface of the belt. The more the belt is glazed, the more it will slip. If the glazing is light, tighten the belt.

Worn cover

The cover of this belt is worn off and is peeling away. The reinforcing cords will begin to wear and the belt will shortly break. When the belt cover wears in spots or has a rough jagged appearance, check the pulley grooves for roughness.

Separation

This belt is on the verge of breaking and leaving you stranded. The layers of the belt are separating and the reinforcing cords are exposed. It's just a matter of time before it breaks completely.

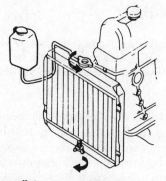

Open the radiator cap and radiator drain petcock to change the coolant

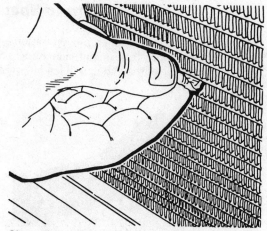

Clean the radiator fins of any debris which impedes air flow

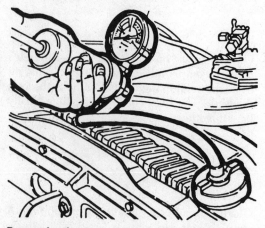

Pressurize the cooling system with the special tool shown to check for leaks

container or in puddles on the ground. This will prove fatal in sufficient quantity. Always drain the coolant into a sealable container. Coolant should be reused unless it is contaminated or several years old.

In the event that the coolant level must be checked when the engine is warm on engines without the expansion tank, place a thick rag over the radiator cap and slowly turn the cap counterclockwise until it reaches the first detent. Allow all the hot steam to escape. This will allow the pressure in the system to drop gradually, preventing an explosion of hot coolant. When the hissing noise stops, remove the cap the rest of the way.

If the coolant level is low, add equal amounts of ethylene glycol based antifreeze and clean water. On models without an expansion tank, add coolant through the radiator filler neck. Fill the expansion tank to the MAX level on cars with that system.

CAUTION: *Never add cold coolant to a hot engine unless the engine is running, to avoid cracking the engine block.*

If the coolant level is chronically low or

rusty, refer to the Troubleshooting chapter for diagnosis of the problem.

The radiator hoses and clamps and the radiator cap should be checked at the same time as the coolant level. Hoses which are brittle, cracked, or swollen should be replaced. Clamps should be checked for tightness (screwdriver tight only. Do not allow the clamp to cut into the hose or crush the fitting). The radiator cap gasket should be checked for any obvious tears, cracks or swelling, or any signs of incorrect seating in the radiator neck.

COOLANT CHANGES

Once every 24 months or 24,000 miles, the cooling system should be drained, thoroughly flushed, and refilled. This should be done with the engine cold.

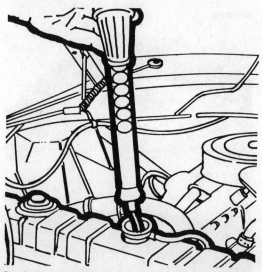

Coolant protection quality can be checked with an inexpensive float-type tester

How to Spot Bad Hoses

Both the upper and lower radiator hoses are called upon to perform difficult jobs in an inhospitable environment. They are subject to nearly 18 psi at under hood temperatures often over 280°F., and must circulate nearly 7500 gallons of coolant an hour—3 good reasons to have good hoses.

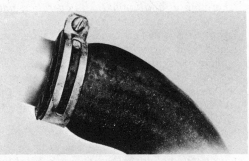

Swollen hose

A good test for any hose is to feel it for soft or spongy spots. Frequently these will appear as swollen areas of the hose. The most likely cause is oil soaking. This hose could burst at any time, when hot or under pressure.

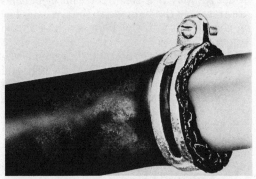

Cracked hose

Cracked hoses can usually be seen but feel the hoses to be sure they have not hardened; a prime cause of cracking. This hose has cracked down to the reinforcing cords and could split at any of the cracks.

Frayed hose end (due to weak clamp)

Weakened clamps frequently are the cause of hose and cooling system failure. The connection between the pipe and hose has deteriorated enough to allow coolant to escape when the engine is hot.

Debris in cooling system

Debris, rust and scale in the cooling system can cause the inside of a hose to weaken. This can usually be felt on the outside of the hose as soft or thinner areas.

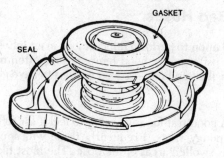

Check the radiator cap seal and gasket condition

1. Remove the radiator cap.
2. There are usually two drain plugs in the cooling system; one at the bottom of the radiator and one at the rear of the driver's side of the engine. Both should be loosened to allow the coolant to drain.
CAUTION: *When draining the coolant, keep in mind that cats and dogs are attracted by the ethylene glycol antifreeze, and are quite likely to drink any that is left in an uncovered container or in puddles on the ground. This will prove fatal in sufficient quantity. Always drain the coolant into a sealable container. Coolant should be reused unless it is contaminated or several years old.*
3. Turn on the heater inside the car to its hottest position. This ensures that the heater core is flushed out completely. Flush out the system thoroughly by refilling it with clean water through the radiator opening as it escapes from the two drain cocks. Continue until the water running out is clear. Be sure to clean out the coolant recovery tank as well if your car has one.
4. If the system is badly contaminated with rust or scale, you can use a commercial flushing solution to clear it out. Follow the manufacturer's instructions. Some causes of rust are air in the system, caused by a leaky radiator cap or an insufficiently filled or leaking system; failure to change the coolant regularly; use of excessively hard or soft water; and failure to use a proper mix of antifreeze and water.
5. When the system is clear, allow all the water to drain, then close the drain plugs. Fill the system through the radiator with a 50/50 mix of ethylene glycol type antifreeze and water.
6. Start the engine and top off the radiator with the antifreeze and water mixture. If your car has a coolant recovery tank, fill it half full with the coolant mix.
7. Replace the radiator and coolant tank caps, and check for leaks. When the engine has reached normal operating temperature, shut it off, allow it to cool, then top off the radiator or coolant tank as necessary.

Air Conditioning System Check

Factory units have a sight glass for checking the refrigerant charge. This is on top of the receiver-dehydrator.
CAUTION: *Do not attempt to charge or discharge the refrigerant system unless you are thoroughly familiar with its operation and the hazards involved. The compressed refrigerant used in the air conditioning system expands and evaporated (boils) into the atmosphere at a temperature of $-29.8°C$ ($-21.7°F$) or less. This will freeze any surface that it contacts, including your eyes. In addition, the refrigerant decomposes into a poisonous gas in the presence of flame.*
NOTE: *If your car is equipped with an aftermarket air conditioner, the following system check may not apply. You should contact the manufacturer of the unit for instructions on system checks.*
This test works best if the outside air temperature is warm (above 70°F).
1. Place the automatic transmission in Park or the manual transmission in Neutral. Set the parking brake.
2. Run the engine at a fast idle (about 1,500 rpm) either with the help of a friend, or by temporarily readjusting the idle speed screw.
3. Set the controls for maximum cold with the blower on high.
4. Locate the sight glass on top of the receiver-dehydrator. If a steady stream of bubbles are present in the sight glass, the system is low on charge. Very likely there is a leak in the system.
5. If no bubbles are present, the system is either fully charged or empty. Feel the high and low pressure lines at the compressor. If no appreciable temperature difference is felt, the system is empty, or nearly so.
6. If one hose (high pressure) is warm and the other (low pressure) is cold, the system may be OK. However, you are probably making these tests because there is something wrong with the system, so proceed to the next step.
7. Either disconnect the compressor clutch wire, or have an assistant in the car turn the fan control on and off to operate the compressor clutch. Watch the sight glass.
8. If bubbles appear when the clutch is disengaged and disappear when it is engaged, the system is properly charged.
9. If the refrigerant takes more than 45 seconds to bubble when the clutch is disengaged, the system is overcharged. This usually causes poor cooling at low speeds.
The air conditioning system should be operated for about five minutes each week, even in

winter. This will circulate lubricating oil within the system to prevent the various seals from drying out.

NOTE: *If it is determined that the system has a leak, it should be repaired as soon as possible. Leaks may allow moisture to enter, causing an expensive rust problem.*

Windshield Wipers

For maximum effectiveness and longest element life, the windshield and wiper blades should be kept clean. Dirt, tree sap, road tar and so on will cause streaking, smearing and blade deterioration if left on the glass. It is advisable to wash the windshield carefully with a commercial glass cleaner at least once a month. Wipe off the rubber blades with the wet

rag afterwards. Do not attempt to move the wipers by hand; damage to the motor and drive mechanism will result.

If the blades are found to be cracked, broken or torn, they should be replaced immediately. Replacement intervals will vary with usage, although ozone deterioration usually limits blade life to about one year. If the wiper pattern is smeared or streaked, or if the blade chatters across the glass, the elements should be replaced. It is easiest and most sensible to replace the elements in pairs.

There are basically three different types of refills, which differ in their method of replacement. One type has two release buttons, approximately ⅓ of the way up from the ends of the blade frame. Pushing the buttons down releases a lock and allows the rubber filler to be

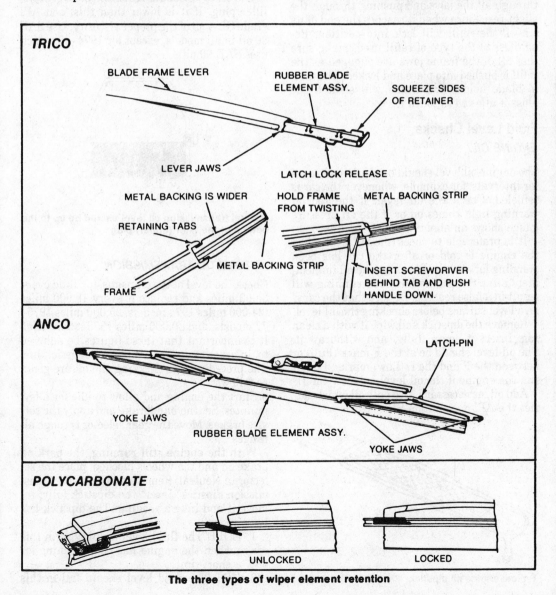

The three types of wiper element retention

removed from the frame. The new filler slides back into the frame and locks in place.

The second type of refill has two metal tabs which are unlocked by squeezing them together. The rubber filler can then be withdrawn from the frame jaws. A new refill is installed by inserting the refill into the front frame jaws and sliding it rearward to engage the remaining frame jaws. There are usually four jaws, be certain when installing that the refill is engaged in all of them. At the end of its travel, the tabs will lock into place on the front jaws of the wiper blade frame.

The third type is a refill made from polycarbonate. The refill has a simple locking device at one end which flexes downward out of the groove into which the jaws of the holder fit, allowing easy release. By sliding the new refill through all the jaws and pushing through the slight resistance when it reaches the end of its travel, the refill will lock into position. Regardless of the type of refill used, make sure that all of the frame jaws are engaged as the refill is pushed into place and locked. The metal blade holder and frame will scratch the glass if allowed to touch it.

Fluid Level Checks

ENGINE OIL

The engine oil level should be checked at regular intervals; for example, whenever the car is refueled. Check the oil level, if the red oil warning light comes on or if the oil pressure gauge shows an abnormally low reading.

It is preferable to check the oil level when the engine is cold or after the car has been standing for a while. Checking the oil immediately after the engine has been running will result in a false reading. Be sure that the car is on a level surface before checking the oil level.

Remove the dipstick and wipe it with a clean rag. Insert it again (fully) and withdraw it. The oil level should be at the F mark (Full) or between the F and the L (Low) marks. Do not run the engine if the oil level is below the L.

Add oil, as necessary. Use only oil which carries the API designation SE.

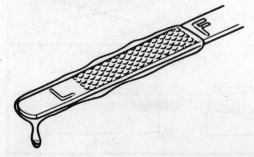

Typical engine oil dipstick

CAUTION: *Do not use unlabeled oil or a lower grade of oil which does not meet SE specifications.*

See the chart in the lubrication section of this chapter for proper oil viscosities. Do not overfill.

MANUAL TRANSMISSION

The oil in the manual transmission should be checked every 6,000 miles and replaced every 18,000 miles (24,000 miles 1974 models, 25,000 miles 1975–77 models, and 30,000 miles 1978–86 models) or 24 months, whichever occurs first.

To check the oil level, remove the transmission filler plug. This is always the upper plug, the lower plug being the drain.

The oil level should reach the bottom of the filler plug. If it is lower than this, add API grade GL-4 oil of the proper viscosity. Use SAE 80 oil in all models, except for 1974–86, which uses SAE 90 oil.

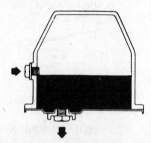

Manual transmission oil level should be up to the bottom of the filler (upper) plug

AUTOMATIC TRANSMISSION

Check the level of the transmission fluid every 3,000 miles and replace it every 18,000 miles (24,000 miles 1974 models, 25,000 miles 1975–77 models, and 30,000 miles 1978–86 models). It is important that these figures be adhered to, in order to ensure a long transmission life. The procedures for checking the oil are given as follows:

Start the engine and allow to idle for a few minutes. Set the handbrake and apply the service brakes. Move the gear selector through all ranges.

With the engine still running, the parking brake on and the wheels blocked, place the selector in Neutral. Remove and clean the transmission dipstick. Insert the dipstick fully, remove it and take a reading. The dipstick has two ranges.

1. COLD The fluid level should fall in this range when the engine has been running for only a short time.

2. HOT The fluid level should fall in this

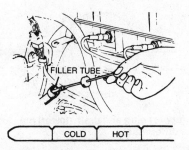

Three-speed automatic transmission dipstick location—insert shows ranges

range when the engine has reached normal running temperatures.

3. Replenish the fluid through the filler tube with type F fluid for all models built until July, 1983; Dexron®II for all models built beginning July 1983. Models using Dexron®II have a DII stamped on the pan or drain plug. Add fluid to the top of the COLD or HOT range, depending upon engine temperature.

CAUTION: *Do not overfill the transmission.*

BRAKE AND CLUTCH MASTER CYLINDERS

The brake and clutch (manual transmission) master cylinder reservoirs are made of a translucent plastic so that the fluid level can be checked without removing the cap. Check the fluid level frequently.

If the fluid is low, fill the reservoir with DOT 3 fluid, pouring so bubbles do not form in the reservoir. Use care not to spill any fluid on the car's paint, damage may result.

CAUTION: *Do not use a lower grade of brake fluid and never mix different types. Either could result in a brake system failure.*

COOLANT

The coolant level should be checked at least once a week or when the temperature gauge registers HOT (H).

CAUTION: *Allow the engine to cool before removing the radiator cap.*

Because the cooling system is under pressure, check the coolant level with the engine

Capacities

Model	Year	Crankcase (qts) w/filter	Crankcase (qts) w/o filter	Transmission (qts) Manual	Transmission (qts) Automatic*	Drive Axle (qts)	Fuel Tank (gal)	Cooling System w/heater (qts)
CORONA								
1900	1970–71	5.3	4.4	2.1	3.7	1.4	13.2	7.8
2000	1972–74	5.3	4.2	2.1①	3.7	1.4	13.2②	8.4
2200	1875–80	4.8	4.1	2.9③	2.3④	⑤	14.5⑥	7.4⑦
2400	1981–82	4.8	4.1	2.9③	2.5	⑤	16.1	8.5
MARK II								
1900	1970–71	5.3	4.3	2.1	3.7	1.4	13.7	7.8
2000	1972	5.2	4.2	2.1	3.7	1.4	13.7	7.8
2300	1972	5.5	4.6	3.6	3.7	1.3	15.8⑧	11.6
2600	1973–76	6.2	5.1	2.9	3.0	1.3	15.9⑧	12.3
CROWN								
2300	1970–71	5.5	4.6	2.1	3.4	1.3	18.5⑨	11.6
2600	1972	5.5	4.6	2.1	3.4	1.3	18.5⑨	11.6
CRESSIDA								
2600	1978–80	4.9	4.3	—	2.5	1.5	17.2⑩	11.6
2800	1981–83	4.9	4.3	—	2.5	1.5	17.2⑩	9.5
	1984–86	5.4	4.9	2.5	2.5	2.6⑪	18.5	9.5
VAN	1984–86	3.7	3.2	2.3	2.5	2.6	15.9	7.5

*Drain and refill
① 4 speed: 2.9
   5 speed: 3.4
② 1974: 14.5 gallons
③ 5 speed: 2.8
④ 1978–80: 2.5

⑤ Unitized type: 1.3
   Banjo type: 1.4
⑥ 1978–79: 15.5 gallons
   1980: 16.1 gallons
⑦ 1979–80: 8.5
⑧ Wagon: 14.5 gallons

⑨ Wagon: 15.8 gallons
⑩ Wagon: 16.2 gallons
⑪ Station wagon: 3.0
   Diesel 4.5 w/Filter; 4.0 w/o
   M.T.: 2.7
   A.T.: 2.1

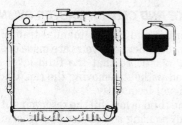

Check the coolant level in the expansion tank on models with a closed cooling system

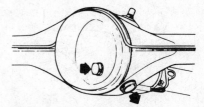

Filler (upper) plug and drain (lower) plug locations on the differential

cold to prevent injury from high pressure, hot water.

The level should be ¾" below the filler neck, when the engine is cold. Replenish with clean, non-alkaline water. If antifreeze is being added, use a type approved for aluminum (ethylene glycol). Most Toyota models have alloy heads.

CAUTION: *Never add cold water to a hot engine; damage to the cooling system and engine block could result. On 2T-C engines, bleed the cooling system by loosening the temperature sending unit after filling the radiator. Tighten the sender.*

Some models are equipped with a closed cooling system, with a tube running from the radiator to a thermal expansion tank. On these models, check the level of the coolant in the expansion tank. The main radiator cap should only be removed when cleaning or draining the cooling system or if the expansion tank is empty.

CAUTION: *The cap on the main radiator is not a pressure/vacuum safety cap. Never remove it when the engine is hot. Severe injury could result.*

The expansion tank should be about ¾ full or coolant should reach the FULL mark. Add coolant as outlined.

REAR AXLE

The oil level in the differential should be checked every 6,000 miles and replaced every 18,000 miles (1974, 24,000 miles; 1975–77, 25,000 miles; 1978–81, 30,000 miles) or 24 months, whichever comes first. The oil should be checked with the car on a level surface. Remove the oil filler and upper plug, located on the back of the differential.

NOTE: *The bottom plug is the drain.*

The oil level should reach to the bottom edge of the filler hole. If low, replenish with API grade GL-5 gear oil of the proper viscosity. The viscosity is determined by the ambient temperature range. If the temperature averages above 10°F, use SAE 90 gear oil. If the temperature averages below 10°F, use SAE 80 oil. Always check for leaks when checking the oil level.

STEERING GEAR

Check the steering gear oil level every 12,000 miles. The level should be up to filler plug hole. All pre-1974 models use SAE 80 gear oil. 1974–81 use SAE 90.

POWER STEERING RESERVOIR

All six cylinder and some other models from 1978–81 use power steering. Check the level of the power steering fluid periodically. The fluid level should fall within the crosshatched area of the gauge attached to the reservoir cap. If the fluid level is below this, add DEXRON® fluid. Remember to check for leaks.

BATTERY

Check the electrolyte level in the battery frequently. The level should be between the upper and lower level lines marked on the battery case or just to the bottom of the filler well, depending on type. Use distilled water to correct the electrolyte level.

CAUTION: *Do not overfill the battery. It could leak and damage the car finish and battery bracket.*

Tires

INFLATION PRESSURE

Tire inflation is the most ignored item of auto maintenance. Gasoline mileage can drop as much as 0.8% for every 1 pound per square inch (psi) of under inflation.

Two items should be permanent fixtures in every glove compartment; a tire pressure gauge and a tread depth gauge. Check the tire air pressure (including the spare) regularly with a pocket type gauge. Kicking the tires won't tell you a thing, and the gauge on the service station air hose is notoriously inaccurate.

The tire pressures recommended for your care are usually found on the glove box door, on the door jam, or in the owner's manual. Ideally, inflation pressure should be checked when the tires are cool. When the air becomes heated it expands and the pressure increases.

Every 10 degree rise (or drop) in temperature means a difference of 1 psi, which also explains why the tire appears to lose air on a very cold night. When it is impossible to check the tires cold, allow for pressure build-up due to heat. If the hot pressure exceeds the cold pressure by more than 15 psi, reduce your speed, load or both. Otherwise internal heat is created in the tire. When the heat approaches the temperature at which the tire was cured, during manufacture, the tread can separate from the body.

CAUTION: *Never counteract excessive pressure build-up by bleeding off air pressure (letting some air out). This will only further raise the tire operating temperature.*

Before starting a long trip with lots of luggage, you can add about 2–4 psi to the tires to make them run cooler, but never exceed the maximum inflation pressure on the side of the tire.

TREAD DEPTH

All tires made since 1968, have 8 built-in tread wear bars that show up as ½" wide smooth bands across the tire when $\frac{1}{16}$" of tread re-

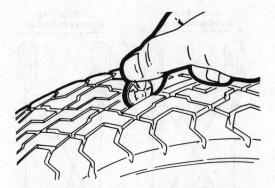

A penny works well for checking the tread depth

mains. The appearance of tread wear indicators means that the tires should be replaced. In fact, many states have laws prohibiting the use of tires with less than $\frac{1}{16}$" tread.

You can check your own tread depth with an inexpensive gauge or by using a Lincoln head penny. Slip the Lincoln penny into several tread grooves. If you can see the top of Lincoln's head in 2 adjacent grooves, the tires have less than $\frac{1}{16}$" tread left and should be replaced. You can measure snow tires in the same manner by using the tails side of the Lincoln penny. If you can see the top of the Lincoln memorial, it's time to replace the snow tires.

TIRE ROTATION

Tire wear can be equalized by switching the position of the tires about every 6000 miles. Including a conventional spare in the rotation pattern can give up to 20% more tire life.

CAUTION: *Do not include the new Space-Saver or temporary spare tires in the rotation pattern.*

There are certain exceptions to tire rotation, however. Studded snow tires should not be rotated, and radials should be kept on the same side of the car (maintain the same direction of rotation). The belts on radial tires get set in a pattern. If the direction of rotation is reversed, it can cause rough ride and vibration.

NOTE: *When radials or studded snows are taken off the car, mark them, so you can maintain the same direction of rotation.*

TIRE STORAGE

Store the tires at proper inflation pressures if they are mounted on wheels. All tires should be kept in a cool, dry place. If they are stored in the garage or basement, do not let them stand on a concrete floor; set them on strips of wood.

Fuel Filter

There are two basic types of fuel filter used on Toyota vehicles: The cartridge type (disposable element) and the totally throwaway type.

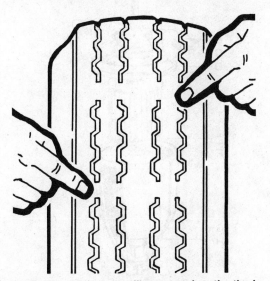

Tread wear indicators will appear when the tire is worn out

Tread depth can also be checked with an inexpensive gauge

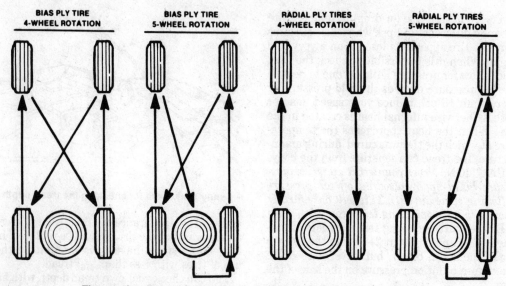

| BIAS PLY TIRE 4-WHEEL ROTATION | BIAS PLY TIRE 5-WHEEL ROTATION | RADIAL PLY TIRES 4-WHEEL ROTATION | RADIAL PLY TIRES 5-WHEEL ROTATION |

Tire rotation diagrams; note that radials should not be cross-switched

CAUTION: *On models with fuel injection; the pressure in the fuel system must be bled before removal of filter. Do not smoke while servicing the fuel filter. Vapors trapped in it could ignite.*

CARTRIDGE TYPE

The cartridge type filter is located in the fuel line. To replace the element, proceed as follows:

1. Loosen and remove the nut on the filter bowl.

2. Withdraw the bowl, element spring, element, and gasket.

3. Wash the parts in solvent and examine them for damage.

4. Install a new filter element and bowl gasket.

5. Install the components in the reverse order of their removal. Do not fully tighten the bail nut.

6. Seat the bowl by turning it slightly. Tighten the bail nut fully and check for leaks. The above service should be performed if the clear glass bowl fills up with gasoline or at the following specified intervals:

NOTE: *Be sure to specify engine and model when buying the element replacement kit. The kits come in several different sizes.*

THROWAWAY TYPE

1971–74

The throwaway type of fuel filter is located in the fuel line. It must be completely removed in order to replace it. The procedure to do this is as follows:

1. Unfasten the fuel intake hose. Use a

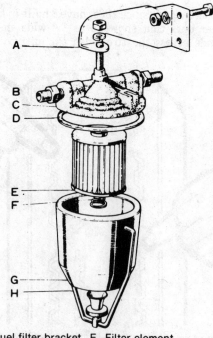

A. Fuel filter bracket
B. Fuel line fitting
C. Body
D. Bowl gasket
E. Filter element
F. Element retaining spring
G. Filter bowl
H. Bowl retaining bail

Cartridge-type fuel filter components

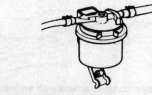

"See-through" fuel filter

wrench to loosen the attachment nut and another wrench on the opposite side to keep the filter body from turning.

2. Unfasten the attaching screws from the filter bracket, if so equipped.

3. Install a completely new fuel filter assembly in the reverse order of removal, above.

1975 and Later

Starting 1975, Toyota passenger cars use a see-through type, disposable fuel filter. This filter should be replaced every 2 years or 25,000 miles on 1975–77 vehicles, and 30,000 miles or 2 years on 1978 and later vehicles, or if the filter appears clogged or dirty.

NOTE: *Fuel Injected Models. To bleed the system pressure:*

1. Place a drain pan under the fuel filter to catch the gasoline.

2. Slowly loosen the lower fitting (or the one coming from the fuel tank) on the fuel filter.

3. After the pressure and the gasoline have bled off, remove and replace the filter in the normal manner.

To replace filter, all engines:

1. Remove the hose clamps from the inlet and outlet hoses.

2. Work the hoses off the filter necks.

3. Snap the filter out of its bracket.

4. Installation is performed in the reverse order of removal. Be sure to install the filter in the proper direction. The arrow on top should point toward the carburetor.

LUBRICATION

Oil Recommendation

Use a good quality motor oil of a known brand, which carries the API classification SE or SF. The proper viscosity of the oil depends on the climate and temperature your car is operated in.

CAUTION: *Do not use unlabeled oil or a lower grade of oil which does not meet SE specifications. If 5W, 10W, or 5W-20 oil is used, avoid prolonged high-speed driving.*

Change the oil at the intervals recommended. If the vehicle is being used in severe service such as trailer towing, change the oil at more frequent intervals.

It is especially important that the oil be changed at the proper intervals in emission controlled engines, as they run hotter than non-controlled, thus causing the oil to break down faster.

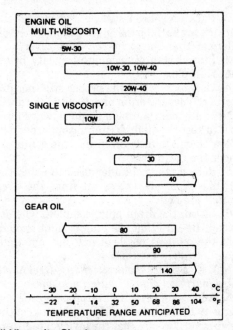

Oil Viscosity Chart

Fuel Recommendations

From 1971 through 1974 all models were designed to run on regular grade gasoline with an octane rating of 90 or higher.

If the engine pings, knocks, or diesels, either the fuel grade is too low or the timing is out of adjustment. Add gasoline of a higher octane and check the timing, as soon as possible.

CAUTION: *Pinging, knocking, or dieseling can rapidly damage the engine. The problem should be cured as quickly as possible.*

Starting in 1975 some Toyota models were equipped with a catalytic converter, because lead ruins the catalyst, the use of unleaded fuel is mandatory. All Toyota models equipped with a catalytic converter therefore, must use unleaded gasoline. The others (non-converter equipped) may use leaded gasoline.

Oil Changes

ENGINE

The oil should be changed at the intervals specified. The amount of oil required for each engine and model may be found in the Capacities chart.

NOTE: *All new cars should have an oil change after the first 1,000 miles. The filter should also be changed at this time.*

To change the oil, proceed in the following manner:

1. Warm the oil by running the engine for a short period of time; this will make the oil flow more freely from the oil pan.

2. Park on a level surface and put on the parking brake. Stop the engine. Remove the oil filler cap from the top of the valve cover.

3. Place a pan of adequate capacity below the drain plug.

4. Use a wrench of the proper size (not pliers) to remove the drain plug. Loosen the drain plug while maintaining a slight upward force on it to keep the oil from running out around it. Allow the oil to fully drain into the container under the drain hole.

5. Remove the container used to catch the oil and wipe any excess oil from the area around the hole.

6. Install the drain plug, complete with its gasket. Be sure that the plug is tight enough that the oil does not leak out, but not tight enough to strip the threads.

NOTE: *Replace the drain plug gasket at every fourth oil change with a new one.*

7. Add clean, new oil of the proper grade and viscosity through the oil filler on the top of the valve cover. Be sure that the oil level registers near the F (full) mark on the dipstick.

OIL FILTER

All Toyota passenger cars use spin-off oil filters. These should be changed at the first 1,000 mile oil change and at the interval specified. The filter should be replaced during the engine oil change procedure. To replace the filter, proceed as follows:

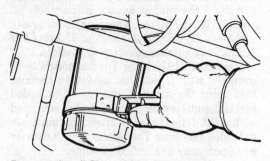

Remove the oil filter with a strap wrench

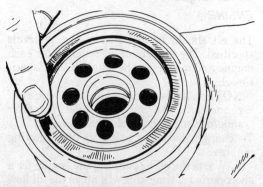

Coat the new oil filter gasket with clean oil

Install the new filter by hand

1. Drain the engine oil as previously outlined. Place a container under the oil filter to catch any excess oil.

2. Use a spin-off (band) wrench to remove the filter unit. Turn the filter counterclockwise in order to remove it.

3. Wipe off the filter bracket with a clean rag.

4. Install a new filter and gasket, after first lubricating the gasket with clean engine oil.

CAUTION: *Do not use the wrench to tighten the filter. Tighten it by hand.*

5. Add engine oil as previously outlined in the appropriate section. Check for leaks.

MANUAL TRANSMISSION

The transmission oil should be replaced every 18,000 miles (1970–73), 24,000 miles (1974), 25,000 miles (1975–77), 30,000 miles (1978–86), or 24 months (all years), whichever occurs first. To change the transmission oil, proceed as follows:

1. Park the car on a level surface and put on the parking brake.

2. Remove the oil filler (upper) plug.

3. Place a container, of a large enough capacity to catch all of the oil, under the drain (lower) plug. Use the proper size wrench to loosen the drain plug slowly, while maintaining a slight upward force to keep the oil from running out. Once the plug is removed, allow all of the oil to drain from the transmission.

4. Install the drain plug and its gasket, if so equipped.

5. Fill the transmission to capacity. (See the Capacities chart.) Use API grade GL4 SAE 80 oil on all 1970–73 passenger cars. Use SAE 90 in 1974–84 models. Be sure that the oil level reaches the bottom of the filler plug.

6. Remember to install the filler plug when finished.

AUTOMATIC TRANSMISSION

Change the fluid in the automatic transmission every 18,000 (1970–73), 24,000 miles (1974), 25,000 (1975–77), 30,000 miles (1978–84), or 25 months, whichever occurs first. To change the fluid, proceed as follows:

1. Park the car on a level surface. Set the parking brake.

2. Place a container, which is large enough to catch all of the transmission fluid, under the transmission oil pan drain plug. Unfasten the drain plug and allow all of the fluid to run out into the container.

3. Check the condition of the transmission fluid. If it is burnt, discolored, or has particles in it, the transmission needs to be overhauled. Consult your local Toyota dealer.

4. Install the drain plug in the transmission oil pan. Be sure that it is tight enough to prevent leakage, but not tight enough to strip the threads.

CAUTION: *Fill the transmission with ATF type F fluid only. Do not use DEXRON®, gear oil or engine oil supplement.*

5. Fill the transmission through the filler tube, after removing the dipstick, with ATF type F transmission fluid.

NOTE: *It may be a good idea to fill to less than the recommended capacity (see the Capacities chart) as some of the fluid will remain in the torque converter.*

6. Start the engine and check the transmission fluid level, as outlined under Fluid Level Checks. Add fluid, if necessary, but do not overfill.

REAR AXLE

All Toyota rear axles use 90 weight, API GL-5 lubricant. Lubricant is changed every 18,000 miles (1970–73), 24,000 miles (1974), 25,000 miles (1975–77), 30,000 miles (1978–84) or 24 months, whichever comes first. To drain and fill the rear axle, proceed as follows:

1. Park the vehicle on a level surface. Set the parking brake.

2. Remove the filler (upper) plug. Place a container which is large enough to catch all of the differential oil, under the drain plug.

3. Remove the drain (lower) plug and gasket, if so equipped. Allow all of the oil to drain into the container.

4. Install the drain plug. Tighten it so that it will not leak, but do not overtighten.

5. Refill with the proper grade and viscosity of axle lubricant. Be sure that the level reaches the bottom of the filler plug.

6. Install the filler plug and check for leakage.

Chassis Greasing

CORONA, MARK II, CROWN 2300 AND CRESSIDA

The chassis lubrication for these models is limited to lubricating the front ball joints every 24,000 miles (1970–74), 25,000 miles (1975–

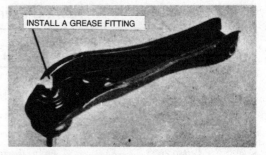

INSTALL A GREASE FITTING

Ball joint grease fitting

77), or 30,000 miles (1978–86) or 24 months, whichever occurs first. To lubricate the ball joints, proceed as follows:

1. Remove the screw plug from the ball joint. Install a grease nipple.

2. Using a hand-operated grease gun, lubricate the ball joint with NGLI No. 1 molybdenum-disulphide lithium-based grease.

CAUTION: *Do not use multipurpose or chassis grease.*

3. Remove the nipple and reinstall the screw plug.

4. Repeat for the other ball joint(s).

CROWN 2600

The ball joints on these models do not normally require lubrication. If the dust boots become torn or damaged, however, the boots should be replaced and the ball joint repacked. (See Chapter 8.)

Body Lubrication

There is no set period recommended by Toyota for body lubrication. However, it is a good idea to lubricate the following body points at least once a year, especially in the fall before cold weather.

  Lubricate with engine oil:
    Door lock latches
    Door lock rollers
    Station wagon tailgate hinges
    Door, hood, and hinge pivots
  Lubricate with silicone grease:
    Trunk lid latch and hinge
    Glove box door latch
  Lubricate with silicone spray:
    All rubber weather stripping
    Hood stops

When finished lubricating a body part, be sure that all the excess lubricant has been wiped off, especially in the areas of the car which may come in contact with clothing.

Wheel Bearings

Refer to the appropriate section in Chapter 9 for wheel bearing assembly and packing procedures. The front wheel bearings should be re-

Towing Points—1970–77

| | Attach the tow line to: | |
Model	Front	Rear
Corona	Towing hook (front crossmember)	Spring hanger
Mark II/4 (RT)	Towing hook (front crossmember)	Spring hanger
Mark II/6 (MX)	Towing hook (front crossmember)	Differential carrier ② ③
Crown 2300	Front bumper stay ①	Rear bumper stay ① ②
Crown 2600	Front crossmember	Towing hook ②

① Towing hook available from dealer (optional)
② Rear spring hanger–station wagon
③ 1974–77 models—rear towing hooks

packed every 24,000 miles on 1970–74 vehicles, 25,000 miles on 1975–77 vehicles, and 30,000 miles on 1978–86 vehicles, or every 24 months, whichever occurs first.

PUSHING AND TOWING

Push-start the car when the engine will not turn over; do not attempt to start the car by towing it.

CAUTION: *If the car is tow-started, it may run into the back of the towing vehicle when it starts.*

To push-start the car, turn the ignition switch to ON. (On models with seat belt interlocks, fasten the seat belts first.) Fully depress the clutch pedal and shift into Second or Third gear. When the car reaches 10 mph, let the clutch pedal up slowly until the engine catches.

NOTE: *It is impossible to push-start models equipped with automatic transmission.*

For information on towing points for 1970–77 cars, see the chart. On 1978–81 cars, tow using the tie down tabs located under front and rear bumpers.

The following precautions should be observed when towing the vehicle:

1. Always place the transmission in Neutral and release the parking brake.

2. Models equipped with automatic transmissions, except 1974–77 models, may be towed with the transmission in Neutral, but only for short distances at speeds below 20 mph. On 1974–77 models, or if the transmission is inoperative, either tow the car with the rear wheels off the ground or disconnect the drive shaft at the differential end. If you are towing a 1978 or later car with an automatic transmission, you may tow the car for up to 50 miles and at speeds of up to 30 miles per hour.

3. If the rear axle is defective, the car must be towed with its rear wheels off the ground.

4. Always turn the steering column lock to ON and then return to ACC. This prevents the steering column from locking.

CAUTION: *The steering column lock is not designed to hold the wheels straight while the car is being towed. Therefore, if the car is being towed with its front end down, place a dolly under the front wheels.*

JACKING

There are certain safety precautions which should be observed when jacking the vehicle. They are as follows:

1. Always jack the car on a level surface.

2. Set the parking brake if the front wheels are to be raised. This will keep the car from rolling backward off the jack.

3. If the rear wheels are to be raised, block the front wheels to keep the car from rolling forward.

4. Block the wheel diagonally opposite the one which is being raised.

NOTE: *The tool which is supplied with Toyota passenger cars includes a wheel block.*

5. If the vehicle is being raised in order to work underneath it, support it with jackstands. Do not place the jackstands against the sheet metal panels beneath the car or they will become distorted.

CAUTION: *Do not work beneath a vehicle supported only by a tire-changing jack.*

6. Do not use a bumper jack to raise the vehicle; the bumpers are not designed for this purpose.

Tips

Whenever you plan to work under the car, you must support it on jackstands or ramps. Never use cinder blocks or stacks of wood to support the car, even if you're only going to be under it for a few minutes.

JUMP STARTING A DEAD BATTERY

The chemical reaction in a battery produces explosive hydrogen gas. This is the safe way to jump start a dead battery, reducing the chances of an accidental spark that could cause an explosion.

Jump Starting Precautions

1. Be sure both batteries are of the same voltage.
2. Be sure both batteries are of the same polarity (have the same grounded terminal).
3. Be sure the vehicles are not touching.
4. Be sure the vent cap holes are not obstructed.
5. Do not smoke or allow sparks around the battery.
6. In cold weather, check for frozen electrolyte in the battery.
7. Do not allow electrolyte on your skin or clothing.
8. Be sure the electrolyte is not frozen.

Jump Starting Procedure

1. Determine voltages of the two batteries; they must be the same.
2. Bring the starting vehicle close (they must not touch) so that the batteries can be reached easily.
3. Turn off all accessories and both engines. Put both cars in Neutral or Park and set the handbrake.
4. Cover the cell caps with a rag—do not cover terminals.
5. If the terminals on the run-down battery are heavily corroded, clean them.
6. Identify the positive and negative posts on both batteries and connect the cables in the order shown.
7. Start the engine of the starting vehicle and run it at fast idle. Try to start the car with the dead battery. Crank it for no more than 10 seconds at a time and let it cool off for 20 seconds in between tries.
8. If it doesn't start in 3 tries, there is something else wrong.
9. Disconnect the cables in the reverse order.
10. Replace the cell covers and dispose of the rags.

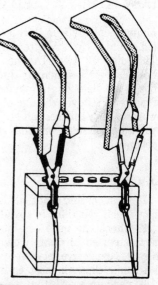

Side terminal batteries occasionally pose a problem when connecting jumper cables. There frequently isn't enough room to clamp the cables without touching sheet metal. Side terminal adaptors are available to alleviate this problem and should be removed after use.

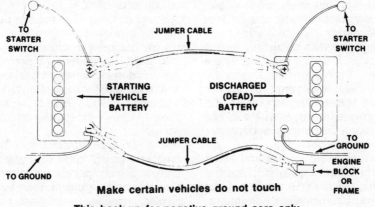

TO STARTER SWITCH

JUMPER CABLE

TO STARTER SWITCH

STARTING VEHICLE BATTERY

DISCHARGED (DEAD) BATTERY

JUMPER CABLE

TO GROUND

TO GROUND

ENGINE BLOCK OR FRAME

Make certain vehicles do not touch

This hook-up for negative ground cars only

Small hydraulic, screw, or scissors jacks are satisfactory for raising the car. Drive-on trestles or ramps are also a handy and safe way to both raise and support the car. These can be bought or constructed from wood or steel.

If your car is to be raised with a hoist such as the type used in service stations, the pads of the hoist should be positioned on the frame rails of the car, or at the points indicated for jackstand support. Never support the car on any suspension member or under-body panel.

HOW TO BUY A USED CAR

Many people believe that a two or three year old, or older, car is a better buy than a new one. This may be true. The new car suffers the heaviest depreciation in the first few years, but is not old enough to present a lot of costly repairs. Whatever the age of the used car you want to buy, this section and a little patience will help you select one that should be safe and dependable.

Shopping Tips

1. First, decide what model you want and how much you want to spend.

2. Check the used car lots and your local newspaper ads. Privately owned cars are usually less expensive, however, you will not get a warranty that, in most cases, comes with a used car purchased from a dealer.

3. Never shop at night. The glare of the lights makes it easy to miss defects in the paint and faults in the body caused by accident or rust repair.

4. Once you've found a car that you're interested in, try to get the name and phone number of the previous owner. Contact that person for details about the car. If he or she refuses information about the car, shop elsewhere. A private seller can tell you about the car and its maintenance history, but there are few laws requiring honesty from private citizens who are selling used vehicles. There are laws forbidding the tampering with or turning back a vehicle's odometer mileage reading. These laws apply to both a private seller as well commercial dealers. The law also requires that the seller, or anyone transferring ownership of a vehicle, must provide the buyer with a signed statement indicating the mileage on the odometer at the time of transfer.

5. Write down the year, model and serial number of the car before you buy it. Then, dial 1–800–424–9393, the toll-free number of the National Highway Traffic Safety Administration, and ask if the car has ever been included on any manufacturer's recall list. If so, make sure the necessary repairs were made.

6. Use the Used Car Checklist in this section, and check all the items on the used car that you are considering. Some items are more important than others. You've already determined how much money you can afford for repairs, and, depending on the price of the car, you should consider doing some of the needed repairs yourself. Beware, however, of trouble in areas involving operation, safety or emissions. Problems in the Used Car Checklist are arranged as follows:

1–8: Two or more problems in this segment indicate a lack of maintenance. You should reconsider your selection.

9–13: Indicates a lack of proper care, however, these can usually be corrected with a tune-up or relatively simple parts replacement.

14–17: Problems in the engine or transmission can be very expensive. Walk away from any car with problems in these areas.

7. If you are satisfied with the apparent condition of the car, take it to an independent diagnostic center or mechanic for a complete checkout. If your state has a state inspection program, have it inspected immediately before purchase, or specify on the invoice that purchase is conditional on the car's passing a state inspection.

8. Road test the car. Refer to the Road Test Checklist in this section. If your original evaluation, and the road test agree, the rest is up to you.

Used Car Checklist

NOTE: *The numbers on the illustration correspond to the numbers in this checklist.*

1. *Mileage:* Average mileage is about 12,000 miles per year. More than average may indicate hard usage. Catalytic converter equipped models may need converter service beyond the 50,000 mile mark.

2. *Paint:* Check around the tailpipe, molding and windows for overspray, indicating that the car has been repainted.

3. *Rust:* Check fenders, doors, rocker panels, window moldings, wheelwells, flooring and in the bed, for signs of rust. Any rust at all will be a problem. There is no way to stop the spread of rust, except to replace the part or panel.

4. *Body Appearance:* Check the moldings, bumpers, grille, vinyl roof, glass, doors, tail gate and body panels for overall condition. Check for misalignment, loose holddown clips, ripples, scratches in the glass, rips or patches in the top. Mismatched paint, welding in the

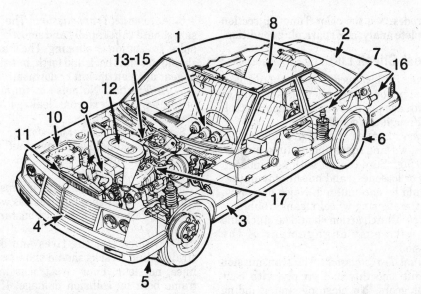

You should check these points when buying a used car. The "Used Car Checklist" gives an explanation of the numbered items

bed, severe misalignment of body panels or ripples may indicate crash work.

5. *Leaks:* Get down under the car and take a good look. There are no "normal" leaks, other than water from the air conditioning condenser drain tube.

6. *Tires:* Check the tire air pressure. A common trick is to pump the tires up hard to make the car roll more easily. Check the tread wear and the spare tire condition. Uneven wear is a sign that the front end is, or was, out of alignment. See the Troubleshooting Chapter for indications of treadwear.

7. *Shock Absorbers:* Check the shocks by forcing downward sharply on each corner of the car. Good shocks will not allow the car to rebound more than twice after you let go.

8. *Interior:* Check the entire interior. You're looking for an interior condition that agrees with the overall condition of the car. Reasonable wear can be expected, but be suspicious of new seatcovers on sagging seats, new pedal pads, and worn armrests. These indicate an attempt to cover up hard usage. Pull back the carpets and/or mats and look for signs of water leaks or flooding. Look for missing hardware, door handles, control knobs, etc. Check lights and signal operations. Make sure that all accessories, such as air conditioner, heater, radio, etc., work. Air conditioning, especially automatic temperature control units, can be very expensive to repair. Check the operation of the windshield wipers.

9. *Belts and Hoses:* Open the hood and check all belts and hoses for wear, cracks, or weak spots. Check around hose connections for stains, indicating leaks.

10. *Battery:* Low electrolyte level, corroded terminals and/or a cracked battery case, indicate a lack of maintenance.

11. *Radiator:* Look for corrosion or rust in the coolant, indicating a lack of maintenance.

12. *Air Filter:* A dirty air filter element indicates a lack of maintenance.

13. *Spark Plug Wires:* Check the wires for cracks, burned spots or wear. Worn wires will have to be replaced.

14. *Oil Level:* If the level is low, chances are that the engine either uses an excessive amount of oil, or leaks. If the oil on the dipstick appears foamy or tan in color, a leakage of coolant into the oil is indicated. Stop here, and go elsewhere for your car. If the oil appears thin or has the smell of gasoline, stop here and go elsewhere for your car.

15. *Automatic Transmission:* Pull the transmission dipstick out when the engine is running in PARK. If the fluid is hot, the dipstick should read FULL. If the fluid is cold, the level will show about one pint low. The fluid itself should be bright red and translucent, with no burned odor. Fluid that is brown or black and has a burned odor is a sign that the transmission needs major repairs.

16. *Exhaust:* Check the color of the exhaust smoke. Blue smoke indicates excessive oil usage, usually due to major internal engine problems. Black smoke can indicate burned valves or carburetor problems. Check the exhaust system for leaks. A leaky system is dangerous and expensive to replace.

17. *Spark Plugs:* Remove one of the spark plugs. An engine in good condition will have spark plugs with a light tan or gray deposit on

the electrodes. See the color Tune-Up section for a complete analysis of spark plug condition.

Road Test Check List

1. *Engine Performance:* The car should have good accelerator response, whether cold or warm, with adequate power and smooth acceleration through the gears.

2. *Brakes:* Brakes should provide quick, firm stops, with no squealing, pulling or fade.

3. *Steering:* Sure control with no binding, harshness or looseness, and no shimmy in the wheel should be encountered. Noise or vibration from the steering wheel means trouble.

4. *Clutch:* Clutch action should be quick and smooth with easy engagement of the transmission.

5. *Manual Transmission:* The transmission should shift smoothly and crisply with easy change of gears. No clashing and grinding should be evident. The transmission should not stick in gear, nor should there be any gear whine evident at road speed.

6. *Automatic Transmission:* The transmission should shift rapidly and smoothly, with no noise, hesitation or slipping. The transmission should not shift back and forth, but should stay in gear until an upshift or downshift is needed.

7. *Differential:* No noise or thumps should be present. No external leakage should be present.

8. *Driveshaft, Universal Joints:* Vibration and noise could mean driveshaft problems. Clicking at low speed or coast conditions means worn U-joints.

9. *Suspension:* Try hitting bumps at different speeds. A car that bounces has weak shock absorbers. Clunks mean worn bushings or ball joints.

10. *Frame:* Wet the tires and drive in a straight line. Tracks should show two straight lines, not four. Four tire tracks indicates a frame bent by collision damage. If the tires can't be wet for this purpose, have a friend drive along behind you and see if the car appears to be traveling in a straight line.

Tune-Up and Performance Maintenance

2

TUNE-UP PROCEDURES

In order to extract the full measure of performance and economy from your engine it is essential that it be properly tuned at regular intervals. A regular tune-up will keep your car's engine running smoothly and will prevent the annoying minor breakdowns and poor performance associated with an untuned engine.

A complete tune-up should be performed every 12,000 miles or twelve months, whichever comes first. This interval should be halved if the car is operated under severe conditions, such as trailer towing, prolonged idling, continual stop and start driving, or if starting or running problems are noticed. It is assumed that the routine maintenance described in Chapter 1 has been kept up, as this will have a decided effect on the results of a tune-up. All of the applicable steps of a tune-up should be followed in order, as the result is a cumulative one.

If the specifications on the tune-up sticker in the engine compartment disagree with the Tune-Up Specifications chart in this chapter, the figures on the sticker must be used. The sticker often reflects changes made during the production run.

Spark Plug

The job of the spark plug is to ignite the air/fuel mixture in the cylinder as the piston approaches the top of the compression stroke. The ignited mixture then expands and forces the piston down on the power stroke. This turns the crankshaft which then turns the remainder of the drive train.

The average life of a spark plug, if the engine is run on leaded fuel, is 12,000 miles, while on unleaded fuel, it may be considerably longer. Spark plug life also depends upon the mechanical condition of the engine and the type of driving you are doing. Plugs usually last longer and stay cleaner if most of your driving is done on long trips at high speeds.

The electrode end of the spark plug (the end that goes into the cylinder) is also a very good indicator of the mechanical condition of your engine. If a spark plug should foul and begin to misfire, you will have to find the condition that caused the plug to foul and correct it. It is also a good idea to occasionally give all the plugs the once-over to get an idea how the inside of your engine is doing. A small amount of deposit on a spark plug, after it has been in use for

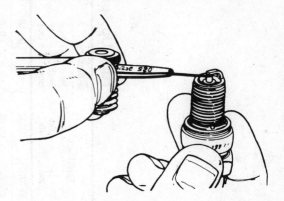

Check the spark plug gap with a wire gauge

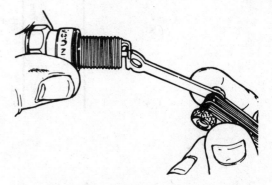

Adjust the spark plug gap with a bending tool

Tune-Up Specifications

Year	Engine Type	Spark Plugs Type	Gap (in.)	Distributor Point Dwell (deg)	Point Gap (in.)	Ignition Timing (deg) ▲ MT	Ignition Timing (deg) ▲ AT	Compression Pressure (psi) @ 250 rpm **	Fuel Pump Pressure (psi)	Idle Speed (rpm) ▲ MT	Idle Speed (rpm) ▲ AT	Valve Clearance (in.) ‡ Intake	Valve Clearance (in.) ‡ Exhaust
1970	8R-C	W20EP	0.031	52	0.018	TDC	TDC	164	2.8–4.3	650	650	0.008	0.014
	2M	W20EP	0.031	41	0.018	TDC	TDC	156	3.6–5.0	650	650	0.007	0.010
1971	8R-C	W20EP	0.031	52	0.018	10B	10B	164	2.8–4.3	650	650	0.008	0.014
	2M	W20EP	0.031	41	0.018	TDC	TDC	156	3.6–5.0	650	650	0.007	0.010
1972	18R-C	W20EP	0.031	52	0.018	7B	7B	164	2.8–4.3	650	650	0.008	0.014
	2M	W16EP	0.030	41	0.018	7B	7B	149	3.4–4.6	700	600	0.007	0.010
	4M	W14EP	0.031	41	0.018	7B	5B	156	4.2–5.4	700	650	0.007	0.010
1973	18R-C	W20EP	0.031	52	0.018	7B	7B	156	2.8–4.3	650	650	0.008	0.014
	4M	W14EP	0.031	41	0.018	7B	5B	156	4.2–5.4	700	650	0.007	0.010
1974	18R-C	W20EP	0.031	52	0.018	7B	7B	156	2.8–4.3	650	850	0.008	0.014
	4M	W16EP	0.031	41	0.018	5B	5B	156	4.2–5.4	700	750	0.007	0.010
1975–76	20R	W16EP	0.030	52	0.018	8B	8B	156	2.2–4.2	850	850	0.008	0.012
	4M ①	W16EP	0.030	41	0.018	10B	10B	156	4.2–5.4	800	750	0.007	0.010
	4M ②	W16EP	0.030	41	0.018	5B	5B	156	4.2–5.4	800	750	0.007	0.010
1977	20R	W16EP	0.031	52	0.018	8B	8B	156	2.8–4.3	850	800	0.008	0.012

Year	Engine	Spark Plug Type	Gap (in.)	Distributor		Ignition Timing				Idle Speed		Valve Clearance	
1978–79	20R	BP5EA-L	0.031	Electronic	—	8B	8B	156	2.2–4.2	800	850	0.008	0.012
	4M	BPR5EA-L	0.031	Electronic	—	10B③	10B③	156	4.2–5.4	750	750	0.011	0.014
1980–82	20R	BPR5EA-L	0.031	Electronic	—	8B	8B	156	2.2–4.3	800	850	0.008	0.012
	22R	BPR5EA-L	0.031	Electronic	—	8B	8B	156	2.2–4.3	800⑤	850⑤	0.008	0.012
	4M-E④	BPR5EA-L	0.031	Electronic	—	—	12B	156	33–38	—	800	0.011	0.014
	5M-E④	BPR5EA-L	0.031	Electronic	—	—	8B	156	33–38	—	800	0.011	0.014
1983–84	2S-E	BPR5EA-L11	0.043	Electronic	—	5B	5B	156	28–36	700	700	Hyd.	Hyd.
1984	3Y-EC	BPR5EP-11	0.043	Electronic	—	8B	8B	171	33–38	950	950	Hyd.	Hyd.
1984–85	5M-GE	BPR5EP-11	0.043	Electronic	—	10B⑥	10B⑥	164	35–38	650	650	Hyd.	Hyd.
1986	5M-GE	BPR5EP-11	0.055	Electronic	—	10B⑥	10B⑥	164	33–38	650	650	Hyd.	Hyd.
1985	3Y-EC	BPR5EP-11	0.043	Electronic	—	8B⑥	8B⑥	171	33–38	700	750	Hyd.	Hyd.
1986	3Y-EC	BPR5EP-11	0.055	Electronic	—	12B⑥	12B⑥	178	33–38	700	750	Hyd.	Hyd.

① USA—except California
② California only
③ Calif.: 8B
④ Electronic fuel injection
⑤ 1982: 700 MT / 750 AT
⑥ Check with connector shorted. See text.

▲ With manual transmission in Neutral and automatic transmission in drive (D).
** Difference between cylinders should not exceed 14 psi. Look for uniformity rather than specific pressures.
‡ Valve clearance checked with engine HOT.

MT—Manual transmission
AT—Automatic transmission
TDC—Top Dead Center
B—Before top dead center

NOTE: If the information given in this chart disagrees with the information on the engine tune-up decal, use the specifications on the decal—changes may have been made during production.

any period of time, should be considered normal. But a black liquid deposit on the plugs indicates oil fouling. You should schedule a few free Saturday afternoons to find the source of it. Because the combustion chamber is supposed to be sealed from the rest of the engine, oil on the spark plug means your engine is hemorrhaging.

Ideally, you should clean and adjust spark plugs every 6,000 miles or so, if you're using leaded fuel, or if the engine shows signs of misfire. Spark plugs should be replaced every 12,000 miles on 1970–74 vehicles, every 12,500 miles on 1975–76 vehicles, and every 15,000 miles on 1975–76 vehicles. On 1980 and later models, the interval for spark plug changes is 30,000 miles.

1. If the spark plug wires are not numbered as to their cylinder, place a piece of masking tape on each wire and number it.

2. Grasp each wire by the rubber boot at the end. Pull the wires from the spark plugs. If the boots stick to the plugs, remove them with a twisting motion. Do not attempt to remove the spark plug wires from the plugs by pulling on the wire itself as this will damage the spark plug wires.

3. Clean any foreign material from around the spark plugs before removing them. Use the spark plug wrench supplied in the tool kit or a ratchet with an extension (if necessary) and a $^{13}/_{16}$″ plug socket.

Compare the condition of the spark plugs to the plugs shown in the Color Insert section of Chapter 4. It should be remembered that any type of deposit will decrease the efficiency of the plug. If the plugs are not to be replaced, they should be thoroughly cleaned before installation. If the electrode ends of the plugs are not worn or damaged and if they are to be reused, wipe off the porcelain insulator on each plug and check for cracks or breaks. If either condition exists, the plug must be replaced.

If the plugs are judged reusable, have them cleaned on a plug cleaning machine (found in most service stations) or remove the deposits with a stiff wire brush.

Check the plug gap on both new and used plugs before installing them in the engine. The ground electrode must be parallel to the center electrode and the specified size wire gauge should pass through the opening with a slight drag.

NOTE: *Do not use a flat gauge; an inaccurate reading will result.*

If the center of ground electrode has worn unevenly, level it off with a file. If the air gap between the two electrodes is not correct, open or close the ground electrode, with the proper tool, to bring it to specifications. Such a tool is usually provided with a gap gauge.

Install the plugs, as follows:

1. Lightly oil the spark plug threads with engine oil.

2. Insert the plugs in the engine and hand tighten them. Do not cross-thread the plugs.

3. Torque the spark plugs to 11–14 ft.lb. Use caution when tightening the spark plugs, since most Toyota engines have aluminum heads.

4. Install each wire on its respective plug, making sure that it is firmly connected.

CHECKING AND REPLACING SPARK PLUG CABLES

At every tune-up, visually inspect the spark plug cables for burns, cuts, or breaks in the insulation. Check the boots and the nipples on the distributor cap and coil. Replace any damaged wiring.

Every 36,000 miles or so, the resistance of the wires should be checked with an ohmmeter. Wires with excessive resistance will cause misfiring, and may make the engine difficult to start in damp weather. Generally, the useful life of the cables is 36,000–50,000 miles.

To check resistance, remove the distributor cap, leaving the wires attached. Connect one lead of an ohmmeter to an electrode within the cap. Connect the other lead to the corresponding spark plug terminal (remove it from the plug for this test). Replace any wire which shows a resistance over 50,000Ω. Generally speaking, however, resistance should not be over 30,000Ω, and 50,000Ω must be considered the outer limit of acceptability. Test the high tension lead from the coil by connecting the ohmmeter between the center contact in the distributor cap and either of the primary terminals of the coil. If resistance is more than 25,000Ω, remove the cable from the coil and check the resistance of the cable alone. Anything over 15,000Ω is cause for replacement. It should be remembered that resistance is also a function of length; the longer the cable, the greater the resistance. Thus, if the cables on your car are longer than the factory originals, resistance will be higher, quite possibly outside these limits.

When installing new cables, replace them one at a time to avoid mixups. Start by replacing the longest one first. Install the boot firmly over the spark plug. Route the wire over the same path as the original. Insert the nipple firmly into the tower on the cap or the coil.

Breaker Points and Condenser

The points and condenser function as a circuit breaker for the primary circuit of the ignition system. The ignition coil must boost the 12 volts (V) of electrical pressure supplied to it by the battery to about 20,000 V in order to fire

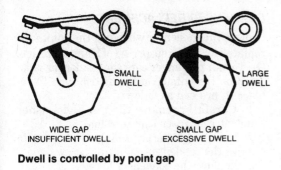

SMALL
DWELL

LARGE
DWELL

WIDE GAP
INSUFFICIENT DWELL

SMALL GAP
EXCESSIVE DWELL

Dwell is controlled by point gap

ACTUAL POINT GAP

FEELER BLADE OF
SPECIFIED THICKNESS

The feeler gauge method of checking point gap is less accurate than the dwell meter method

the spark plugs. To do this, the coil depends on the points and condenser for assistance.

The coil has a primary and a secondary circuit. When the ignition key is turned to the ON position, the battery supplies voltage to the primary side of the coil which passes the voltage on to the points. The points are connected to ground to complete the primary circuit. As the cam in the distributor turns, the points open and the primary circuit collapses. The magnetic force in the primary circuit of the coil cuts through the secondary circuit and increases the voltage in the secondary circuit to a level that is sufficient to fire the spark plugs. When the points open, the electrical charge contained in the primary circuit jumps the gap that is created between the two open contacts of the points. If this electrical charge was not transferred elsewhere, the material on the contacts of the points would melt and that all important gap between the contacts would start to change. If this gap is not maintained, the points will not break the primary circuit. If the

primary circuit is not broken, the secondary circuit will not have enough voltage to fire the spark plugs. Enter the condenser.

The function of the condenser is to absorb the excessive voltage from the points when they open and thus prevent the points from becoming pitted or burned.

If you have ever wondered why it is necessary to tune-up your engine occasionally, consider the fact that the ignition system must complete the above cycle each time a spark plug fires. On a four-cylinder, four-cycle engine, two of the four plugs must fire once for every engine revolution. If the idle speed of your engine is 800 revolutions per minute (800 rpm), the breaker points open and close two times for each revolution. For every minute your engine idles, your points open and close 1,600 times (2 800 = 1,600). And that is just at idle. What about at 60 mph?

There are two ways to check breaker point gap: with a feeler gauge or with a dwell meter. Either way you set the points, you are adjusting the amount of time (in degrees of distributor rotation) that the points will remain open. If you adjust the points with a feeler gauge, you are setting the maximum amount the points will open when the rubbing block on the points is on a high point of the distributor cam. When you adjust the points with a dwell meter, you are measuring the number of degrees (of distributor cam rotation) that the points will remain closed before they start to open as a high point of the distributor cam approaches the rubbing block of the points.

If you still do not understand how the points function, take a friend, go outside, and remove the distributor cap from your engine. Have your friend operate the starter (make sure the transmission is not in gear) as you look at the exposed parts of the distributor.

There are two rules that should always be followed when adjusting or replacing points. The points and condenser are a matched set. Never replace one without replacing the other. If you change the point gap or dwell of the engine, you also change the ignition timing. Therefore, if you adjust the points, you must also adjust the timing.

INSPECTION AND CLEANING

The breaker points should be inspected and cleaned at 6,000 mile intervals. To do so, perform the following steps:

1. Disconnect the high tension lead from the coil.

2. Unsnap the two distributor cap retaining clips and lift the cap straight up. Leave the leads connected to the cap and position it out of the way.

3. Remove the rotor and dust cover by pulling them straight up.

4. Place a screwdriver against the breaker points and pry them open. Examine their condition. If they are excessively worn, burned, or pitted, they should be replaced.

5. Polish the points with a point file. Do not use emery cloth or sandpaper. These may leave particles on the points causing them to arc.

6. Clean the distributor cap and rotor with alcohol. Inspect the cap terminals for looseness and corrosion. Check the rotor tip for excessive burning. Inspect both cap and rotor for cracks. Replace either if they show any of the above signs of wear or damage.

7. Check the operation of the centrifugal advance mechanism by turning the rotor clockwise. Release the rotor. It should return to its original position. If it doesn't, check for binding parts.

8. Check the vacuum advance unit, by removing the plastic cap and pressing on the octane selector. It should return to its original position. Check for binding if it doesn't.

9. If the points do not require replacement, proceed with the adjustment section below. Otherwise perform the point and condenser replacement procedures.

POINT REPLACEMENT

The points should be replaced every 12,000 miles (24,000 miles with transistorized ignition), or if they are badly pitted, worn, or burned. To replace them, proceed as follows:

1. If you have not already done so, perform Steps 1 through 3 of the preceding Inspection and Cleaning procedure.

2. Unfasten the point lead connector.

3. Remove the point retaining clip and unfasten the point holddown screw(s). It is a good idea to use a magnetic or locking screwdriver to remove the small screws inside the distributor, since they have been dropped.

4. Lift out the point set.

5. Install the new point set in the reverse order of removal. Adjust the points as detailed below, after completing installation.

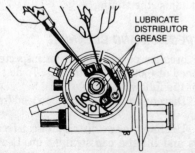

LUBRICATE DISTRIBUTOR GREASE

Adjusting the points

CONDENSER REPLACEMENT

Replace the condenser whenever the points are replaced, or if it is suspected of being defective. On Toyota passenger cars the condenser is located on the outside of the distributor. To replace it, proceed as follows:

1. Carefully remove the nut and washer from the condenser lead terminal.

2. Use a magnetic or locking screwdriver to remove the condenser mounting screw.

3. Remove the condenser.

4. Installation of a new condenser is performed in the reverse order of removal.

ADJUSTMENT

Perform the gap adjustment procedure whenever new points are installed, or as part of routine maintenance. If you are adjusting an old set of points, you must check the dwell as well, since the feeler gauge is only really accurate with a new point set.

1. Rotate the engine by hand or by using a remote starter switch, so that the rubbing block is on the high point of the cam lobe.

2. Insert a 0.45mm feeler gauge between the points. A slight drag should be felt.

3. If no drag is felt or if the feeler gauge cannot be inserted at all, loosen, but do not remove, the point holddown screw.

4. Insert a screwdriver into the adjustment slot. Rotate the screwdriver until the proper point gap is attained. The point gap is increased by rotating the screwdriver counterclockwise and decreased by rotating it clockwise.

5. Tighten the point holddown screw.

Lubricate the cam lobes, breaker arm, rubbing block, arm pivot, and distributor shaft with special high temperature distributor grease.

Transistorized Ignition

Transistorized ignition was first used on 1974 4M engines sold in California. With the introduction of 1975 models, usage has been extended to all Toyota vehicles sold in the United States.

The transistorized ignition system employed by Toyota works very much like the conventional system previously described. Regular breaker points are used, but instead of switching primary current to the coil off-and-on, they are used to trigger a switching transistor. The transistor, in turn, switches the coil primary current on and off.

Since only a very small amount of current is needed to operate the transistor, the points will not become burned or pitted, as they

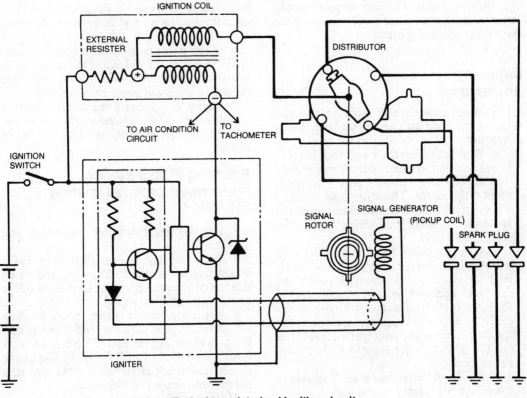

Typical transistorized ignition circuit

would if they had full primary current passing through them. This also allows the primary current to be higher than usual because the use of a higher current would normally cause the points to fail much more rapidly.

As already stated, the condenser is used to absorb any extra high voltage passing through the points. Since, in the transistorized system, there is no high current, no condenser is needed or used.

As a result of the lower stress placed on them, the points only have to be replaced every 24,000 miles instead of the usual 12,000 miles.

The Toyota transistorized ignition system may be quickly identified by the lack of a condenser on the outside of the distributor and by the addition of a control box, which is connected between the distributor and the primary side of the coil.

A fully transistorized ignition system was introduced in 1977. The system, including an ignition signal generating mechanism instead of the normal contact points, became the standard ignition system on all models from 1978.

The mechanism consists of a timing rotor, a magnet and a pick-up coil, all mounted in place of the points inside the distributor. As the signal rotor spins, the teeth on it pass a projection leading form the pick-up coil. When

this happens voltage is allowed to pass through the system, firing the spark plugs. There is no physical contact and no electric arcing, hence no need to replace burnt or worn parts.

SERVICE PRECAUTIONS

Basically, the transistorized ignition is serviced just like its conventional counterpart. The points must be checked, adjusted, and replaced in the same manner. Point gap and dwell must be checked and set. The points should also be kept clean and should be replaced at 24,000 mile intervals. Of course, since there is no condenser, it does not have to be replaced when the points are.

However, there are several precautions to observe when servicing the transistorized ignition system.

1. Use only pure alcohol to clean the points. Shop solvent or an oily rag will leave a film on the points which will not allow the low current to pass.

CAUTION: *Hook up a tachometer, dwell meter, or a combination dwell/tachometer to the negative (−) side of the coil, NOT to the distributor or the positive (+) side. Damage to the switching transistor will result if the meter is connected in the usual manner.*

2. See the previous section for point installation and Chapter 3 for troubleshooting the fully transistorized ignition.

Dwell Angle
ADJUSTMENT

1. Connect a dwell meter to the ignition system, according to the manufacturer's instructions.

a. When checking the dwell on a conventional ignition system, connect meter lead (usually black) to a metallic part of the car to ground the meter. The other lead (usually red) is connected to the coil primary post (the one with the small lead which runs to the distributor body).

b. When checking dwell on a model with transistorized ignition, ground one meter lead (usually black) to a metallic part of the car. Hook up the other lead (usually red) to the negative (−) coil terminal. Under no circumstances should the meter be connected to the distributor or the positive (+) side of the coil. (See the preceding Service Precautions.)

2. If the dwell meter has a set line, adjust the needle until it rests on the line.

3. Start the engine. It should be warmed up and running at the specified idle speed.

NOTE: *It is not necessary to check the dwell on the fully transistorized system. It is set at the factory and requires no adjustment.*

CAUTION: *Be sure to keep fingers, tools, clothes, hair, and wires clear of the engine fan. The transmission should be in Neutral (or Park), parking brake set, and the engine running in a well ventilated area.*

4. Check the reading on the swell meter. If you have a Toyota with a 4-cylinder engine and your meter doesn't have a 4-cylinder scale, multiply the 8-cylinder reading by two.

5. If the meter reading is within the range specified in the Tune-Up Specifications chart, shut the engine off and disconnect the dwell meter.

6. If the dwell is not within specifications, shut the engine off and adjust the point gap as previously outlined. Increasing the point gap decreases the dwell angle and vice versa.

7. Adjust the points until dwell is within specifications, then disconnect the dwell meter. Adjust the timing; see the following section.

Adjusting Pickup Air Gap
FULLY TRANSISTORIZED IGNITION SYSTEM

1. Remove the distributor cap, rotor, and dust shield.

2. Turn the engine over (you may use a socket wrench on the front pulley bolt to do this) until the projection on the pickup coil is directly opposite the signal rotor tooth.

3. Get a non-ferrous (paper, brass, or plastic) feeler gauge of 0.30mm, and insert it into the pickup air gap. DO NOT USE AN ORDINARY METAL FEELER GAUGE! The gauge should just touch either side of the gap (the permissible range is 0.2–0.4mm).

4. If the gap is either too wide or too narrow, loosen the two Phillips screws mounting the pickup coil onto the distributor base plate. Then, wedge a screwdriver between the notch in the pickup coil assembly and the two dimples on the base plate, and turn the screwdriver back and forth until the pickup gap is correct.

5. Tighten the screws and recheck gap, readjusting if necessary.

SERVICING

Fully Transistorized Ignition System

A troubleshooting guide is found in the beginning of chapter three. Since dwell adjustment is not necessary, and air gap adjustment infrequent, the only other things to keep your eye on are the condition of the plug wires, and cap and rotor.

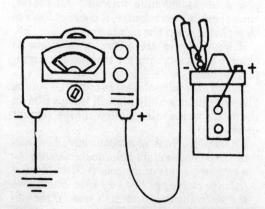

Dwell meter connections with transistorized ignition

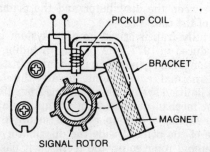

Parts of the fully transistorized ignition system signal generator

Ignition Timing

Ignition timing is the measurement in degrees of crankshaft rotation of the instant the spark plugs in the cylinders fire, in relation to the location of the piston, while the piston is on its compression stroke.

Ignition timing is adjusted by loosening the distributor locking device and turning the distributor in the engine.

Ideally, the air/fuel mixture in the cylinder will be ignited (by the spark plug) and just beginning its rapid expansion as the piston passes top dead center (TDC) of the compression stroke. If this happens, the piston will be beginning the power stroke just as the compressed (by the movement of the piston) and ignited (by the spark plug) air/fuel mixture starts to expand. The expansion of the air/fuel mixture will then force the piston down on the power stroke and turn the crankshaft.

It takes a fraction of a second for the spark from the plug to completely ignite the mixture in the cylinder. Because of this, the spark plug must fire before the piston reaches TDC, if the mixture is to be completely ignited as the piston passes TDC. This measurement is given in degrees of top dead center (BTDC). If the ignition timing setting for your engine is seven degrees (7°) BTDC, this means that the spark plug must fire at a time when the piston for that cylinder is 7° before top dead center of the compression stroke. However, this only holds true while your engine is at idle speed.

As you accelerate from idle, the speed of your engine (rpm) increases. The increase in rpm means that the pistons are now traveling up and down much faster. Because of this, the spark plugs will have to fire even sooner if the mixture is to be completely ignited as the piston passes TDC. To accomplish this, the distributor incorporates means to advance the timing of the spark as engine speed increases.

The distributor in your Toyota has two means of advancing the ignition timing. One is called centrifugal advance and is actuated by weights in the distributor. The other is called vacuum advance and is controlled by that large circular housing on the side of the distributor.

In addition, some distributors have a vacuum-retard mechanism which is contained in the same housing on the side of the distributor as the vacuum advance. The function of this mechanism is to retard the timing of the ignition spark under certain engine conditions. This causes more complete burning of the air/fuel mixture in the cylinder and consequently lowers exhaust emissions.

Because these mechanisms change ignition timing, it is necessary to disconnect and plug the one or two vacuum lines from the distributor when setting the basic ignition timing.

Because these mechanisms change ignition timing, it is necessary to disconnect and plug the one or two vacuum lines from the distributor when setting the basic ignition timing.

If ignition timing is set too far advanced (BTDC), the ignition and expansion of the air/fuel mixture in the cylinder will try to force the piston down the cylinder while it is still traveling upward. This causes engine ping, a sound which resembles marbles being dropped into an empty tin can. If the ignition timing is too far retarded (after, or ATDC), the piston will have already started down on the power stroke when the air/fuel mixture ignites and expands. This will cause the piston to be forced down only a portion of its travel and will result in poor engine performance and lack of power.

Ignition timing adjustment is checked with a timing light. This instrument is connected to the number one (No. 1) spark plug of the engine. The timing light flashes every time an electrical current is sent from the distributor, through the No. 1 spark plug wire, to the spark plug. The crankshaft pulley and the front cover of the engine are marked with a timing pointer and a timing scale. When the timing pointer is aligned with the 0 mark on the timing scale, the piston in No. 1 cylinder is at TDC of its compression stroke. With the engine running, and the timing light aimed at the timing pointer and timing scale, the stroboscopic flashes from the timing light will allow you to check the ignition timing setting of the engine. The timing light flashes every time the spark plug in the No. 1 cylinder of the engine fires. Since the flash from the timing light makes the crankshaft pulley seem stationary for a moment, you will be able to read the exact position of the piston in the No. 1 cylinder on the timing scale on the front of the engine.

CHECKING AND ADJUSTMENT

Single Point Distributor

1. Warm up the engine. Connect a tachometer and check the engine idle speed to be sure

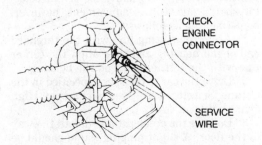

CHECK
ENGINE
CONNECTOR

SERVICE
WIRE

Shorting the check connector—3Y–EC and 4Y–EC

that it is within the specification given in the Tune-Up Specifications chart at the beginning of the chapter.

2. If the timing marks are difficult to see, use a dab of paint or chalk to make them more visible.

3. Connect a timing light according to the manufacturer's instructions. If the light has three wires, one (usually blue or green) must

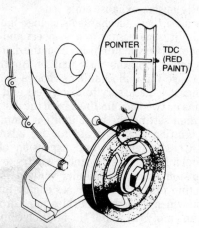

POINTER   TDC (RED PAINT)

8R-C and 18R-C timing marks

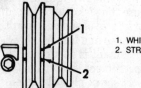

1. WHITE V-GROOVE IS 8° BTDC
2. STRAIGHT GROOVE IS TDC

20R and 22R timing marks

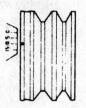

"M" series timing marks

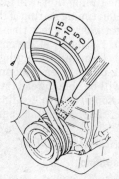

5M-E, 5M-GE timing marks

be installed with an adapter between the No. 1 spark plug lead and the spark plug. The other leads are connected to the positive (+) battery terminal (usually a red lead) and the other to the negative (–) battery terminal (usually a black lead).

4. Disconnect the vacuum line(s) from the distributor vacuum unit. Plug it (them) with a pencil or golf tee(s).

5. Be sure that the timing light wires are clear of the fan and start the engine.

CAUTION: *Keep fingers, clothes, tools, hair, and leads clear of the spinning engine fan. Be sure that you are running the engine in a well ventilated area.*

6. Allow the engine to run at the specified idle speed with the gearshift in Neutral with manual transmission and Drive (D) with automatic transmission.

CAUTION: *Be sure that the parking brake is set and that the front wheels are blocked to prevent the car from rolling forward, especially when Drive is selected with an automatic.*

7. Point the timing marks at the marks indicated in the chart and illustrations. With the engine at idle, timing should be at the specification given on the Tune-Up Specifications chart at the beginning of the chapter.

8. If the timing is not at the specification, loosen the pinch bolt at the base of the distributor just enough so that the distributor can be turned. Turn the distributor to advance or retard the timing as required. Once the proper marks are seen to align with the timing light, timing is correct.

9. Stop the engine and tighten the pinch bolt. Start the engine and recheck timing. Stop the engine. Disconnect the tachometer and timing light. Connect the vacuum line(s) to the distributor vacuum unit.

Octane Selector

The octane selector is used as a fine adjustment to match the vehicle's ignition timing to the grade of gasoline being used. It is located near the distributor vacuum unit, beneath a plastic dust cover. Normally the octane selector should not require adjustment, however, adjustment is as follows:

1. Align the setting line with the threaded end of the housing and then align the center line with the setting mark on the housing.

2. Drive the car to the speed specified in the Octane Selector Test Speeds chart in High gear on a level road.

3. Depress the accelerator pedal all the way to the floor. A slight pinging sound should be heard. As the car accelerates, the sound should

gradually go away. If the pinging sound is loud or if it fails to disappear as the vehicle speed increases, retard the timing by turning the knob toward R (Retard).

4. If there is no pinging sound at all, advance the timing by turning the knob toward A (Advance).

NOTE: *Do not turn the octane selector more than ½ turn toward R. Do not turn it toward A at all.*

5. When the adjustment is completed, replace the plastic dust cover.

NOTE: *One graduation of the octane selector is equal to about ten degrees of crankshaft angle.*

Octane Selector Test Speeds

Engine Type	Test Speed (mph)
2T-C, 8R-C, 20R and 18R-C	16–22
2M and 4M	25

Valve Adjustment

Toyota models equipped with mechanical valve lifters should be adjusted at the factory recommended intervals (every 12,000 miles, 15,000 miles for late models).

Valve adjustment is one factor which determines how far the intake and exhaust valves will open into the cylinder.

If the valve clearance is too large, part of the lift of the camshaft will be used up in removing the excessive clearance, thus the valves will not be opened far enough. This condition has two effects, the valve train components will emit a tapping noise as they take up the excessive clearance, and the engine will perform poorly, since the less the intake valves open, the smaller the amount of air/fuel mixture that will be admitted to the cylinders. The less the exhaust valves open, the greater the back-pressure in the cylinder which prevents the proper air/fuel mixture from entering the cylinder.

If the valve clearance is too small, the intake and exhaust valves will not fully seat on the cylinder head when they close. When a valve seats on the cylinder head it does two things. It seals the combustion chamber so none of the gases in the cylinder can escape and it cools itself by transferring some of the heat it absorbed from the combustion process through the cylinder head and into the engine cooling system. Therefore, if the valve clearance is too small, the engine will run poorly (due to gases escaping from the combustion chamber), and

the valves will overheat and warp (since they cannot transfer heat unless they are touching the seat in the cylinder head).

While all valve adjustments must be as accurate as possible, it is better to have the valve adjustment slightly loose than slightly tight, as burnt valves may result form overly tight adjustments.

ADJUSTMENT PROCEDURES

8R-C and 18R-C Engines

1. Start the engine and allow it to reach normal operating temperature (above 175° F).

2. Stop the engine. Remove the air cleaner assembly, its hoses, and bracket. Remove any other cables, hoses, wires, etc., which are attached to the valve cover. Remove the valve cover. Be careful, some metal parts get quite hot.

3. Check the torque of the valve rocker shaft bolts and the camshaft bearing bolts. They should be 12–17 ft.lb.

4. Check the torque specification of the camshaft bearing cap union bolts. They should be torqued to 11–16 ft.lb.

5. Set the No. 1 cylinder to TDC on its compression stroke. Disconnect the high tension lead from the coil. Remove the spark plug from the No. 1 cylinder and place a screwdriver handle over the hole. Crank the engine until a pressure is felt, then line the V-notch on the crankshaft pulley with the pointer on the timing chain cover. The No. 1 cylinder is now at TDC.

CAUTION: *Do not cover the spark plug hole with your finger when determining the compression stoke. The cylinder head is hot and a burn could occur.*

NOTE: *Do not start the engine. Valve clearances are checked with the engine stopped to prevent hot oil from being splashed out by the timing chain.*

6. Check the clearances (see the Tune-Up Specifications chart) and adjust valves 1, 2, 3,

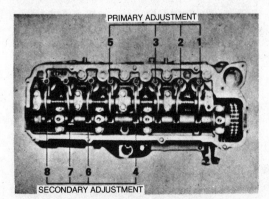

8R-C and 18R-C valve adjusting sequence

and 5 to the proper specifications, if necessary.

7. To adjust the valve clearance, loosen the locknut and turn the adjusting screw until the specified clearance is obtained. Tighten the locknut and check the clearance again.

8. Crank the engine one revolution (360 degress) and perform Steps 6 and 7 for valves 4, 6, 7, and 8 in the illustration.

9. Install the spark plug in the No. 1 cylinder. Connect the high tension lead to the coil. Install the valve cover, air cleaner assembly, and any other components which were removed.

20R and 22R Engines

1. Start the engine and allow it to reach normal operating temperature (above 180° F).

2. Stop the engine. Remove the air cleaner assembly, its hoses, and bracket. Remove any other cables, hoses, wires, etc., which are attached to the valve cover. Remove the valve cover.

3. Set the No. 1 cylinder at top dead center (TDC) of its compression stroke. Remove the high tension lead from the coil. Remove the spark plug from the No. 1 cylinder and place a screwdriver handle over the hole. Crank the engine until pressure is felt and the TDC notch is lined up with the pointer. The No. 1 cylinder is now at TDC.

CAUTION: *Do not cover the spark plug hole with your finger when determining the compression stroke. The cylinder head is hot and a burn could occur.*

4. Measure the clearance between the valve stem and the rocker arm with a feeler gauge for the valves marked FIRST in the illustration. See the Tune-Up Specifications chart for the correct clearance.

5. To adjust the valve clearance, loosen the locknut and turn the adjusting screw until the proper clearance is obtained. Tighten the locknut and check the clearance again.

6. Crank the engine one revolution (360°) and perform Steps 4 and 5 for the set of valves marked SECOND in the illustration.

7. Install the spark plug in the No. 1 cylinder and reconnect the coil lead. Install the valve cover, air cleaner, assembly, and any other components which were removed.

M Series

1. Allow the engine to reach normal operating temperature. Stop the engine.

2. Remove the air cleaner assembly, air cleaner bracket, spark plug cable guides, and any other components attached to the valve cover. Remove the valve cover. Be careful, some metal parts get very hot.

3. Disconnect the high tension lead from the coil. Crank the engine until the No. 1 cylinder is at TDC of it compression stroke. To determine this, remove the spark plug from the No. 1 cylinder and place a screwdriver handle over the spark plug hole. Crank the engine until pressure is felt against the screwdriver handle and the slot in the crankshaft pulley aligns with the 0 (TDC) on the timing scale.

CAUTION: *Do not cover the spark plug hole with your finger when determining the compression stroke, as the nearness of the hole to the exhaust manifold could result in a severe burn.*

4. Check and adjust the clearance of the intake valve on 1, 2, and 4 cylinders and of the exhaust valves on 1, 3, and 5 cylinders.

5. Measure the clearance between the valve stem and the adjusting screw with a feeler gauge of the proper size. (See the Tune-Up Specifications chart at the beginning of this chapter.).

6. If the valves require adjustment, loosen the locknut and turn the adjusting screw until the proper clearance is obtained. Tighten the locknut. Check the clearance again.

7. Crank the engine one revolution (360°) and repeat Steps 5 and 6 for the remaining valves.

8. Install the cylinder head cover, spark plug cable guides, air cleaner bracket, air cleaner assembly and any other components which were removed. Replace the No. 1 spark

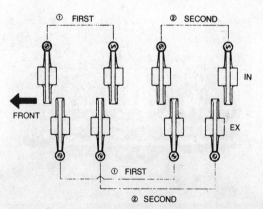

20R and 22R valve adjusting sequence

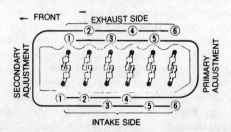

"M" series valve adjusting sequence

plug and reconnect the coil high tension lead, as well.

Diesel Engines

1. Run the engine to normal operating temperature.

2. Remove the cylinder head cover.

3. With a wrench, turn the crankshaft pulley until the notch in the pulley aligns with the timing pointer on the front cover. The engine will now be at TDC #1 cylinder. The lifters on #1 cylinder should both be loose, and both those on #4 should be tight.

4. Using a flat feeler gauge measure the gap between the lifter and the camshaft lobe on each valve of the #1 cylinder. Then, check each valve marked FIRST in the accompanying illustration. If the clearance is not within specifications, note what it is.

5. Turn the crankshaft 360°, in the direction of normal rotation, and align the pointer and notch. Measure the clearance on the valves marked SECOND.

6. If all measurements were within specifications, you can stop here. If not, record the measurements and go on.

7. Turn the crankshaft so that the intake lobe of the camshaft on any cylinder in need of adjustment, is pointing straight up. Both valves on that cylinder may now be adjusted.

8. Using a small screwdriver, turn the lifter so that the notch is easily accessible.

9. Install SST#09248-64010 between the two lobes and turn the handle so that the tool presses down both lifters evenly.

10. Using a small screwdriver and magnet, remove the shims.

11. Using the accompanying thickness chart, measure the thickness of the old shims and locate the previosuly recorded gap measurement in the chart. Index the two columns to determine the new shim thickness.

12. Install the new shims and remove the tool. Recheck the gaps.

13. Repeat this procedure for each affected valve.

Carburetor

This section contains only carburetor adjustments as they normally apply to engine tune-up. Descriptions of the carburetor and complete adjustment procedures can be found in Chapter 4.

When the engine in your Toyota is running, air/fuel mixture from the carburetor is being drawn into the engine by a partial vacuum which is created by the downward movement of the pistons on the intake stroke of the four-stroke engine. The amount of air/fuel mixture

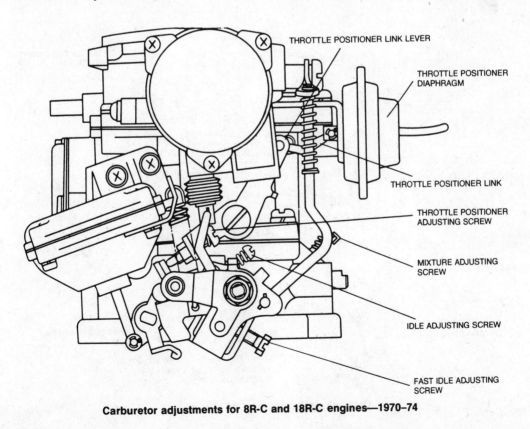

THROTTLE POSITIONER LINK LEVER

THROTTLE POSITIONER DIAPHRAGM

THROTTLE POSITIONER LINK

THROTTLE POSITIONER ADJUSTING SCREW

MIXTURE ADJUSTING SCREW

IDLE ADJUSTING SCREW

FAST IDLE ADJUSTING SCREW

Carburetor adjustments for 8R-C and 18R-C engines—1970–74

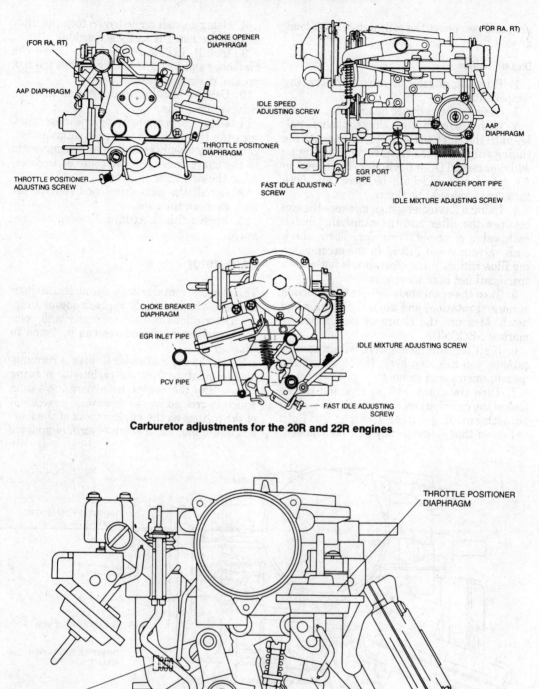

(FOR RA, RT)

AAP DIAPHRAGM

CHOKE OPENER DIAPHRAGM

THROTTLE POSITIONER DIAPHRAGM

THROTTLE POSITIONER ADJUSTING SCREW

(FOR RA, RT)

IDLE SPEED ADJUSTING SCREW

AAP DIAPHRAGM

FAST IDLE ADJUSTING SCREW

EGR PORT PIPE

ADVANCER PORT PIPE

IDLE MIXTURE ADJUSTING SCREW

CHOKE BREAKER DIAPHRAGM

EGR INLET PIPE

IDLE MIXTURE ADJUSTING SCREW

PCV PIPE

FAST IDLE ADJUSTING SCREW

Carburetor adjustments for the 20R and 22R engines

THROTTLE POSITIONER DIAPHRAGM

IDLE ADJUSTING SCREW

MIXTURE ADJUSTING SCREW

THROTTLE POSITIONER LINK

THROTTLE POSITIONER LINK LEVER

FAST IDLE ADJUSTING SCREW

THROTTLE POSITIONER ADJUSTING SCREW

Carburetor adjustments—"M" series

that enters the engine is controlled by throttle plates in the bottom of the carburetor. When the engine is not running, the throttle plates are closed, completely blocking off the bottom of the carburetor from the inside of the engine. The throttle plates are connected, through the throttle linkage, to the gas pedal in the passenger compartment of the car. After you start the engine and put the transmission in gear, you depress the gas pedal to start the car moving. What you actually are doing when you depress the gas pedal is opening the throttle plates in the carburetor to admit more of the air/fuel mixture to the engine. The further you open the throttle plates in the carburetor, the higher the engine speed becomes.

As previously stated, when the engine is not running, the throttle plates in the carburetor are closed. When the engine is idling, it is necessary to open the throttle plates slightly. To prevent having to keep your foot on the gas pedal. The idle speed adjusting screw was added to the carburetor. This screw has the same effect as keeping your foot slightly depressed on the gas pedal. The idle speed adjusting screw contacts a lever (the throttle lever) on the outside of the carburetor. When the screw is turned in, it opens the throttle plate on the carburetor, raising the idle speed of the engine. This screw is called the curb idle adjusting screw, and the procedures in this section will tell you how to adjust it.

Since it is difficult for the engine to draw the air/fuel mixture from the carburetor with the small amount of throttle plate opening that is present when the engine is idling, an idle mixture passage is provided in the carburetor. This passage delivers air/fuel mixture to the engine from a hole which is located in the bottom of the carburetor below the throttle plates. This idle mixture passage contains an adjusting screw which restricts the amount of air/fuel mixture that enters the engine at idle. The procedures given in this section will tell how to set the idle mixture adjusting screw.

IDLE SPEED AND MIXTURE

1970–74

NOTE: *Perform the following adjustments with the air cleaner in place. When adjusting the idle speed and mixture, the gear selector should be placed in Drive (D) on 1970–73 models equipped with an automatic transmission. Be sure to set the parking brake and block the front wheels. On all cars equipped with manual transmissions and all 1974 automatics, adjust the idle speed with the gearshift in Neutral (N).*

1. Run the engine until it reaches normal operating temperature. Stop the engine.

Vacuum at Idle (in. Hg)

Year	Engine	Transmission	Minimum Vacuum Gauge Reading
1970–72	8R-C	All	15.7
	18R-C	MT	17.7
		AT	15.7
	2M and 4M	All	15.7
1973	18R-C	MT	17.7
		AT	15.7
	4M	MT	16.3
		AT	13.8
1974	18R-C	All	17.7
	4M	MT	16.3
		AT	13.8
	20R	All	16.5

MT—Manual transmission
AT—Automatic transmission

2. Connect a tachometer to the engine as detailed in the manufacturer's instructions.

a. On models having a conventional ignition system, one lead (usually black) goes to a good chassis ground. The other lead (usually red) goes to the distributor primary side of the coil (the terminal with small wire running to the distributor body).

b. On models with transistorized ignition, connect one lead (usually black) of the tachometer to a good chassis ground. Connect the other lead (usually red) to the negative (–) coil terminal, NOT to the distributor or positive (+) side. Connecting the tach to the wrong side will damage the switching transistor.

3. Remove the plug and install a vacuum gauge in the manifold vacuum port by using a suitable metric adapter.

4. Start the engine and allow it to stabilize at idle.

5. Turn the mixture screw in or out, until the engine runs smoothly at the lowest possible engine speed without stalling.

6. Turn the idle speed screw until the vacuum gauge indicates the highest specified reading (see the Vacuum At Idle chart) at the specified idle speed. (See the Tune-Up Specifications chart at the beginning of the chapter.).

7. Tighten the idle speed screw to the point just before the engine rpm and vacuum readings drop off.

8. Remove the tachometer and the vacuum gauge. Install the plug back in the manifold vacuum port. Road test the vehicle.

9. In some states, emission inspection is re-

quired. In such cases, you should take your car to a diagnostic center which has an HC/CO meter, and have the idle emission level checked to be sure that it is in accordance with state regulations. Starting 1974, CO levels at idle are given on the engine tune-up decal under the hood.

1975–77

The idle speed and mixture should be adjusted under the following conditions: the air cleaner must be installed, the choke fully opened, the transmission should be in Neutral (N), all accessories should be turned off, all vacuum lines should be connected, and the ignition timing should be set to specification.

1. Start the engine and allow it to reach normal operating temperature (180° F).

2. Check the float setting. The fuel level should be just about even with the spot on the sight glass. If the fuel level is too high or low, adjust the float level. (See Chapter 4).

3. Connect a tachometer in accordance with the manufacturer's instructions. However, connect the tachometer positive (+) lead to the coil Negative (–) terminal. Do NOT hook it up to the distributor or positive (+) side; damage to the transistorized ignition will result.

4. Adjust the speed to the highest rpm it will attain with the idle mixture adjusting screw.

5. Set the rpm with the idle speed adjusting screw to:
    20R: 900 rpm
    4M (auto. trans.): 820 rpm
    4M (man. trans.): 870 rpm

6. Repeat steps four and five until the highest rpm can be reached with the mixture screw and then readjust to rpm in step five.

7. Now set the speed by turning the idle mixture adjusting screw in (clockwise), to the initial idle speed of:
    20R: 850 + 50 rpm
    4M (man. trans.): 800 rpm
    4M (auto. trans.): 750 rpm

8. Disconnect the tachometer.

1978–81

Use the same procedure for 1975–77 models, described above. However, substitute different idle mixture and idle speeds as specified below: You will note that some late models use Step 5 as final idle adjustment.
For idle speeds (Step 5), use the following specifications:
    1978–79 4M: 820
    1978 20R: 850
    1979 20R: 870 Manual, 920 Automatic
    1980 22R: 750 4 speed Manual
                    920 Automatic

1980 22R California models. Idle speed adjusted with idle speed screw only
    800 Manual
    850 Manual
1981 22R
    700 Manual
    750 USA-Auto
    850 Canada-Auto
For idle speed adjusted by mixture screw (Step 6), use the following figures:
    1978–79 4M: 750
    1978 20R: 800
    1979 20R: 800 Manual, 850 Automatic
    1980 22R: 700 4 speed Manual
    (exc. Calif.) 800 5 speed Manual
                    850 Automatic

3Y-EC, 4Y-EC

1. Run the engine to normal operating temperature.

2. The air cleaner should be in place and all wires and vacuum hoses connected. All accessories should be off and the transmission in neutral.

3. Connect a tachometer to the engine. The positive lead of the tach should be connected to the negative side of the coil.
CAUTION: *Never allow the tachometer or coil terminals to be grounded. This will damage the injection system.*

4. Run the engine at 2500 rpm for 2 minutes.

5. Let the engine return to idle and set the idle speed for MT to 550 rpm or 750 rpm for AT.

6. Remove the tachometer.

Diesels

1. Run the engine to normal operating temperature.

2. The air cleaner should be in place and all accessories off.

3. The transmission should be in Neutral.

4. Install a tachometer compatible with diesels.

Diesel idle speed adjustment

5. Turn the idle adjusting screw to obtain 700 rpm.

6. Remove the tachometer.

Fuel Injection

IDLE ADJUSTMENT

1. Make sure the following conditions prevail before adjusting the idle speed of fuel injected 4M-E, 5M-E and 5M-GE engines:

    a. Air cleaner installed.

    b. Engine has reached normal operating temperature.

    c. All pipes and hoses of the air intake system are connected.

    d. All accessories are switched off.

    e. Electronic fuel injection (EFI) wiring connections tightly connected.

    f. Ignition timing correct.

    g. Transmission in Neutral, parking brake set and wheels blocked.

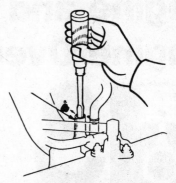

Idle speed adjustment for fuel injected models

2. Remove the rubber plug (1981 and later) from the side of the throttle body exposing the idle adjustment screw. The screw is exposed on 1980 models.

3. Adjust the idle speed to 800 rpm and reinstall the rubber plug.

Engine and Engine Overhaul

3

ENGINE ELECTRICAL SYSTEM

Transistorized Ignition System

TROUBLESHOOTING THE FULLY TRANSISTORIZED IGNITION SYSTEM

Troubleshooting the fully transistorized ignition system is easy, but you must have an accurate ohmmeter and voltmeter and take certain precautions as follow.

IGNITION SYSTEM PRECAUTIONS

1. Do not allow the ignition switch to be ON for more than 10 minutes if the engine will not start.

2. Some tachometers are not compatible with the fully transistorized system. Check the tach's instruction sheet or its manufacturer if there is any doubt in your mind about compatibility.

3. When connecting a tachometer: On USA models, connect the tachometer (plus) terminal to the ignition coil (minus) terminal. On some Canadian models a service wiring connector (covered with a rubber boot) is provided for tachometer connection.

4. Never allow the ignition coil terminals to touch ground. Damage to the ignitor or coil could result if the terminals are grounded.

5. Do not disconnect the battery when the engine is running.

6. Make sure that the ignitor is properly grounded to the body.

TESTING

Before testing the signal generator and the ignitor, several other ignition system components should be checked.

1. Connect a timing light to each plug wire in turn. Crank the engine, if the light flashes it can be assumed that voltage is reaching the plugs. If there is no flash from the timing light, see Step 2.

2. Inspect the spark plug wires. Carefully

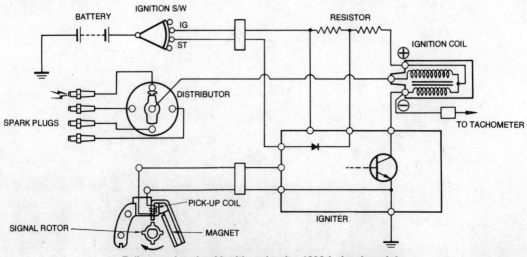

Fully transistorized ignition circuit—1980 federal models

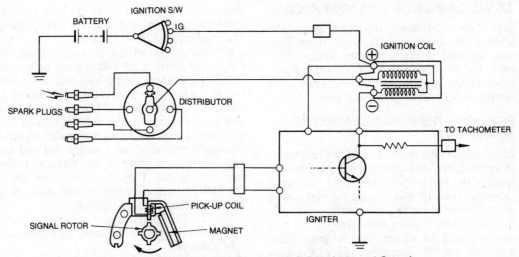

Fully transistorized ignition circuit—1980 California and Canada

remove the wires from the spark plugs by twisting the boots. Do not pull or bend the wire, damage to the inside conductor will occur. Inspect the terminals for dirt, looseness and corrosion. If the outside insulation is cracked or broken, replace the wire. Check the resistance of the wire with an ohmmeter. Do not disconnect the wire from the distributor cap. Remove the distributor cap, connect one lead of the ohmmeter to the distributor cap contact and the other to the terminal of the connected plug wire. Replace any wires with excessive resistance, over 8000Ω per foot of cable length (more than 25 kilo-ohms), or any that have no continuity. Inspect the distributor cap and ignition rotor for cracks, damage or carbon tracking. Replace as necessary.

3. Remove the spark plugs and check for electrode wear, carbon deposits, thread damage and insulator damage. If any problem is found, replace the plugs. If the old plugs are to be reused, clean them with a wire brush or have them cleaned in a spark plug cleaner. (Check your local gas station). After cleaning the plugs, check the gap (see Chapter two) and reinstall.

NOTE: *If the engine still will not start, or the timing light test shows no spark, check the ignition coil resistances.*

IGNITION COIL TESTS

Primary Resistance

With an ohmmeter, check between the positive (plus) and negative (minus) terminals of the ignition coil. With the coil cold, the resistances should be:

   1977–79 All models: 1.3–1.7Ω
   1980 Fed. models: 0.5–0.6Ω

1980 Canada & Calif.: 0.8–1.0Ω
1981 22R engine: 0.8–1.0Ω (USA)
1981 Canada: 0.4–0.5Ω
1981 5M-E engine: 0.5–0.6Ω

Secondary Resistance

With an ohmmeter, check between the positive (plus) coil terminal and the high tension (coil wire) terminal. Clean the coil wire terminal with a wire brush before testing. The resistance on all models except 1981 and later Canadian models should be 11.5–15.5kΩ; Canadian models (1981 and later): 8.5–11.5 kΩ.

BALLAST RESISTOR/RESISTOR WIRE TEST

On models with a coil mounted resistor, connect the ohmmeter leads to the end terminals of the resistor. Resistance should measure 1.2–1.4Ω. On models with a resistor wire, disconnect the plastic connector at the igniter. Connect one ohmmeter lead to the yellow wire and the other to the brown wire. Resistance should measure 1.2–1.4Ω.

NOTE: *If the tests on the coil or the resistor show values far from the standard, replace the part or wire, perform the timing light test or attempt to start the engine.*

CHECKING THE AIR GAP

Remove the distributor cap and ignition rotor. Check the air gap between the timing rotor spoke and the pick up coil. When aligned, the air gap should be 0.2–0.4mm. You will probably have to bump the engine around with the starter to line up the timing rotor. Refer to air gap adjustment in Chapter 2 for adjustment procedure.

SIGNAL GENERATOR TEST (PICKUP COIL)

Check the resistance of the signal generator. Unplug the connector to the distributor. Connect one lead of the ohmmeter to the white wire, the other lead to the pink wire. Resistance should be 130–190Ω. If resistance is not correct, replace the signal generator.

REPLACING THE SIGNAL GENERATOR (PICKUP COIL)

Remove the distributor cap and ignition rotor. Disconnect the distributor wiring connector. Remove the two screws that mount the signal generator (pickup coil). Install the new signal generator with the two mounting screws, do not completely tighten the screws until you have adjusted the air gap. (See air gap adjustment, Chapter 2). Reconnect the wiring harness, install the rotor and distributor cap. Check for engine starting. If the engine will not start, check the ignitor.

TESTING THE IGNITOR

1977–80 All Models and 1981 Canadian

1. Connect the negative (minus) probe of the voltmeter to the negative (minus) terminal of the ignition coil and the positive (plus) probe of the voltmeter to the yellow resistor wire at the connector unplugged from the ignitor. With the ignition switch ON (not start) the voltage should read 12 volts.

2. Check the voltage between the negative (minus) coil terminal and the yellow resistor wire again, but this time use the ohmmeter as resistance. Connect the positive (plus) ohmmeter lead to the pink wire in the plug connector. Connect the negative (minus) ohmmeter lead to the white wire in the connector.

CAUTION: *Do not reverse the connection of the ohmmeter.*

Select either the 1Ω or 10Ω range on the ohmmeter. With the voltmeter connected as in Step one and the ignition switch turned ON, the voltage should measure nearly zero. If a problem is found, replace the ignitor.

1981 Models (Except Canada)

NOTE: *To test the ignitor on 1981 Canadian models, refer to the above section.*

1. Connect the positive (plus) probe of the voltmeter to the positive (plus) terminal of the ignition coil. Connect the negative (minus) probe of the voltmeter to the car body ground. Turn the ignition switch to the ON position. The voltage should read 12 volts.

2. To check the power transistor in the ignitor, connect the positive (plus) probe of the voltmeter to the negative (minus) terminal of the ignition coil and the negative (minus)

probe of the voltmeter to the car body ground. Turn the ignition switch to the ON position. The reading should be 12 volts.

3. Unplug the wiring connector from the distributor. With a 1.5 volt dry cell battery in circuit, i.e. connect the positive pole of the battery to the pink terminal of the connector plug, and the negative pole of the battery to the white wire. Connect the voltmeter with the positive (plus) probe connected to the negative (minus) terminal of the ignition coil and the negative (minus) probe of the voltmeter to the car body ground. Turn the ignition switch to the ON position. Voltage should measure 5 volts, less than battery voltage.

CAUTION: *Do not apply voltage for more than five seconds or the power transistor will be destroyed.*

If a problem is found, replace the ignitor.

Distributor

REMOVAL

1970–83

On all four-cylinder engines, except the 20R and 22R, and the distributor is on the right (passenger's) side. On 20R and 22R engines and all sixes, the distributor is located at the front of the engine on the left driver's side. To remove the distributor, proceed in the following order:

1. Unfasten the retaining clips and lift the distributor cap straight up. It will be easier to install the distributor if the wiring is left connected to the cap. If the wires must be removed from the cap, mark their positions to aid in installation.

2. Remove the dust cover and mark the position of the rotor relative to the distributor body. Then mark the position of the body relative to the block.

3. Disconnect the coil primary wire and the vacuum line(s). If the distributor vacuum unit has two vacuum lines, mark which is which for installation.

4. Remove the pinch bolt and lift the distributor straight up, away from the engine. The rotor and body are marked so that they can be returned to the position from which they were removed. Do not turn or disturb the engine (unless absolutely necessary, such as for engine rebuilding), after the distributor has been removed.

1984

1. On the Van, remove the right front seat and engine service hole cover.

2. On all engines, disconnect the battery ground, disconnect the electrical leads, vacu-

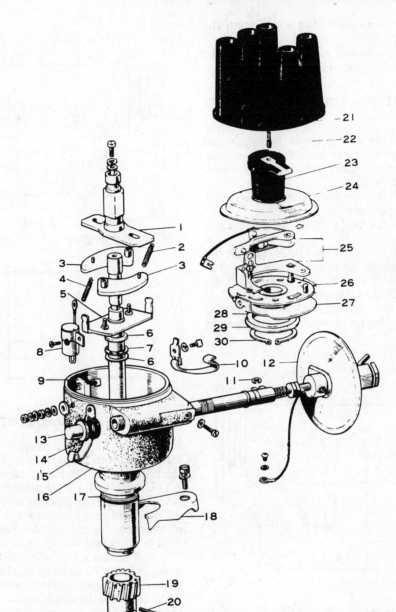

1. Cam
2. Governor spring
3. Governor weight
4. Governor spring
5. Distributor shaft
6. Metal washer
7. Bakelite washer
8. Condenser (not used w/transistor ignition)
9. Insulator
10. Cap spring clip
11. Snap-ring
12. Vacuum advance unit
13. Octane selector assembly
14. Rubber washer
15. Cap spring clip
16. Distributor housing
17. O-ring
18. Distributor clamp
19. Spiral gear
20. Pin
21. Distributor cap
22. Spring
23. Rotor
24. Dust cover
25. Breaker point assembly
26. Movable plate
27. Stationary plate
28. Adjusting washer
29. Wave washer
30. Snap-ring

Typical point-type distributor

um hoses and spark plug wires from the distributor.

3. Remove the hold down bolts, and pull the distributor from the engine.

INSTALLATION – TIMING NOT DISTURBED

1970–83

1. Insert the distributor in the block and align the matchmarks made during removal.

2. Engage the distributor driven gear with the distributor drive.

3. Install the distributor clamp and secure it with the pinch bolt.

4. Install the cap, primary wire, and vacuum line(s).

5. Install the spark plug leads. Consult the marks made during removal to be sure that the proper lead goes to each plug. Install the high tension wire if it was removed.

6. Start the engine. Check the timing and adjust it and the octane selector, as outlined in Chapter 2.

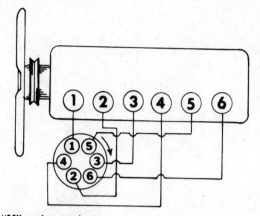

"M" series engines

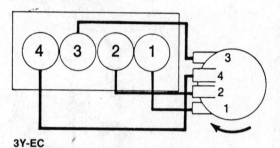

3Y-EC

INSTALLATION – TIMING LOST

1970–83

If the engine has been cranked, dismantled, or the timing otherwise lost, proceed as follows:

1. Determine top dead center (TDC) of the No. 1 cylinder's compression stroke by removing the spark plug from the No. 1 cylinder and placing your thumb over the spark plug hole. This is important because the timing marks will also line up with the last cylinder in the firing order in its exhaust stroke. Crank the engine until compression pressure starts to build up. Continue cranking the engine until the timing marks indicate TDC (or 0).

2. Next, align the timing marks to the specifications given in the Ignition Timing column of the Tune-Up Specifications chart at the beginning of Chapter 2.

3. Temporarily install the rotor in the distributor without the dust cover. Turn the distributor shaft so that the rotor is pointing toward the No. 1 terminal in the distributor cap. The points should be just about to open.

4. Use a small screwdriver to align the slot on the distributor drive (oil pump driveshaft) with the key on the bottom of the distributor shaft.

5. Align the matchmarks on the distributor body and the blocks which were made during the removal. Install the distributor in the block by rotating it slightly (no more than one

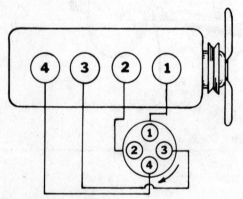

8RC and 18RC engines

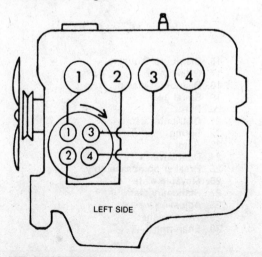

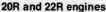

LEFT SIDE

20R and 22R engines

gear tooth in either direction) until the driven gear meshes with the drive.

NOTE: *Oil the distributor spiral gear and the oil pump driveshaft end before distributor installation.*

6. Rotate the distributor, once it is installed, so that the points are just about to open or the projection on the pickup coil is almost opposite the signal rotor tooth. Temporarily tighten the pinch bolt.

7. Remove the rotor and install the dust cover. Replace the rotor and the distributor cap.

8. Install the primary wire and the vacuum line(s).

9. Install the No. 1 spark plug. Connect the cables to the spark plugs in the proper order by using the marks made during removal. Install the high tension lead if it was removed.

10. Start the engine. Adjust the ignition timing and the octane selector, as outlined in Chapter 2.

1984

1. Set the engine at TDC of #1 cylinder's firing stroke. This can be accomplished by removing #1 spark plug and turn the engine by hand with your thumb over the spark plug hole. As #1 is coming up on its firing stroke, you'll feel the pressure against your thumb. Make sure the timing marks are set at 0.

2. On all except the Van, coat the spiral gear and governor shaft tip with clean engine oil. Align the protrusion on the distributor housing with the pin on the spiral gear drill mark side. Insert the distributor, aligning the center of the flange with the bolt hole on the cylinder head. Tighten the bolts.

3. On the Van, align the drilled mark on the driven gear with the groove on the distributor housing. Insert the distributor, aligning the stationary flange center with the bolt hole in the head. Tighten the bolts.

Alternator

ALTERNATOR PRECAUTIONS

1. Always observe proper polarity of the battery connections. Be especially careful when jump-starting the car.

2. Never ground or short out any alternator or alternator regulator terminals.

3. Never operate the alternator with any of its or the battery's leads disconnected.

4. Always remove the battery or disconnect both cables (ground cable first) before charging.

5. Always disconnect the ground cable when replacing any electrical components.

6. Never subject the alternator to excessive

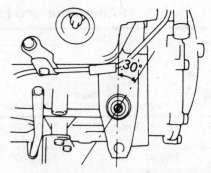

Drive rotor slot alignment—3Y–EC and 4Y–EC

heat or dampness if the engine is being steam-cleaned.

7. Never use arc welding equipment with the alternator connected.

REMOVAL AND INSTALLATION

NOTE: *On some models the alternator is mounted very low in the engine. On these models it may be necessary to remove the gravel shield and work from underneath the car in order to gain access to the alternator.*

1. Disconnect the battery ground (negative) cable. Unfasten the starter-to-battery cable at the battery end.

2. Remove the air cleaner, if necessary, to gain access to the alternator.

3. Unfasten the bolts which attach the adjusting link to the alternator. Remove the alternator drive belt.

4. Unfasten the alternator wiring connections.

5. Remove the alternator attaching bolt and then withdraw the alternator from its bracket.

6. Installation is performed in the reverse order of removal. After installing the alternator, adjust the belt tension as detailed in Chapter 1.

Regulator, Except IC

NOTE: *IC regulators are built onto the alternator. For testing procedures refer to the next section in this chapter.*

REMOVAL AND INSTALLATION

1. Remove the cable from the negative (–) battery terminal and then remove the cable from the positive (+) battery terminal.

2. Disconnect the wiring harness connector at the regulator.

3. Unfasten the bolts which secure the regulator. Remove the regulator and its condenser.

4. Installation is the reverse of removal.

VOLTAGE ADJUSTMENT

1. Connect a voltmeter up to the battery terminals. Negative (black) lead to the negative

Alternator and Regulator Specifications

| Engine Type | Alternator | | | Regulator | | | | | | |
| | | | | Field Relay | | | Regulator | | | |
	Manufacturer	Output (amps)	Manufacturer	Contact Spring Deflection (in.)	Point Gap (in.)	Volts to Close	Air Gap (in.)	Point Gap (in.)	Volts	
20R ⑤	Nippon Denso	40 ③	Nippon Denso	0.008– 0.024	0.016– 0.047 ④	4.5– 5.8	0.012	0.010– 0.018	13.8– 14.8 ②	
4M	Nippon Denso	55	Nippon Denso	0.008– 0.024	0.016– 0.047	4.5– 5.8	0.012	0.008– 0.024	13.8– 14.8	
4M-E	Nippon Denso	55	Nippon Denso	————————Not adjustable————————					14.0– 14.7 ⑥	
5M-GE	Nippon Denso	60	Nippon Denso	————————Not adjustable————————					13.5– 15.1	
3Y-EC	Nippon Denso	60 ⑦	Nippon Denso	————————Not adjustable————————					13.5– 15.1	

① 1976–79: 50 and 55
② W/55 amp alt.: 14.0–14.7
③ Optional: 55
④ 1975–79: 0.0118–0.0177
⑤ 1980 has non-adjustable regulator
⑥ 1980: 14.3–14.9
⑦ 70 on 1986 and later models

(–) terminal; positive (red) lead to positive (+) terminal.

2. Start the engine and gradually increase its speed to about 1,500 rpm.

3. At this speed, the voltage reading should fall within the range specified in the Alternator and Regulator Specifications chart.

4. If the voltage does not fall within the specifications, remove the cover from the regulator and adjust it by bending the adjusting arm.

5. Repeat Steps 2 and 3 if the voltage cannot be brought to specification, proceed with the mechanical adjustments which follow.

MECHANICAL ADJUSTMENTS

NOTE: *Perform the voltage adjustment outlined above, before beginning the mechanical adjustments.*

Field Relay

1. Remove the cover form the regulator assembly.

2. Use a feeler gauge to check the amount that the contact spring is deflected while the armature is being depressed.

3. If the measurement is not within specifications (see the Alternator and Regulator Specifications chart), adjust the regulator by bending point holder P2. (See the illustration.).

4. Check the point gap with a feeler gauge against the specifications in the chart.

5. Adjust the point gap, as required, by bending the point holder P1. (See the illustration).

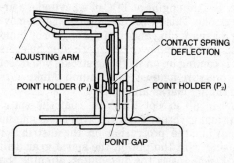

Field-relay components

6. Clean off the points with emery cloth if they are dirty and wash them with solvent.

Voltage Regulator

1. Use a feeler gauge to measure the air (armature) gap. If it is not within the specifications (see the Alternator and Regulator Specifications chart), adjust it by bending the low speed point holder. (See the illustration).

2. Check the point gap with a feeler gauge. If it is not within specifications, adjust it by bending the high speed point holder. (See the illustration.) Clean the points with emery cloth and wash them off with solvent.

3. Check the amount of contact spring deflection while depressing the armature. The specification should be the same as that for the contact spring on the field relay. If the amount of deflection is not within specification, replace, do not adjust, the voltage regulator.

Go back and perform the steps outlined under Voltage Adjustment. If the voltage still

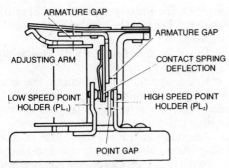

ARMATURE GAP

ARMATURE GAP

ADJUSTING ARM

CONTACT SPRING
DEFLECTION

LOW SPEED POINT
HOLDER (PL₁)

HIGH SPEED POINT
HOLDER (PL₂)

POINT GAP

Voltage regulator components

fails to come within specifications, the alternator is probably defective and should be replaced.

IC Regulator

The IC regulator is mounted on the alternator housing, is transistorized and is non-adjustable.

REMOVAL AND INSTALLATION

1. Disconnect the negative (ground) battery cable from the battery.
2. Remove the end cover of the regulator.
3. Remove the three screws that go through the terminals.
4. Remove the (two) top mounting screws that mount the regulator to the alternator. Remove the regulator.
5. To install the new IC regulator. Place the regulator in position on the alternator. Install and secure the (two) top mounting screws. Install the (three) terminal screws. Install the end cover.
6. Reconnect the battery ground cable.

TESTING THE IC REGULATOR

To test the IC regulator you will need a voltmeter and an ammeter.

1. Disconnect the wire connected to the B terminal of the alternator. Connect the wire (that you disconnected) to the negative (minus) terminal of the ammeter.

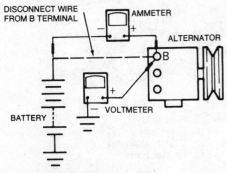

DISCONNECT WIRE
FROM B TERMINAL

AMMETER

ALTERNATOR

B

BATTERY

VOLTMETER

Testing the IC regulator

2. Connect the test lead from the positive (plus) terminal of the ammeter to the B terminal of the alternator.
3. Connect the positive (plus) lead of the voltmeter to the B terminal of the alternator.
4. Connect the negative (minus) lead of the voltmeter to ground.
5. Start the engine and run at about 2000 rpm. Check the reading on the ammeter and voltmeter. Standard amperage should be less than 10 amps. Standard voltage should be from 14 to 14.7 volts (Temperature 77°F).
6. If the voltage is greater than 15 volts, replace the IC regulator.
7. If the voltage reading is less than 13.5 volts, shut off the engine and check the regulator and alternator as follows.
8. Turn the ignition switch to ON. Check the voltage at the IG terminal of the alternator. If no voltage, check the ENGINE fuse and/or the ignition switch. No problems found, go to next step.
9. Remove the end cover from the IC regulator. Check the voltage reading at the regulator L terminal. If the voltage reading is zero to 2 volts, suspect the alternator.
10. If the voltage is the same as battery voltage, turn off the ignition switch (OFF position) and check for continuity between the regulator L and F terminals.
11. If there is no continuity, suspect the alternator. If there is continuity (approx. 4Ω) replace the IC regulator.

Starter

REMOVAL AND INSTALLATION

1. Disconnect the negative (ground) cable from the battery.
2. Disconnect the wires/cables connected to the starter motor.
3. On some models it may be necessary to remove the air cleaner, splash shields or linkage that is in the way of easy access to the starter motor.
4. Loosen and remove the starter motor mounting nuts/bolts while supporting the motor.
5. Remove the starter motor.
6. Installation is in the reverse order of removal.

STARTER SOLENOID AND BRUSH REPLACEMENT

Direct Drive Type

NOTE: *The starter must be removed from the car in order to perform this operation.*

1. Disconnect the field coil lead from the solenoid terminal.

Remove direct-drive starter solenoid in direction of arrow

2. Unfasten the solenoid retaining screws. Remove the solenoid by tilting it upward and withdrawing it.

3. Unfasten the end frame bearing cover screws and remove the cover.

4. Unfasten and withdraw the thru-bolts. Remove the commutator endframe.

5. Withdraw the brushes from their holder it they are to be replaced.

6. Check the brush length against the speci-

fication in the Battery and Starter Specifications chart. Replace the brushes with new ones if required.

7. Dress the new brushes with emery cloth so that they will make proper contact.

8. Use a spring scale to check the brush spring tensions against the specification in the chart. Replace the springs if they do not meet specification.

9. Assembly is the reverse order of disassembly. Remember to pack the end bearing cover with multipurpose grease before installing it.

Gear Reduction Type

NOTE: *The starter must be removed from the car in order to perform this operation.*

1. Disconnect the solenoid lead terminal.

2. Loosen the two bolts on the starter housing and separate the field frame from the solenoid. Remove the O-ring and felt dust seal.

3. Unfasten the two screws and separate the starter drive from the solenoid.

4. Withdraw the clutch and gears. Remove the ball from the clutch shaft bore or solenoid.

5. Remove the brushes from the holder.

6. Measure the brush length and compare it

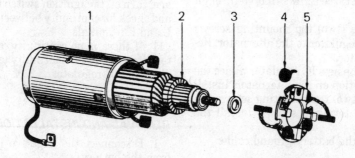

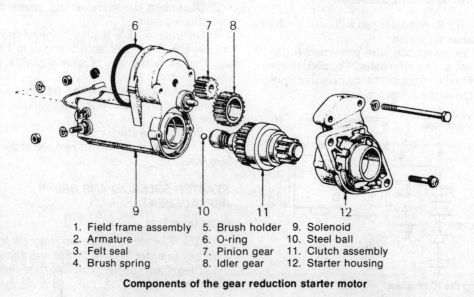

1. Field frame assembly	5. Brush holder	9. Solenoid
2. Armature	6. O-ring	10. Steel ball
3. Felt seal	7. Pinion gear	11. Clutch assembly
4. Brush spring	8. Idler gear	12. Starter housing

Components of the gear reduction starter motor

Oil Pump Clearance Specifications

All measurements are given in inches unless noted

Engine	Tip Clearance (Driven)	Side Clearance	Body Clearance	Relief Valve Spring Installed Length
4M	0.016	0.0012–0.0035	0.0012–0.0024	1.89
20R	0.0059–0.0083	0.0012–0.0035	0.0035–0.0059	—
4ME	—	0.0012–0.0035	0.0012–0.0024	②

① Drive—0.0040–0.0100 inch
② 1980–81 opening pressure 71–85 psi

to the figure in the Battery and Starter Specifications chart. Replace the brushes with new ones if they are too short.

7. Replace any worn or chipped gears.

8. Assembly is performed in the reverse order of disassembly. Lubricate all gears and bearings with high temperature grease. Grease the ball before inserting it in the clutch shaft bore. Align the tab on the brush holder with the notch on the field frame. Check the positive (+) brush leads to ensure that they aren't grounded. Align the solenoid marks with the field frame bolt anchors.

STARTER DRIVE REPLACEMENT

Direct Drive Starter

NOTE: *The starter must be removed from car.*

1. Loosen the locknut or bolt and remove the connection going to the terminal of the solenoid. Remove the securing screws and remove the solenoid.

2. Remove the front dust cover, E-ring, thrust washers, and the two screws retaining the brush holder assembly. Remove the brush cover thru-bolts and remove the cover assembly.

3. Lift the brushes to free them from the commutator and remove the brush holder.

4. Tap the yoke assembly lightly with a wooden hammer and remove it from the field and case.

5. Remove the nut and bolt which serve as a pin for the shift lever, carefully retaining the associated washers.

6. Remove the armature assembly and shift lever.

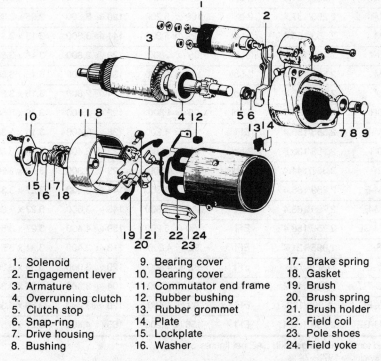

1. Solenoid	9. Bearing cover
2. Engagement lever	10. Bearing cover
3. Armature	11. Commutator end frame
4. Overrunning clutch	12. Rubber bushing
5. Clutch stop	13. Rubber grommet
6. Snap-ring	14. Plate
7. Drive housing	15. Lockplate
8. Bushing	16. Washer

17. Brake spring
18. Gasket
19. Brush
20. Brush spring
21. Brush holder
22. Field coil
23. Pole shoes
24. Field yoke

Components of the direct-drive starter motor

7. Push the stop ring (located at the end of the armature shaft) toward the clutch and remove the snapring. Remove the stop ring.

8. Remove the clutch assembly from the armature shaft.

To install the drive:

1. Install the clutch assembly onto the armature shaft.

2. Put the stop ring on and hold it toward the clutch while installing the snapring.

3. Install the armature assembly and shift lever into the yoke.

4. Install the washers, nut and bolt which serve as a shift lever pivot pin.

5. Install the field back onto the yoke assembly.

6. Lift the brushes and install the brush holder. Install the brush cover and thru-bolts.

7. Replace the brush holder set screws, the thrust washers, E-ring, and the dust cover.

8. Install the solenoid. Reconnect the wire to the terminal of the solenoid.

Gear Reduction Type

1. Remove the starter.

2. Remove the solenoid and the shift lever.

3. Remove the bolts securing the center housing to the front cover and separate the parts.

4. Remove the gears and the starter drive. CAUTION: *Be careful not to lose the steel ball installed in the drive. Remember to reinstall when replacing the drive.*

5. Installation is the reverse of removal.

Battery

Refer to Chapter 1 for details on battery maintenance.

REMOVAL AND INSTALLATION

1. Disconnect the negative (ground) cable from the terminal, and then the positive cable. Special pullers are available to remove the cable clamps.

General Engine Specifications

Year	Engine Type	Engine Cu In. Displacement (cm³/cu in.)	Carburetor Type	Horsepower @ rpm ①	Torque @ rpm (ft. lbs.) ①	Bore x Stroke (in.)	Compression Ratio
1970–71	8R-C	1,858/113.4	2-bbl	108 @ 5,500	113 @ 3,800	3.38 x 3.15	9.0:1
	2M	2,253/137.5	2-bbl	115 @ 5,200	117 @ 3,600	2.96 x 3.35	9.0:1
1972–74	18R-C	1,980/123.0	2-bbl	97 @ 5,500	106 @ 3,600	3.48 x 3.15	8.5:1
	2M ②	2,253/137.5	2-bbl	109 @ 5,200	120 @ 3,600	2.95 x 3.35	8.5:1
	4M	2,563/156.4	2-bbl	122 @ 5,200	141 @ 3,600	3.15 x 3.35	8.5:1
1975–77	20R	2,189/133.6	2-bbl	96 @ 4,800	120 @ 2,800	3.48 x 3.50	8.4:1
	4M	2,563/151.4	2-bbl	108 @ 5,000	130 @ 2,800	3.15 x 3.35	8.5:1
1978–79	4M	2,563/156.4	2-bbl	108 @ 5,000	134 @ 2,800	3.15 x 3.35	8.5:1
	20R	2,189/133.6	2-bbl	95 @ 4,800	122 @ 2,400	3.48 x 3.50	8.4:1
1980	4M-E	2,563/156.4	EFI	110 @ 4,800	136 @ 2,400	3.15 x 3.35	8.5:1
	20R	2,189/133.6	2-bbl	90 @ 4,800	122 @ 2,400	3.48 x 3.50	8.4:1
1981	22R	2,367/144.4	2-bbl	96 @ 4,800	129 @ 2,800	3.62 x 3.50	9.0:1
	5M-E	2,759/168.4	EFI	116 @ 4,800	145 @ 3,600	3.27 x 3.35	8.8:1
1982–84	5M-E	2,759/168.4	EFI	116 @ 4,800	145 @ 3,600	3.27 x 3.35	8.8:1
	5M-GE	2,759/168.4	EFI	150 @ 5,200	159 @ 4,400	3.27 x 3.55	8.8:1
	2S-E	1,995/121.7	EFI	92 @ 4,200	113 @ 2,400	3.31 x 3.54	8.7:1
	3Y-EC	1,998/122	EFI	82 @ 4,400	120 @ 3,000	3.39 x 3.39	8.8:1
	1C-TL	1,839/112.2	Diesel	72 @ 4,500	104 @ 3,000	3.27 x 3.35	22.5:1
1985–86	3Y-EC	1,998/122	EFI	90 @ 4,400	120 @ 3,000	3.39 x 3.39	8.8:1
	5M-GE	2,759/168.4	EFI	156 @ 5,200	165 @ 4,400	3.27 x 3.55	8.8:1

① Horsepower and torque ratings given in SAE net figures
② 2M engine not available 1973–74
EFI: Electronic fuel injection

Valve Specifications

Engine Type	Seat Angle (deg)	Face Angle (deg)	Spring Test Pressure (lbs.)		Spring Installed Height (in.)		Stem to Guide Clearance (in.) ▲		Stem Diameter (in.)	
			Inner	Outer	Inner	Outer	Intake	Exhaust	Intake	Exhaust
8R-C and 18R-C	45	45	15.2	50.6	1.480	1.640	0.0010–0.0022	0.0014–0.0030	0.3140	0.3136
2M	45	45	11.9	68.0 ①	1.535	1.654 ②	0.0006–0.0018	0.0014–0.0030	0.3153	0.3121
4M	45	44.5	25.7 ⑥	63.1 ③	1.504	1.642 ④	0.0006–0.0018	0.0010–0.0024	0.3146	0.3140
4M-E	45	44.5	15.6	41.6	1.49	1.63	0.0010–0.0024	0.0014–0.0028	0.3141	0.3137
20R	45	44.5	—	60.0 ⑤	—	1.594	0.0006–0.0024	0.0012–0.0026	0.3141	0.3140
2S-E	45.5	45.5	—	68.0	—	1.555	0.0010–0.0024	0.0012–0.0026	0.3141	0.3139
3Y-EC	45	45.5 ⑧	—	63.0	—	1.589	0.0010–0.0024	0.0012–0.0026	0.3141	0.3139
1C-TL	45	44.5	—	53.0	—	1.587	0.0008–0.0022	0.0012–0.0026	0.3143	0.3139
5M-E	45	44.5	15.5	42.0	1.492	1.630	0.0010–0.0024	0.0012–0.0028	0.3141	0.3137
5M-GE	45	44.5	—	⑦	—	⑧	0.0010–0.0024	0.0012–0.0026	0.3141	0.3139

▲ Valve guides are removable
① Exhaust valve spring test pressure: inner—11.5 lbs.; outer—66.6 lbs.
② Exhaust valve installed height: inner—1.535 in.; outer—1.661 in.
③ Exhaust valve spring test pressure: inner—24.6 lbs.; outer—59.4 lbs.
1978–79 intake and exhaust: 41.9
④ Exhaust valve installed height: inner—1.520 in.; outer—1.657 in.
⑤ 1977–79: 55.1 lbs.
⑥ 1978–79: 15.5
⑦ Int.: 76.5–84.4
Exh.: 73.4–80.9
⑧ Int.: 1.575
Exh.: 1.693
⑨ 1985–86: 44.5

Crankshaft and Connecting Rod Specifications
(All measurements are given in inches)

Engine Type	Crankshaft				Connecting Rod		
	Main Brg Journal Dia	Main Brg Oil Clearance	Shaft End-Play	Thrust on No.	Journal Diameter	Oil Clearance	Side Clearance
8R-C	2.3613–2.3622	0.0008–0.0020	0.0020–0.0100	3	2.0857–2.0866	0.0008–0.0020	0.0043–0.0097
18R-C	2.3613–2.3622	0.0008–0.0020	0.0008–0.0080	3	2.0857–2.0866	0.0010–0.0021	0.0060–0.0100
2M	2.3616–2.3622	0.0007–0.0017	0.0020–0.0170	4	2.0466–2.0472	0.0006–0.0020	0.0040–0.0100
4M, 4M-E	2.3617–2.3627	0.0012–0.0021	0.0020–0.0100	4	2.0463–2.0472	0.0008–0.0021	0.0020–0.0100 ②
20R	2.3614–2.3622	0.0010–0.0022	0.0008–0.0079 ①	3	2.0862–2.0866	0.0010–0.0022	0.0063–0.0100
5M-E, 5M-GE	2.3617–2.3627	0.0013–0.0023	0.0020–0.0098	4	2.0463–2.0472	0.0008–0.0021	0.0063–0.0117
2S-E	2.1648–2.1654	0.0008–0.0020	0.0008–0.0037	3	1.8892–1.8898	0.0008–0.0020	0.0063–0.0083
1C-TL	2.2435–2.2441	0.0013–0.0020	0.0010–0.0094	3	1.9877–1.9987	0.0014–0.0025	0.0039–0.0118
3Y-EC	2.2829–2.2835	0.0008–0.0020	0.0008–0.0087	3	1.8892–1.8898	0.0008–0.0020	0.0063–0.0123

Dia—Diameter
Brg—Bearing
① 1978–79: 0.0010–0.0080
② 1978–79: 0.0063–0.0117

Piston and Ring Specifications
(All measurements in inches)

Year	Engine Type	Piston Clearance 68°F	Ring Gap			Ring Side Clearance		
			Top Compression	Bottom Compression	Oil Control	Top Compression	Bottom Compression	Control Oil
All	8R-C	0.0010–0.0020	0.004–0.012	0.004–0.012	0.004–0.012	0.0012–0.0028	0.0012–0.0028	0.0008–0.0028
All	18R-C	0.0020–0.0030	0.004–0.012	0.004–0.012	0.004–0.012	0.0012–0.0028	0.0012–0.0028	0.0008–0.0028
All	2M and 4M	0.0010–0.0020	0.006–0.014	0.006–0.014	0.008–0.020	0.0012–0.0028	0.0008–0.0024	—
1975	4M	0.0020–0.0030	0.004–0.011	0.004–0.011	0.008–0.020	0.0012–0.0028	0.0008–0.0024	—
1976–77	4M	0.0020–0.0030	0.006–0.012	0.003–0.020	0.007–0.040	0.0012–0.0014	0.0008–0.0024	—
1978–79	4M	0.0020–0.0030	0.0039–0.0110	0.0059–0.0110	0.007–0.040	0.0012–0.0014	0.0008–0.0035	—
All	4M-E	0.0020–0.0028	0.0039–0.0110	0.0039–0.0110	0.0079–0.0200	0.0012–0.0028	0.0008–0.0024	NA
All	20R	0.0012–0.0020	0.004–0.012	0.004–0.012	NA	0.008	0.008	NA
All	1C-TL	0.0016–0.0024	0.0098–0.0193	0.0079–0.0173	0.0079–0.0193	0.0079–0.0081	0.0079–0.0081	Snug
All	5M-E	0.0020–0.0028	0.0039–0.0110	0.0039–0.0110	0.0079–0.0200	0.0012–0.0028	0.0008–0.0024	Snug
1982–84	5M-GE	0.0020–0.0028	0.0083–0.0146	0.0067–0.0209	0.0079–0.0276	0.0012–0.0028	0.0008–0.0024	Snug
1985–86	5M-GE	0.0020–0.0028	0.0091–0.0161	0.0098–0.0217	0.0067–0.0335	0.0012–0.0028	0.0008–0.0024	Snug
All	2S-E	0.0008–0.0014	0.0110–0.0197	0.0078–0.0177	0.0078–0.0311	0.0012–0.0028	0.0012–0.0028	Snug
1982–84	3Y-EC	0.0030–0.0037	0.0087–0.0138	0.0059–0.0118	0.0079–0.0311	0.0012–0.0028	0.0012–0.0028	Snug
1985	3Y-EC	0.0030–0.0037	0.0087–0.0185	0.0059–0.0165	0.0079–0.0323	0.0012–0.0028	0.0012–0.0028	Snug
1986	3Y-EC	0.0026–0.0033	0.0091–0.0189	0.0063–0.0173	0.0051–0.0185	0.0012–0.0028	0.0012–0.0028	Snug

NA—Not available

Torque Specifications
(All readings in ft. lbs.)

Engine Type	Cylinder Head Bolts	Rod Bearing Bolts	Main Bearing Bolts	Crankshaft Pulley Bolt	Flywheel to Crankshaft Bolts	Manifold	
						Intake	Exhaust
8R-C	75.0–85.0	42.0–48.0	72.0–80.0	43.0–51.0	42.0–49.0	20.0–25.0 [1]	
18R-C	72.0–82.0	39.0–48.0	69.0–83.0	43.0–51.0	51.0–58.0	30.0–35.0 [1]	
2M	[2]	25.0–30.0	72.0–79.0	43.0–51.0	41.0–46.0 [3]	22.0–29.0 [4]	18.0–25.0 [5]
4M	[6]	30.0–36.0	72.0–78.0	69.0–76.0 [10][17]	41.0–46.0 [7][18]	17.0–21.0 [4]	12.0–17.0 [5]
4M-E	55–61 [6]	31–34	72–78	98–119	51–57	10–15	13–16
20R	52.0–64.0	39.0–48.0	69.0–83.0	80.0–94.0 [15]	62.0–68.0 [16]	11.0–15.0	29.0–36.0
5M-E	55–61	31–34	72–78	98–119	51–57	10–15	13–16
5M-GE	55–61	31–34	72–78	98–119 [20]	51–57	15–17	26–32
2S-E	45–50	33–38	40–45	78–82	70–75	30–33	30–33
1C-TL	60–65	45–50	75–78	70–75	63–68	10–15	32–36
3Y-EC	[19]	33–38	55–60	78–82	60–63	7–11	33–38

[1] Intake and exhaust manifolds combined
[2] 8 mm bolts—11–14 ft. lbs.
  13 mm bolts—54–61 ft. lbs.
[3] Flex-plate (automatic) 14–22 ft. lbs.
[4] Intake manifold stud bolt—14–18 ft. lbs.
[5] Exhaust manifold stud bolt—6–7 ft. lbs.
[6] 8 mm bolts—7–12 ft. lbs.
[7] 10 mm bolts—54–61 ft. lbs.
[8] 1975—43–51 ft. lbs.; 1976—116–145 ft. lbs.
[9] 1975–76—58–64 ft. lbs.
[10] 1975–76—51–58 ft. lbs.
[11] 1977—32.5–39.8
[12] 1977–79—61.5–68.7
[13] 1978–79—14–18
[14] 1978–79—22–32
[15] 1978–79—102–130
[16] 1978–79—73–79
[17] 1978–79—98–119
[18] 1978–79—51–57
[19] 12 mm bolt: 12–16
  14 mm bolt: 63–68
[20] 1985–86: 155–163

NOTE: *To avoid sparks, always disconnect the ground cable first, and connect it last.*

2. Remove the battery holddown clamp.

3. Remove the battery, being careful not to spill the acid.

NOTE: *Spilled acid can be neutralized with a baking soda/water solution. If you somehow get acid into your eyes, flush it out with lots of water and get to a doctor.*

4. Clean the battery posts thoroughly before reinstalling, or when installing a new battery.

5. Clean the cable clamps, using a wire brush, both inside and out.

6. Install the battery and the holddown clamp or strap. Connect the positive, then the negative cable. Do not hammer them in place. The terminals should be coated lightly (externally) with grease to prevent corrosion. There are also felt washers impregnated with an anti-corrosion substance which are slipped over the battery posts before installing the cables. These are available in auto parts stores.

CAUTION: *Make absolutely sure that the battery is connected properly before you turn on the ignition switch. Reversed polarity can burn out your alternator and regulator within a matter of seconds.*

ENGINE MECHANICAL

Design

8R-C AND 18R-C ENGINES

The 8R-C/18R-C family of four cylinder engines was used in the Mark II/4 and the Corona in the early nineteen seventies.

The engine has an overhead cam, and aluminum head and a cast iron block. Displacement of the 8R-C engine is 1858cc and was enlarged to 1980cc (in 1972) to beome the 18R-C engine.

20R AND 22R ENGINES

The 20R (2189cc) four cylinder, overhead cam engine was introduced in 1975 and used in the Corona. Features included:

A gear driven oil pump

Single timing chain (instead of two)

Cross-flow head

Hemispherical combustion chambers

With an eye on the future, Toyota designed the engine to help control emissions by casting EGR and air injection passages in the aluminum head.

The 22R engine was introduced in 1981. Based on the 20R, the new engine has a displacement of 2367cc, a higher compression ratio as well as other refinements which contribute to even better fuel economy than before.

2M, 4M-E AND 5M-E ENGINES

The M family of engines is the most sophisticated in the Toyota line. Their basic design is similar to that used in some European luxury cars, which they rival in smoothness and power.

These six cylinder, overhead cam engines (featuring cross-flow heads and hemispherical combustion chambers) first appeared in the luxury Crown series. The 2M (2.3 liter) engine was used until 1971. In 1972 the 4M (2.6 liter) engine was introduced and used, in various forms, until 1979. The 4M-E engine, used in the 1980 Cressida, featured electronic fuel injection and was replaced in 1981 by the new 5M-E (2.8 liter) electronic fuel injected engine.

Engine

REMOVAL AND INSTALLATION

All exc. 3Y-EC, 4Y-EC

These instructions provide for removal of the engine and transmission as a unit.

All operations involving hoisting the engine-transmission unit should be done with extreme care and should be carefully planned beforehand. Read the procedure through before beginning. It is best to use fender covers on both fenders and on the firewall cowl to protect the metal and paint form damage or scratches during removal or installation.

CAUTION: *Be sure to bleed the fuel system on fuel injected engines before disconnecting the fuel lines. (See chapter one, Fuel Filters). Before working underneath the car, be sure it is blocked and supported safely on jackstands.*

1. Disconnect the battery cables, negative (ground) cable first. Remove the battery hold down and the battery.

2. Mark the location of each hood hinge with a scribe, this will help you with alignment when reinstalling the hood.

3. Support the hood so that its weight is not

Lift the engine out as illustrated

on the hinge bolts. Then, remove the bolts. With the help of an assistant, remove the hood from the car and store in a safe place.

4. Remove the air cleaner assembly and mounting supports.

5. Drain the radiator, the engine crankcase, and the transmission fluid. On some models where splash shields interfere with easy access while working under the car, remove the shields.

6. If you car has an automatic transmission, disconnect and plug the cooler lines from the radiator.

7. Disconnect the radiator hoses from the radiator. On some six cylinder models, an auxiliary engine oil cooler is mounted on the radiator support, disconnect and remove it. Models that have an expansion tank: remove the hose to the radiator and remove the tank.

8. On some four cylinder models, it may be necessary to remove the radiator grille and headlight bezels.

9. Remove the radiator shroud, the hood lock base and support, the upper radiator supports and the condenser (models with air conditioning). Remove the radiator.

NOTE: *On some models it may be possible to remove the radiator and shroud as an assembly.*

10. On some models with air conditioning, loosen the compressor mounting bolts and remove the drive belt. Unbolt the compressor and move it aside, but do not disconnect any of the refrigerant lines. If there is not enough slack in the lines (this may be the case on some older models), the system will have to be discharged and the lines disconnects.

CAUTION: *Unless you are thoroughly familiar with air conditioning systems, this job should be referred to a specialist with proper training. The escaping refrigerant is extremely dangerous.*

11. On models with power steering, loosen the mounting bolts and remove the drive belt. Remove the mounting bolts and move the pump away from the engine. Do not disconnect the power steering hoses unless there is not enough slack.

12. Disconnect the accelerator linkage on carbureted models.

13. Disconnect and label:

    a. battery ground cable at engine.

    b. starter wiring.

    c. coil to distributor high tension cable.

    d. primary wiring harness to the distributor.

    e. wire to temperature sender.

    f. all other sensor wire connectors.

    g. alternator wiring.

    h. choke heat wire or hoses connecting the choke housing.

    i. fuel lines: on fuel injected systems, bleed line at lower fuel filter hose before disconnecting (see chapter one, Fuel Filter).

    j. EGR solenoid connector wire, if equipped.

    k. all wiring harness and air hoses to the fuel injection.

    l. heater hoses.

    m. vacuum lines to the power brake unit from the intake manifold.

    n. all other wires harnesses and vacuum lines connected to the engine that would interfere with removal.

    o. heater control cable at valve, if equipped.

14. On cars equipped with an hydraulic clutch. Disconnect the line from the master cylinder to the slave cylinder and cap the line.

15. Remove the clutch slave cylinder (manual transmission).

16. Disconnect the speedometer cable from the transmission.

17. Disconnect the transmission control linkage or cross shaft, if equipped (column shift and automatic).

18. Disconnect the wiring to the neutral safety switch, or any other wiring or vacuum lines to the transmission that would interfere with removal.

19. Remove the shift lever (floor mounted controls). On some models it may be necessary to remove the center console.

20. To remove the center console: take out the mounting screws, remove the gear shift knob and the boot. Disconnect the wiring and lift the console off over the shift lever.

21. Remove the shift lever by loosening and removing the four mounting screws and lifting the lever form the shift tower.

22. Automatic transmission models with a floor mounted gear selector: unfasten the connecting rod swivel nut and detach the control rod from the gear selector lever.

23. Disconnect the parking brake lever rod, return spring, intermediate rod and the cable from the equalizer.

24. Disconnect the exhaust pipe from the exhaust manifold. Remove the front splash shield.

NOTE: *On some models, it may be necessary to disconnect and remove the steering relay rod. If so, disconnect the idler arm from the frame, etc.*

25. Mark the driveshaft companion flange and the driveshaft (for installation in the same place). Disconnect the driveshaft at the rear by removing the four bolts. Remove the driveshaft. Plug the rear of the transmission with a clean rag to prevent any fluid form spilling.

26. Support the transmission carefully to remove all weight from the rear mounts. Remove

the bolts securing the mounts and crossmember. Remove the rear crossmember and the mounts.

27. Attach an adequate cable or chain between the lifting points on the engine. Hook the cable or chain to a hoist and apply just enough lift to take the weight off of the front mounts. Remove the front motor mount bolts.

28. Work carefully to avoid damage to the engine or body parts. Tilt the engine, lowering the transmission as necessary, until the engine/transmission unit can be pulled up and out of the engine compartment. Mount the engine on a secure stand as soon as possible. Do not work on the engine while it is hanging on the hoist.

29. Before reinstalling the engine, carefully inspect the front and rear mounts. If any part of the mount is damaged or if the bonded surface is deteriorated or separated, replace the mount.

30. Engine installation is in the reverse order of removal. Adjust the linkages as detailed in the appropriate chapters. Bleed the clutch as outlined in chapter six and replenish the fluid levels as outlined in chapter one.

3Y-EC, 4Y-EC

1. Disconnect the battery.
2. Remove the right front seat.
3. Remove the engine cover.
4. Drain the coolant.

CAUTION: *When draining the coolant, keep in mind that cats and dogs are attracted by the ethylene glycol antifreeze, and are quite likely to drink any that is left in an uncovered container or in puddles on the ground. This will prove fatal in sufficient quantity. Always drain the coolant into a sealable container. Coolant should be reused unless it is contaminated or several years old.*

5. Disconnect the radiator and heater hoses.
6. Disconnect and tag all vacuum hoses attached to various engine parts.
7. Disconnect and tag all wires attached to various engine parts.
8. Disconnect and tag all cables attached to various engine parts.
9. Remove the air cleaner.
10. Unbolt the power steering pump and secure it out of the way.
11. Remove the fan shroud.
12. Remove the fan and fan clutch. Do not lay the fan on its side. If you do, the fluid will leak out and the fan clutch will be permanently ruined.
13. Unbolt the air conditioning compressor and secure it out of the way.
14. Raise the vehicle about 40" off the floor and support is securely.
15. Drain the engine oil.

16. Disconnect the driveshaft.
17. Disconnect the remove the exhaust system.
18. Remove the transmission control cable.
19. Remove the clutch release starter.
20. Remove the starter.
21. Remove the speedometer cable.
22. Disconnect all remaining hoses and cable from the transmission.
23. Remove the engine tensioner cable.
24. Remove the engine underpan.
25. Remove the strut bar.
26. Place an engine jack under the engine and take up the weight. Unbolt and remove the engine mounts and lower the engine from the vehicle.
27. Installation is the reverse of removal. Torque the engine mount bolts to 58 ft.lb.

Cylinder Head
REMOVAL AND INSTALLATION
8R-C and 18R-C Engines

CAUTION: *Do not perform this operation on a warm engine.*

1. Bring the engine to No. 1 cylinder TDC. (See the beginning of this chapter.) Disconnect the battery and drain the cooling system.

CAUTION: *When draining the coolant, keep in mind that cats and dogs are attracted by the ethylene glycol antifreeze, and are quite likely to drink any that is left in an uncovered container or in puddles on the ground. This will prove fatal in sufficient quantity. Always drain the coolant into a sealable container. Coolant should be reused unless it is contaminated or several years old.*

2. Remove the air cleaner assembly, including the mounting brackets and attached hoses.
3. Disconnect the accelerator cable from the support on the cylinder head cover and from the throttle arm.
4. Remove the water hose bracket from the cylinder head cover.
5. Unfasten the hose clamps and remove the hoses from the water pump and water valve.
6. Remove the vacuum lines form the distributor vacuum unit. Remove the lines which run from various emission control components mounted on the cylinder head. Be sure to label all lines disconnected so that you can reinstall them in the proper place. Disconnect the EGR valve, if equipped.
7. Remove the piper or hoses to the choke control heat stove.
8. Unfasten the spark plug wires from the plugs. Remove the spark plugs.
9. Remove the cylinder head cover (valve cover) mounting bolts and remove the cover.

NOTE: *Use a clean cloth, placed over the*

ENGINE OVERHAUL

Most engine overhaul procedures are fairly standard. In addition to specific parts replacement procedures and complete specifications for your individual engine, this chapter also is a guide to accepted rebuilding procedures. Examples of standard rebuilding practice are shown and should be used along with specific details concerning your particular engine.

Competent and accurate machine shop services will ensure maximum performance, reliability and engine life. Procedures marked with the symbol shown above should be performed by a competent machine shop, and are provided so that you will be familiar with the procedures necessary to a successful overhaul.

In most instances it is more profitable for the do-it-yourself mechanic to remove, clean and inspect the component, buy the necessary parts and deliver these to a shop for actual machine work.

On the other hand, much of the rebuilding work (crankshaft, block, bearings, pistons, rods, and other components) is well within the scope of the do-it-yourself mechanic.

Tools

The tools required for an engine overhaul or parts replacement will depend on the depth of your involvement. With a few exceptions, they will be the tools found in a mechanic's tool kit (see Chapter 1). More in-depth work will require any or all of the following:
* a dial indicator (reading in thousandths) mounted on a universal base
* micrometers and telescope gauges
* jaw and screw-type pullers
* scraper
* valve spring compressor
* ring groove cleaner
* piston ring expander and compressor
* ridge reamer
* cylinder hone or glaze breaker

* Plastigage®
* engine stand

Use of most of these tools is illustrated in this chapter. Many can be rented for a one-time use from a local parts jobber or tool supply house specializing in automotive work.

Occasionally, the use of special tools is called for. See the information on Special Tools and the Safety Notice in the front of this book before substituting another tool.

Inspection Techniques

Procedures and specifications are given in this chapter for inspecting, cleaning and assessing the wear limits of most major components. Other procedures such as Magnaflux and Zyglo can be used to locate material flaws and stress cracks. Magnaflux is a magnetic process applicable only to ferrous materials. The Zyglo process coats the material with a flourescent dye penetrant and can be used on any material. Check for suspected surface cracks can be more readily made using spot check dye. The dye is sprayed onto the suspected area, wiped off and the area sprayed with a developer. Cracks will show up brightly.

Overhaul Tips

Aluminum has become extremely popular for use in engines, due to its low weight. Observe the following precautions when handling aluminum parts:
* Never hot tank aluminum parts (the caustic hot-tank solution will eat the aluminum)
* Remove all aluminum parts (identification tag, etc.) from engine parts prior to hot-tanking.
* Always coat threads lightly with engine oil or anti-seize compounds before installation, to prevent seizure.
* Never over-torque bolts or spark plugs, especially in aluminum threads.

Stripped threads in any component can be repaired using any of several commercial repair kits (Heli-Coil, Microdot, Keenserts, etc.)

When assembling the engine, any parts that will be in frictional contact must be prelubed to provide lubrication at initial start-up. Any product specifically formulated for this purpose can be used, but engine oil is not recommended as a pre-lube.

When semi-permanent (locked, but removable) installation of bolts or nuts is desired, threads should be cleaned and coated with Loctite® or other similar, commercial non-hardening sealant.

Repairing Damaged Threads

Several methods of repairing damaged threads are available. Heli-Coil® (shown here), Keenserts® and Microdot® are among the most widely used. All involve basically the same principle—drilling out stripped threads, tapping the hole and installing a pre-wound insert—making welding, plugging and oversize fasteners unnecessary.

Two types of thread repair inserts are usually supplied—a standard type for most Inch Coarse, Inch Fine, Metric Coarse and Metric Fine thread sizes and a spark plug type to fit most spark plug port sizes. Consult the individual manufacturer's catalog to determine exact applications. Typical thread repair kits will contain a selection of pre-wound threaded inserts, a tap (corresponding to the outside diameter threads of the insert) and an installation tool. Spark plug inserts usually differ because they require a tap equipped with pilot threads and a combined reamer/tap section. Most manufacturers also supply blister-packed thread repair inserts separately in addition to a master kit containing a variety of taps and inserts plus installation tools.

Before effecting a repair to a threaded hole, remove any snapped, broken or damaged bolts or studs. Penetrating oil can be used to free frozen threads; the offending item can be removed with locking pliers or with a screw or stud extractor. After the hole is clear, the thread can be repaired, as follows:

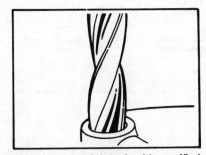

Drill out the damaged threads with specified drill. Drill completely through the hole or to the bottom of a blind hole

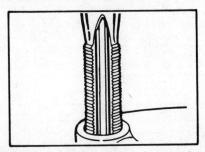

With the tap supplied, tap the hole to receive the thread insert. Keep the tap well oiled and back it out frequently to avoid clogging the threads

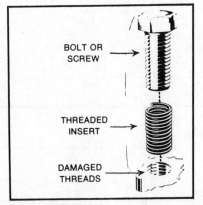

BOLT OR SCREW

THREADED INSERT

DAMAGED THREADS

Damaged bolt holes can be repaired with thread repair inserts

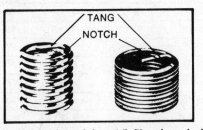

TANG

NOTCH

Standard thread repair insert (left) and spark plug thread insert (right)

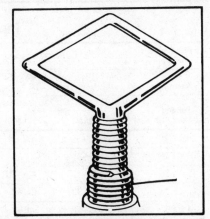

Screw the threaded insert onto the installation tool until the tang engages the slot. Screw the insert into the tapped hole until it is ¼–½ turn below the top surface. After installation break off the tang with a hammer and punch

Standard Torque Specifications and Fastener Markings

In the absence of specific torques, the following chart can be used as a guide to the maximum safe torque of a particular size/grade of fastener.

- There is no torque difference for fine or coarse threads.
- Torque values are based on clean, dry threads. Reduce the value by 10% if threads are oiled prior to assembly.
- The torque required for aluminum components or fasteners is considerably less.

U.S. Bolts

SAE Grade Number → Number of lines always 2 less than the grade number.	1 or 2			5			6 or 7		
	Maximum Torque			Maximum Torque			Maximum Torque		
Bolt Size (Inches)—(Thread)	Ft./Lbs.	Kgm	Nm	Ft./Lbs.	Kgm	Nm	Ft./Lbs.	Kgm	Nm
¼ — 20	5	0.7	6.8	8	1.1	10.8	10	1.4	13.5
— 28	6	0.8	8.1	10	1.4	13.6			
⁵⁄₁₆ — 18	11	1.5	14.9	17	2.3	23.0	19	2.6	25.8
— 24	13	1.8	17.6	19	2.6	25.7			
⅜ — 16	18	2.5	24.4	31	4.3	42.0	34	4.7	46.0
— 24	20	2.75	27.1	35	4.8	47.5			
⁷⁄₁₆ — 14	28	3.8	37.0	49	6.8	66.4	55	7.6	74.5
— 20	30	4.2	40.7	55	7.6	74.5			
½ — 13	39	5.4	52.8	75	10.4	101.7	85	11.75	115.2
— 20	41	5.7	55.6	85	11.7	115.2			
⁹⁄₁₆ — 12	51	7.0	69.2	110	15.2	149.1	120	16.6	162.7
— 18	55	7.6	74.5	120	16.6	162.7			
⅝ — 11	83	11.5	112.5	150	20.7	203.3	167	23.0	226.5
— 18	95	13.1	128.8	170	23.5	230.5			
¾ — 10	105	14.5	142.3	270	37.3	366.0	280	38.7	379.6
— 16	115	15.9	155.9	295	40.8	400.0			
⅞ — 9	160	22.1	216.9	395	54.6	535.5	440	60.9	596.5
— 14	175	24.2	237.2	435	60.1	589.7			
1 — 8	236	32.5	318.6	590	81.6	799.9	660	91.3	894.8
— 14	250	34.6	338.9	660	91.3	849.8			

Metric Bolts

Relative Strength Marking → Bolt Markings →	4.6, 4.8			8.8		
	Maximum Torque			Maximum Torque		
Bolt Size Thread Size x Pitch (mm)	Ft./Lbs.	Kgm	Nm	Ft./Lbs.	Kgm	Nm
6 x 1.0	2–3	.2–.4	3–4	3–6	.4–.8	5–8
8 x 1.25	6–8	.8–1	8–12	9–14	1.2–1.9	13–19
10 x 1.25	12–17	1.5–2.3	16–23	20–29	2.7–4.0	27–39
12 x 1.25	21–32	2.9–4.4	29–43	35–53	4.8–7.3	47–72
14 x 1.5	35–52	4.8–7.1	48–70	57–85	7.8–11.7	77–110
16 x 1.5	51–77	7.0–10.6	67–100	90–120	12.4–16.5	130–160
18 x 1.5	74–110	10.2–15.1	100–150	130–170	17.9–23.4	180–230
20 x 1.5	110–140	15.1–19.3	150–190	190–240	26.2–46.9	160–320
22 x 1.5	150–190	22.0–26.2	200–260	250–320	34.5–44.1	340–430
24 x 1.5	190–240	26.2–46.9	260–320	310–410	42.7–56.5	420–550

CHECKING ENGINE COMPRESSION

A noticeable lack of engine power, excessive oil consumption and/or poor fuel mileage measured over an extended period are all indicators of internal engine wear. Worn piston rings, scored or worn cylinder bores, blown head gaskets, sticking or burnt valves and worn valve seats are all possible culprits here. A check of each cylinder's compression will help you locate the problems.

As mentioned in the "Tools and Equipment" section of Chapter 1, a screw-in type compression gauge is more accurate than the type you simply hold against the spark plug hole, although it takes slightly longer to use. It's worth it to obtain a more accurate reading. Follow the procedures below for gasoline and diesel-engined cars.

Gasoline Engines

1. Warm up the engine to normal operating temperature.
2. Remove all spark plugs.

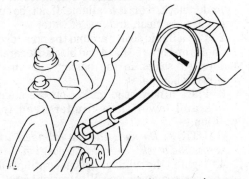

The screw-in type compression gauge is more accurate

3. Disconnect the high-tension lead from the ignition coil.
4. On carbureted cars, fully open the throttle either by operating the carburetor throttle linkage by hand or by having an assistant "floor" the accelerator pedal. On fuel-injected cars, disconnect the cold start valve and all injector connections.
5. Screw the compression gauge into the No. 1 spark plug hole until the fitting is snug.
NOTE: *Be careful not to crossthread the plug hole. On aluminum cylinder heads use extra care, as the threads in these heads are easily ruined.*
6. Ask an assistant to depress the accelerator pedal fully on both carbureted and fuel-injected cars. Then, while you read the compression gauge, ask the assistant to crank the engine two or three times in short bursts using the ignition switch.

7. Read the compression gauge at the end of each series of cranks, and record the highest of these readings. Repeat this procedure for each of the engine's cylinders. Compare the highest reading of each cylinder to the compression pressure specifications in the "Tune-Up Specifications" chart in Chapter 2. The specs in this chart are maximum values.

A cylinder's compression pressure is usually acceptable if it is not less than 80% of maximum. The difference between each cylinder should be no more than 12–14 pounds.

8. If a cylinder is unusually low, pour a tablespoon of clean engine oil into the cylinder through the spark plug hole and repeat the compression test. If the compression comes up after adding the oil, it appears that that cylinder's piston rings or bore are damaged or worn. If the pressure remains low, the valves may not be seating properly (a valve job is needed), or the head gasket may be blown near that cylinder. If compression in any two adjacent cylinders is low, and if the addition of oil doesn't help the compression, there is leakage past the head gasket. Oil and coolant water in the combustion chamber can result from this problem. There may be evidence of water droplets on the engine dipstick when a head gasket has blown.

Diesel Engines

Checking cylinder compression on diesel engines is basically the same procedure as on gasoline engines except for the following:

1. A special compression gauge adaptor suitable for diesel engines (because these engines have much greater compression pressures) must be used.
2. Remove the injector tubes and remove the injectors from each cylinder.
NOTE: *Don't forget to remove the washer underneath each injector; otherwise, it may get lost when the engine is cranked.*

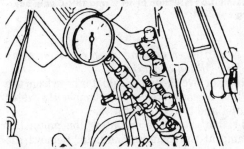

Diesel engines require a special compression gauge adaptor

3. When fitting the compression gauge adaptor to the cylinder head, make sure the bleeder of the gauge (if equipped) is closed.
4. When reinstalling the injector assemblies, install new washers underneath each injector.

8R-C and 18R-C rocker shaft bolt removal sequence

8R-C and 18R-C engine head bolt removal sequence

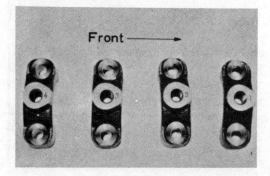

Installation direction of 8R-C and 18R-C cam bearing cap

timing cover opening, to prevent anything from falling down into it.

10. Remove the upper radiator hose from the cylinder head water outlet. Remove the water outlet and the thermostat.

11. Unfasten the exhaust pipe mounting clamp at the exhaust manifold. Remove the combination intake/exhaust manifold from the cylinder head.

12. Loosen the rocker arm shaft mounting bolts, evenly in stages. Remove the mounting bolts and the rocker arm shaft assembly and oil delivery tube.

13. Remove the timing gear from the camshaft. Be careful to support the gear and chain

so they do not fall down into the timing cover.

14. Remove the camshaft bearing caps and the camshaft. Mark the bearing caps as to direction and position.

15. Remove the cam bearings from the head. Place them, in order, with the caps you just removed.

16. Separate the timing gear and chain. Fasten the chain so that it will not fall into the timing cover.

17. Loosen the head bolts in two or three stages (see sequence illustration). Remove the bolts, keep them in order of removal, they are different lengths and must be installed in the proper direction.

18. Lift the cylinder head from the engine block.

NOTE: *The head is positioned on dowels, do not try to slide it from the engine.*

Prior to installation, thoroughly clean the cylinder block and head mating surfaces. Refer to the Engine Rebuilding section (in this chapter) for details on checking the head and block for flatness, and other services that may be necessary.

1. Blow out the mounting bolt holes in the cylinder block, if air is available. If not, be sure the holes are clean and free of water.

2. Use a liquid sealer around the oil and water holes on both the head and block. Be careful not to get sealer in the passages or in the mounting bolt holes.

3. Place a new head gasket on the engine block and lower the cylinder head into position.

CAUTION: *Do not slide the cylinder head across the block; lower it into position.*

4. Tighten the cylinder head mounting bolts in proper sequence (see illustration) and in three or four stages. Tighten the bolts to the specifications given in the Torque Specifications chart.

5. Install the lower camshaft bearings into the seat from which they were removed. Install

Aligning the timing marks on the 8R-C/18R-C camshaft, sprocket, and timing chain

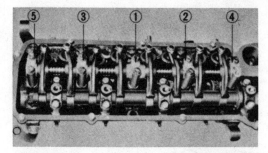

8R-C and 18R-C valve rocker support tightening sequence

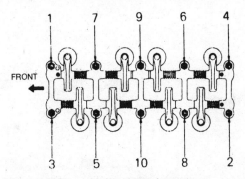

20R and 22R head bolt removal sequence

the camshaft and the bearing caps, numbers facing forward. Tighten the cap nuts to 12–17 ft.lb.

NOTE: *Cam bearings may be checked the same way as engine main and connecting rod bearings for oil clearance. Refer to the Engine Rebuilding section on how to use Plastigage®. The oil clearance should be 0.025–0.050mm; the end play should be 0.043–0.167mm.*

6. If you did not have the engine at TDC when the cylinder head was removed or if the engine has been turned from TDC, realign the engine to No. 1 piston TDC (see beginning of this chapter).

7. Align the mark on the timing chain with the dowel hole on the camshaft timing gear and the stamped mark on the camshaft. All three marks should be aligned so that they are facing upward.

8. Install the chain and gear on the camshaft.

9. Install the rocker arm assembly. Tighten the mounting bolts to 12–17 ft.lb., in sequence and in two or three stages.

10. Attach the oil delivery tube to the rocker arm assembly and the camshaft bearing caps. Tighten the mounting bolts to 11–16 ft.lb.

11. Adjust the valve clearance as outlined in chapter two, to the following cold specifications:

Intake: 0.1778mm
Exhaust: 0.3302mm

12. The rest of the cylinder head installation is in the reverse order of removal. Change the engine oil before starting the engine because it could be contaminated by the coolant when the cylinder head was removed.

20R and 22R Engines

CAUTION: *Do not perform this operation on a warm engine.*

NOTE: *The cylinder head removal procedure that follows allows the intake and exhaust manifold to remain on the head. If you wish to remove them before the cylinder*

head, refer to the manifold removal section contained in this chapter.

1. Disconnect the battery.

2. Remove the three exhaust pipe flange nuts and separate the pipe from the manifold.

3. Drain the cooling system (both radiator and block). If the coolant is to be reused, place a large, clean container underneath the drains.

CAUTION: *When draining the coolant, keep in mind that cats and dogs are attracted by the ethylene glycol antifreeze, and are quite likely to drink any that is left in an uncovered container or in puddles on the ground. This will prove fatal in sufficient quantity. Always drain the coolant into a sealable container. Coolant should be reused unless it is contaminated or several years old.*

4. Remove the air cleaner assembly, complete with hoses, from the carburetor.

NOTE: *Cover the carburetor with a clean shop cloth so that nothing can fall into it.*

5. Mark all vacuum hoses to aid installation and disconnect them. Remove all linkages, fuel lines, etc., from the carburetor, cylinder head, and manifolds. Remove the wire supports.

6. Mark the spark plug leads and disconnect them form the plugs.

7. Matchmark the distributor housing and block. Disconnect the primary lead and remove the distributor. Installation will be easier if you leave the cap and leads in place.

8. Unfasten the four 14mm nuts which secure the valve cover.

9. Remove the rubber camshaft seals. Use a 19mm wrench to remove the cam sprocket bolt. Slide the distributor drive gear off the cam and wire the cam sprocket in place.

10. Remove the 14mm bolt at the front of the head that connects the head to the timing cover. This must be done before the head bolts are removed.

11. Remove the cylinder head bolts in the order shown below. Improper removal could cause head damage.

12. Remove the rocker arm shaft assembly. It

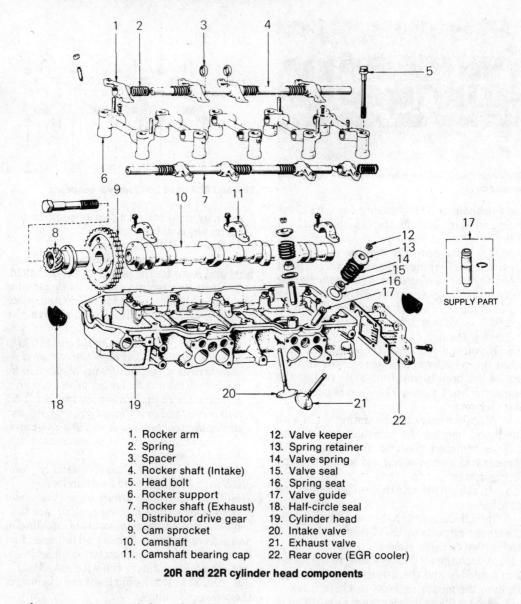

1. Rocker arm
2. Spring
3. Spacer
4. Rocker shaft (Intake)
5. Head bolt
6. Rocker support
7. Rocker shaft (Exhaust)
8. Distributor drive gear
9. Cam sprocket
10. Camshaft
11. Camshaft bearing cap
12. Valve keeper
13. Spring retainer
14. Valve spring
15. Valve seal
16. Spring seat
17. Valve guide
18. Half-circle seal
19. Cylinder head
20. Intake valve
21. Exhaust valve
22. Rear cover (EGR cooler)

20R and 22R cylinder head components

may be necessary to pry it from the mounting dowel. Using pry bars applied evenly at the front and the rear of the valve rocker assembly, pry the assembly off its mounting dowels.

13. Lift the head off its dowels. Do NOT pry it off.

14. Support the head solidly on a work bench and remove the intake and exhaust manifolds.

15. Drain the engine oil from the crankcase after the head has been removed, because the oil will become contaminated with coolant while the head is being removed.

Prior to installation, thoroughly clean the cylinder block and head mating surfaces. Refer to the Engine Rebuilding section (in this chapter) for details on checking the head and block for flatness, and other services that may be necessary.

1. Apply liquid sealer to the front corners of the block and install the head gasket.

2. Lower the head over the locating dowels. Do not attempt to slide it into place.

3. Rotate the camshaft so that the sprocket aligning pin is at the top. Remove the wire and hold the cam sprocket. Manually rotate the engine so that the sprocket hole is also at the top. Wire the sprocket in place again.

4. Install the rocker arm assembly over its positioning dowels.

5. Tighten the cylinder head bolts evenly, in three stages, and in the order shown, under Torque Sequences, to a specified torque of 52–63 ft.lb.

6. Install the timing chain cover bolt and tighten it to 7–11 ft.lb.

7. Remove the wire and fit the sprocket over

Apply liquid sealer to the front corners of the cylinder block

Rotate the cam till the pin is at the top—20R and 22R engines

the camshaft dowel. If the chain won't allow the sprocket to reach, rotate the crankshaft back and forth, while lifting up on the chain and sprocket.

8. Install the distributor drive gear and tighten the crankshaft bolt to 51–65 ft.lb.

9. Set the No. 1 piston to TDC of its compression stroke and adjust the valves as outlined in Chapter 2.

10. After completing valve adjustments, rotate the crankshaft 352 degrees, so that the 8 degree BTDC mark on the pulley aligns with the pointer.

11. Install the distributor, as outlined in the beginning of this chapter.

12. Install the spark plugs and leads.

13. Make sure that the oil drain plug is installed. Fill the engine with oil after installing the rubber cam seals. Pour the oil over the distributor drive gear and the valve rockers.

14. Install the rocker cover and tighten the bolts to 8–11 ft.lb.

15. Connect all the vacuum hoses and electrical leads which were removed during disassembly. Install the spark plug lead supports. Fill the cooling system. Install the air cleaner.

16. Tighten the exhaust pipe-to-manifold flange bolts to 25–33 ft.lb.

17. Reconnect the battery. Start the engine

and allow it to reach normal operating temperature. Check and adjust the timing and valve clearance. Adjust the idle speed and mixture. Road test the vehicle.

M Series

CAUTION: *Do not perform this operation on a warm engine.*

CARBURETOR EQUIPPED MODELS

1. Disconnect the battery (negative cable first) and drain the cooling system.

CAUTION: *When draining the coolant, keep in mind that cats and dogs are attracted by the ethylene glycol antifreeze, and are quite likely to drink any that is left in an uncovered container or in puddles on the ground. This will prove fatal in sufficient quantity. Always drain the coolant into a sealable container.*

Valve rocker shaft removal sequence for "M" series—remove the oil union bolt (1) and then the union (2)—models equipped

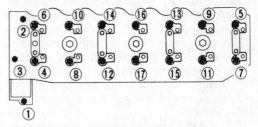
2M engine head bolt removal sequence

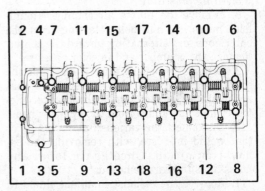
4M engine head bolt removal sequence

Coolant should be reused unless it is contaminated or several years old.

2. Remove the air cleaner assembly and mounting brackets, complete with attached hoses.

3. Mark (for identification) and disconnect the hoses from the air injection system and the vacuum switching valve (if equipped).

4. Disconnect the following:

Accelerator cable from both the support on the cylinder head and the throttle arm.

The automatic transmission linkage connected to the carburetor and intake manifold.

The water hoses, upper and lower, from the engine, and from the heater control valve.

Control cable from the heater valve control.

PCV valve hose to the cylinder head cover.

Fuel lines to the carburetor.

Choke lines and/or hoses to the choke.

Disconnect all other vacuum lines, hoses and wire connectors that are attached to the intake manifold. Label them for identification.

5. Remove the intake manifold mounting nuts/bolts starting from the outer ends and alternating toward the center. Remove the intake manifold and carburetor as an assembly.

6. On fuel injected models, disconnect the battery (negative cable first) and drain the cooling system. Remove the radiator hoses and heater hoses attached to the cylinder head or manifolds.

CAUTION: *When draining the coolant, keep in mind that cats and dogs are attracted by the ethylene glycol antifreeze, and are quite likely to drink any that is left in an uncovered container or in puddles on the ground. This will prove fatal in sufficient quantity. Always drain the coolant into a sealable container. Coolant should be reused unless it is contaminated or several years old.*

7. Refer to the illustration provided and disconnect or remove the parts in the numerical order shown.

CAUTION: *The fuel system is under pressure. Refer to chapter one, Fuel Filters, for bleeding procedure.*

8. Remove the intake air chamber (manifold) mounting nuts/bolts starting from the outer ends and alternating toward the center. Remove the chamber and injector as a unit.

9. Remove the spark plug wires from the spark plugs and from the wire supports that are mounted on the cylinder head cover. Remove the spark plugs from the cylinder head.

10. Disconnect the various lines/hoses to, or that would interfere with, removing the exhaust manifold. Once again label any hoses/lines that are removed.

11. Remove the exhaust manifold shield (if equipped) and loosen and remove the exhaust pipe mounting bolts/nuts.

12. Remove the exhaust manifold by unfastening the mounting bolts/nuts. Start from the outer ends and work your way toward the center, alternating as you go.

13. Unfasten the retaining bolts that hold the cylinder head cover (valve cover) to the head. Remove the valve cover.

CAUTION: *Take care not to drop any bolts, nuts, etc. into the timing chain cover.*

14. Turn the engine to No. 1 piston TDC.

15. Remove the timing chain tensioner. It is located on the right side front (exhaust manifold side) of the cylinder head.

16. The match marks on the timing chain and gear should be aligned. It might be helpful to highlight them with some paint.

17. Straighten out the locking tab on the camshaft timing gear retaining bolt. Remove the bolt.

NOTE: *The timing gear retaining bolt has left hand threads. To loosen turn clockwise.*

18. Remove the timing gear form the camshaft.

19. Loosen and remove the rocker arm shaft mounting bolts. Follow the sequence shown, uniformly loosening them in two or three passes.

20. Remove the rocker arm shaft assembly.

21. Remove the camshaft bearing caps, keep them in order (mark the caps so they cannot get mixed up). Remove the camshaft.

22. Loosen and remove the cylinder head mounting bolts. Follow the sequence shown, uniformly loosening them in two or three passes.

23. Lift the cylinder head form the engine block. Locating dowel pins are installed in the front and the rear of the engine, making it impossible to slide off the head.

Prior to installation, thoroughly clean the cylinder block and head mating surfaces. Refer to the Engine Rebuilding section (in this chapter)

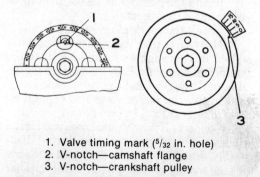

1. Valve timing mark (5/32 in. hole)
2. V-notch—camshaft flange
3. V-notch—crankshaft pulley

Correct alignment of the crankshaft and camshaft timing marks—"M" series

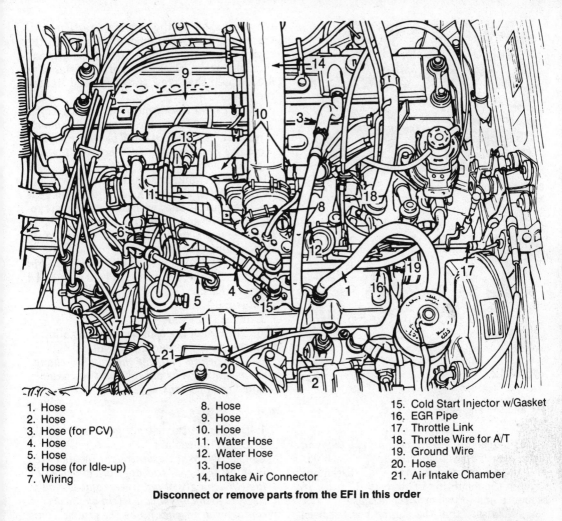

1. Hose
2. Hose
3. Hose (for PCV)
4. Hose
5. Hose
6. Hose (for Idle-up)
7. Wiring
8. Hose
9. Hose
10. Hose
11. Water Hose
12. Water Hose
13. Hose
14. Intake Air Connector
15. Cold Start Injector w/Gasket
16. EGR Pipe
17. Throttle Link
18. Throttle Wire for A/T
19. Ground Wire
20. Hose
21. Air Intake Chamber

Disconnect or remove parts from the EFI in this order

for details on checking the head and block for flatness, and other services that may be necessary.

1. Blow out the mounting bolt holes in the cylinder block, if air is available. If not, be sure the holes are clean and free of water.

2. Use a liquid sealer around the oil and water holes on both the head and the block and on the timing cover upper surfaces. Be careful not to get sealer in the passages or in the mounting holes.

3. Place a new head gasket on the engine block and lower the cylinder head into position.

4. Tighten the cylinder head mounting bolts in proper sequence (see illustration) and in three or four stages. Tighten the bolts to the specifications given in the Torque Specifications chart.

5. Install the lower camshaft bearings if removed. Install the camshaft and bearing caps. Tighten the cap nuts to 12–17 ft.lb.

NOTE: *Cam bearings may be checked the same way as engine main and connecting rod bearings for oil clearance. Refer to the Engine Rebuilding section on how to use*

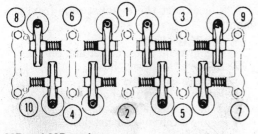

20R and 22R engines

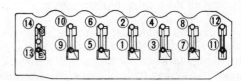

2M engine

8R-C and 18R-C engines

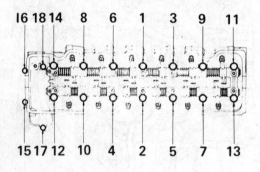

4M′ and 5M′ engines

Plastigage®. Oil clearance limit is 0.099mm; end play limit is 0.304mm.

6. Install the rocker arm shaft assembly. Tighten the mounting bolts to 12–17 ft.lb., in sequence and in two or three stages.

7. Make sure that the engine has not been turned from No. 1 piston TDC. The crankshaft pulley should have its V notch aligned with the zero mark on the timing cover scale.

8. Align the V-notch on the camshaft with the 4mm hole on the No. 1 camshaft bearing cap, or the pin on the camshaft flange with the embossed pointer on the No. 1 rocker shaft support.

9. Install the timing chain (marked link up) on the camshaft gear (mark on gear aligned with marked link) and install on the end of the camshaft. Align the pin on the camshaft flange with the hole in the cam gear.

10. Install the timing gear bolt (left hand thread) with the locking tab. Bolt torque is 47–54 ft.lb.

11. Install the timing chain tensioner. Tighten to 22–29 ft.lb.

12. Turn the crankshaft two complete revolutions. If, at the end of the two revolutions, the timing marks do not align, repeat steps 7 through 11. If they still will not align, see step 14.

13. Adjust the timing chain tensioner. Turn

the crankshaft in the regular direction until there is a maximum amount of slack in the chain. Loosen the locknut on the tensioner and turn the screw clockwise until resistance is felt. Loosen the screw two turns and tighten the locknut.

NOTE: *If the timing marks do not align after once again turning the engine two complete revolutions the chain could be stretched. Toyota has provided other pin holes in the cam gear to correct this problem.*

14. If the crankshaft pulley notch will not align with the zero mark while the cam gear and chain are aligned with the rocker arm support, remove and reposition the cam gear to the second pin hole position. Recheck crankshaft timing marks.

15. Adjust the valve clearance, as outlined in chapter two, to the following cold specifications:

Intake: 0.15mm
Exhaust: 0.20mm

16. The rest of the cylinder head installation is in the reverse order of removal.

NOTE: *Before starting the engine, change the motor oil. The old oil could be contaminated from coolant.*

1C-L

1. Disconnect the battery ground.
2. Drain the coolant.

CAUTION: *When draining the coolant, keep in mind that cats and dogs are attracted by the ethylene glycol antifreeze, and are quite likely to drink any that is left in an uncovered container or in puddles on the ground. This will prove fatal in sufficient quantity. Always drain the coolant into a sealable container. Coolant should be reused unless it is contaminated or several years old.*

3. Remove the cruise control actuator.
4. Disconnect and tag all wires connected to or running across the head.
5. Disconnect and tag all vacuum hoses connected to or running across the head.
6. Disconnect and tag all cables and linkage rods connected to or running across the head.
7. Raise and support the car on jackstands.
8. Drain the oil.
9. Disconnect the exhaust pipe from the manifold.
10. Lower the car.
11. Remove the water outlet and pipe.
12. Remove the heater hoses.
13. Remove the heater pipe.
14. Remove the bypass hoses.
15. Remove the glow plugs.
16. Remove the injector nozzles.
17. Remove the level gauge guide support mounting bolt.

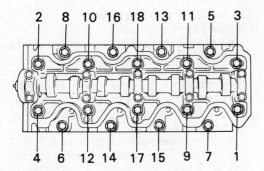

Diesel head bolt loosening sequence

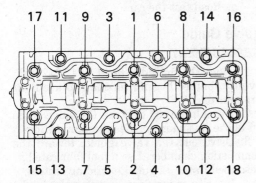

Diesel head bolt tightening sequence

18. Remove the number 2 timing cover.

19. Turn the engine so that #1 cylinder is at TDC of the firing stroke. Make sure that the line mark on the camshaft pulley is aligned with the top surface of the head.

20. Remove the timing belt and camshaft pulley.

21. Remove the belt tension spring.

22. Remove the #1 idler pulley. Remove the camshaft #3 cover.

23. Remove the valve cover.

24. Remove the front head lifting eye.

25. Loosen the head bolts gradually, in three passes, in the order shown. Lift off the head. If the head is difficult to break loose, there is a recess at the front end in which you may pry with a suitable tool.

26. Installation is the reverse of removal. Note the following points:

    a. Always use a new head gasket.

    b. Make sure that all sealing surfaces are absolutely clean.

    c. Coat all bolt threads with clean engine oil, lightly.

    d. Tighten the head bolts, in three passes, in the order shown, to 62 ft.lb.

    e. When installing the valve cover, note that RTV silicone gasket compound is used in place of a gasket.

    f. Torque the valve cover bolts to 65 in.lb.

    g. Torque the camshaft pulley bolt to 72 ft.lb.

    h. Make sure that the timing marks align by rotating the engine 2 full revolutions and rechecking the alignment.

    i. Torque the #1 idler pulley bolt to 27 ft.lb.

    j. Road test the car.

3Y-EC, 4Y-EC

1. Disconnect the battery ground.
2. Remove the right front seat.
3. Remove the engine cover.
4. Drain the coolant.

CAUTION: *When draining the coolant, keep in mind that cats and dogs are attracted by the ethylene glycol antifreeze, and are quite likely to drink any that is left in an uncovered container or in puddles on the ground. This will prove fatal in sufficient quantity. Always drain the coolant into a sealable container. Coolant should be reused unless it is contaminated or several years old.*

5. Drain the oil.
6. Remove the power steering pump.
7. Disconnect the exhaust pipe at the manifold.
8. Disconnect and tag all wires, vacuum

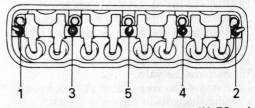

Rocker arm shaft loosening sequence—3Y–EC and 4Y–EC

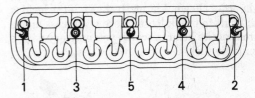

3Y-EC Rocker arm bolt loosening sequence

Front

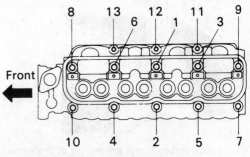

3Y-EC Head bolt tightening sequence

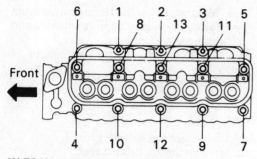

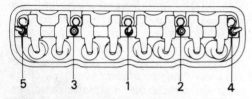

3Y-EC Head bolt loosening sequence

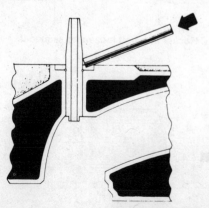

3Y-EC Rocker arm bolt tightening sequence

hoses and cables attached to or running across the head.

9. Remove the throttle body.

10. Remove the EGR valve.

11. Disconnect the coolant bypass hoses.

12. Remove the air intake chamber.

13. Remove the fuel lines form the injectors.

14. Disconnect the fuel line and fuel return line.

15. Remove the spark plugs and tubes.

16. Remove the valve cover.

17. Remove the rocker arm shaft assembly, loosening the bolts in the order shown.

18. Remove the pushrods. Keep them in order for installation.

19. Loosen the head bolts, in three passes, in the order shown. Lift off the head. If the head is difficult to break loose, there is a recess at the front of the head in which you may pry with a suitable tool.

20. Installation is the reverse of removal. Note the following points:

a. Always use a new head gasket. Make sure that all sealing surfaces are clean.

b. Tighten the head bolts gradually, in three passes, in the order shown, to 65 ft.lb. for 14mm bolts and 14 ft.lb. for 12mm bolts.

c. Tighten the rocker shaft bolts, in the order shown, to 17 ft.lb.

d. Torque the spark plugs to 13 ft.lb.

e. Torque the air intake chamber bolts to 9 ft.lb.

f. Torque the throttle body bolts to 9 ft.lb.

g. Road test the car.

Valve Guide

REPLACEMENT

1. Heat the cylinder head to 176–212°F, evenly, before beginning the replacement procedure.

2. Use a brass rod to break the valve guide off above its snaring. (See the illustration).

3. Drive out the valve guide, toward the combustion chamber. Use a tool fabricated as described in the Engine Rebuilding section.

4. Install a snaring on the new valve guide. Apply liquid sealer. Drive in the valve guide until the snaring contacts the head. Use the tool previously described.

5. Measure the guide bore. If the stem-to-guide clearance is below specification, ream it out, using a valve guide reamer.

Valve Rocker Shaft

REMOVAL AND INSTALLATION

Valve rocker shaft removal and installation is given as part of the various Cylinder Head Removal and Installation procedures.

Perform only the steps of the appropriate Cylinder Head Removal and Installation procedures necessary to remove and install the rocker shafts.

Intake Manifold

REMOVAL AND INSTALLATION

20R and 22R Engines

1. Disconnect the battery.

2. Drain the cooling system.

CAUTION: *When draining the coolant, keep in mind that cats and dogs are attracted by the ethylene glycol antifreeze, and are quite likely to drink any that is left in an uncovered container or in puddles on the ground. This will prove fatal in sufficient quantity. Always drain the coolant into a sealable container. Coolant should be reused unless it is contaminated or several years old.*

Use a brass drift to break the top off of the valve guide

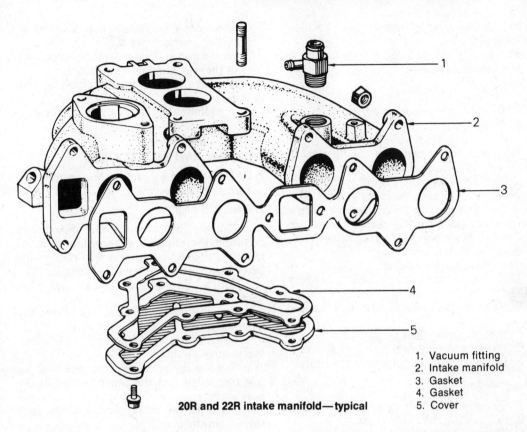

20R and 22R intake manifold—typical

1. Vacuum fitting
2. Intake manifold
3. Gasket
4. Gasket
5. Cover

3. Remove the air cleaner assembly, complete with hoses, from the carburetor.

4. Disconnect the vacuum lines from the EGR valve and carburetor. Mark them first to aid in installation.

5. Remove the fuel lines, electrical leads, accelerator linkage, and water hose from the carburetor.

6. Remove the water by-pass hose from the manifold.

7. Unbolt and remove the intake manifold, complete with carburetor and EGR valve.

8. Cover the cylinder head ports with clean shop cloths to keep anything from falling into the cylinder head or block.

9. Installation is the reverse of removal. Replace the gasket with a new one. Torque the mounting bolts to the figure given in the Torque Specifications chart. Tighten the bolts in several stages working form the inside bolts outward. Remember to refill the cooling system.

M Series

NOTE: *For fuel injected models refer to the Cylinder Head removal section of this chapter.*

1. Drain the cooling system.

CAUTION: *When draining the coolant, keep in mind that cats and dogs are attracted by the ethylene glycol antifreeze, and are quite likely to drink any that is left in an uncovered container or in puddles on the ground. This will prove fatal in sufficient quantity. Always drain the coolant into a sealable container. Coolant should be reused unless it is contaminated or several years old.*

2. Remove the air cleaner assembly, complete with hoses, from its mounting bracket.

3. Remove the distributor cap.

4. Remove the upper radiator hose from the elbow.

5. Remove the wiring from the temperature gauge sender.

6. Remove the following from the carburetor: fuel lines; vacuum line; choke stove hoses, emission control system hoses (and wires); accelerator torque rod; and automatic transmission linkage (if so equipped).

7. Remove the emission control system lines and wiring from the manifold when equipped with a vacuum switching valve on engines with EGR, remove the EGR lines and fittings.

8. Remove the water by-pass hose from the manifold.

9. Unbolt and remove the manifold, complete with the carburetor.

10. Installation is in the reverse order of removal. Remember to replace the gaskets with new ones. Torque the mounting bolts to the

specifications given in the Torque Specifications chart.

NOTE: *Tighten the bolts, in stages, working from the inside out.*

1C-L, 1C-TL

1. Disconnect the battery ground.
2. Drain the coolant.

CAUTION: *When draining the coolant, keep in mind that cats and dogs are attracted by the ethylene glycol antifreeze, and are quite likely to drink any that is left in an uncovered container or in puddles on the ground. This will prove fatal in sufficient quantity. Always drain the coolant into a sealable container. Coolant should be reused unless it is contaminated or several years old.*

3. Remove the air cleaner.
4. Disconnect and tag any wire, hose or cable in the way of manifold removal.
5. Remove the turbocharger as described later.
6. Remove the coolant by-pass pipe.
7. Unbolt and remove the manifold.
8. Installation is the reverse of removal.

3Y-EC, 4Y-EC

1. Disconnect the battery ground.
2. Remove the right front seat.
3. Remove the engine cover.
4. Drain the coolant.

CAUTION: *When draining the coolant, keep in mind that cats and dogs are attracted by the ethylene glycol antifreeze, and are quite likely to drink any that is left in an uncovered container or in puddles on the ground. This will prove fatal in sufficient quantity. Always drain the coolant into a sealable container.*

Coolant should be reused unless it is contaminated or several years old.

5. Disconnect and tag any wires, hoses or cables in the way of manifold removal.
6. Remove the air intake chamber and manifold.
7. Installation is the reverse of removal.

Exhaust Manifold

REMOVAL AND INSTALLATION

CAUTION: *Do not perform this operation on a warm or hot engine.*

20R and 22R Engines

1. Remove the three exhaust pipe flange bolts and disconnect the exhaust pipe from the manifold. It may be necessary to remove the outer heat shield first on some models.
2. Mark and disconnect the spark plug leads.
3. Remove the air cleaner tube from the heat stove.
4. Use a 14mm wrench to remove the manifold securing nuts.
5. Remove the manifold, complete with air injection tubes and the inner portion of the heat stove.
6. Separate the inner portion of the heat stove from the manifold.
7. Installation is the reverse of removal. Tighten the retaining nuts to 29–36 ft.lb., working form the inside out, and in several stages. Tighten the exhaust pipe flange nuts to 25–32 ft.lb.

3Y-EC, 4Y-EC and M Series exc. 5M-GE

1. Raise the front and the rear of the car and support it with jackstands.

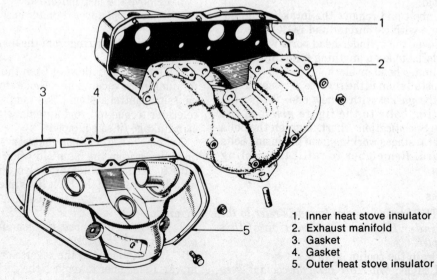

1. Inner heat stove insulator
2. Exhaust manifold
3. Gasket
4. Gasket
5. Outer heat stove insulator

20R and 22R exhaust manifold—typical

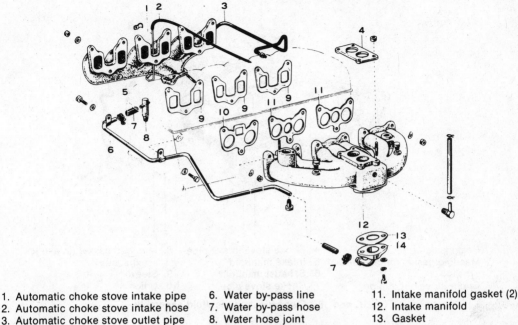

1. Automatic choke stove intake pipe
2. Automatic choke stove intake hose
3. Automatic choke stove outlet pipe
4. Carburetor heat insulator
5. Exhaust manifold
6. Water by-pass line
7. Water by-pass hose
8. Water hose joint
9. Exhaust manifold gasket
10. Intake manifold gasket (1)
11. Intake manifold gasket (2)
12. Intake manifold
13. Gasket
14. Water by-pass outlet

2M and 4M intake and exhaust manifolds

CAUTION: *Be sure that the car is securely supported.*

2. Remove the right hand gravel shield from beneath the engine.

3. Remove the downpipe support bracket.

4. Unfasten the bolts from the flange and detach the downpipe from the manifold. It may be necessary to remove the outer heat shield first.

5. Remove the automatic choke and air cleaner stove hoses from the exhaust manifold.

6. Remove or move aside, any of the air injection system components which may be in the way when removing the manifold. Unfasten the EGR valve and pipes.

7. In order to remove the manifold, unfasten the manifold retaining bolts.

CAUTION: *Remove and tighten the bolts in two or three stages and, starting from the inside, working out.*

8. Installation is performed in the reverse order of removal. Always use a new gasket. Tighten the retaining bolts to the specifications given in two or three stages.

5M-GE

NOTE: *The air intake hose may have to be removed to give access to all the manifold nuts.*

1. Jack up the front end of the car and safely support it with jackstands.

2. Remove the right hand gravel shield from underneath the car.

3. Remove the exhaust pipe support stay.

4. Unbolt the exhaust pipe from the exhaust manifold flange.

5. Disconnect the oxygen sensor connector.

6. Remove the seven nuts and remove the exhaust manifold.

7. Installation is the reverse of removal. Use a new manifold gasket and torque all nuts evenly to 25–33 ft.lb.

Combination Manifold

REMOVAL AND INSTALLATION

CAUTION: *Do not perform this procedure on a warm engine.*

8R-C and 18R-C Engines

1. Remove the air cleaner assembly, complete with hoses, from its mounting bracket.

2. Remove the fuel line, vacuum lines, automatic choke stove hoses, PCV hose, and accelerator linkage from the carburetor.

3. Unfasten the carburetor securing nuts. Remove the torque rod support, carburetor, and heat insulator.

4. Use a jack to raise the front of the car. Support the car with jackstands.

CAUTION: *Be sure that the car is securely supported.*

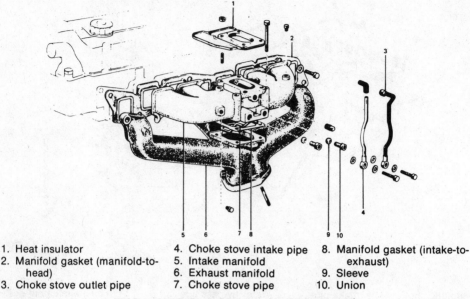

1. Heat insulator
2. Manifold gasket (manifold-to-head)
3. Choke stove outlet pipe
4. Choke stove intake pipe
5. Intake manifold
6. Exhaust manifold
7. Choke stove pipe
8. Manifold gasket (intake-to-exhaust)
9. Sleeve
10. Union

8R-C and 18R-C combination manifold assembly

5. Unfasten the bolts which attach the downpipe flange to the exhaust manifold.

6. In order to remove the manifold assembly, unfasten the manifold retaining bolts. On 1974 California engines, remove the EGR valve and tubes first.

CAUTION: *Remove and tighten the bolts in two or three stages, starting from the inside and working out.*

7. Installation is performed in the reverse order of removal. Always use new gaskets. Tighten the manifold securing bolts to the figure shown in the Torque Specifications chart, in the reverse sequence of removal.

Timing Gear Cover

REMOVAL AND INSTALLATION

8R-C, 19R-C, 20R, 22R and M series, exc. 5M-GE

1. Perform the Cylinder Head Removal procedure as detailed in the appropriate previous sections.

2. Remove the radiator.

3. Remove the alternator.

4. On engines equipped with air pumps, unfasten the adjusting link bolts and the drive belt. Remove the hoses form the pump. Remove the pump and bracket from the engine.

NOTE: *If the car is equipped with power steering, see Chapter 8 for its pump removal procedure.*

5. Remove the fan and water pump as a complete assembly.

CAUTION: *To prevent the fluid from running out of the fan coupling, do not tip the assembly over on its side.*

6. Unfasten the crankshaft pulley securing bolt and remove the pulley with a gear puller.

CAUTION: *Do not remove the 10mm bolt from its hole, if installed as it is used for balancing.*

7. Loosen the bolts securing the front of the oil pan, after draining the engine oil. Lower the front of the oil pan. It may be necessary to loosen the front motor mounts and jack up the engine slightly on some models.

8. Remove the bolts securing the timing chain cover. Withdraw the cover.

NOTE: *The M series engines use two gaskets on the timing chain cover.*

9. Tighten the timing chain cover bolts to the specifications below:

8R-C and 18R-C engines, all bolts: 11–15 ft.lb.

20R and 22R engines, all bolts: 7–12 ft.lb.

M Series 6 cylinder Engines
  8mm bolts: 7–12 ft.lb.
  10mm bolts: 14–22 ft.lb.

1C-L

1. Remove the right front wheel.

2. Remove the fender liner.

3. Remove the alternator belt.

4. Remove the cruise control actuator and bracket.

5. Remove the power steering reservoir and belt.

6. Using a wood block on the jack, raise the engine slightly.

7. Remove the right engine mount.

8. Remove the timing covers.

9. Installation is the reverse of removal.

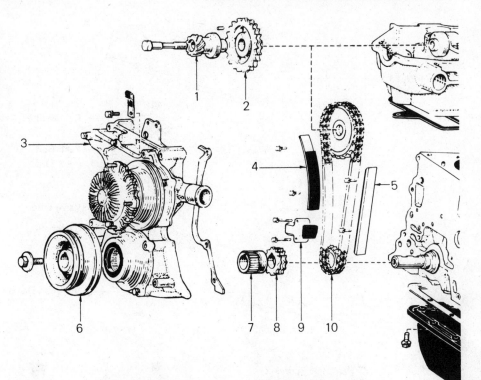

1. Distributor drive gear
2. Camshaft sprocket
3. Chain cover
4. Chain damper No. 2
5. Chain damper No. 1
6. Crankshaft pulley
7. Pump drive spline
8. Crankshaft sprocket
9. Chain tensioner
10. Chain

Front cover and timing chain components—20R and 22R engines

3Y-EC, 4Y-EC

1. Remove the radiator.
2. Remove the water pump pulley and belt.
3. Remove the distributor.
4. Remove the cold start injector.
5. Remove the crankshaft pulley. A puller must be used.
6. Unbolt and remove the cover.
7. Installation is the reverse of removal. Always use a new gasket and clean the gasket mating surfaces.

5M-GE

The 5M-GE engine uses three timing belt covers: front upper, front lower, and rear upper. To gain access to the timing belt, only the front covers need to be removed. Refer to the Timing Belt Removal and Installation procedure to remove these covers.

Timing Chain Cover Oil Seal
REPLACEMENT
All Engines

1. Remove the timing chain cover, as previously detailed in the appropriate section.

2. Inspect the oil seal for signs of wear, leakage, or damage.
3. If worn, pry the old oil seal out, using a small pry bar. Remove it toward the front of the cover.

NOTE: *Once the oil seal has been removed, it must be replaced with a new one.*

4. Use a socket, pipe, or block of wood and a hammer to drift the oil seal into place. Work from the front of the cover.

CAUTION: *Be extremely careful not to damage the seal or else it will leak.*

5. Install the timing chain cover as previously outlined.

Timing Chain and Tensioner
REMOVAL AND INSTALLATION
8R-C and 18R-C Engines

1. Remove the cylinder head and timing chain cover as previously detailed.
2. Remove the timing chain (front) together with the camshaft drive sprocket.
3. Remove the crankshaft sprocket and oil pump jack shaft, complete with the pump jack

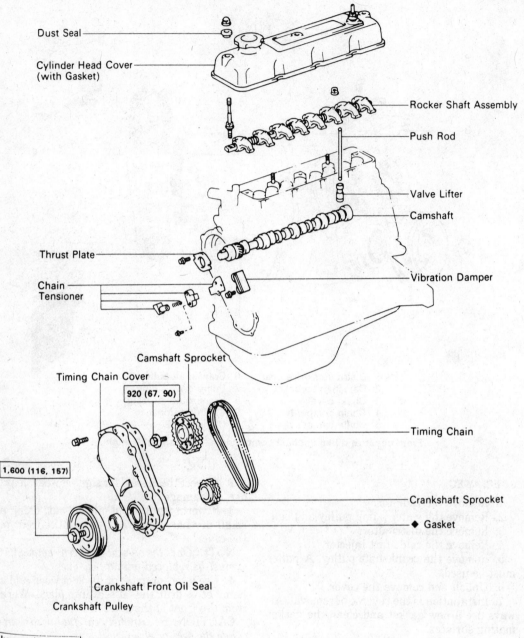

Dust Seal

Cylinder Head Cover
(with Gasket)

Rocker Shaft Assembly

Push Rod

Valve Lifter

Camshaft

Thrust Plate

Chain
Tensioner

Vibration Damper

Camshaft Sprocket

Timing Chain Cover

920 (67, 90)

Timing Chain

1,600 (116, 157)

Crankshaft Sprocket

Gasket

Crankshaft Front Oil Seal

Crankshaft Pulley

kg-cm (ft-lb, N·m) : Specified torque
◆ Non-reusable part

Front cover and related components—3Y–EC and 4Y–EC

shaft, complete with the pump drive chain (rear). Remove the chain vibration damper.

CAUTION: *Both timing chains are identical. Tag them for proper identification during installation.*

4. Inspect the chains and sprockets for wear or damage. Clean the chains with solvent.

5. Use a vernier caliper to measure the amount of stretch of both chains. Measure any

17 links while pulling the chain which is being measured taut.

6. Repeat Step 5 at two other places on each chain. Replace either of the chains if any of the 17 link measurements exceed 147mm or if the difference between the minimum and maximum readings is more than 2mm, on any one chain.

7. Remove the plunger and spring form one

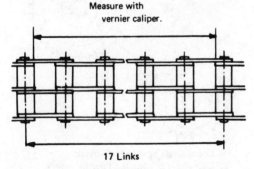

1. Camshaft timing chain
2. Camshaft drive gear
3. Chain tensioner
4. Chain tensioner

8R-C and 18R-C camshaft timing chain removal (engine inverted)

Measure with vernier caliper.

17 Links

Timing chain stretch measurement—8R-C and 18R-C

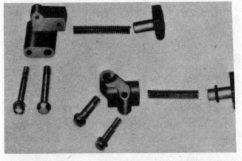

8R-C and 18R-C chain tensioner assemblies

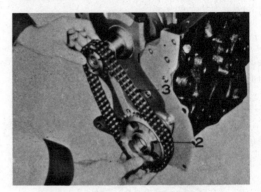

1. Crankshaft timing gear mark
2. Oil pump driveshaft mark
3. Oil pump chain timing mark

Aligning the timing marks on the oil pump drive chain (engine inverted)

3. Align the marks on the timing sprocket and the oil pump drive sprocket with each of the marks on the chain.

4. Install the chain and sprocket assembly over the keyways, while retaining alignment of the chain/sprocket timing marks.

CAUTION: *Use care not to disengage the welch plug at the rear of the oil pump driveshaft by forcing the sprocket over the keyway.*

6. Install the gasket for the timing chain cover.

NOTE: *Use liquid sealer on the gasket before installation.*

7. Install both of the chain tensioners in their respective places, being careful not to mix them up. Tighten their securing bolts to 12–17 ft.lb.

CAUTION: *Use care when installing the chain tensioner bolts; they have oil holes tapped in them.*

8. Fit the camshaft drive sprocket over the keyway on the oil pump driveshaft. Tighten its securing nut to 58–72 ft.lb.

9. Install the camshaft drive chain over the camshaft drive sprocket. Align the mating marks on the chain and sprocket.

10. Apply tension to the chain by tying it to

of the chain tensioners. Inspect all of the parts of the tensioner for wear or damage. Fill it with oil and assemble it if it is not defective.

8. Repeat Step 7 for the other tensioner.

CAUTION: *Do not mix the parts of the two chain tensioners together.*

Installation is performed in the following manner:

1. Position the No. 1 piston at TDC by having the crankshaft keyway point straight up (perpendicular to) toward the cylinder head.

2. Align the oil pump jack shaft, with the keyway pointing straight up as well.

the chain tensioner. This will prevent it from falling back into the timing chain cover once it is installed.

20R and 22R Engines

1. Remove the cylinder head and timing chain cover as previously outlined.

2. Separate the chain from the damper, and remove the chain, complete with the camshaft sprocket.

3. Remove the crankshaft sprocket and the oil pump drive with a puller.

4. Inspect the chain for wear or damage. Replace it if necessary.

5. Inspect the chain tensioner for wear. If it measures less than 11mm, replace it.

6. Check the dampers for wear. If their measurements are below the following specifications, replace them:

Upper damper: 5mm
Lower damper: 4.5mm

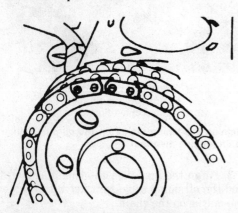

Timing mark alignment—20R and 22R

1. Timing chain tensioner gear
2. Timing chain tensioner arm
3. Damper guide
4. Vibration damper
5. Vibration damper
6. Crankshaft oil slinger

Removing the 2M and 4M timing chain (engine inverted)

Installation is performed in the following order:

1. Rotate the crankshaft until its key is at TDC. Slide the sprocket in place over the key.

2. Place the chain over the sprocket so that its single bright link aligns with the mark on the camshaft sprocket.

3. Install the cam sprocket so that the timing mark falls between the two bright links on the chain.

4. Fit the oil pump drive spline over the crankshaft key.

5. Install the timing cover gasket on the front of the block.

6. Rotate the camshaft sprocket counterclockwise to remove the slack from the chain.

7. Install the timing chain cover and cylinder head as previously outlined.

M Series

1. Remove the cylinder head and timing chain cover as previously outlined.

2. Remove the chain tensioner assembly (arm and gear).

3. Unfasten the bolts retaining the chain damper and damper guide and withdraw the damper and guide.

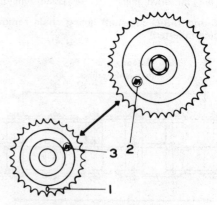

1. Crankshaft sprocket O-mark
2. Camshaft sprocket "Toyota" mark
3. Crankshaft sprocket "Toyota" mark

Timing mark—"M" series engine

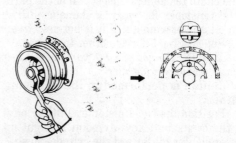

Timing mark alignment 4M engine

4. Remove the oil slinger from the crankshaft.

5. Withdraw the timing chain.

6. Inspect the chain for wear or damage. Replace it if necessary.

Installation is performed in the following manner:

1. Position the No. 1 cylinder at TDC.

2. Position the crankshaft sprocket 0 mark downward, facing the oil pan.

3. Align the Toyota trademarks on the sprockets as illustrated.

4. Fit the tensioner gear assembly on the block.

NOTE: *Its dowel pin should be positioned 38mm from the surface of the block.*

5. Install the chain over the two gears while maintaining tension.

6. Install both of the vibration dampers and the damper guide.

7. Fit the oil slinger to the crankshaft.

8. Tie the chain to the upper vibration damper, to keep it from falling into the chain cover, once the cover is installed.

9. Install the timing chain cover as previously detailed.

10. Perform the cylinder head installation procedure as detailed previously.

NOTE: *If proper valve timing cannot be obtained, it is possible to adjust it by placing the camshaft slotted pin in the second or third hole on the camshaft timing gear, as required. If the timing is out by more than 15 degrees, replace the chain and both of the sprockets.*

1C-L

1. Disconnect the battery ground.

2. Remove the right front wheel.

3. Remove the fender liner.

4. Remove the washer bottle and radiator overflow.

5. Remove the cruise control actuator.

6. Remove the power steering pump and bracket.

7. Remove the AC idler pulleys and bracket.

8. Remove the alternator.

9. Remove the lower belt cover.

10. Turn the engine to #1 cylinder at TDC compression.

11. Using a puller, remove the crankshaft pulley.

12. Remove the upper belt cover.

13. Remove the belt guide.

14. Jack up the engine slightly.

15. Remove the right side engine mount.

16. If the belt is to be reused, matchmark the belt and the pulleys with paint.

17. Remove the belt tensioner spring.

18. Loosen the idler pulley bolt and remove the belt.

19. Installation is the reverse of removal.

3Y-EC, 4Y-EC

1. Remove the radiator.

2. Remove the water pump drive belt and pulley.

3. Remove the distributor.

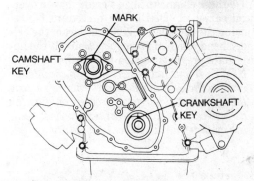

3Y-EC valve timing marks aligned

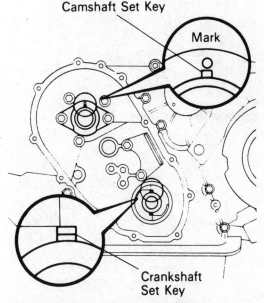

Set key alignment on the 3Y-EC and 4Y-EC

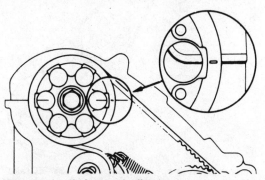

Diesel valve timing mark alignment

4. Remove the cold start injector.

5. Remove the crankshaft pulley with a puller.

6. Remove the chain cover.

7. Check the chain slack at the center point of the left side. Free play should not exceed 12.7mm If it does, replace the chain.

8. Set the engine to #1 piston TDC.

9. Remove the crankshaft and camshaft pulleys and chain.

10. Installation is the reverse of removal.

11. If the engine was turned while the chain was off, make sure that the camshaft and crankshaft keys are in the upper side position and aligned with the marks on their thrust plates.

Camshaft

REMOVAL AND INSTALLATION

8R-C, 18R-C, 20R, 22R, 4M, 4M-E, 5M-E

All of these engines utilize a chain driven overhead camshaft (OHC). The procedure for removing the camshaft is given as part of the cylinder head removal procedure. Consult the appropriate previous section for details.

NOTE: *It will not be necessary to completely remove the cylinder head in order to remove the camshaft. Therefore, proceed only as far as is necessary, to remove the camshaft, with the cylinder head removal procedure.*

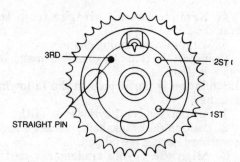

Camshaft sprocket—valve timing retarded 9 to 12°

1C-L

1. Remove the cylinder head.

2. Remove the camshaft pulley.

3. Remove the thrust plate.

4. Unbolt and remove the cam bearing caps.

5. Turning the camshaft slowly, slide the camshaft from the head.

6. Installation is the reverse of removal.

3Y-EC, 4Y-EC

1. Remove the timing chain as described above.

2. Remove the camshaft thrust plate.

3. Turning the camshaft slowly, slide it from the block.

4. Installation is the reverse of removal. Coat the camshaft with clean engine oil prior to insertion.

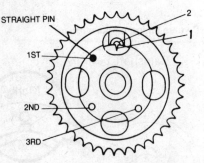

Camshaft sprocket—normal valve timing

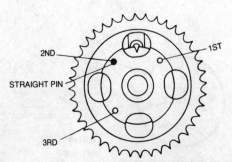

Camshaft sprocket—valve timing retarded 3 to 9°

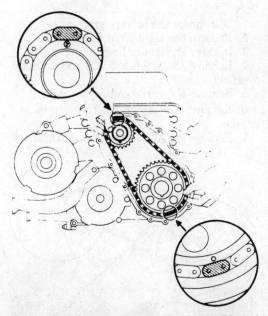

Timing chain-to-sprocket alignment—3Y-EC and 4Y-EC

5M-GE

1. Remove the two camshaft covers.

2. Remove the timing belt assembly and gears as previously detailed.

3. Following the sequence shown, loosen the camshaft housing nuts and bolts in three passes. Remove the housings (with camshafts) from the cylinder head.

4. Remove the camshaft housing rear covers. Squirt clean oil down around the cam journals in the housing, to lubricate the lobes, oil seals and bearings as the cam is removed. Begin to pull the camshaft out of the back of the housing slowly, turning it as you pull. Remove the cam completely.

5. To install, lubricate the entire camshaft with clean oil. Insert the cam into the housing from the back, and slowly turn it as you push it into the housing. Install new O-rings and the housing end covers.

6. Installation of the remaining components is in the reverse order of removal. Tighten camshaft housing bolts to 15–17 ft.lb. in the proper sequence.

CAMSHAFT INSPECTION

Prior to removal of the camshaft, measure the end play with a feeler gauge. Refer to the Specifications Chart, if the end play is beyond specs, it may be necessary to replace the cylinder head or camshaft.

Measure the bearing oil clearance by placing a piece of Plastigage® on each bearing journal. Replace the bearing caps and tighten the bolts to 13–16 ft.lb.

NOTE: *Do not turn the camshaft.*

Remove the caps and measure each piece of Plastigage®. If the clearance is greater than the values on the Specifications Chart, replace the bearings, head or cam, depending on which engine you are working on.

Place the camshaft in V-block supports and measure its run-out at the center bearing journal with a dial indicator. If the run-out exceeds specs, replace the cam.

Use a micrometer and measure the bearing journals and the cam lobe heights. If the bearing journals are not within specs, or the lobes differ greatly in size from wear, replace the camshaft.

Pistons and Connecting Rods

REMOVAL AND INSTALLATION

All Engines

1. Remove the cylinder head as outlined in the appropriate preceding section.

2. Remove the oil pan and pump.

3. Ream the ridges from the top of the cylinder bores, as detailed in Engine Rebuilding, at the end of this chapter. Remove the oil strainer if it is in the way.

4. Unbolt the connecting rod caps. Mark the caps with the number of the cylinder from which they were removed.

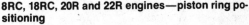
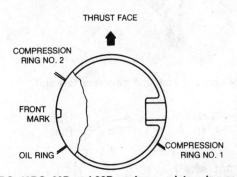

8RC, 18RC, 20R and 22R engines—piston ring positioning

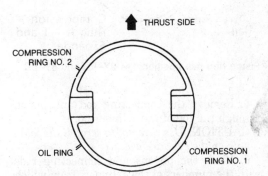

"M" series engines—piston ring positioning

8RC, 18RC, 20R and 22R—piston and rod positioning

2M engine—piston and rod positioning

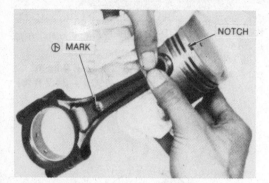

4M engine (notch and mark face forward)

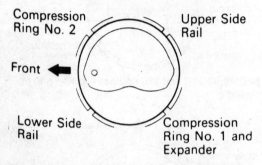

Piston ring gap positioning—3Y–EC and 4Y–EC

5. Remove the connecting rod and piston through the top of the cylinder bore.

CAUTION: *Use care not to scratch the journals or the cylinder walls.*

6. Mark the pistons and connecting rods with the numbers of the cylinders from which they were removed.

Installation is performed in the following order:

1. Apply a light coating of engine oil to the pistons, rings, and wrist pins.

2. Examine the piston to ensure that it has been assembled with its parts positioned correctly. (See the illustrations.) Be sure that the ring gaps are not pointed toward the thrust face of the piston and that they do not overlap.

3. Install the pistons, using a ring compressor, into the cylinder bore. Be sure that the appropriate marks on the piston are facing the front of the cylinder.

CAUTION: *It is important that the pistons, rods, bearings, etc., be returned to the same cylinder bore from which they were removed.*

4. Install the connecting rod bearing caps and tighten them to the torque figures given in the Torque Specifications chart.

CAUTION: *Be sure that the mating marks on the connecting rods and rod bearing caps are aligned.*

5. The rest of the removal procedure is performed in the reverse order of installation.

Oil Pan

REMOVAL AND INSTALLATION

Corona, Crown, Mk. II, Cressida

NOTE: *It may be easier to remove the engine, on some models (Crown 2300 and 2600), in order to remove the oil pan. However, with a little patience it is possible to remove the pan with the engine installed in the car.*

1. Open the hood. Drain the coolant from the radiator and disconnect the upper and lower hoses from the radiator connections. Disconnect the negative battery cable.

CAUTION: *When draining the coolant, keep in mind that cats and dogs are attracted by the ethylene glycol antifreeze, and are quite likely to drink any that is left in an uncovered container or in puddles on the ground. This will prove fatal in sufficient quantity. Always drain the coolant into a sealable container. Coolant should be reused unless it is contaminated or several years old.*

2. Loosen the front wheel lugs slightly. Raise the front of the car and support with jackstands. Remove the front wheels.

CAUTION: *Be sure the car is supported securely. Remember, you will be working underneath it.*

3. Drain the engine oil.

4. Detach the steering relay rod and the tie rod ends from the idler arm, pitman arm and the steering knuckles. (Refer to Chapter eight).

5. Remove the splash shields. Remove the engine stiffening plates (supports between the engine and transmission-if equipped).

6. Support the front of the engine with a jack and remove the front motor mount bolts.

7. Raise the engine and place blocks between the mount and the frame. Lower the engine on the blocks, make sure it is supported securely.

8. Check the clearance between the oil pan and the crossmember. It may be necessary to raise the rear of the engine as well.

9. To raise the rear of the engine, place a jack under the bell housing (between the engine and transmission) remove the rear motor mount bolts and raise the rear of the engine. Place blocks between the rear mounts and the crossmember. Slowly lower the engine onto the blocks. Make sure it is secure.

10. Remove the oil pan mounting bolts and remove the oil pan.

NOTE: *If you still do not have enough room to remove the oil pan it may be necessary to place thicker blocks under the front or rear of the engine. Do so carefully.*

11. Installation is the reverse of removal. Ap-

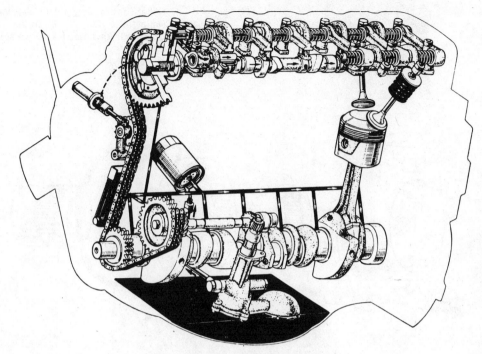

"M" series engine lubrication system

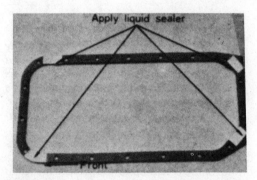

Apply sealer to the corners of the engine oil pan gasket

ply liquid sealer to the corners of the oil pan and install a new pan gasket.

Van

1. Raise and support the support the front end on jackstands.
2. Drain the oil.
3. Remove the left and right stiffener plates.
4. Unbolt and remove the pan.
5. Installation is the reverse of removal. Clean the pan and block mating surfaces. Apply a 5mm bead of RTV gasket material to the groove around the pan flange. Install the pan within 15 min. Torque the pan bolts to 9 ft.lb.

Rear Main Oil Seal
REPLACEMENT
All Engines

NOTE: *This procedure applies only to those models with manual transmissions. If your car has an automatic transmission, leave removal of the oil seal to your dealer.*

1. Remove the transmission as detailed in Chapter 6.
2. Remove the clutch cover assembly and flywheel. See Chapter 6 also.
3. Remove the oil seal retaining plate, complete with the oil seal.
4. Use a screwdriver to pry the oil seal from the retaining plate. Be careful not to damage the plate.
5. Install the new seal, carefully, by using a block of wood to drift it into place.
CAUTION: *Do not damage the seal. A leak will result.*
6. Lubricate the lips of the seal with multi-purpose grease.
7. Installation is performed in the reverse order from removal.

Oil Pump
REMOVAL AND INSTALLATION

NOTE: *It may be necessary to remove the radiator on some models, to gain the necessary room.*

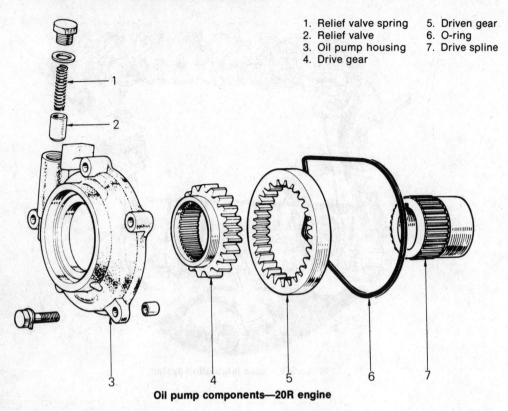

1. Relief valve spring
2. Relief valve
3. Oil pump housing
4. Drive gear
5. Driven gear
6. O-ring
7. Drive spline

Oil pump components—20R engine

All Engines Except 20R and 22R

1. Remove the oil pan, as outlined in the appropriate preceding section.

2. Unbolt the oil pump securing bolts and remove it as an assembly.

3. Installation is the reverse of removal.

20R and 22R Engines

1. Remove the oil pan as previously outlined.

2. Unfasten the three bolts which secure the oil strainer.

3. Remove the drive belts, the pulley bolt, and the crankshaft pulley.

4. Unfasten the bolts which secure the oil pump housing to the timing chain cover, and remove the pump assembly.

5. Remove the oil pump drive spline and the rubber O-ring.

6. Installation is performed in the reverse order of removal. Apply sealer to the top oil pump housing bolt. Use a new oil strainer gasket.

Radiator

REMOVAL AND INSTALLATION

All Models

1. Drain the cooling system.

CAUTION: *When draining the coolant, keep*

in mind that cats and dogs are attracted by the ethylene glycol antifreeze, and are quite likely to drink any that is left in an uncovered container or in puddles on the ground. This will prove fatal in sufficient quantity. Always drain the coolant into a sealable container. Coolant should be reused unless it is contaminated or several years old.

2. Unfasten the clamps and remove the radiator upper and lower hoses. If equipped with an automatic transmission, remove the oil cooler lines.

3. Detach the hood lock cable and remove the hood lock from the radiator upper support.

NOTE: *It may be necessary to remove the*

Removing the radiator

grille in order to gain access to the hood lock/radiator support assembly.

4. Remove the fan shroud, if so equipped.

5. On models equipped with a coolant recovery system, disconnect the hose from the thermal expansion tank and remove the tank from its bracket.

6. Unbolt and remove the radiator upper support.

7. Unfasten the bolts and remove the radiator.

CAUTION: *Use care not to damage the radiator fins on the cooling fan.*

8. Installation is performed in the reverse order of removal. Remember to check the transmission fluid level on cars with automatic transmissions. Fill the radiator to the specified level, as detailed under Fluid Level Checks, in Chapter 1. Remember to check for leaks after installation is completed.

Water Pump
REMOVAL AND INSTALLATION
All Engines

1. Drain the cooling system.

CAUTION: *When draining the coolant, keep in mind that cats and dogs are attracted by the ethylene glycol antifreeze, and are quite likely to drink any that is left in an uncovered container or in puddles on the ground. This will prove fatal in sufficient quantity. Always drain the coolant into a sealable container. Coolant should be reused unless it is contaminated or several years old.*

2. Unfasten the fan shroud securing bolts and remove the fan shroud, if so equipped.

3. Loosen the alternator adjusting link bolt and remove the drive belt.

4. Repeat Step 3 for the air and/or power steering pump drive belt, if so equipped.

5. Detach the by-pass hose from the water pump. On the 5M-GE, remove the air cleaner case.

6. Unfasten the water pump retaining bolts and remove the water pump and fan assembly, using care not to damage the radiator with the fan.

CAUTION: *If the fan is equipped with a fluid coupling, do not tip the fan/pump assembly on its side, as the fluid will run out.*

7. Installation is performed in the reverse order of removal. Always use a new gasket between the pump body and its mounting.

Thermostat
REMOVAL AND INSTALLATION
All Engines

1. Drain the cooling system.

CAUTION: *When draining the coolant, keep in mind that cats and dogs are attracted by the ethylene glycol antifreeze, and are quite likely to drink any that is left in an uncovered container or in puddles on the ground. This will prove fatal in sufficient quantity. Always drain the coolant into a sealable container. Coolant should be reused unless it is contaminated or several years old.*

2. Unfasten the clamp and remove the supper radiator hose from the water outlet elbow.

3. Unbolt and remove the water outlet (thermostat housing).

4. Withdraw the thermostat.

5. Installation is performed in the reverse order of the removal procedure. Use a new gasket on the water outlet.

CAUTION: *Be sure that the thermostat is installed with the spring pointing down.*

Emission Controls and Fuel System

EMISSION CONTROL SYSTEMS

Positive Crankcase Ventilation

A positive crankcase ventilation (PCV) system is used on all Toyotas sold in the United States. Blow-by gases are routed from the crankcase to the carburetor, where they are combined with the fuel/air mixture and burned during combustion.

A valve (PCV) is used in the line to prevent the gases in the crankcase from being ignited in case of a backfire. The amount of blow-by gases entering the mixture is also regulated by the PCV Valve, which is spring-loaded and has a variable orifice.

On Toyotas, the valve is either mounted on the valve cover or in the line which runs from the intake manifold to the crankcase.

The valve should be replaced at the following intervals:
- 1970–71 models – 12,000mi/12mo
- 1972–74 models – 24,000mi/24mo
- 1975–77 models – 25,000mi/24mo
- 1978–81 models – 30,000mi/24mo
- 1980–81 Calif. – 69,000 mi/48mo

REMOVAL AND INSTALLATION

Remove the PCV valve from the cylinder head cover or from the manifold-to-crankcase hose. Check the attaching hoses for cracks or clogs. Install a new PCV valve into the hoses, or reinstall in the cylinder head cover.

TESTING

Check the PCV system hoses and connections, to ensure that there are no leaks, then replace or tighten, as necessary.

To check the valve, remove it and blow through both of its ends. When blowing from the side which goes toward the intake manifold, very little air should pass through. When blowing from the crankcase (valve cover) side, air should pass through freely.

Replace the valve with a new one, if the valve fails to function as outlined.

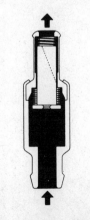

IDLE SPEED OR DECELERATION
(HIGH MANIFOLD VACUUM)

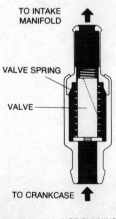

TO INTAKE MANIFOLD

VALVE SPRING

VALVE

TO CRANKCASE

NOT RUNNING
OR BACKFIRE

PCV valve operation

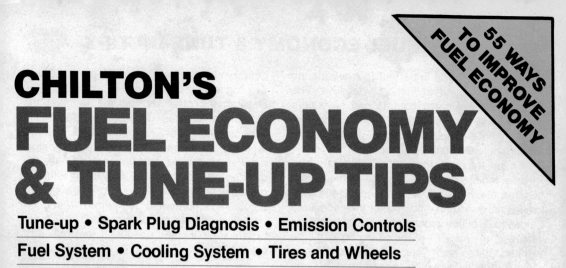

CHILTON'S
FUEL ECONOMY
& TUNE-UP TIPS

Tune-up • Spark Plug Diagnosis • Emission Controls

Fuel System • Cooling System • Tires and Wheels

General Maintenance

CHILTON'S FUEL ECONOMY & TUNE-UP TIPS

Fuel economy is important to everyone, no matter what kind of vehicle you drive. The maintenance-minded motorist can save both money and fuel using these tips and the periodic maintenance and tune-up procedures in this Repair and Tune-Up Guide.

There are more than 130,000,000 cars and trucks registered for private use in the United States. Each travels an average of 10-12,000 miles per year, and, and in total they consume close to 70 billion gallons of fuel each year. This represents nearly ⅔ of the oil imported by the United States each year. The Federal government's goal is to reduce consumption 10% by 1985. A variety of methods are either already in use or under serious consideration, and they all affect you driving and the cars you will drive. In addition to "down-sizing", the auto industry is using or investigating the use of electronic fuel delivery, electronic engine controls and alternative engines for use in smaller and lighter vehicles, among other alternatives to meet the federally mandated Corporate Average Fuel Economy (CAFE) of 27.5 mpg by 1985. The government, for its part, is considering rationing, mandatory driving curtailments and tax increases on motor vehicle fuel in an effort to reduce consumption. The government's goal of a 10% reduction could be realized — and further government regulation avoided — if every private vehicle could use just 1 less gallon of fuel per week.

How Much Can You Save?

Tests have proven that almost anyone can make at least a 10% reduction in fuel consumption through regular maintenance and tune-ups. When a major manufacturer of spark plugs sur-

TUNE-UP

1. Check the cylinder compression to be sure the engine will really benefit from a tune-up and that it is capable of producing good fuel economy. A tune-up will be wasted on an engine in poor mechanical condition.

2. Replace spark plugs regularly. New spark plugs alone can increase fuel economy 3%.

3. Be sure the spark plugs are the correct type (heat range) for your vehicle. See the Tune-Up Specifications.

Heat range refers to the spark plug's ability to conduct heat away from the firing end. It must conduct the heat away in an even pattern to avoid becoming a source of pre-ignition, yet it must also operate hot enough to burn off conductive deposits that could cause misfiring.

The heat range is usually indicated by a number on the spark plug, part of the manufacturer's designation for each individual spark plug. The numbers in bold-face indicate the heat range in each manufacturer's identification system.

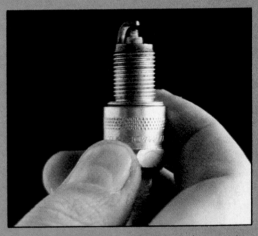

Periodically, check the spark plugs to be sure they are firing efficiently. They are excellent indicators of the internal condition of your engine.

Manufacturer	Typical Designation
AC	R **45** TS
Bosch (old)	WA **145** T30
Bosch (new)	HR **8** Y
Champion	RBL **15** Y
Fram/Autolite	**415**
Mopar	P-**62** PR
Motorcraft	BRF-**42**
NGK	BP **5** ES-15
Nippondenso	W **16** EP
Prestolite	14GR **5** 2A

On AC, Bosch (new), Champion, Fram/Autolite, Mopar, Motorcraft and Prestolite, a higher number indicates a hotter plug. On Bosch (old), NGK and Nippondenso, a higher number indicates a colder plug.

4. Make sure the spark plugs are properly gapped. See the Tune-Up Specifications in this book.

5. Be sure the spark plugs are firing efficiently. The illustrations on the next 2 pages show you how to "read" the firing end of the spark plug.

6. Check the ignition timing and set it to specifications. Tests show that almost all cars have incorrect ignition timing by more than 2°.

veyed over 6,000 cars nationwide, they found that a tune-up, on cars that needed one, increased fuel economy over 11%. Replacing worn plugs alone, accounted for a 3% increase. The same test also revealed that 8 out of every 10 vehicles will have some maintenance deficiency that will directly affect fuel economy, emissions or performance. Most of this mileage-robbing neglect could be prevented with regular maintenance.

Modern engines require that all of the functioning systems operate properly for maximum efficiency. A malfunction anywhere wastes fuel. You can keep your vehicle running as efficiently and economically as possible, by being aware of your vehicle's operating and performance characteristics. If your vehicle suddenly develops performance or fuel economy problems it could be due to one or more of the following:

PROBLEM	POSSIBLE CAUSE
Engine Idles Rough	Ignition timing, idle mixture, vacuum leak or something amiss in the emission control system.
Hesitates on Acceleration	Dirty carburetor or fuel filter, improper accelerator pump setting, ignition timing or fouled spark plugs.
Starts Hard or Fails to Start	Worn spark plugs, improperly set automatic choke, ice (or water) in fuel system.
Stalls Frequently	Automatic choke improperly adjusted and possible dirty air filter or fuel filter.
Performs Sluggishly	Worn spark plugs, dirty fuel or air filter, ignition timing or automatic choke out of adjustment.

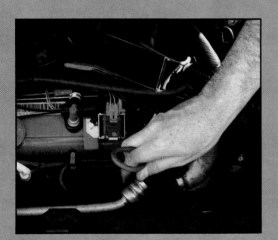

Check spark plug wires on conventional point type ignition for cracks by bending them in a loop around your finger.

Be sure that spark plug wires leading to adjacent cylinders do not run too close together. (Photo courtesy Champion Spark Plug Co.)

7. If your vehicle does not have electronic ignition, check the points, rotor and cap as specified.

8. Check the spark plug wires (used with conventional point-type ignitions) for cracks and burned or broken insulation by bending them in a loop around your finger. Cracked wires decrease fuel efficiency by failing to deliver full voltage to the spark plugs. One misfiring spark plug can cost you as much as 2 mpg.

9. Check the routing of the plug wires. Misfiring can be the result of spark plug leads to adjacent cylinders running parallel to each other and too close together. One wire tends to

pick up voltage from the other causing it to fire "out of time".

10. Check all electrical and ignition circuits for voltage drop and resistance.

11. Check the distributor mechanical and/or vacuum advance mechanisms for proper functioning. The vacuum advance can be checked by twisting the distributor plate in the opposite direction of rotation. It should spring back when released.

12. Check and adjust the valve clearance on engines with mechanical lifters. The clearance should be slightly loose rather than too tight.

SPARK PLUG DIAGNOSIS

Normal

APPEARANCE: This plug is typical of one operating normally. The insulator nose varies from a light tan to grayish color with slight electrode wear. The presence of slight deposits is normal on used plugs and will have no adverse effect on engine performance. The spark plug heat range is correct for the engine and the engine is running normally.

CAUSE: Properly running engine.

RECOMMENDATION: Before reinstalling this plug, the electrodes should be cleaned and filed square. Set the gap to specifications. If the plug has been in service for more than 10-12,000 miles, the entire set should probably be replaced with a fresh set of the same heat range.

Oil Deposits

APPEARANCE: The firing end of the plug is covered with a wet, oily coating.

CAUSE: The problem is poor oil control. On high mileage engines, oil is leaking past the rings or valve guides into the combustion chamber. A common cause is also a plugged PCV valve, and a ruptured fuel pump diaphragm can also cause this condition. Oil fouled plugs such as these are often found in new or recently overhauled engines, before normal oil control is achieved, and can be cleaned and reinstalled.

RECOMMENDATION: A hotter spark plug may temporarily relieve the problem, but the engine is probably in need of work.

Incorrect Heat Range

APPEARANCE: The effects of high temperature on a spark plug are indicated by clean white, often blistered insulator. This can also be accompanied by excessive wear of the electrode, and the absence of deposits.

CAUSE: Check for the correct spark plug heat range. A plug which is too hot for the engine can result in overheating. A car operated mostly at high speeds can require a colder plug. Also check ignition timing, cooling system level, fuel mixture and leaking intake manifold.

RECOMMENDATION: If all ignition and engine adjustments are known to be correct, and no other malfunction exists, install spark plugs one heat range colder.

Carbon Deposits

APPEARANCE: Carbon fouling is easily identified by the presence of dry, soft, black, sooty deposits.

CAUSE: Changing the heat range can often lead to carbon fouling, as can prolonged slow, stop-and-start driving. If the heat range is correct, carbon fouling can be attributed to a rich fuel mixture, sticking choke, clogged air cleaner, worn breaker points, retarded timing or low compression. If only one or two plugs are carbon fouled, check for corroded or cracked wires on the affected plugs. Also look for cracks in the distributor cap between the towers of affected cylinders.

RECOMMENDATION: After the problem is corrected, these plugs can be cleaned and reinstalled if not worn severely.

MMT Fouled

APPEARANCE: Spark plugs fouled by MMT (Methycyclopentadienyl Maganese Tricarbonyl) have reddish, rusty appearance on the insulator and side electrode.

CAUSE: MMT is an anti-knock additive in gasoline used to replace lead. During the combustion process, the MMT leaves a reddish deposit on the insulator and side electrode.

RECOMMENDATION: No engine malfunction is indicated and the deposits will not affect plug performance any more than lead deposits (see Ash Deposits). MMT fouled plugs can be cleaned, regapped and reinstalled.

High Speed Glazing

APPEARANCE: Glazing appears as shiny coating on the plug, either yellow or tan in color.

CAUSE: During hard, fast acceleration, plug temperatures rise suddenly. Deposits from normal combustion have no chance to fluff-off; instead, they melt on the insulator forming an electrically conductive coating which causes misfiring.

RECOMMENDATION: Glazed plugs are not easily cleaned. They should be replaced with a fresh set of plugs of the correct heat range. If the condition recurs, using plugs with a heat range one step colder may cure the problem.

Ash (Lead) Deposits

APPEARANCE: Ash deposits are characterized by light brown or white colored deposits crusted on the side or center electrodes. In some cases it may give the plug a rusty appearance.

CAUSE: Ash deposits are normally derived from oil or fuel additives burned during normal combustion. Normally they are harmless, though excessive amounts can cause misfiring. If deposits are excessive in short mileage, the valve guides may be worn.

RECOMMENDATION: Ash-fouled plugs can be cleaned, gapped and reinstalled.

Detonation

APPEARANCE: Detonation is usually characterized by a broken plug insulator.

CAUSE: A portion of the fuel charge will begin to burn spontaneously, from the increased heat following ignition. The explosion that results applies extreme pressure to engine components, frequently damaging spark plugs and pistons.

Detonation can result by over-advanced ignition timing, inferior gasoline (low octane) lean air/fuel mixture, poor carburetion, engine lugging or an increase in compression ratio due to combustion chamber deposits or engine modification.

RECOMMENDATION: Replace the plugs after correcting the problem.

Photos Courtesy Champion Spark Plug Co.

EMISSION CONTROLS

13. Be aware of the general condition of the emission control system. It contributes to reduced pollution and should be serviced regularly to maintain efficient engine operation.

14. Check all vacuum lines for dried, cracked or brittle conditions. Something as simple as a leaking vacuum hose can cause poor performance and loss of economy.

15. Avoid tampering with the emission control system. Attempting to improve fuel econ-

FUEL SYSTEM

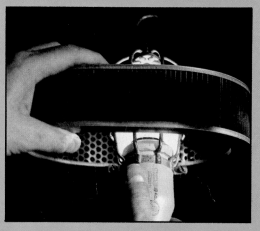

Check the air filter with a light behind it. If you can see light through the filter it can be reused.

Extremely clogged filters should be discarded and replaced with a new one.

18. Replace the air filter regularly. A dirty air filter richens the air/fuel mixture and can increase fuel consumption as much as 10%. Tests show that ⅓ of all vehicles have air filters in need of replacement.

19. Replace the fuel filter at least as often as recommended.

20. Set the idle speed and carburetor mixture to specifications.

21. Check the automatic choke. A sticking or malfunctioning choke wastes gas.

22. During the summer months, adjust the automatic choke for a leaner mixture which will produce faster engine warm-ups.

COOLING SYSTEM

29. Be sure all accessory drive belts are in good condition. Check for cracks or wear.

30. Adjust all accessory drive belts to proper tension.

31. Check all hoses for swollen areas, worn spots, or loose clamps.

32. Check coolant level in the radiator or expansion tank.

33. Be sure the thermostat is operating properly. A stuck thermostat delays engine warm-up and a cold engine uses nearly twice as much fuel as a warm engine.

34. Drain and replace the engine coolant at least as often as recommended. Rust and scale

TIRES & WHEELS

38. Check the tire pressure often with a pencil type gauge. Tests by a major tire manufacturer show that 90% of all vehicles have at least 1 tire improperly inflated. Better mileage can be achieved by over-inflating tires, but never exceed the maximum inflation pressure on the side of the tire.

39. If possible, install radial tires. Radial tires deliver as much as ½ mpg more than bias belted tires.

40. Avoid installing super-wide tires. They only create extra rolling resistance and decrease fuel mileage. Stick to the manufacturer's recommendations.

41. Have the wheels properly balanced.

omy by tampering with emission controls is more likely to worsen fuel economy than improve it. Emission control changes on modern engines are not readily reversible.

16. Clean (or replace) the EGR valve and lines as recommended.

17. Be sure that all vacuum lines and hoses are reconnected properly after working under the hood. An unconnected or misrouted vacuum line can wreak havoc with engine performance.

---

23. Check for fuel leaks at the carburetor, fuel pump, fuel lines and fuel tank. Be sure all lines and connections are tight.

24. Periodically check the tightness of the carburetor and intake manifold attaching nuts and bolts. These are a common place for vacuum leaks to occur.

25. Clean the carburetor periodically and lubricate the linkage.

26. The condition of the tailpipe can be an excellent indicator of proper engine combustion. After a long drive at highway speeds, the inside of the tailpipe should be a light grey in color. Black or soot on the insides indicates an overly rich mixture.

27. Check the fuel pump pressure. The fuel pump may be supplying more fuel than the engine needs.

28. Use the proper grade of gasoline for your engine. Don't try to compensate for knocking or "pinging" by advancing the ignition timing. This practice will only increase plug temperature and the chances of detonation or pre-ignition with relatively little performance gain.

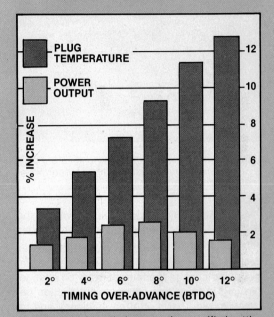

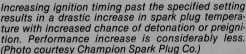

Increasing ignition timing past the specified setting results in a drastic increase in spark plug temperature with increased chance of detonation or preignition. Performance increase is considerably less. (Photo courtesy Champion Spark Plug Co.)

---

that form in the engine should be flushed out to allow the engine to operate at peak efficiency.

35. Clean the radiator of debris that can decrease cooling efficiency.

36. Install a flex-type or electric cooling fan, if you don't have a clutch type fan. Flex fans use curved plastic blades to push more air at low speeds when more cooling is needed; at high speeds the blades flatten out for less resistance. Electric fans only run when the engine temperature reaches a predetermined level.

37. Check the radiator cap for a worn or cracked gasket. If the cap does not seal properly, the cooling system will not function properly.

---

42. Be sure the front end is correctly aligned. A misaligned front end actually has wheels going in differed directions. The increased drag can reduce fuel economy by .3 mpg.

43. Correctly adjust the wheel bearings. Wheel bearings that are adjusted too tight increase rolling resistance.

Check tire pressures regularly with a reliable pocket type gauge. Be sure to check the pressure on a cold tire.

GENERAL MAINTENANCE

Check the fluid levels (particularly engine oil) on a regular basis. Be sure to check the oil for grit, water or other contamination.

A vacuum gauge is another excellent indicator of internal engine condition and can also be installed in the dash as a mileage indicator.

44. Periodically check the fluid levels in the engine, power steering pump, master cylinder, automatic transmission and drive axle.

45. Change the oil at the recommended interval and change the filter at every oil change. Dirty oil is thick and causes extra friction between moving parts, cutting efficiency and increasing wear. A worn engine requires more frequent tune-ups and gets progressively worse fuel economy. In general, use the lightest viscosity oil for the driving conditions you will encounter.

46. Use the recommended viscosity fluids in the transmission and axle.

47. Be sure the battery is fully charged for fast starts. A slow starting engine wastes fuel.

48. Be sure battery terminals are clean and tight.

49. Check the battery electrolyte level and add distilled water if necessary.

50. Check the exhaust system for crushed pipes, blockages and leaks.

51. Adjust the brakes. Dragging brakes or brakes that are not releasing create increased drag on the engine.

52. Install a vacuum gauge or miles-per-gallon gauge. These gauges visually indicate engine vacuum in the intake manifold. High vacuum = good mileage and low vacuum = poorer mileage. The gauge can also be an excellent indicator of internal engine conditions.

53. Be sure the clutch is properly adjusted. A slipping clutch wastes fuel.

54. Check and periodically lubricate the heat control valve in the exhaust manifold. A sticking or inoperative valve prevents engine warm-up and wastes gas.

55. Keep accurate records to check fuel economy over a period of time. A sudden drop in fuel economy may signal a need for tune-up or other maintenance.

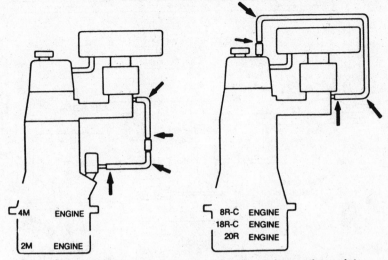

4M   ENGINE

2M   ENGINE

8R-C ENGINE
18R-C ENGINE
20R   ENGINE

Hose routing for PCV system—arrows indicate inspection points

NOTE: *Do not attempt to clean or adjust the valve. Replace it with a new one.*

Air Injection System

A belt-driven pump supplies air to an injection manifold which has nozzles in each exhaust port. Injection of air at this point causes combustion of unburned hydrocarbons in the exhaust manifold rather than allowing them to escape into the atmosphere. An anti-backfire valve controls the flow of air from the pump to prevent backfiring which results from an overly rich mixture under closed throttle conditions. There are two types of antibackfire valve used on Toyota models: 1970–71 models use gulp valves; 1972–81 models air by-pass valves.

A check valve prevents hot exhaust gas backflow into the pump and hoses, in case of a pump failure, or when the antibackfire valve is not working.

In addition, all 1975–81 engines have an air switching valve (ASV). On engines without catalytic converters, the ASV is used to stop air injection under a constant heavy engine load condition.

On engines with catalytic converters, the ASV is also used to protect the catalyst from overheating, by blocking the injector air necessary for the operation of the converter.

Since 1975 on most passenger car engines, the pump relief valve is built into the ASV.

REMOVAL AND INSTALLATION

Air Pump

1. Disconnect the air hoses from the pump.
2. Loosen the bolt on the adjusting link and remove the drive belt.

3. Remove the mounting bolts and withdraw the pump.
CAUTION: *Do not pry on the pump housing. It may be distorted.*
4. Installation is in the reverse order of removal. Adjust the drive belt tension after installation. Belt deflection should be ½–¾" with 22 lbs. pressure.

Anti-backfire Valve and Air Switching Valve

1. Detach the air hoses from the valve, and electrical leads (if equipped).
2. Remove the valve securing bolt.
3. Withdraw the valve.
4. Installation is performed in the reverse order of removal.

Check Valve

1. Detach the intake hose from the valve.
2. Use an open-end wrench to remove the valve from its mounting.
3. Installation is the reverse of removal.

Relief Valve

NOTE: *From 1975 on models with ASV-mounted relief valves, replace the entire ASV/relief valve as an assembly.*
1. Remove the air pump from the car.
2. Support the pump so that it cannot rotate.
CAUTION: *Never clamp the pump in a vise. The aluminum case will be distorted.*
3. Use a bridge to remove the relief valve from the top of the pump.
4. Position the new relief valve over the opening in the pump.
NOTE: *The air outlet should be pointing toward the left.*
5. Gently tap the relief valve home, using a block of wood and a hammer.

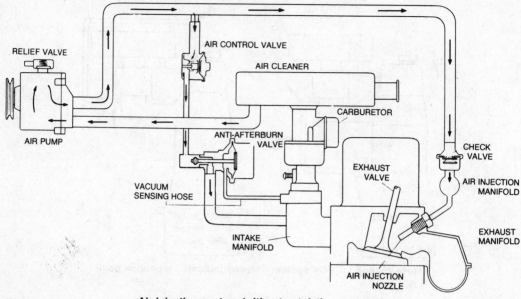

Air injection system (without catalytic converter)

6. Install the pump on the engine, as outlined above.

Air Injection Manifold

1. Remove the check valve, as previously outlined.
2. Loosen the air injection manifold attachment nuts and withdraw the manifold.
NOTE: *On some engines it may be necessary to remove the exhaust manifold first.*
3. Installation is in the reverse order of removal.

Air Injection Nozzles

1. Remove the air injection manifold as previously outlined.
2. Remove the cylinder head, as detailed in Chapter 3.
3. Place a new nozzle on the cylinder head.
4. Install the air injection manifold over it.

5. Install the cylinder head on the engine block.

TESTING

Air Pump

CAUTION: *Do not hammer, pry, or bend the pump housing while tightening the drive belt or testing the pump.*

BELT TENSION AND AIR LEAKS

1. Before proceeding with the tests, check the pump drive belt tension to ensure that it is within specifications.
2. Turn the engine. If the pump has seized, the belt will slip, making a noise. Disregard any chirping, squealing, or rolling sounds from inside the pump. These are normal when it is turned by hand.
3. Check the hoses and connections for leaks. Hissing or a blast of air indicates a leak.

Removing the check valve

Removing the pump-mounted relief valve

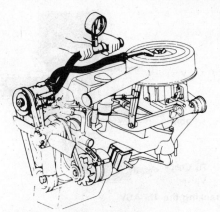

Checking the air pump output

Soapy water, applied lightly around the area in question, is a good method for detecting leaks.

AIR OUTPUT

1. Disconnect the air supply hose at the antibackfire valve.

2. Connect a vacuum gauge, using a suitable adaptor, to the air supply hose.

NOTE: *If there are two hoses, plug the second one.*

3. With the engine at normal operating temperature, increase the idle speed and watch the vacuum gauge.

4. The airflow from the pump should be steady (between 2 and 6 psi). If it is unsteady or falls below specs, the pump is defective and must be replaced.

PUMP NOISE DIAGNOSIS

The air pump is normally noisy. As engine speed increases, the noise of the pump will rise in pitch. The rolling sound the pump bearings make is normal. But if this sound becomes objectionable at certain speeds, the pump is defective and will have to be replaced.

A continual hissing sound from the air pump pressure relief valve at idle, indicates a defective valve. Replace the relief valve.

If the pump rear bearing fails, a continual knocking sound will be heard. Since the rear bearing is not separately replaceable, the pump will have to be replaced as an assembly.

Anti-backfire Valve Tests

There are two different types of anti-backfire valve used with air injection systems. A by-pass valve is used on 1971–81 engines, while 1970–71 engines use a gulp type anti-backfire valve. Test procedures for both types are given below.

GULP VALVE

1. Detach the air supply hose which runs between the pump and the gulp valve.

2. Connect a tachometer and run the engine to 1,500–2,000 rpm.

3. Allow the throttle to snap shut. This should produce a loud sucking sound from the gulp valve.

4. Repeat this operation several times. If no sound is present, the valve is not working or else the vacuum connections are loose.

5. Check the vacuum connections. If they are secure, replace the gulp valve.

BY-PASS VALVE

1. Detach the hose, which runs from the by-pass valve to the check valve, at the by-pass valve hose connection.

2. Connect a tachometer to the engine. With the engine running at normal idle speed, check to see that air is flowing from the by-pass valve hose connection.

3. Speed up the engine so that it is running at 1,500–2,000 rpm. Allow the throttle to snap shut. The flow of air from the by-pass valve at the check valve hose connection should stop momentarily and air should then flow from the exhaust port on the valve body or the silencer assembly.

4. Repeat Step 3 several times. If the flow of air is not diverted into the atmosphere from the valve exhaust port or if it fails to stop flowing from the hose connection, check the vacuum lines and connections. If these are tight, the valve is defective and requires replacement.

5. A leaking diaphragm will cause the air to flow out both the hose connection and the exhaust port at the same time. If this happens, replace the valve.

Check Valve Test

1. Before starting the test, check all of the hoses and connections for leaks.

2. Insert a suitable probe into the check valve and depress the plate. Release it. The plate should return to its original position against the valve seat. If binding is evident, replace the valve.

3. With the engine running at normal operating temperature, gradually increase its speed to 1,500 rpm. Check for exhaust gas leakage. If any is present, replace the valve assembly.

NOTE: *Vibration and flutter of the check valve at idle speed is a normal condition and does not mean that the valve should be replaced.*

Air Switching Valve (ASV) Tests

1975–81 20R and 22R ENGINES

1. Start the engine and allow it to reach normal operating temperature and speed.

2. At curb idle, the air from the by-pass valve should be discharged through the hose which runs to the ASV.

3. When the vacuum line to the ASV is disconnected, the air from the by-pass valve should be diverted out through the ASV to-air cleaner hose. Reconnect the vacuum line.

4. Disconnect the ASV-to-check valve hose and connect a pressure gauge to it.

5. Increase the engine speed. The relief valve should open when the pressure gauge registers 2.7–6.5 psi.

6. If the ASV fails any of the above tests, replace it. Reconnect all hoses.

1975–79 M ENGINES

1. Start the engine and allow it to reach normal operating temperature and speed.

2. At curb idle, air from the pump should be discharged through the hose which runs to the check valve.

3. Race the engine and allow the throttle valve to snap shut. The air from the pump should be discharged into the air cleaner.

4. Disconnect the ASV-to-check valve hose and connect a pressure gauge to it.

5. Increase the engine speed gradually. The relief valve should open when the gauge registers 3.7–7.7 psi. Reconnect the check valve hose.

6. Unfasten the wiring connector and the hoses from the solenoid valve, which is attached to the ASV. Air should pass through

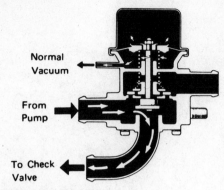

Normal Vacuum

From Pump

To Check Valve

Checking the 4M ASV

the solenoid valve when either the top or bottom port is blown into.

7. Connect a 12v power source to the terminals on the valve. No air should flow through the valve when either port is blown into.

8. If the solenoid valve or the ASV fail any of the above tests, replace either or both of them, as necessary.

Vacuum Delay Valve Test

1975–81 20R and 22R ENGINES

The vacuum delay valve is located in the line which runs from the intake manifold to the vacuum surge tank. To check it, proceed as follows:

1. Remove the vacuum delay valve from the vacuum line. Be sure to note which end points toward the intake manifold.

2. When air is blown in from the ASV (surge tank) side, it should pass through the valve freely.

Air Injection System Diagnosis Chart

Problem	Cause	Cure
1. Noisy drive belt	Loose belt	Tighten belt
	Seized pump	Replace
2. Noisy pump	Leaking hose	Trace and fix leak
	Loose hose	Tighten hose clamp
	Hose contacting other parts	Reposition hose
	Diverter or check valve failure	Replace
	Pump mounting loose	Tighten securing bolts
	Defective pump	Replace
3. No air supply	Loose belt	Tighten belt
	Leak in hose or at fitting	Trace and fix leak
	Defective antibackfire valve	Replace
	Defective check valve	Replace
	Defective pump	Replace
	Defective ASV	Replace
4. Exhaust backfire	Vacuum or air leaks	Trace and fix leak
	Defective antibackfire valve	Replace
	Sticking choke	Service choke
	Choke setting rich	Adjust choke

3. When air is blown in from the intake manifold side, a resistance should be felt.

4. Replace the valve if it fails either of the above tests.

5. Install the valve in the vacuum line, being careful not to install it backward.

Evaporative Emission Control System

To prevent hydrocarbon emissions from entering the atmosphere, Toyota vehicles use evaporative emission control (EEC) systems. Models produced between 1970 and 1971 use a case storage system, while later models use a charcoal canister storage system.

The major components of the case storage system are a purge control or vacuum switching valve, a fuel vapor storage case, an air filter, a thermal expansion tank, and a special fuel tank.

When the vehicle is stopped or the engine is running at a low speed, the purge control or vacuum switching valve is closed. Fuel vapor travels only as far as the case where it is stored.

When the engine is running at a high speed (cruising speed), the purge control valve is opened by pressure from the air pump or else the vacuum switching valve opens, depending upon the type of emission control system used (see the Evaporative Emission Control System Usage chart). This allows the vapor stored in the case to be drawn into the intake manifold along with fresh air which is drawn in from the filter.

The charcoal canister storage system functions in a similar manner to the case system, except that the fuel vapors are stored in a canister filled with activated charcoal, rather than in a case, and that all models use a vacuum switching valve to purge the system. The air filter is not external as it is on the case system. Rather, it is an integral part of the charcoal canister.

REMOVAL AND INSTALLATION

Removal and installation of the various evaporative emission control system components consists of unfastening hoses, loosening securing screws, and removing the part which is to be replaced from its mounting bracket. Installation is the reverse of removal.

NOTE: *When replacing any EEC system hoses, always use hoses that are fuel-resistant or are marked 'EVAP'.*

TESTING

EEC System Troubleshooting

There are several things which may be checked if a malfunction of the evaporative emission control system is suspected.

1. Leaks may be traced by using a hydrocarbon tests. Run the test probe along the lines and connections. The meter will indicate the presence of a leak by a high hydrocarbon (HC) reading. This method is much more accurate than visual inspection which would only indicate the presence of a leak large enough to pass liquid.

2. Leaks may be caused by any of the following:

    a. Defective or worn hoses.

    b. Disconnected or pinched hoses.

    c. Improperly routed hoses.

    d. A defective filler cap or safety valve (sealed cap system).

NOTE: *If it becomes necessary to replace any of the hoses used in the evaporative emission*

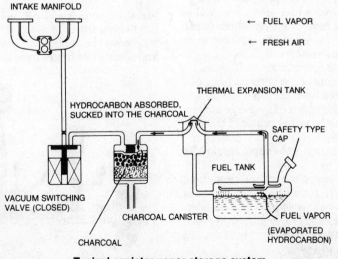

Typical canister vapor storage system

control system, use only hoses which are fuel-resistant or are marked "EVAP."

3. If the fuel tank, storage case or thermal expansion tank collapses, it may be the fault of clogged or pinched vent lines, a defective vapor separator, or a plugged or incorrect filler cap.

4. To test the filler cap (if it is the safety valve type), clean it and place it against your mouth. Blow into the relief valve housing. If the cap passes pressure with light blowing, or fails to release with hard blowing, it is defective and must be replaced.

NOTE: *Use the proper cap for the type of system in your car. Either a sealed cap or safety valve cap is required.*

Purge Control Valve

1970–71 Cars with Air Injection

1. Disconnect the line which runs from the storage case to the valve, at the valve.

2. Connect a tachometer to the to the engine, according to the manufacturer's instructions.

3. Start the engine, set the parking brake, place the transmission in neutral and slowly increase engine speed to 2,500 rpm.

4. Place your finger over the hose fitting on the valve.

5. If there is no vacuum felt, the air pump is probably defective. If the air pump is good, replace the valve.

Purge Control Valve

1974 and Later

The purge control valve is connected to a carburetor port, which is located above the throttle control valve. When the engine is stopped or at idle, there is no vacuum signal at the purge control valve, so, it remains closed.

When the throttle valve opens, the carburetor port is uncovered and a vacuum signal is sent to the purge control valve, which opens and allows vapors stored in the canister to be pulled into the carburetor.

To test the valve operation:

1. Note the routing of the vacuum lines and remove the canister from the car.

2. Place your finger over the purge control valve opening, located at the center of the canister on its top side.

3. Gently blow through the vapor intake. No resistance should be felt.

4. Uncover the purge control valve opening and blow through it. No air should come out of the vapor intake or the bottom of the canister.

5. If the purge control valve fails either test, replace the canister. If the valve is okay, put the canister back in the car.

6. If the valve once again, appears to be mal-functioning after installation, you have either defective vacuum lines or a clogged carburetor port.

Check Valve

The check valve is located in the line which runs from the fuel tank or vapor separator, to the canister. On all 1973 models, it is located in the trunk. On all other models, it is in the engine compartment, near the canister. To test the check valve, proceed as follows:

1. Remove the check valve from the fuel tank-to-canister line.

2. Blow into the fuel tank end. A slight resistance should be felt at first.

3. Blow through the canister end. No resistance should be felt.

4. If the check valve is defective, replace it.

Carburetor Auxiliary Slow System

A carburetor auxiliary slow system is used on 1970–71 2M engines. It provides uniform combustion during deceleration. The components of the auxiliary slow system consist of a vacuum operated valve, a fresh air intake, and a fuel line which is connected to the carburetor float chamber.

During deceleration, manifold vacuum acts on the valve which opens it causing additional air/fuel mixture to flow into the intake manifold.

REMOVAL AND INSTALLATION

1. Remove the hoses from the auxiliary slow system.

2. Unfasten the recessed screws and remove the system as a unit.

3. Installation is the reverse of removal.

TESTING

1.

Start the engine and run it to normal operating temperature.

2.Remove the rubber cap from the diaphragm and place your finger over the opening. There

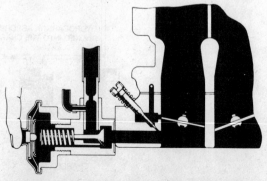

Inspecting the auxiliary slow system diaphgram

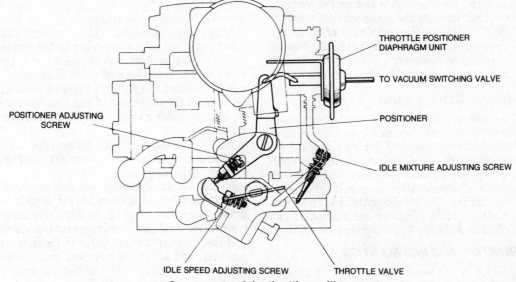

Components of the throttle positioner

should be no vacuum at idle speed. If there is, the diaphragm must be replaced.

3. Pinch the air intake hose which runs from the air cleaner to the auxiliary slow system. There should be no change in the engine idle with the hose pinched.

4. Disconnect the air intake hose at the auxiliary slow system. Race the engine. Place your finger over the air intake. Release the throttle. Suction should be felt at the air intake.

5. If any of the tests indicate a failed component, replace the system as a unit.

Throttle Positioner

The throttle positioner reduces emissions during deceleration. It prevents the throttle from closing completely. Vacuum is reduced under the throttle which, in turn, acts on the retard chamber of the distributor vacuum unit. This compensates for the loss of engine braking caused by the partially opened throttle.

Once the vehicle speed drops below a predetermined value, the vacuum switching valve provides vacuum to the throttle positioner diaphragm. The throttle positioner retracts, allowing the throttle valve to close completely.

ADJUSTMENT

1. Start the engine and run it to normal operating temperature.

2. Adjust the idle speed as described in Chapter 1

NOTE: *Leave the tachometer connected after completing the idle adjustments.*

3. Detach the vacuum line from the positioner diaphragm unit and plug the line up.

4. Accelerate the engine slightly to set the throttle positioner in place.

5. Check the engine speed with a tachometer when the throttle positioner is set.

6. If necessary, adjust the engine speed, with the throttle positioner adjusting screw, to the specifications given in the Throttle Positioner Settings chart at the end of this section.

7. Connect the vacuum hose to the positioner diaphragm.

8. The throttle lever should be freed form the positioner as soon as the vacuum hose is connected. Engine idle should return to normal.

9. If the throttle positioner fails to function properly, check its linkage, and vacuum diaphragm. If there are no defects in either of

Throttle Positioner Settings (rpm)

Year	Engine	Engine rpm (positioner set)
1970	8R-C	1,400
1971	8R-C	1,400
1972–74	18R-C	1,400
	2M, 4M	1,300 MT 1,400 AT
1975–77	20R	1,400 MT 1,050 AT
	4M	1,200 AT
1978–80	20R/22R	1,050
	4M	950

MT—Manual transmission
AT—Automatic transmission

these, the fault probably lies in the vacuum switching valve or the speed marker unit.

NOTE: *Due to the complexity of these two components, and also because they require special test equipment, their service is best left to an authorized facility.*

Mixture Control Valve

The mixture control valve, used on some models with manual transmissions, aids in combustion of unburned fuel during periods of deceleration. The mixture control valve is operated by the vacuum switching valve during periods of deceleration to admit additional fresh air into the intake manifold. The extra air allows more complete combustion of the fuel, thus reducing hydrocarbon emissions.

REMOVAL AND INSTALLATION

1. Unfasten the vacuum switching valve line from the mixture control valve.
2. Remove the intake manifold hose from the valve.
3. Remove the valve from its engine mounting.
4. Installation is performed in the reverse order of removal.

TESTING

1. Start the engine and allow it to idle (warmed up).
2. Place your hand over the air intake at the bottom of the valve.
CAUTION: *Keep your fingers clear of the engine fan.*
3. Increase the engine speed and then release the throttle.
4. Suction should be felt at the air intake only while the engine is decelerating. Once the engine has returned to idle, no suction should be felt.

If the above test indicates a malfunction, proceed with the next step. If not, the mixture

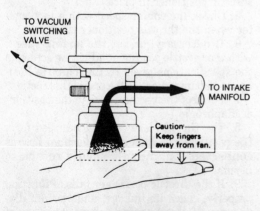

TO VACUUM SWITCHING VALVE

TO INTAKE MANIFOLD

Caution
Keep fingers away from fan.

Testing the mixture control valve

control valve is functioning properly and requires no further adjustment.

5. Disconnect the vacuum line from the mixture control valve. If suction can be felt underneath the valve with the engine at idle, the valve seat is defective and must be replaced.

6. Reconnect the vacuum line to the valve. Disconnect the other end of the line from the vacuum switching valve and place it in your mouth.

7. With the engine idling, suck on the end of the vacuum line to duplicate the action of the vacuum switching valve.

8. Suction at the valve air intake should only be felt for an instant. If air cannot be drawn into the valve at all, or if it is continually drawn in, replace the mixture control valve.

If the mixture control valve is functioning properly, and all of the hose and connections are in good working order, the vacuum switching valve is probably at fault.

Auxiliary Accelerator Pump System

When the engine is cold, an auxiliary accelerator pump system unit (AAP) in the carburetor is operated to squirt extra fuel into the acceleration circuit in order to prevent the mixture from becoming too lean.

A thermostatic vacuum valve (warmup-sensing valve), which is threaded into the intake manifold, controls the operation of the enrichment circuit. Below a specified temperature, the valve is opened and manifold vacuum is allowed to act on a diaphragm in the carburetor. The vacuum pulls the diaphragm down, allowing fuel to flow into a special chamber above it.

Under sudden acceleration manifold vacuum drops momentarily, allowing the diaphragm to be pushed up by spring tension. This in turn forces the fuel from the chamber through a passage and out the accelerator pump jet.

When the coolant temperature goes above specification, the thermostatic vacuum valve closes, preventing the vacuum from reaching the diaphragm which makes the enrichment system inoperative.

TESTS

1. Check for clogged, pinched, disconnected, or misrouted vacuum lines.
2. With the engine cold (below 75°F), remove the top of the air cleaner, and allow the engine to idle.
3. Disconnect the vacuum line from the carburetor AAP unit. Gasoline should squirt out the accelerator pump jet.
4. If gas doesn't squirt out of the jet, check for vacuum at the AAP vacuum line with the

engine idling. If there is no vacuum and the hoses are in good shape, the thermostatic vacuum valve is defective and must be replaced.

5. If the gas doesn't squirt out and vacuum is present at the vacuum line in Step 4, the AAP unit is defective and must be replaced.

NOTE: *On later models, a diaphragm kit is available.*

6. Repeat Step 3 with the engine at normal operating temperature. If gasoline squirts out of the pump jet, the thermostatic vacuum valve is defective and must be replaced.

7. Reconnect all of the vacuum lines and install the top of the air cleaner.

Auxiliary Enrichment System

This system is used on the 4M engine to improve driveability. It cuts air supplied to the main nozzle of the carburetor under certain conditions to improve performance.

If the system is suspected to be operating improperly, test the VCV valve as described below. If any of the tests are failed, replace the valve.

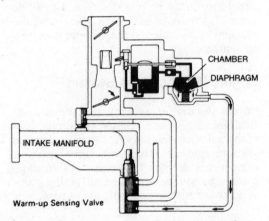

Components of the auxiliary enrichment system

TESTS

1. Disconnect hoses 10 and 15 at the carburetor. Start the engine.

2. Blow air into hose No. 10 at idle speed. Check to see that air is expelled from hose 15.

3. Connect the VCV S pipe to the intake manifold as shown in the illustration. Again, blow air into hoses 10 at idle speed. Check to see that air comes out of hose 15.

4. Stop the engine. Again blow air into hose 10. Check to see that air does not come out of hose.

Spark Delay Valve

The spark delay valve (SDV) is located in the distributor vacuum line. The valve has a small orifice in it, which slows down the vacuum flow to the vacuum advance unit on the distributor. By delaying the vacuum to the distributor, a reduction in HC and CO emissions is possible.

When the coolant temperature is below 95°F, a coolant temperature operated vacuum control valve is opened, allowing the distributor to receive undelayed, ported vacuum through a separate vacuum line. Above 95°F, this line is blocked and all ported vacuum must go through the spark delay valve.

TESTING

1. Allow the engine to cool, so that the coolant temperature is below 95°F.

2. Disconnect the vacuum line which runs from the coolant temperature operated vacuum valve to the vacuum advance unit at the advance unit end. Connect a vacuum gauge to this line.

3. Start the engine. Increase the engine speed. The gauge should indicate a vacuum.

4. Allow the engine to warm-up to normal operating temperature. Increase the engine speed. This time the vacuum gauge should read zero.

5. Replace the coolant temperature operat-

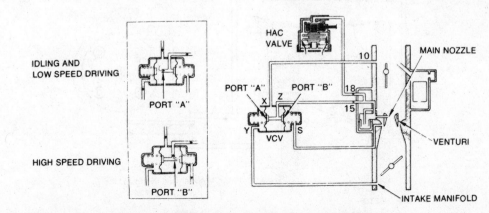

Schematic of 1978–79 auxiliary enrichment system

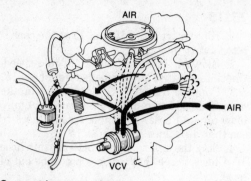

Connect hoses as shown

ed vacuum valve, if it fails either of these tests. Disconnect the vacuum gauge and reconnect the vacuum lines.

6. Remove the spark delay valve from the vacuum line, noting which side faces the distributor.

7. Connect a hand-operated vacuum pump which has a built-in vacuum gauge to the carburetor side of the spark delay valve.

8. Connect a vacuum gauge to the distributor side of the valve.

9. Operate the hand pump to create a vacuum. The vacuum gauge on the distributor side should show a hesitation before registering.

10. The gauge reading on the pump side should drop slightly, taking several seconds for it to balance with the reading on the other gauge.

11. If Steps 9 and 10 are negative, replace the spark delay valve.

12. Remove the vacuum gauge from the distributor side of the valve. Cover the distributor side of the valve with your finger and operate the pump to create a vacuum of 15 in. Hg.

13. The reading on the pump gauge should remain steady. If the gauge reading drops, replace the valve.

14. Remove your finger. The reading of the gauge should drop slowly. If the reading goes to zero rapidly, replace the valve.

Dual Diaphragm Distributor

Some Toyota models are equipped with a dual diaphragm distributor unit. This distributor has a retard diaphragm, as well as a diaphragm for advance.

TESTING

1. Connect a timing light to the engine. Check the ignition timing.
   NOTE: *Before proceeding with the tests, disconnect any spark control devices, distributor vacuum valves, etc. If these are left connected, inaccurate results may be obtained.*

2. Remove the retard hose from the distributor and plug it. Increase the engine speed. The timing should advance. If it fails to do so, then the vacuum unit is faulty and must be replaced.

3. Check the timing with the engine at normal idle speed. Unplug the retard hose and connect it to the vacuum unit. The timing should instantly be retarded from 4 to 10 degrees. If this does not occur, the retard diaphragm has a leak and the vacuum unit must be replaced.

Engine Modifications System

Toyota also uses an assortment of engine modifications to regulate exhaust emissions. Most of these devices fall into the category of engine vacuum controls. There are three principal components used on the engine modifications system, as well as a number of smaller parts. The three major components are: a speed sen-

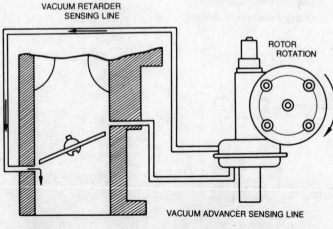

VACUUM RETARDER
SENSING LINE

ROTOR
ROTATION

VACUUM ADVANCER SENSING LINE

CARBURETOR

Dual-diaphgram distributor with vacuum switching valve

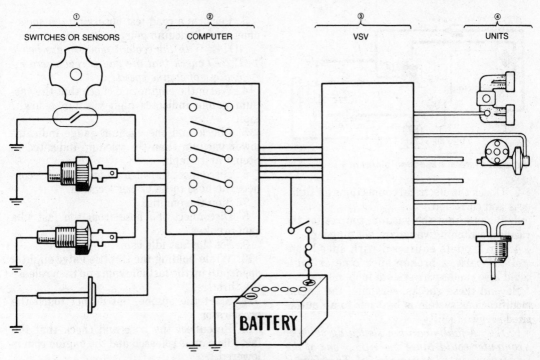

① SWITCHES OR SENSORS   ② COMPUTER   ③ VSV   ④ UNITS

BATTERY

Engine modification system—typical

sor, a computer (speed marker), and a vacuum switching valve.

The vacuum switching valve and computer circuit operate most of the emission control components. Depending upon year and engine usage, the vacuum switching valve and computer may operate the pure control for the evaporative emission control system, the transmission controlled spark (TCS) or speed controlled spark (SCS), the dual diaphragm distributor, the throttle positioner systems, the EGR system, the catalyst protection system, etc.

The functions of the evaporative emission control system, the throttle positioner, and the dual diaphragm distributor are described in detail in the preceding sections. However, a word is necessary about the functions of the TCS and SCS systems before discussing the operation of the vacuum switching valve/computer circuit.

The major difference between the transmission controlled spark and speed controlled spark systems is the manner in which system operation is determined. Toyota TCS systems use a speed sensor built into the speedometer cable.

Below a predetermined speed, or any gear other than Fourth, the vacuum advance unit on the distributor is rendered inoperative or the timing retarded. By changing the distributor advance curve in this manner, it is possible to reduce emissions of oxides of nitrogen NOx).

NOTE: *Some engines are equipped with a thermo-sensor so that the TCS or SCS system only operates when the coolant temperature is 140°–212°F.*

Aside from determining the preceding conditions, the vacuum switching valve computer circuit operates other devices in the emission control system (EGR, Catalytic converter, etc.)

The computer acts as a speed marker. At certain speeds it sends a signal to the vacuum switching valve which acts as a gate, opening and closing the emission control system vacuum circuits.

The vacuum switching valve on all 1970 and some 1971 engines is a simple affair. A single solenoid operates a valve which uncovers certain vacuum ports at the same time others are covered.

The valve used on all 1972–81 and some 1971 engines contains several solenoid and valve assemblies so that different combinations of opened and closed vacuum ports are possible. This allows greater flexibility of operation for the emission control system.

SYSTEM CHECKS

Due to the complexity of the components involved, about the only engine modification system checks which can be made, are the following:

1. Examine the vacuum lines to ensure that they are not clogged, pinched, or loose.

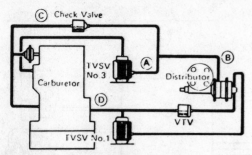

Vacuum system inspection diagram

2. Check the electrical connections for tightness and corrosion.

3. Be sure that the vacuum sources for the vacuum switching valve are not plugged.

4. On models equipped with speed controlled spark, a broken speedometer cable could also render the system inoperative.

Beyond these checks, servicing the engine modifications system is best left to an authorized service facility.

NOTE: *A faulty vacuum switching valve or computer could cause more than one of the emission control systems to fail. Therefore, if several systems are out, these two units (and the speedometer cable) would be the first things to check.*

Choke Opener System

This system holds the choke open during warmup to prevent an overly rich mixture from emitting pollutants above acceptable limits. When the coolant temperature rises above 140°F, a thermostatic vacuum switching valve allows vacuum from the manifold to pull in on the choke opener diaphragm which is connected to the choke valve. Thus the choke valve is opened sooner than if just the automatic choke was operating it. When the coolant is below 95°F, the choke opener works with the automatic choke to close the choke valve and permit the choke to close until the engine is warm. Some models use two thermosensor switches and a speed sensor to trigger a miniature computer, which in turn triggers the vacuum switching valve.

Fast Idle Cam Breaker

After warm up this system forcibly releases the fast idle cam which lowers the engine speed.

TESTING

1. Use a 3-way connector to connect a vacuum gauge to the fast idle cam breaker.

2. Use enough vacuum line to bring the gauge into the vehicle and set it on the drivers seat.

3. Perform a road test observing the speedometer and vacuum gauge.

NOTE: *With the coolant temperature below (122°F) check that the gauge reads zero regardless of engine speed.*

4. Warm the engine and check that the vacuum gauge indicates high vacuum below 7 mph.

5. Check that the vacuum gauge indicates lower vacuum than the vacuum indicated in Step 4 at 16 mph.

6. Disconnect the vacuum gauge and reconnect the hose to its proper location.

7. Stop the engine.

8. Disconnect the hose from the fast idle cam breaker.

9. Set the fast idle cam.

10. While holding the throttle valve slightly open, pull up the fast idle cam and then release the throttle.

11. Start the engine, but do not touch the accelerator.

12. Reconnect the hose and check that the fast idle cam is released and the engine rpm is lowered.

NOTE: *If the above tests are positive, this procedure is complete. If not, inspect the breaker diaphragm, TVSV valve, speed sensor or VSV.*

Choke Break

ADJUSTMENT

20R and 22R Engine

1. Push the rod which comes out of the upper (choke break) diaphragm so that the choke valve opens.

2. Measure the choke valve opening angle. It should be 40 degrees (38 degrees 1976–79).

3. Adjust the angle, if necessary, by bending the relief lever link.

Hot Idle Compensation Valve

This system allows the air controlled by the HIC valve to enter the intake manifold to maintain proper air fuel mixture during high temperatures at idle.

TESTING

1. Close the pipe to the intake manifold with your finger.

2. Blow air into the open end. The passage should be closed at temperatures below 86°F.

3. Heat the valve in hot water.

CAUTION: *Do not allow water to get in the valve.*

4. Blow air into the valve again. As the temperature nears 104°F the passage should open.

5. A small amount of air should flow

through the valve when the temperature of the valve is 104°F to 158°F.

6. A large amount of air should flow through the valve when the temperature is above 176°F.

7. If air does not flow through the valve replace it.

Secondary Slow Circuit Fuel Cut System

This system cuts off part of the fuel in the secondary slow circuit of the carburetor to prevent dieseling.

TESTING

1. Completely open and close the throttle valve.
2. Measure the stroke of the valve. (1.5–2.0mm).
3. If necessary adjust the stroke.
NOTE: *The stroke should be set to specifications before the secondary throttle valve opens.*

Deceleration Fuel Cut System

This system cuts off part of the fuel in the slow circuit of the carburetor to prevent overheating and afterburning in the exhaust system.

TESTING

1. Start the engine.
2. Check that the engine runs normally.
3. Pinch the vacuum hose to the vacuum switch.
4. Gradually increase the engine speed to 2500 rpm. Check that the engine misfires between 2000–2500 rpm.
CAUTION: *Perform this procedure quickly to prevent overheating of the catalytic converter.*
5. Release the pinched hose and see that the engine returns to normal operation.
6. Unplug the solenoid valve until the engine misfires or stalls.
7. Stop the engine and reconnect the wire.
NOTE: *If the above tests are positive the procedure is complete. If not, inspect the solenoid valve and vacuum switch.*

FUEL SOLENOID TEST

1. Remove the solenoid.
2. Using two test wires, hook one to the positive and the other to the negative battery terminals.
3. Touch these two wires to the solenoid to determine if it clicks.
4. If it does click, it is operational. If not, discard it and replace it with a new one.

VACUUM SWITCH TEST

1. Use a ohmmeter to check the continuity between the switch and the terminal body.
2. Start the engine.
3. Check that there is no continuity between the switch and the terminal body. If there, is replace the switch.

High Altitude Compensation System

For all engines to be sold in areas over 4000 ft. in altitude, a system has been installed to automatically lean out the fuel mixture by supplying additional air. This also results in lower emissions.

Low atmospheric pressure allows the bellows in the system to expand the close a port, allowing more air to enter from different sources.

In the 20R and 22R engines, this also results in a timing advance to improve driveability.

All parts in this system must be replaced. The only adjustment available is in the timing.

Bi-Metal Vacuum Switching Valve

TESTING

1. Drain the engine coolant.
2. Remove the vacuum hoses and remove the BVSV.
3. Cool the BVSV to 86°F.
4. Blow air through the valve. At this time the valve should be closed and not allow air to pass.
5. Heat the valve to 111°F. The valve should open and allow air to pass through.
6. Repeat Step 4.
7. If the valve is inoperative it must be replaced.
8. Apply a liquid sealer to the threads and replace the valve.
9. Reconnect the vacuum lines.
10. Refill the coolant.

Hot Air Intake

In order to keep the temperature of the air drawn into the carburetor as constant as possible, all engines are equipped with a Hot Air Intake System (HAI).

In all engines, the system depends on a thermo valve to control the temperature.

At normal temperatures the air is drawn into the inlet in the air filter. When the temperature drops, the valve switches position, opening the way for air to be drawn from around the exhaust manifold.

When inspecting, check all hoses for poor connections or damage and visually check the air control valve in the air duct.

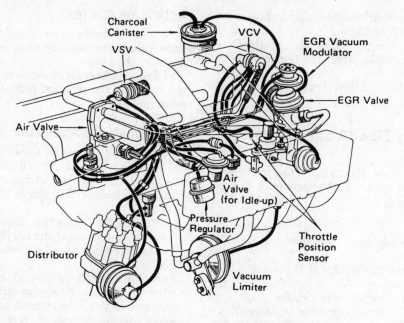

Vacuum limiter and other controls—EFI

NOTE: *When checking valve movement, do not push too strongly on the control face.* Should there be a malfunction, replace the part involved.

Exhaust Gas Recirculation (EGR)

Starting with 1974 models, exhaust gas recirculation (EGR) was used on 18R-C, and 4M engines sold in California. All engines, since 1975 use EGR.

In all cases, the EGR valve is controlled by the same computer and vacuum switching valve which is used to operate other emission control system components.

On four cylinder engines, the EGR valve is operated by vacuum supplied from a port above the throttle blades and fed through the vacuum switching valve.

On M engines, vacuum from the carburetor vacuum advance port flows through the vacuum switching valve to an EGR vacuum control valve. The vacuum from the advance port opens the vacuum control valve which then allows venturi vacuum to act on the chamber above the EGR valve diaphragm, causing the EGR valve to open. When exhaust gas recirculation is not required, the vacuum switching valve stops sending the advance port vacuum signal to the EGR vacuum control valve which closes, sending intake manifold vacuum to the chamber below the EGR valve diaphragm. This closes the EGR valve, blocking the flow of exhaust gases to the intake manifold.

On all engines there are several conditions, determined by the computer and vacuum switching valve, which permit exhaust gas recirculation to take place:

1. Vehicle speed.
2. Engine coolant temperature.
3. EGR valve temperature (4 cylinder).
4. Carburetor flange temperature (4 cylinder).

On 4 cylinder engines equipped with EGR, the exhaust gases are carried from the exhaust manifold to the EGR valve and from the EGR valve to the carburetor, via external tubing. Some later engines have an exhaust gas cooler mounted on the back of the cylinder head.

On M engines, the EGR valve is mounted on the exhaust manifold and exhaust gases from it are carried through external tubing to the intake manifold.

EGR VALVE CHECKS

18R-C, 20R and 22R Engines

1. Allow the engine to warm up and remove the top from the air cleaner.
NOTE: *Do not remove the entire air cleaner assembly.*
2. Disconnect the hose (white tape coded), which runs from the vacuum switching valve to the EGR valve, at its EGR valve end.
3. Remove the intake manifold hose (red coded) from the vacuum switching valve and connect it to the EGR valve. When the engine is at idle, a hollow sound should be heard coming from the air cleaner.
4. Disconnect the hose from the EGR valve. The hollow sound should disappear.

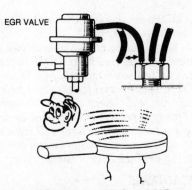

Checking the EGR valve—18R-C and 20R engines

5. If the sound doesn't vary, the EGR valve is defective and must be replaced.

6. Reconnect the vacuum hoses as they were originally found. Install the top on the air cleaner.

M Engines

1. Warm up the engine and allow it to idle.

2. Disconnect the vacuum sensing line from the upper vacuum chamber of the EGR valve.

3. Disconnect the sensing line from the lower chamber of the EGR valve.

4. Now, take the hose which was disconnected from the lower chamber and connect it to the upper EGR valve chamber.

NOTE: *Leave the lower chamber vented to the atmosphere.*

5. The engine idle should become rough or the engine should stall with the hoses connected in this manner. If the engine runs normally, check the EGR vacuum control valve (see below). If the vacuum control valve is in good working order, then replace the EGR valve.

6. Reconnect the vacuum sensing lines as they were originally found.

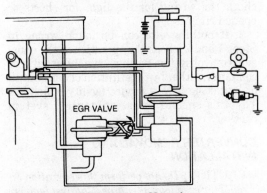

Checking the EGR valve—4M engine

EGR VALVE THERMO-SENSOR

18R-C, 20R and 22R Engines

1. Disconnect the electrical lead which runs to the EGR valve thermo-sensor.

2. Remove the thermo-sensor from the side of the EGR valve.

3. Heat the thermo-sensor in a pan of water to 260°F.

4. Connect an ohmmeter, in series with a 10 ohm resistor, between the thermo-sensor terminal and case.

5. With the ohmmeter set on the $K\Omega$ scale, the reading should be 2.55 $K\Omega$.

6. Replace the thermo-sensor if the ohmmeter readings vary considerably from those specified.

7. To install the thermo-sensor on the EGR valve, tighten it to 15–21 ft.lb.

CAUTION: *Do not tighten the thermo-sensor with an impact wrench.*

EGR VACUUM CONTROL VALVE

M Engines

1. Connect the EGR vacuum control valve hoses up, so that carburetor advance port vacuum operates directly on its diaphragm (top hose connection).

2. Disconnect the two hoses from the EGR vacuum control valve which run to the upper and lower diaphragm chambers of the EGR valve.

3. Take two vacuum gauges and connect one to each of the ports from which you removed a hose in Step 2.

4. Race the engine. The vacuum gauges should indicate the following:

Upper chamber port — Venturi vacuum

Lower chamber port — Atmospheric pressure

5. Disconnect the sensing hose from the carburetor advance port.

6. The vacuum gauges should now show the following:

Upper chamber port — Atmospheric pressure

Lower chamber port — Intake manifold vacuum.

NOTE: *The atmospheric pressure reading*

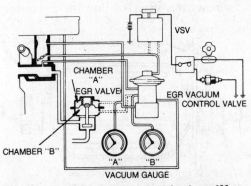

Checking the EGR vacuum control valve—4M engine

should be nearly equal to that obtained in Step 4.

7. Replace the EGR vacuum control valve if the readings on the vacuum gauges are incorrect.

8. Hook up the vacuum lines as they were originally found.

SYSTEM CHECKS

If, after having completed the above tests, the EGR system still doesn't work right and everything else checks out OK, the fault probably lies in the computer or the vacuum switching valve systems. If this is the case, it is best to have the car checked out by test facility which has the necessary Toyota emission system test equipment.

NOTE: *A good indication that the fault doesn't lie in the EGR system, but rather in the vacuum supply system, would be if several emission control systems were not working properly.*

Catalytic Converters

All Mark II and all California models were equipped with catalytic converters in 1975. Since 1975, till today, stricter emission level standards have made it necessary for all Toyota models to utilize one or another (or both) type(s) of catalytic converter(s).

Earlier models and today's Canadian models use an oxidation converter. That is, one that converts carbon monoxide and hydrocarbons into carbon dioxide and water.

A three-way (TWC) catalytic converter is used (by itself or with an oxidation converter) on late models. The TWC acts on all three major pollutants. Hydrocarbons and carbon monoxide are oxidized in the usual manner (into carbon dioxide and water) and the oxides of nitrogen are reduced to free oxygen and nitrogen.

An air pump is used to supply air to the exhaust system to aid in the reaction. A thermosensor, inserted into the converter,

shuts off the air supply if the catalyst temperature becomes excessive.

The same sensor circuit also causes a dash warning light labeled EXH TEMP to come one when the catalyst temperature gets too high.

NOTE: *It is normal for the light to come on temporarily if the car is being driven downhill for long periods of time (such as descending a mountain). The light will come on and stay on if the air injection system is malfunctioning or if the engine is misfiring.*

PRECAUTIONS

1. Use only unleaded fuel.

2. Avoid prolonged idling. The engine should run no longer than 20 minutes at curb idle, nor longer than 10 minutes at fast idle.

3. Reduce the fast idle speed, by quickly depressing and releasing the accelerator pedal, as soon as the coolant temperature reaches 120°F.

4. Do not disconnect any spark plug leads while the engine is running.

5. Make engine compression checks as quickly as possible.

6. Do not dispose of the catalyst in a place where anything coated with grease, gas, or oil is present. Spontaneous combustion could result.

WARNING LIGHT CHECKS

NOTE: *The warning light comes on while the engine is being cranked, to test its operation, just like any of the other warning lights.*

1. If the warning light comes on and stays on, check the components of the air injection system as previously outlined. If these are not defective, check the ignition system for faulty leads, plugs, points, or control box.

2. If no problems can be found in Step 1, check the wiring for the light for shorts or opened circuits.

3. If nothing else can be found wrong in Steps 1 and 2, check the operation of the emission control system vacuum switching valve or computer, either by substitution of a new unit, or by taking it to a service facility which has Toyota's special emission control system checker.

CONVERTER REMOVAL AND INSTALLATION

CAUTION: *Do not perform this operation on a hot (or even warm) engine. Catalyst temperatures may go as high as 1,700°F, so that any contact with the catalyst could cause severe burns.*

1. Disconnect the lead from the converter thermosensor.

2. Remove the wiring shield.

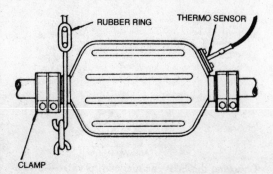

Catalytic converter installation

3. Unfasten the pipe clamp securing bolts at either end of the converter. Remove the clamps.

4. Push the tailpipe rearward and remove the converter, complete with thermosensor.

5. Carry the converter with the thermo-sensor upward to prevent the catalyst from falling out.

6. Unfasten the screws and withdraw the thermosensor and gasket.

Installation is performed in the following order:

1. Place a new gasket on the thermosensor. Push the thermosensor into the converter and secure it with its two bolts. Be careful not to drop the thermosensor.

NOTE: *Service replacement converters are provided with a plastic thermosensor guide. Slide the sensor into the guide to install it. Do not remove the guide.*

2. Install new gaskets on the converter mounting flanges.

3. Secure the converter with its mounting clamps.

4. If the converter is attached to the body with rubber O-rings, install the O-rings over the body and converter mounting hooks.

5. Install the wire protector and connect the lead to the thermosensor.

GENERAL FUEL SYSTEM COMPONENTS

Fuel Filter

REPLACEMENT

Carbureted Engines

All engines employ a disposable, inline filter. When dirty, or at recommended intervals, remove from line and replace.

Fuel Injected Engines

1. Unbolt the retaining screws and remove the protective shield for the fuel filter.

2. Place a pan under the delivery pipe (large connection) to catch the dripping fuel and SLOWLY loosen the union bolt to bleed off the fuel pressure.

3. Remove the union bolt and drain the remaining fuel.

4. Disconnect and plug the inlet line.

5. Unbolt and remove the fuel filter.

NOTE: *When tightening the fuel line bolts to the fuel filter, you must use a torque wrench. The tightening torque is very important, as under or over tightening may cause fuel leakage. Insure that there is no fuel line interference and that there is sufficient clearance between it and any other parts.*

6. Coat the flare nut, union nut and bolt threads with engine oil.

7. Hand tighten the inlet line to the fuel filter.

8. Install the fuel filter and then tighten the inlet bolt to 23–33 ft.lb.

9. Reconnect the delivery pipe using new gaskets and then tighten the union bolt to 18–25 ft.lb.

10. Run the engine for a few minutes and check for any fuel leaks.

11. Install the protective shield.

Mechanical Fuel Pump

REMOVAL AND INSTALLATION

1. Disconnect both of the fuel lines from the pump.

2. Unfasten the bolts which attach the fuel pump to the cylinder block.

3. Withdraw the pump assembly.

4. Installation is performed in the reverse order of removal. Always use a new gasket when installing the fuel pump. After the pump is installed check its discharge rate against the Tune-Up Specifications chart at the beginning of Chapter 2.

Some pumps are equipped with a fuel return cut valve installed. This valve is designed to vary the amount of fuel returned to the gas tank according to the engine load. It helps to avoid gas percolation when the engine is hot and lightly loaded.

NOTE: *Failure to use a gasket of the correct thickness could result in an improper pump discharge rate.*

Electrical Fuel Pump

REMOVAL AND INSTALLATION

Carbureted Engines and the Van

1. Disconnect the negative (–) cable from the battery.

2a. On sedans and hardtops, remove the trim panel from inside the tank.

2b. On station wagons, raise the rear of the vehicle, in order to gain access to the pump. Support it securely.

3. Remove the screws which secure the pump access plate to the tank. Withdraw the plate, gasket, and pump assembly.

4. Disconnect the leads and hoses from the pump.

5. Installation is performed in the reverse order of removal. Use a new gasket on the pump access plate.

Fuel Injected Engines, except Van

The pump used on these models is removed by simply disconnecting the fuel lines and electrical connector from the pump and dismounting the pump.

TESTING
Carbureted Engines

CAUTION: *Do not operate the fuel pump unless it is immersed in gasoline and connected to its resistor.*

1. Disconnect the lead from the oil pressure warning light sender.

2. Unfasten the line from the outlet side of the fuel filter.

3. Connect a pressure gauge to the filter outlet with a length of rubber hose.

4. Turn the ignition switch to the ON position, but do not start the engine.

5. Check the pressure gauge reading against the figure given in the Tune-Up Specifications chart in Chapter 2.

6. Check for a clogged filter or pinched lines if the pressure is not up to specification.

7. If there is nothing wrong with the filter or lines, replace the fuel pump.

8. Turn the ignition off and reconnect the fuel line to the filter. Connect the lead to the oil pressure sender also.

Fuel Injected Engines

1. Turn the ignition switch to the ON position, but don't start the engine.

2. Remove the rubber cap from the fuel pump check connector and short both terminals.

3. Check that there is pressure in the hose to the cold start injector.

NOTE: *At this time you should be able to hear the fuel return noise from the pressure regulator.*

4. If no pressure can be felt in the line, check the fuses and all other related electrical connections. If everything is all right, the fuel pump will probably require replacement.

5. Remove the service wire, reinstall the rubber cap and turn off the ignition switch.

Fuel Tank
REMOVAL AND INSTALLATION
Except EFI

1. Disconnect the negative battery cable.

2. Remove the drain plug and drain all fuel from the tank.

3. Remove mat and access cover from the luggage compartment. Disconnect the gauge unit electrical wiring. Disconnect the outlet or outlet and return hose(s) at the tank. Label the wires.

4. Remove the nuts form the two tank securing bands and lower the tank slightly.

5. Disconnect and label the three ventilation hoses used on models with evaporative emission control. Disconnect the fuel tank filler pipe. Remove the tank.

6. The tank should be checked carefully for dents or cracks which might cause leaks. Replace the tank as necessary.

7. Installation is the reverse of removal. Be sure to connect the filler hose after the tank has been mounted, to prevent leakage at the connection. Be careful not to kink hoses or overtighten fittings when reconnecting.

Models with EFI

1. Reduce the fuel pressure to zero. See Chapter one under fuel filters for correct procedure.

2. Disconnect the fuel outlet hose from the fuel pipe and drain the tank if no drain plug is provided.

3. Remove the luggage compartment mat. Remove the cover over the tank sending unit and hose connections. Disconnect the gauge electrical harness and the ventilation, fuel feed and fuel return hoses.

4. Remove the nut and the fuel tank retaining straps. Remove the tank.

5. Installation is the reverse of removal. Be careful not to twist or kink any of the hoses.

CARBURETED FUEL SYSTEM COMPONENTS

The carburetors used on Toyota models are conventional two-barrel, downdraft types similar to domestic carburetors. The main circuits are: primary, for normal operational requirements; secondary, to supply high speed fuel needs; float, to supply fuel to the primary and secondary circuits; accelerator, to supply fuel for quick and safe acceleration; choke, for reliable starting in cold weather; and power valve, for fuel economy. Although slight differences in appearance may be noted, these carburetors are basically alike. Of course, different jets and settings are demanded by the different engines to which they are fitted.

Carburetor
REMOVAL AND INSTALLATION

1. Remove the air filter housing, disconnect all air hoses from the filter base, and disconnect the battery ground cable.

NOTE: *On 20R and 22R engines, drain the cooling system to prevent coolant from running into the intake manifold.*

2. Disconnect the fuel line, choke pipe, and distributor vacuum line. On 20R and 22R engines, disconnect the choke coolant hose. Dis-

connect any electrical leads which run to the carburetor.

3. Remove the accelerator linkage. (With an automatic transmission, also remove the throttle rod to the transmission).

4. Remove the four nuts which secure the carburetor to the manifold and lift off the carburetor and gasket.

5. Cover the open manifold with a clean rag to prevent small objects from dropping into the engine.

6. Installation is performed in the reverse order of removal. After the engine is warmed up, check for fuel leaks and float level settings.

GENERAL OVERHAUL NOTES

Efficient carburetion depends greatly on careful cleaning and inspection during overhaul since dirt, gum, water, or varnish in or on the carburetor parts are often responsible for poor performance.

Overhaul your carburetor in a clean, dust-free area. Carefully disassemble the carburetor, referring often to the exploded views. Keep all similar and lookalike parts segregated during disassembly and cleaning to avoid accidental interchange during assembly. Make a note of all jet sizes.

When the carburetor is disassembled, wash all parts (except diaphragms, electrical choke units, pump plunger, and any other plastic, leather, fiber, or rubber parts) in clean carburetor solvent. Do not leave parts in the solvent any longer than is necessary to sufficiently loosen the deposits. Excessive cleaning may remove the special finish from the float bowl and choke valve bodies, leaving these parts unfit for service. Rinse all parts in clean solvent and blow them dry with compressed air or allow them to air dry. Wipe clean all cork, plastic, leather, and fiber parts with a clean, lint-free cloth.

Blow out all passages and jets with compressed air and be sure that there are no restrictions or blockages. Never use wire or similar tools to clean jets, fuel passages, or air bleeds. Clean all jets and valves separately to avoid accidental interchange.

Check all parts for wear or damage. If wear or damage is found, replace the defective parts. Especially check the following:

1. Check the float needle and seat for wear. If wear is found, replace the complete assembly.

2. Check the flat hinge pin for wear. If wear is found, replace the complete assembly.

3. Check the throttle and choke shaft bores for wear or an out-of-round condition. Damage or wear to the throttle arm, shaft, or shaft bore will often require replacement of the throttle body. These parts require a close tolerance of fit. Wear may allow air leakage, which could affect starting and idling.

NOTE: *Throttle shafts and bushings are not included in overhaul kits. They can be purchased separately.*

4. Inspect the idle mixture adjusting needles for burrs or grooves. Any such condition requires replacement of the needle, since you will not be able to obtain a satisfactory idle.

5. Test the accelerator pump check valves. They should pass air one way but not the other. Test for proper seating by blowing and sucking on the valve. Replace the valve if necessary. If the valve is satisfactory, wash the valve again to remove breath moisture.

6. Check the bowl cover for warped surfaces with a straightedge.

7. Closely inspect the valves and seats for wear and damage, replacing as necessary.

8. After the carburetor is assembled, check the choke valve for freedom of operation.

Carburetor overhaul kits are recommended for each overhaul. These kits contain all gaskets and new parts to replace those that deteriorate most rapidly and complete instructions for rebuilding, Failure to replace all parts supplied with the kit (especially gaskets) can result in poor performance later.

Some carburetor manufacturers supply overhaul kits of 3 basic types: minor repair, major repair, and gasket kits. Basically, they contain the following:

Minor Repair Kits
• All gaskets
• Float needle valve
• Volume control screw
• All diaphragms

Major Repair Kits
• All jets and gaskets
• All diaphragms
• Float needle valve
• Volume control screw
• Pump ball valve
• Float
• Complete intermediate rod
• Intermediate pump lever
• Some cover holddown screws and washers

Gasket Kits
• All gaskets

After cleaning and checking all components, reassemble the carburetor, using new parts and referring to the exploded view. When reassembling, make sure that all screws and jets are tight in their seats, but do not overtighten, as the tips will be distorted. Tighten all screws gradually, in rotation. Do not tighten needle valves into their seats. Uneven jetting will result. Always use new gaskets. Be sure to adjust the float level when reassembling.

FLOAT LEVEL ADJUSTMENT

Float level adjustments are unnecessary on models equipped with a carburetor sight glass, if the fuel level falls within the lines when the engine is running.

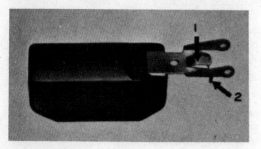

To adjust the float level bend the upper tab (1) or the lower tab (2)

8RC, 18RC, 20R and 22R-lowered

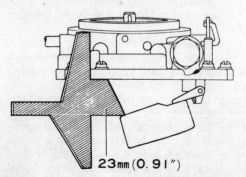

8RC, 18RC, 20R and 22R-raised

There are two float level adjustments which may be made on Toyota carburetors. One is with the air horn inverted, so that the float is in a fully raised position. The other is with the air horn in an upright position, so that the float falls to the bottom of its travel.

The float level is either measured with a special carburetor float level gauge, which comes with a rebuilding kit, or with a standard wire gauge. For the proper type of gauge, as well as the points to be measured, see the Float Level Adjustments chart at the end of this section.

NOTE: *Gap specifications are also given so*

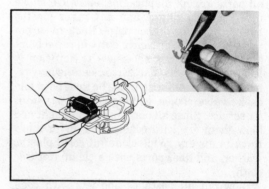

2M—raised

9. 5mm (0. 37")

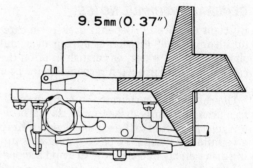

4M—lowered

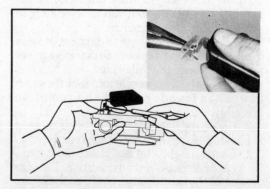

4M—raised

23mm (0. 91")

2M—lowered

Float Level Adjustments

Engine	Float Raised			Float Lowered		
	Gauge Type	Machine Distance Between:	Gap (in.)	Gauge Type	Measure Distance Between:	Gap (in.)
8R-C	Special	Float and air horn	0.370	Wire	Needle valve bushing pin and float tab	0.039
18R-C	Special	Float and air horn	0.200 ①	Wire	Needle valve bushing pin and float tab	0.039
20R	Special	Float and air horn	0.197 ②	Special	Needle valve bushing pin and float tab	0.039
2M and 4M	Special	Float end and air horn	0.370 ③	Special	Float end and air horn	0.910 ④

① 1976–77—0.236 in.
② 1978–79—0.276 in.
③ 1975–76—0.394 in.
④ 1975–76—0.039 in.

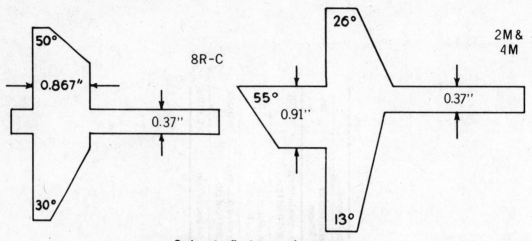

Carburetor float measuring gauges

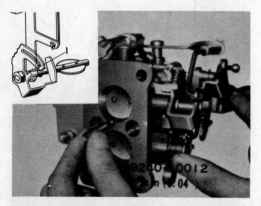

Make fast idle adjustments by bending the linkage

Screw-type fast idle adjustment (1)

that a float level gauge may be fabricated. Several different gauges are illustrated below.

Adjust the float level by bending the tabs on the float levers, either upper or lower, as required.

FAST IDLE ADJUSTMENT

Off Vehicle

The fast idle adjustment is performed with the choke valve fully closed. Adjust the gap between the throttle valve edge and bore to the specifications, where given, in the Fast Idle Adjustment chart. Use a wire gauge to determine the gap.

The chart also gives the proper primary throttle valve opening angle, where necessary, and the proper means of fast idle adjustment. NOTE: *The throttle valve opening angle is measured with a gauge supplied in the carburetor rebuilding kit. It is also possible to make one out of cardboard by using a protractor to obtain the correct angle.*

On Vehicle – 1975–81 Only

NOTE: *Disconnect the EGR valve vacuum line on 20R and 22R engines.*
1. Perform the idle speed/mixture adjustments as outlined in Chapter 2. Leave the tachometer connected.
2. Remove the top of the air cleaner.
3. Open the throttle valve slightly and close the choke valve. Next, hold the choke valve with your finger and close the throttle valve. The choke valve is now fully closed.
4. Without depressing the accelerator pedal, start the engine.
5. Check the engine fast idle speed against the following chart.
6. If the reading on the tachometer is not within specifications, adjust the fast idle speed by turning the fast idle screw.
7. Disconnect the tachometer, install the air cleaner cover, and connect the EGR valve vacuum line if it was disconnected.

AUTOMATIC CHOKE ADJUSTMENT

The automatic choke should be adjusted with the carburetor installed and the engine running.

Fast Idle Speed

	Engine	Speed (rpm)
1975–77	20R (All)	2400
	4M (US)	2600
	4M (Calif)	2400
1978–81	20R	2400
	22R	2400
	4M	2500

US—United States
Calif—California

Begin adjustment by aligning the setting marks

SETTING MARKS

DO NOT LOOSE

On 20R engines, do not loosen the center bolt

1. Check to ensure that the choke valve will close from fully opened when the coil housing is turned counterclockwise (2M and 4M engines clockwise).
CAUTION: *On models equipped with a 20R*

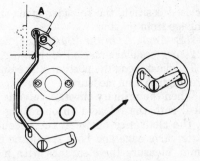

Measure the angle at "A" (20°)

or 22R engine, do not loosen the center bolt or coolant will run out.
2. Align the mark on the coil housing with the center line on the thermostat case. In this position, the choke valve should be fully closed when the ambient temperature is 77°F.
3. If necessary, adjust the mixture by turning the coil housing. If the mixture is too rich, rotate the housing clockwise. If too lean, rotate the housing counterclockwise. On models equipped with the 2M and 4M engines, rotate the housing in exactly the reverse direction of the above.
NOTE: *Each graduation on the thermostat case is equivalent to 9°F.*

UNLOADER ADJUSTMENT

Make the unloader adjustment with the primary valve fully opened. Adjust by performing the procedure indicated on the Choke Unloader Adjustment chart. The total angle of choke valve opening, in the chart, is measured with either a special gauge, supplied in the carburetor rebuilding kit, or a gauge of the proper angle fabricated from cardboard.

RELOADER ADJUSTMENT

A reloader is used on the 8R-C engine to prevent the throttle valve from opening during automatic choke operation.
1. When the choke valve is opened 45° from

Fast Idle Adjustment

Engine	Throttle Valve to Bore Clearance (in.)	Primary Throttle Angle (deg)	To Adjust Fast Idle:
8R-C	0.029	11—from closed	Turn the fast idle adjusting screw
18R-C	0.041	13—from closed	Turn the fast idle adjusting screw
20R	0.047	—	Turn the fast idle screw
2M	—	24—from closed	Turn the fast idle adjusting screw
4M	—	16—from closed ①	Turn the fast idle adjusting screw

—Not available
① 1977–81: 9°

the closed position, the reloader lever should disengage from its stop.

NOTE: *Angle A, in the illustration, should be 20 degrees when measured with a gauge.*

2. To adjust, bend the portion of the linkage where angle A was measured.

3. When the primary throttle valve is fully opened, with the reloader in operating position, the clearance between the secondary throttle valve edge and bore should be 0.35–0.76mm. Measure the clearance with a wire gauge and bend the reloader tab to adjust it.

4. Fully open the choke valve by hand. The reloader lever should be disengaged from its stop by the weight on its link.

CHOKE BREAKER ADJUSTMENT

1. Push the rod which comes out of the upper (choke breaker) diaphragm so that the choke valve opens.

2. Measure the choke valve opening angle. It should be 40°.

3. Adjust the angle, if necessary, by bending the relief lever link.

KICK-UP ADJUSTMENT

1. Open the primary throttle valve the amount specified in the Kick-Up Adjustment chart.

2. Measure the secondary throttle valve-to-bore clearance with a 0.2mm (0.2–0.4mm – 1970–74 2M/4M engines) gauge.

3. Adjust the clearance by bending the secondary throttle lever.

INITIAL IDLE MIXTURE SCREW ADJUSTMENT

When assembling the carburetor, turn the idle mixture screw the number of turns specified below. After the carburetor is installed, perform the appropriate idle speed/mixture adjustment as outlined in Chapter 2.

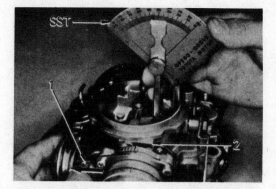

Push the breaker rod (1) to open the choke and bend the relief lever (2) to adjust the breaker

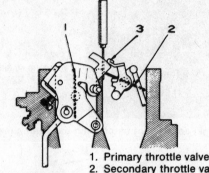

Kick-up adjustment

1. Primary throttle valve
2. Secondary throttle valve
3. Secondary throttle lever

Kick-Up Adjustment

Engine	Primary Throttle Valve Opening Angle (deg)
18R-C	64 from bore
20R	fully opened
2M/4M	55 from closed
4M (1975–79)	64–90 from closed

Choke Unloader Adjustment

Year	Engine	Throttle Valve Fully Closed (deg)	From Closed to Fully Open (deg)	Throttle Valve Open (total) (deg)	To Adjust Bend:
			Choke Valve Angle (deg)		
1970–75	20R	30	—	50	Fast idle lever
	8R-C	32	19	51	Fast idle cam follower or choke shaft tab
	18R-C	—	27	47	Fast idle cam follower or choke shaft tab
	4M	20	15	35 ①	Fast idle lever
1976–82	20R	—	50	90	Fast idle lever, follower or choke shaft tab
	4M	20	15	90	Fast idle lever

—Not available
① 1975—50°

• 8R-C engine — 2 turns from seating
• 18R-C engine — 2½ turns from fully closed
• 20R, 22R engine — 1¾ turns from fully closed
• 2M/4M engines — 1½ turns out
CAUTION: *Seat the idle mixture screw lightly. Overtightening will damage its tip.*

CHOKE RETURN SYSTEM

Some engines have a choke return system to protect the catalytic converter. Because of the chance of overheating the exhaust system and damaging the catalytic converter by running with the choke out, a thermoswitch and return spring system automatically close the choke when the coolant temperature reaches 104°F.

A holding coil and holding plate surround the choke cable and retain it when the temperature is low enough. When the temperature reaches 104°F the thermoswitch opens, freeing the return spring to pull in the choke. There are no adjustments on the system. If a malfunction occurs, trace the loss and replace that segment of the unit.

Vacuum Limiter System

4M-E and 4M-E Engines 1980–81

This system allows fresh air to enter the air intake chamber upon sudden deceleration to reduce hydrocarbons and carbon dioxide emissions.

REMOVAL AND INSTALLATION

1. Remove the two vacuum lines.
2. Remove the intake chamber line.
3. Remove the valve from its mounting.
4. Installation is the reverse of removal.

TESTING

1. Disconnect the air inlet hose of the vacuum limiter from the air connector and plug the air connector port.
2. Start the engine.
3. Close the inlet of the vacuum limiter with your finger.
4. Increase the speed of the engine and then release the throttle.
5. When the throttle valve is opened and closed you should momentarily feel vacuum. If not the vacuum limiter is defective and must be replaced.

GASOLINE FUEL INJECTION SYSTEM COMPONENTS

The 4M-E and 5M-E engines are equipped with electronic fuel injection. The EFI system precisely controls fuel injection to match engine requirements, reducing emissions and increasing driveability.

The electric fuel pump pumps fuel through a damper and filter to the pressure regulator. The six fuel injectors are electric solenoid

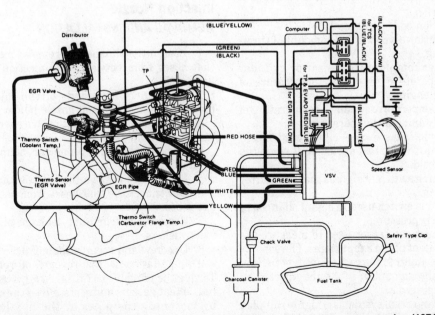

The vacuum lines and wiring for the emission control system can become very complex (1974 California 18R-C engine)

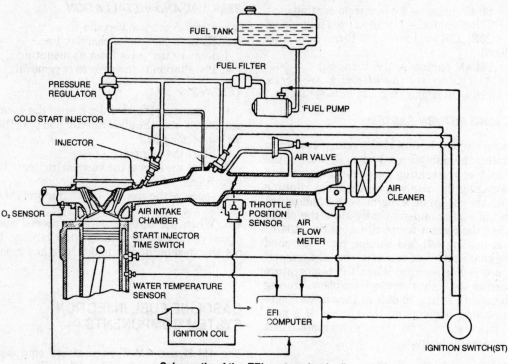

Schematic of the EFI system (typical)

valves which open and close by signals from the control unit.

The EFI computer receives input from various sensors to determine engine operating condition.

1. Air flow meter — measures the amount of intake air.

2. Ignition coil — engine RPM.

3. Throttle valve switch — amount of throttle opening.

4. Water temperature sensor or cylinder head temperature sensor — temperature of coolant or engine.

5. Air temperature sensor — temperature of intake air (ambient temperature).

6. Thermotime switch — signal used to control cold start valve fuel enrichment when the engine is cold.

7. Starting switch — signals that the starter is operating.

8. Altitude switch used to signal changes in atmospheric pressure.

9. Exhaust gas sensor used to measure the oxygen content of the exhaust gas. The sensors provide the input to the control unit, which determines the amount of fuel to be injected by its preset program.

The fuel injection system is a highly complex unit. All repair or adjustment should be left to an expert Toyota technician.

DIESEL FUEL SYSTEM COMPONENTS

Injection Nozzle

REMOVAL AND INSTALLATION

1. Loosen the clamps and remove the injection hoses from between the injection pump and pipe.

2. Disconnect both ends of the injection pipes from the pump and nozzle holders.

3. Disconnect the fuel cut off wire from the connector clamp.

4. Remove the nut, connector clamp and bond cable.

5. Unbolt and remove the injector pipes.

6. Disconnect the fuel hoses from the leakage pipes.

7. Remove the four nuts, leakage pipe and four washers.

8. Unscrew and remove the nozzles.

9. Installation is the reverse of removal. Torque the nozzles to 47 ft.lb. Always use new nozzle seat gaskets and seats. Bleed the system by loosening the pipes at the nozzles and cranking the engine until all air is expelled and fuel sprays.

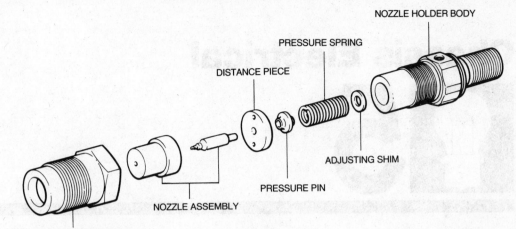

Diesel injector

Injection Pump

REMOVAL AND INSTALLATION

1. Drain the cooling system.

2. Disconnect the accelerator and cruise control cables from the pump.

3. Disconnect the fuel cut off wire at the pump.

4. Disconnect the fuel inlet and outlet hoses, the water by-pass hoses, the boost compensator hoses, the A/C or heater idle-up vacuum hoses and the heater hose.

5. Remove the injector pipes at the pump.

6. Remove the pump pulley.

7. Matchmark the raised timing mark on the pump flange with the block. Unbolt and remove the pump.

8. Installation is the reverse of removal. There must be no clearance between the pump bracket and stay.

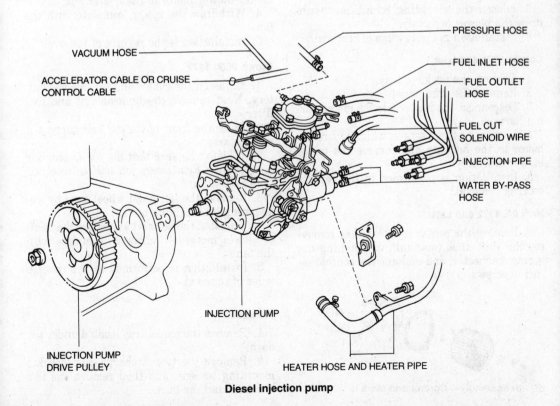

Diesel injection pump

Chasis Electrical

5

HEATER

On some models the air conditioner, if so equipped, is integral with the heater, and therefore, heater removal may differ from the procedures detailed below.

Blower

REMOVAL AND INSTALLATION

Corona (1970–73) and Mark II/4

1. Working from under the instrument panel, unfasten the defroster hoses from the heater box.
2. Unplug the multiconnector.
3. Loosen the mounting screws and withdraw the blower assembly.
4. Installation is the reverse of removal.

Corona 1974 and later

1. Remove the package tray.
2. Remove the trim panel.
3. Disconnect the heater blower motor wiring harness.
4. Loosen the three screws which secure the motor to the housing and remove the motor blower assembly.
5. Installation is performed in the reverse order of removal.

Mark II/6 1972 and Later

1. Remove the center console, after removing the shift knob (manual), unfastening the wiring, connector, and undoing the console securing screws.

Blower assembly—Corona and Mark II

2. Unfasten the heater blower wiring connector.
3. Remove the three bolts which secure the blower motor to the heater box.
4. Withdraw the motor, complete with fan, from the box.
5. Installation is the reverse of removal.

Crown 2300 1970–71

1. Remove the air cleaner, complete with its attendant hoses.
2. Remove the left hand front fender and the wheel arch. (Both are bolted in place).
3. Unfasten the three bolts which secure the heater blower motor to the heater box.
4. Withdraw the motor, complete with the fan.
5. Installation is the reverse of removal.

Crown 2600 1972

1. Unfasten the cables and remove the battery. Next remove the ignition coil and fuel filter.
2. Raise the front of the car and support it with jackstands.
CAUTION: *Be sure that the car is securely supported. Remember, you will be working underneath it.*
3. Remove the left hand wheel arch by unfastening its retaining bolts.
4. Unfasten the bolts which secure the heater blower motor; withdraw it, complete with the fan.
5. Installation is performed in the reverse order of removal.

Cressida

1. Remove the parcel tray located under the dash.
2. Remove the two discharge duct bracket mounting screens, and then remove the two brackets and the duct.

3. Remove the mounting screw, and remove the right side forward console cover.

4. Unscrew the mounting screw and remove the relay bracket located under the motor.

5. Remove the three mounting screws, and remove the motor, gasket, and blower assembly. If necessary, remove the blower mounting nut and washers, and remove the blower from the shaft.

6. Install in reverse order.

Core

REMOVAL AND INSTALLATION

Corona (1970–73) and Mark II

1. Drain the cooling system.

2. Remove the console, if so equipped, by removing the shift knob (manual), wiring connector, and console attaching screws.

3. Remove the carpeting from the tunnel.

4. If necessary, remove the cigarette lighter and ash tray.

5. Remove the package tray, if it makes access to the heater core difficult.

6. Unfasten the securing screws and remove the center air outlet on the Mark II/6.

7. Remove the bottom cover/intake assembly screws and withdraw the assembly.

8. Remove the cover from the water valve.

9. Remove the water valve.

10. Unfasten the hose clamps and remove the hoses from the core.

11. Withdraw the core.

12. Installation is performed in the reverse order of removal.

Corona 1974 and Later

1. Disconnect the negative battery cable.

2. Drain the cooling system.

3. Disconnect the heater hoses from the engine.

4. Remove the center console, if so equipped.

5. Remove the package tray and disconnect the heater air duct.

6. Unfasten the screws and take the glove compartment out of the dash.

7. Working through the glove compartment opening, remove the rear duct.

8. Detach the fresh air ventilation duct.

9. Remove the instrument cluster, as detailed in the appropriate section.

10. Remove the radio, if installed, as detailed in the appropriate section.

11. Remove the heater control assembly.

12. Take the defroster duct assembly out.

13. Tilt the heater assembly to the right and withdraw it from the package tray side.

14. Remove the water valve and outlet hose from the heater assembly.

15. Take off the retaining band and remove the bolt.

16. Take out the core.

17. Installation is performed in the reverse order of removal.

Crown 2300 1970–71

1. Drain the cooling system.

2. Remove the glove box and the package tray.

3. Unfasten both water hoses.

4. Detach the control cable.

5. Remove the dash panel ducts.

6. Remove the core from beneath the heater.

Removing the Crown 2300 heater core

Crown 2600 1972

1. Disconnect the fusible link.

2. Perform Steps 1–3 of the Crown 2300 heater core removal procedure.

3. Detach the air intake door and heater control cables from the core.

4. Remove the air ducts, center, left hand, and right hand, as well as both defroster hoses.

5. Remove the heater core from the top of the heater box.

6. Installation is performed in the reverse of removal.

1. Water valve cover   3. Core
2. Water valve   4. Duct/cover assembly

Core removal—Corona (1970–73) and Mark II

Cressida

1. Disconnect the battery ground and drain the radiator. Remove parts as described in steps 1–4 in the blower motor removal procedure above.
2. Remove the console.
3. remove the two remaining air ducts.
4. Remove:
   a. Right and left side cowl trim panels.
   b. Fuse box and steering column covers.
   c. Glove box.
   d. Radio (see below).
5. Remove the center air discharge panel.
6. Remove the instrument cluster.
7. Disengage damper operating cables and spring.
8. Remove the lower duct plenum by lifting it up at the rear.
9. Remove the heater valve and disconnect the two core hoses.
10. Remove the two heater unit retaining bolts and the mounting nuts, and pull the unit out on the passenger's side. Pull the heater core upward out of the unit.
11. Installation is the reverse of removal.

Radio

NOTE: *Never operate the radio without a speaker. Severe damage to the output transistors will result. If the speaker must be replaced, use a speaker of the correct impedance (ohms) or else the output transistors will be damaged and require replacement.*

REMOVAL AND INSTALLATION

Corona (1970–73)

1. Remove the center air outlet from under the dash.
2. Unfasten the radio control mounting bracket.
3. Remove the radio control knobs and then the retaining nuts from the control shafts.
4. Detach the speaker, and the power and antenna leads from the radio.
5. Withdraw the radio from underneath the dashboard.
6. Unfasten the speaker retaining nuts and remove the speaker.
7. Installation is performed in the reverse order of removal.

Corona 1974 and Later

INSTRUMENT PANEL MOUNTED

1. Remove the two screws securing the instrument cluster trim panel and remove the trim panel.

2. Remove the knobs from the heater controls and remove the heater control face.
3. Remove the four screws which secure the center trim panel (two are behind the heater control opening).
4. Remove the radio knobs and remove the center trim panel.
5. Remove the four screws which secure the radio bracket.
6. Pull the radio far enough out to remove the antenna, power, and speaker leads.
7. Remove the radio.
8. Installation is performed in the reverse order of removal.

CONSOLE MOUNTED

1. Remove the screws which secure the console and remove the console, by lowering the armrest and lifting up on the center of the console.
2. Unplug the multiconnector from the radio and disconnect the antenna lead.
3. Remove the radio knobs.
4. Remove the radio bracket and then remove the radio.
5. Installation is performed in the reverse order of removal.

Mark II/4 1970–72 (Early)

1. Disconnect the battery.
2. Remove the left and right instrument panel moldings.
3. Remove the heater control knobs, unfasten the screws, and remove the heater control trim panel.
4. Remove the five screws and withdraw the center crash pad from the instrument panel area around the heater controls.
5. Working from beneath the dash, disconnect the radio and clock leads.
6. Unfasten the screws securing the radio and clock trim panel.
7. Remove the radio bracket attaching screws. Remove the trim panel, radio and clock.
8. Remove the knobs and unfasten the nuts which secure the radio to the face plate.
9. Installation is the reverse of removal.

Mark II/6 1972 and Later

1. Remove the instrument cluster housing.
2. Remove the heater control panel.
3. Remove the two radio attaching bolts.
4. Disconnect all radio leads.
5. Remove the radio.
6. Installation is the reverse of removal.

Crown 2300 1970–71

1. Remove the glove compartment.
2. Remove all leads from the radio.

3. Remove the radio control knobs.

4. Remove the radio shaft nuts.

5. Slide the radio sideways, and out through the glove compartment opening.

6. Installation is the reverse of removal.

1972 Crown 2600

1. Remove the center and right side heater ducts.

2. Disconnect all leads from the radio.

3. Remove the control knobs, and the nuts from the top of the radio trim panel.

4. Remove the trim panel.

5. Remove the tape deck mounting screws and remove the tape deck.

6. Unfasten the radio mounting bracket and remove the radio.

7. Installation is the reverse of removal.

Cressida

1. Remove the radio knobs and face plate.

2. Remove the bezel nuts from the control shafts and remove the bezel from the dash.

3. Remove the driver's side forward console trim board.

4. Remove the radio forward mounting bolt, disconnect the wiring, and remove the radio.

5. Installation is the reverse of removal.

WINDSHIELD WIPERS

Blade and Arm

REPLACEMENT

1. To remove the wiper blades, lift up on the spring release tab on the wiper blade-to-arm connector.

2. Pull the blade assembly off the wiper arm.

3. There are two types of replacements for Toyotas:

   a. Pre-1973, replace the entire wiper blade as an assembly. Simply snap the replacement into pace on the arm.

b. Post-1973, press the old blade insert down, away from the blade assembly to free it from the retaining clips on the blade ends. Slide the insert out of the blade carrier, slide the new insert in and bend the insert upwards slightly to engage the retaining clips.

4. To replace a wiper arm, unscrew the acorn nut which secures it to the pivot and carefully pull the arm upwards and off of the pivot. Installation is the reverse of removal.

Motor

REMOVAL AND INSTALLATION

Corona and Crown

1. Disconnect the wiper motor multiconnector.

2. Remove the service cover and loosen the motor mounting bolts.

3. Use a screwdriver to separate the wiper link-to-motor connection.

CAUTION: *Be careful not to bend the linkage.*

4. Remove the wiper motor.

5. Installation is the reverse of removal.

Mark II/4

1. Remove the access hole cover.

2. Separate the wiper link from the motor by prying gently.

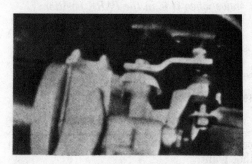

Remove the wiper arm with the crank in this position—Celica and Mark II/4

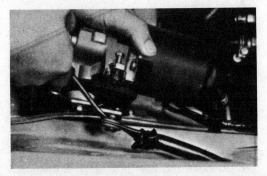

Separate the wiper link from the motor with a screwdriver

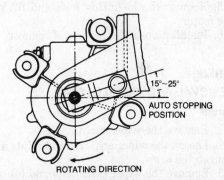

Install the wiper motor with the crank in this position—Celica and Mark II/4

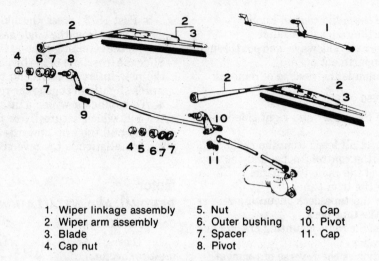

1. Wiper linkage assembly
2. Wiper arm assembly
3. Blade
4. Cap nut
5. Nut
6. Outer bushing
7. Spacer
8. Pivot
9. Cap
10. Pivot
11. Cap

Windshield wiper linkage assembly—Corona (typical)

3. Remove the left and right cowl ventilators by lifting the retaining clips.

4. Remove the wiper arms and linage retaining nuts. Push the pivots into the ventilators.

5. Loosen the wiper link connectors at their ends.

6. Start the wiper motor and turn the ignition key OFF when the motor crank is at the position illustrated.

NOTE: *The wiper motor is difficult to remove when it is in the PARK position.*

7. Unplug the multiconnector at the motor.

8. Remove the motor mounting bolts and lift out the motor.

9. Installation is the reverse of removal. Assemble the crank as illustrated.

1972–76 Mark II/6 and Cressida

1. Remove the cover from the service hole.

2. Set the wiper crank 180° from the PARK position by turning the ignition switch OFF at that point.

3. Separate the link from the motor crank.

4. Unplug the multiconnector at the motor.

5. Remove the mounting nuts and lift out the motor.

6. Installation is the reverse of removal.

Linkage

REMOVAL AND INSTALLATION

Corona

1. Remove the wiper motor.

2. Loosen the wiper arm retaining nuts and remove the arms.

3. Remove the wiper pivot nuts and lift out the linkage through the access hole.

4. Installation is the reverse of removal.

Mark II/4

The linkage is removed along with the motor.

Mark II/6 and Cressida

1. Remove the wiper arms.

2. Remove the left and right cowl ventilators.

3. Remove the ventilator service hole cover.

4. Remove the linkage attaching screws.

5. Remove the wiper motor access cover.

6. Unfasten the wiper linkage from the motor crank. (See the wiper motor removal procedures).

7. Withdraw the linkage through the access hole.

8. Installation is performed in the reverse order of removal.

Crown

1. Perform Steps 1–5 of the Mark II/6 Linkage Removal procedure.

2. Remove both of the pivots and the connecting linkage. Be careful not to damage the windshield washer nozzle.

3. Installation is performed in the reverse order of removal.

INSTRUMENT PANEL

Cluster

REMOVAL AND INSTALLATION

Corona

1970–73

1. Disconnect the battery.

2. Remove the fuse box block attachment bolts.

3. Remove the parking brake bracket.

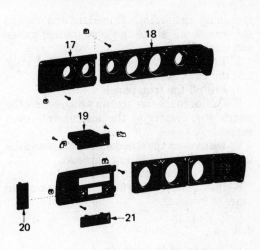

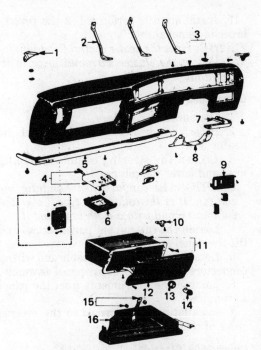

1. Instrument panel side bracket
2. Cowl-to-instrument panel brace
3. Instrument panel
4. Ash tray retainer
5. Instrument panel reinforcement No. 1
6. Ash tray
7. Instrument panel reinforcement No. 2
8. Steering column lower trim panel
9. Switch bezel
10. Glovebox retainer
11. Glovebox

12. Glovebox door
13. Glovebox door lock bezel
14. Glovebox lock cylinder
15. Instrument panel parcel tray bracket No. 1
16. Instrument panel parcel tray
17. Instrument center panel
18. Instrument surround
19. Tape player opening cover
20. Heater control panel
21. Radio opening cover

Components of a typical Corona instrument panel

4. Detach the fuel gauge/warning light pod wiring harness and remove its mounting screws. Pull out the pod.

5. Perform Step 4 for the clock.

6. Disconnect the speedometer wiring harness and cable.

7. Unfasten the wiring harness clamp then push the harness toward the front.

8. Loosen the speedometer attaching screws and remove the speedometer.

NOTE: *Cover the lens with a cloth during removal.*

9. Installation is performed in the reverse order of removal.

1974 AND LATER

1. Disconnect the negative (–) battery cable.

2. Remove the two instrument cluster surround securing screws. One is located above the speedometer lens and the other above the

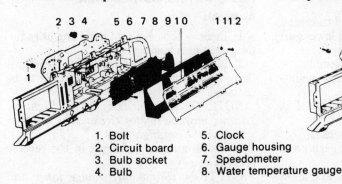

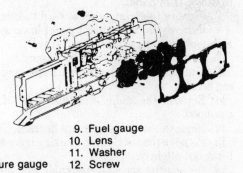

1. Bolt
2. Circuit board
3. Bulb socket
4. Bulb
5. Clock
6. Gauge housing
7. Speedometer
8. Water temperature gauge
9. Fuel gauge
10. Lens
11. Washer
12. Screw

Mark II/6 instrument cluster assemblies—sedan and wagon at left; hardtop at right

fuel gauge on hardtops. On sedans and wagons the screws are above the combination gauge and clock.

3. Remove the side air outlet control knob and the clock setting knob.

4. Lift off the trim panel.

5. Unfasten the five screws which secure the instrument cluster to the instrument panel support.

6. Disconnect the speedometer cable and the instrument cluster wiring harness.

7. Lift out the cluster assembly.

8. Installation is performed in the reverse order of removal.

Mark II/4

1. Disconnect the battery.

2. Remove the package shelf from beneath the dashboard.

3. Remove the fuse block bracket.

4. Remove the lower left side crash pad and the left hand trim molding.

5. Unfasten the instrument cluster securing screws and tip the cluster slightly forward.

6. Detach the cluster wiring harness and the speedometer cable. Remove the cluster.

NOTE: *If the car is not equipped with a radio, it is much easier to remove the glove box and then remove the instrument cluster through the opening.*

7. Installation is performed in the reverse order of removal.

Mark II/6

1. Remove the housing from the steering column.

2. Remove the control knobs from the heater and radio.

3. Loosen the heater control floodlight and pull it out slightly.

4. Remove the nine screws which attach the cluster surround.

5. Push the upper crash pad away from the trim panel and slightly pull out the trim panel.

6. Remove the heater control floodlight from the trim panel.

7. Remove the trim panel toward the right.

8. Remove the instrument panel lower garnish moldings. Remove the ash tray.

9. Remove the heater control assembly.

10. Unfasten the dash side ventilator mounting screws.

11. Remove the radio and tape deck, if so equipped.

12. Remove the heater control bracket.

13. Remove the six cluster securing bolts and lift it out slightly.

14. Detach the speedometer cable and all of the wiring harnesses. Remove the cluster.

15. Installation is performed in the reverse order of removal.

NOTE: *Have the heater control floodlight installed in the cluster surround prior to its installation.*

Crown 2300

1. Disconnect the battery.

2. Detach the heater control cables at the heater box.

3. Loosen the steering column clamping nuts and lower the column.

CAUTION: *Be careful when handling the column. It is the collapsible type. Cover the column shroud with a cloth to protect it.*

4. Loosen the instrument panel screws and tilt the panel forward.

5. Detach the speedometer cable and wiring connectors. Remove the entire panel assembly.

6. Remove the instruments from the panel as required.

7. Installation is performed in the reverse order of removal.

Crown 2600, Cressida

1. Disconnect the battery.

2. Remove the air duct from the center air outlet.

3. Remove the radio trim panel from the center instrument panel.

4. Remove the radio.

5. Unfasten the screws and remove the instrument cluster trim panel. Remove the cluster housing.

6. Detach the speedometer drive cable and wiring connectors by reaching through the radio opening.

7. Withdraw the instrument cluster.

8. Installation is performed in the reverse order of removal.

LIGHTS

Headlights

REMOVAL AND INSTALLATION

All Models

1. Remove the headlight bezel and/or radiator grille, as necessary.

2. Repeat Steps 2–3 of the Corona Headlight Removal procedure of each lamp unit to be replaced.

NOTE: *On some models, the headlight retainer must be rotated clockwise in order to remove the headlight unit.*

3. Installation is performed in the reverse order of removal.

CAUTION: *Do not interchange inner and outer headlight units.*

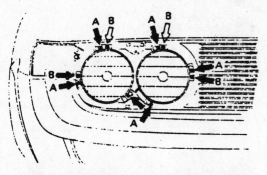

To remove the headlights, remove the retaining screws "A"; but do not loosen adjusting screws "B"

Turn Signals and Flashers
ALL EXCEPT CROWN

These models' turn signals and hazard warning flashers are combined in a single unit. It is located on the left hand side, underneath the dashboard, next to the fuse block.

NOTE: *On some models it may be necessary to remove the fuse block bracket in order to gain access to the flasher.*

CROWN 2300

The turn signal and hazard warning flasher is located on a bracket next to the parking brake handle.

CROWN 2600

The turn signal/hazard flasher is located behind the left hand (driver's) ash tray. In order to remove the flasher, first take out the ash tray.

FUSES AND FUSIBLE LINK
1970–79

The fuse box is located on the left hand side, underneath the dashboard, on all models except the Crown 2600. On the Crown 2600, the fuse box is located behind a door on the driver's side kick panel.

All models are equipped with fusible links on the battery cables running from the positive (+) battery terminal.

On all Mark II-6 models, and on all other passenger cars made in 1974 and later, the headlights are protected by a relay and the fusible link, rather than by individual fuses.

The circuits protected by the fuses and the fuse ratings (amps) are given below for each model.

1980–81

These models have two fuse blocks. One is located behind a panel in the dash (same as 1978–79, while the other can be found on the left front fender apron.

1982–86

A single fuse block unit is located under the hood (driver's side) on these models.

WIRING DIAGRAMS

Wiring diagrams have been left out of this book. As cars have become more complex, and available with longer and longer option lists, wiring diagrams have grown in size and complexity also. It has become virtually impossible to provide a readable reproduction in a reasonable number of pages. Information on ordering wiring diagrams from the vehicle manufacturer can be found in the owners manual.

Clutch and Transmission

6

MANUAL TRANSMISSION

Understanding the Manual Transmission and Clutch

Because of the way an internal combustion engine breathes, it can produce torque, or twisting force, only within a narrow speed range. Most modern, overhead valve engines must turn at about 2,500 rpm to produce their peak torque. By 4,500 rpm they are producing so little torque that continued increases in engine speed produce no power increases.

The transmission and clutch are employed to vary the relationship between engine speed and the speed of the wheels so that adequate engine power can be produced under all circumstances. The clutch allows engine torque to be applied to the transmission input shaft gradually, due to mechanical slippage. The car can, consequently, be started smoothly from a full stop.

The transmission changes the ratio between the rotating speeds of the engine and the wheels by the use of gears. 3-speed or 4-speed transmissions are most common. The lower gears allow full engine power to be applied to the rear wheels during acceleration at low speeds.

The clutch drive plate is a thin disc, the center of which is splined to the transmission input shaft. Both sides of the disc are covered with a layer of material which is similar to brake lining and which is capable of allowing slippage without roughness or excessive noise.

The clutch cover is bolted to the engine flywheel and incorporates a diaphragm spring which provides the pressure to engage the clutch. The cover also houses the pressure plate. The driven disc is sandwiched between the pressure plate and the smooth surface of the flywheel when the clutch pedal is released,

thus forcing it to turn at the same speed as the engine crankshaft.

The transmission contains a mainshaft which passes all the way through the transmission, from the clutch to the driveshaft. This shaft is separated at one point, so that front and rear portions can turn at different speeds.

Power is transmitted by a countershaft in the lower gears and reverse. The gears of the countershaft mesh with gears on the mainshaft, allowing power to be carried from one to the other. All the countershaft gears are integral with that shaft, while several of the mainshaft gears can either rotate independently of the shaft or be locked to it. Shifting from one gear to the next causes one of the gears to be freed from rotating with the shaft and locks another to it. Gears are locked and unlocked by internal dog clutches which slide between the center of the gear and the shaft. The forward gears usually employ synchronizers, friction members which smoothly bring gear and shaft to the same speed before the toothed dog clutches are engaged.

The clutch is operating properly if:

1. It will stall the engine when released with the vehicle held stationary.

2. The shift lever can be moved freely between first and reverse gears when the vehicle is stationary and the clutch disengaged.

A clutch pedal free play adjustment is incorporated in the linkage. If there is about 25–51mm of motion before the pedal begins to release the clutch, it is adjusted properly. Inadequate free play wears all parts of the clutch releasing mechanisms and may cause slippage. Excessive free play may cause inadequate release and hard shifting of gears.

Some clutches use a hydraulic system in place of mechanical linkage. If the clutch fails to release, fill the clutch master cylinder with fluid to the proper level and pump the clutch pedal to fill the system with fluid. Bleed the system in the same way as a brake system. If leaks are located, tighten loose connections or overhaul the master or slave cylinder as necessary.

LINKAGE ADJUSTMENT

All Toyota passenger cars equipped with floor mounted shifters have internally mounted shift linkage. On some older models, the linkage is contained in the side cover which is bolted on the transmission case. All of the other models have the linkage mounted inside the top of the transmission case, itself.

No external adjustments are needed or possible.

REMOVAL AND INSTALLATION

Corona (1970–73) and Mark II/4

Working under the hood, perform the following:

1. Unfasten the cable from the negative battery terminal.
2. Remove the accelerator torque rod from its valve cover mounting.
3. Separate the downpipe from the flange and remove the flange. Remove the exhaust pipe bracket.
4. Raise the car with a jack and support it with jackstands.

CAUTION: *Be sure that the car is securely supported. Remember, you will be working underneath it.*

4. Remove the parking brake equalizer support bracket.
5. Unfasten the speedometer cable and back up lamp wiring harness from the transmission.
6. Remove the control shaft lever retainer.
7. Remove the clutch release cylinder from the transmission and set it up, out of the way.

NOTE: *Do not disconnect the hydraulic line from the release cylinder.*

8. Drain the transmission oil.
9. Remove the driveshaft.

NOTE: *To prevent oil from draining out of the transmission, cover the opening with a plastic bag secured by a rubber band.*

10. Support the transmission with a jack.

NOTE: *Place a support under the engine to prevent the total weight from being supported by the front mounts. Be careful of oil pan damage.*

11. Unfasten the rear engine mounts and remove the engine rear support crossmember (see Chapter 3).
12. Lower the jack.
13. Unfasten the bolts securing the clutch housing to the cylinder block.
14. Remove the transmission toward the rear of the car.
15. Installation is the reverse of removal. However, before installing the transmission apply a light coating of multipurpose grease to the input shaft end, input shaft spline, clutch release bearing and the driveshaft end. After installation, fill the transmission and the cooling system. Adjust the clutch.

Mark II/6 and Crown 2600

Working from inside of the car, perform the following:

1. Place the gear selector in Neutral. Remove the center console, if so equipped.
2. Remove the trim boot at the base of the shift lever and the boot underneath it on the shift tower.
3a. Unfasten the four shift lever plate returning screws.
3b. Withdraw the shift lever assembly.
3c. Remove the gasket.

NOTE: *Cover the hole with a clean cloth to prevent anything from falling into the transmission case.*

Working in the engine compartment perform the following:

4. Drain the cooling system and disconnect the cable from the negative side of the battery.
5. Remove the radiator hoses.

Disconnecting the shift linkage securing bolts (1), and lever housing (2)—Corona (1970–73) and Mark II/4 (1970–72)

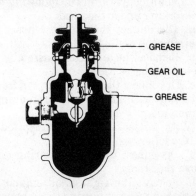

GREASE

GEAR OIL

GREASE

Floorshift lever lubricating points—Mark II/6 and Crown 2600

6. Separate the downpipe from the flange and remove the flange. Remove the exhaust pipe bracket.

7. Raise the car with a jack and support it with jackstands.

CAUTION: *Be sure that the car is securely support with jackstands. Remember, you will be working underneath it.*

8. Drain the transmission oil.

9. Detach the exhaust pipe from the manifold and remove the exhaust pipe support bracket.

10. Remove the driveshaft.

NOTE: *It will be necessary to plug the opening in the end of the transmission with an old yoke or, if none is available, cover it with a plastic bag secured by a rubber band.*

11. Unfasten the speedometer cable from the right side of the transmission.

12a. Remove the clutch release cylinder assembly from the transmission and tie it aside, so that it is out of the way.

12b. Unplug the back-up lamp switch connector.

13. Support the transmission with a jack.

14. Unfasten the engine rear mounts. (See Chapter 3). Remove the rear crossmember.

NOTE: *Be sure to support the engine so that total weight will not be on the front mounts. Be careful of oil pan damage.*

15. Unbolt the clutch housing from the engine and withdraw the transmission assembly.

16. Installation is performed in the reverse order of removal, but remember to perform the following during installation.

Apply a light coating of multipurpose grease to the input shaft end, input shaft spline, clutch release bearing, and driveshaft end.

After installation, fill the transmission and the cooling system. Adjust the clutch.

Crown 2300

Perform the removal procedure as previously outlined for the Corona (1970–73) and Mark II/4. In addition, perform the following steps:

1. Working under the hood:

    a. Disconnect the radiator hoses after draining the cooling system.

    b. Remove the air cleaner assembly complete with hoses.

    c. Disconnect the connecting rod from the accelerator linkage, before removing the torque rod.

2. With car jacked up and supported, perform the following:

    a. Disconnect the starter wiring and remove the starter.

    b. Remove the right hand engine stone shield before disconnecting the exhaust pipe from the manifold.

    c. Detach the parking brake operating lever from the intermediate lever. Remove the return spring and the intermediate lever from its support bracket. Unfasten the parking brake cable.

    d. Jack up the front of the engine, once the jack has been removed from the transmission, to facilitate transmission removal.

1974 and Later Corona (4 and 5-Speed)

1. Disconnect the negative battery cable and then the positive battery-to-starter cable, complete with the fusible link.

2. Drain the coolant from the radiator into a suitable clean container for reuse. Unfasten the upper radiator hose.

3. Detach the accelerator rod and link at the firewall side.

4. Raise both ends of the car and support them with jackstands.

CAUTION: *Be sure that the car is securely supported.*

5. Working underneath the car, remove the exhaust pipe clamp and clutch release cylinder (Don't disconnect its hydraulic line, set the cylinder out of the way). Next, disconnect the back-up light switch lead and speedometer cable. Drain the transmission oil.

6. Remove the driveshaft from the transmission, after matchmarking it and the companion flange for assembly.

NOTE: *To prevent oil from draining out of the transmission, cover the opening with a plastic bag secured with a rubber band.*

7. Place a block of wood on the lift pad of a jack to protect the transmission, and support the transmission with the jack.

8. Cover the back end of the valve cover with shop towels, remove the rear crossmember (see Chapter 3) and lower the jack.

9. Unfasten the bolts which secure the shift lever, and withdraw the shift lever.

10. Remove the starter motor from the clutch housing.

11. Unfasten the bolts which secure the clutch housing to the engine block.

12. Move the transmission and jack rearward, until the input shaft has cleared the clutch cover. Remove the transmission from underneath the car.

13. Installation is performed in the reverse order of removal. Be sure to apply a thin coating of grease to the input shaft splines. The clutch housing-to-cylinder block bolts should be tightened to 37–58 ft.lb. Adjust the clutch and fill the transmission with API GL-4 SAE 90 gear oil (see the Capacities chart in Chapter 1). Grease the shift lever spring seat and shift lever tip. Use the matchmarks to install the driveshaft.

Cressida

Perform the removal procedures as outlined for the Corona. In addition, perform the following:

1. Remove the accelerator connecting rod from the linkage.
2. With the car jacked up and supported:
   a. Remove the left hand, rear stone shield before removing the clutch release cylinder.
   b. Remove the flywheel housing lower cover and its braces.
3. Installation is the reverse or removal.
NOTE: *Use a clutch guide tool, during installation, to locate the clutch disc.*

Van

1. Disconnect the battery ground.
2. Raise and support the vehicle on jackstands.
3. Drain the transmission.
4. Matchmark the driveshaft and remove it from the vehicle.
5. Remove the transmission control cables.
6. Remove the clutch release cylinder.
7. Remove the starter.
8. Disconnect the speedometer cable.
9. Disconnect the back-up light switch.
10. Remove the exhaust clamp and bracket from the case.
11. Remove the stiffener plate.
12. Take up the weight of the transmission with a floor jack.
13. Remove the engine rear mount and bracket.
14. Remove the engine-to-transmission attaching bolts and slide the transmission from the engine.
15. Installation is the reverse of removal. Coat the input shaft splines with chassis lube prior to installation. Observe the following torques:
- Transmission attaching bolts: 53 ft.lb.
- Engine rear mount bolts: 20 ft.lb.
- Fill the unit with 80W-90 gear oil.

CLUTCH

The clutch is a single plate, dry disc type. Some early models use a coil spring pressure plate. Later models use a diaphragm spring pressure plate. Clutch release bearings are sealed ball bearing units which need no lubrication and should never be washed in any kind of solvent.

PEDAL HEIGHT ADJUSTMENT

Adjust the pedal height to the specification given in the following chart, by rotating the pedal stop (nut).

FREE PLAY ADJUSTMENT

1. Adjust the clearance between the master cylinder piston and the pushrod to the specifications given in the Clutch Pedal Free Play Adjustments chart. Loosen the pushrod locknut and rotate the pushrod while depressing the clutch pedal lightly with your finger.
2. Tighten the locknut when finished with the adjustment.
3. Adjust the release cylinder free play by loosening the release cylinder pushrod locknut and rotating the pushrod until the specification in the chart is obtained.
4. Measure the clutch pedal free play after performing the above adjustments. If it fails to fall within specifications, repeat Steps 1–3 until it does.

REMOVAL AND INSTALLATION

CAUTION: *Do not allow grease or oil to get on any of the disc, pressure plate, or flywheel surfaces.*

1. Remove the transmission from the car as previously detailed.
2. Remove the clutch cover and disc from the bellhousing.
3. Unfasten the release fork bearing clips. Withdraw the release bearing hub, complete with the release bearing.

Pedal Height Specifications

Model	Height (in.)	Measure Between:
Corona ('70–'73)	5.7–6.1	Pedal pad and floor mat
Corona ('74–'77)	6.3–6.7	Pedal pad and top of asphalt
Corona ('78–'82)	6.5–6.9	Pedal pad and floor mat
Mark II/4	6.0–6.2	Pedal pad and top of floor panel
Mark II/6	6.2–6.6 ①	Pedal pad and asphalt seat
Crown 2300	5.7	Pedal pad and floor
Crown 2600	6.8	Pedal pad and asphalt seat
Cressida	6.1–6.5	From floor mat
Camry	7.6–8.0	Pedal pad and kickpanel
Van	6.5–8.0	Pedal pad and floor mat

① 1976—6–6.4

Clutch Pedal Free-Play Adjustments

Model	Master Cylinder Piston to Pushrod Clearance (in.)	Release Cylinder to Release Fork Free-Play (in.)	Pedal Free-Play (in.)
Corona 2000	0.02–0.12	0.08–0.14	1.00–1.75
Corona 2000/2200 ④	—	0.08–0.12 ⑥	0.04–0.28 ⑤
Corona 1978–80	Not adj	Not adj	0.51–0.91
Mark II/4	①	0.08–0.14	0.79–1.58 ⑦
Mark II/6	0.02–0.12	0.08–0.12	1.20–1.80
Crown 2300	0.02–0.10 ②	0.08–0.14	1.40–2.00
Crown 2600	0.02–0.12	0.08–0.14 ③	1.40–2.20
Van	Not adj.	Not adj.	0.20–0.59
Camry	Not adj.	Not adj.	0.20–0.59

① Not adjustable
② Measured at clutch pedal
③ Adjustable type only
④ 1975–79
⑤ 1978–79: 0.2–0.6
⑥ 1978–79: Not adjustable
⑦ 1976—0.04–0.28

4. Remove the tension spring from the clutch linkage.

5. Remove the release fork and support.

6. Punch matchmarks on the clutch cover and the pressure plate so that the pressure plate can be returned to its original position during installation.

7. Slowly unfasten the screws which attach the retracting springs.

NOTE: *If the screws are released too fast, the clutch assembly will fly apart, causing possible injury or loss of parts.*

8. Separate the pressure plate from the clutch cover/spring assembly.

9. Inspect the parts for wear or deterioration. Replace parts as required.

10. Installation is performed in the reverse order of removal. Several points should be noted, however:

a. Be sure to align the matchmarks on the clutch cover and pressure plate which were made during disassembly.

b. Apply a thin coating of multipurpose grease to the release bearing hub and release fork contact points. Also, pack the

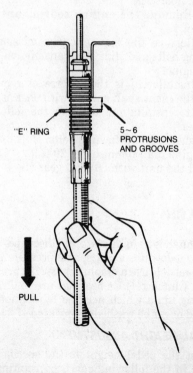

"E" RING

5~6 PROTRUSIONS AND GROOVES

PULL

PEDAL FREE-PLAY

PEDAL HEIGHT

1. Master cylinder pushrod
2. Pushrod locknut
3. Clevis
4. Pedal stop (bolt)

Clutch pedal adjustment

Adjusting the clutch release cable (typical)

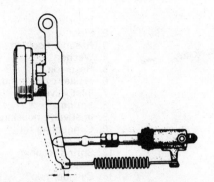

Release cylinder free-play is the distance between the arrows

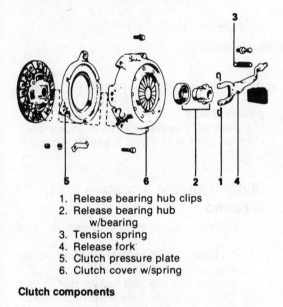

1. Release bearing hub clips
2. Release bearing hub w/bearing
3. Tension spring
4. Release fork
5. Clutch pressure plate
6. Clutch cover w/spring

Clutch components

Lightly apply multipurpose grease to points "1" and "2"

groove inside the clutch hub with multipurpose grease.

c. Center the clutch disc by using a clutch pilot tool or an old input shaft. Insert the pilot into the end of the input shaft front bearing and bolt the clutch to the flywheel.

NOTE: *Bolt the clutch assembly to the flywheel in two or three stages, evenly and to the torque specified in the chart below.*

d. Adjust the clutch as outlined below.

Master Cylinder (Clutch)

REMOVAL AND INSTALLATION

1. Remove the clevis pin.
2. Detach the hydraulic line from the tube.
CAUTION: *Do not spill brake fluid on the painted surfaces of the vehicle.*
3. Unfasten the bolts which secure the master cylinder to the firewall. Withdraw the assembly.
4. Installation is the reverse of removal. Bleed the system as detailed following. Adjust the clutch pedal height and free play as previously detailed.

OVERHAUL

1. Clamp the master cylinder body in a vise with soft jaws.
2. Separate the reservoir assembly from the master cylinder.
3. Remove the snapring and remove the pushrod/piston assembly.
4. Inspect all of the parts and replace any which are worn or defective.
NOTE: *Honing of the cylinder may be necessary to smooth pitting.*
Assembly is performed in the following order:
1. Coat all parts with clean brake fluid, prior to assembly.
2. Install the piston assembly in the cylinder bore.
3. Fit the pushrod over the washer and secure them with the snapring.
4. Install the reservoir.

Clutch Torque Specifications (ft. lbs.)

Model	Release Fork	Retracting Spring Bolts	Clutch Cover-to-Flywheel Bolts
Corona	13.7–22.4	10.9–15.9	7.2–11.6 ②
Mark II/4	14–22	—	11
Mark II/6	—	2.9–5.1	10.8–15.9
Crown 2300	—	3–5	6–9.5
Crown 2600	—	2.9–5.1	7.2–11.6

① 1975 Corolla—15–16 ft. lbs.; 1976 and later—10.9–15.9 ft. lbs.
② 1976 and later—10.9–15.9 ft. lbs.

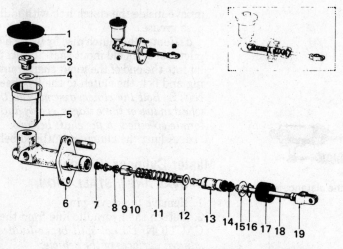

1. Filler cap
2. Float
3. Reservoir setbolt
4. Washer
5. Reservoir
6. Master cylinder body
7. Inlet valve
8. Spring
9. Inlet valve housing
10. Connecting rod
11. Spring
12. Spring retainer
13. Piston
14. Cylinder cup
15. Plate
16. Snap-ring
17. Boot
18. Pushrod
19. Clevis

Clutch master cylinder components

Clutch Slave Cylinder

REMOVAL AND INSTALLATION

CAUTION: *Avoid spilling brake fluid on any painted surface.*

1. Raise and support the front end on jackstands.
2. Remove the gravel shield to gain access to the slave cylinder.
3. Remove the clutch fork return spring.
4. Disconnect the hydraulic line from the slave cylinder.
5. Screw the threaded end of the pushrod in.
6. Remove the cylinder attaching nuts and pull out the cylinder.
7. Installation is the reverse of removal.

OVERHAUL

1. Remove the pushrod and rubber boot.
2. Remove the piston, with cup. Don't remove the cup unless you are replacing it.
3. Wash all parts in clean brake fluid. Inspect all parts for wear or damage. The bore can be honed to remove minor imperfections. If

it is severely pitted or scored, the cylinder must be replaced. If piston-to-bore clearance is greater than 0.006″, replace the unit.

4. Assembly is the reverse of disassembly. Coat all parts with clean brake fluid prior to assembly.

Clutch Hydraulic System

BLEEDING

1. Fill the master cylinder reservoir with brake fluid.

CAUTION: *Do not spill brake fluid on the painted surfaces of the vehicle.*

2. Remove the cap and loosen the bleeder plug. Block the outlet hole with your finger.
3. Pump the clutch pedal several times, then take your finger from the hole while depressing the clutch pedal. Allow the air to flow out. Place your finger back over the hole and release the pedal.
4. After fluid pressure can be felt (with your finger), tighten the bleeder plug.
5. Fit a bleeder tube over the plug and place

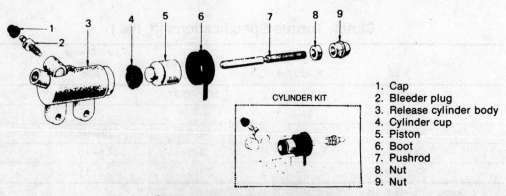

CYLINDER KIT

1. Cap
2. Bleeder plug
3. Release cylinder body
4. Cylinder cup
5. Piston
6. Boot
7. Pushrod
8. Nut
9. Nut

Clutch release cylinder components

the other end into a clean jar half filled with brake fluid.

6. Depress the clutch pedal, loosen the bleeder plug with a wrench, and allow the fluid to flow into the jar.

7. Tighten the plug and then release the clutch pedal.

8. Repeat Steps 6–7 until no air bubbles are visible in the bleeder tube.

9. When there are no more air bubbles, tighten the plug while keeping the clutch pedal fully depressed. Replace the cap.

10. Fill the master cylinder to the specified level. (See Chapter 1).

11. Check the system for leaks.

AUTOMATIC TRANSMISSION

Understanding Automatic Transmissions

The automatic transmission allows engine torque and power to be transmitted to the rear wheels within a narrow range of engine operating speeds. The transmission will allow the engine to turn fast enough to produce plenty of power and torque at very low speeds, while keeping it at a sensible rpm at high vehicle speeds. The transmission performs this job entirely without driver assistance. The transmission uses a light fluid as the medium for the transmission of power. This fluid also works in the operation of various hydraulic control circuits and as a lubricant. Because the transmission fluid performs all of these three functions, trouble within the unit can easily travel from one part to another. For this reason, and because of the complexity and unusual operating principles of the transmission, a very sound understanding of the basic principles of operation will simplify troubleshooting.

THE TORQUE CONVERTER

The torque converter replaces the conventional clutch. It has three functions:

1. It allows the engine to idle with the vehicle at a standstill even with the transmission in gear.

2. It allows the transmission to shift from range to range smoothly, without requiring that the driver close the throttle during the shift.

3. It multiplies engine torque to an increasing extent as vehicle speed drops and throttle opening is increased. This has the effect of making the transmission more responsive and reduces the amount of shifting required.

The torque converter is a metal case which is shaped like a sphere that has been flattened on opposite sides. It is bolted to the rear end of the engine's crankshaft. Generally, the entire metal case rotates at engine speed and serves as the engine's flywheel.

The case contains three sets of blades. One set is attached directly to the case. This set forms the torus or pump. Another set is directly connected to the output shaft, and forms the turbine. The third set is mounted on a hub which, in turn, is mounted on a stationary shaft through a one-way clutch. This third set is known as the stator.

A pump, which is driven by the converter hub at engine speed, keeps the torque converter full of transmission fluid at all times. Fluid flows continuously through the unit to provide cooling.

Under low speed acceleration, the torque converter functions as follows: The torus is turning faster than the turbine. It picks up fluid at the center of the converter and, through centrifugal force, slings it outward. Since the outer edge of the converter moves faster than the portions at the center, the fluid picks up speed.

The fluid then enters the outer edge of the turbine blades. It then travels back toward the center of the converter case along the turbine blades. In impinging upon the turbine blades, the fluid loses the energy picked up in the torus.

If the fluid were now to immediately be returned directly into the torus, both halves of the converter would have to turn at approximately the same speed at all times, and torque input and output would both be the same.

In flowing through the torus and turbine, the fluid picks up two types of flow, or flow in two separate directions. It flows through the turbine blades, and it spins with the engine. The stator, whose blades are stationary when the vehicle is being accelerated at low speeds, converts one type of flow into another. Instead of allowing the fluid to flow straight back into the torus, the stator's curved blades turn the fluid almost 90 degrees toward the direction of rotation of the engine. Thus the fluid does not flow as fast toward the torus, but is already spinning when the torus picks it up. This has the effect of allowing the torus to turn much faster than the turbine. This difference in speed may be compared to the difference in speed between the smaller and larger gears in any gear train. The result is that engine power output is higher, and engine torque is multiplied.

As the speed of the turbine increases, the fluid spins faster and faster in the direction of engine rotation. As a result, the ability of the stator to redirect the fluid flow is reduced. Under cruising conditions, the stator is eventually forced to rotate on its one-way clutch in the direction of engine rotation. Under these conditions, the torque converter begins to behave almost like a solid shaft, with the torus and turbine speeds being almost equal.

THE PLANETARY GEARBOX

The ability of the torque converter to multiply engine torque is limited. Also, the unit tends to be more efficient when the turbine is rotating at relatively high speeds. Therefore, a planetary gearbox is used to carry the power output of the turbine to the driveshaft.

Planetary gears function very similarly to conventional transmission gears. However, their construction is different in that three elements make up one gear system, and in that all three elements are different from one another. The three elements are: an outer gear that is shaped like a hoop, with teeth cut into the inner surface. A sun gear, mounted on a shaft and located at the very center of the outer gear, and a set of three planet gears, held by pins in a ring-like planet carrier and meshing with both the sun gear and the outer gear. Either the outer gear or the sun gear may be held stationary, providing more than one possible torque multiplication factor for each set of gears. Also, if all three gears are forced to rotate at the same speed, the gearset forms, in effect, a solid shaft.

Most modern automatics use the planetary gears to provide either a single reduction ratio of about 1.8:1, or two reduction gears: a low of about 2.5:1, and an intermediate of about 1.5:1. Bands and clutches are used to hold various portions of the gearsets to the transmission case or to the shaft on which they are mounted. Shifting is accomplished, then, by changing the portion of each planetary gearset which is held to the transmission case or to the shaft.

THE SERVOS AND ACCUMULATORS

The servos are hydraulic pistons and cylinders. They resemble the hydraulic actuators used on many familiar machines, such as bulldozers. Hydraulic fluid enters the cylinder, under pressure, and forces the piston to move to engage the band or clutches.

The accumulators are used to cushion the engagement of the servos. The transmission fluid must pass through the accumulator on the way to the servo. The accumulator housing contains a thin piston which is sprung away from the discharge passage of the accumulator. When fluid passes through the accumulator on the way to the servo, it must move the piston against spring pressure, and this action smooths out the action of the servo.

THE HYDRAULIC CONTROL SYSTEM

The hydraulic pressure used to operate the servos comes from the main transmission oil pump. This fluid is channeled to the various servos through the shift valves. There is generally a manual shift valve which is operated by the transmission selector lever and an automatic shift valve for each automatic upshift the transmission provides: i.e., two-speed automatics have a low-high shift valve, while three-speeds have a 1–2 valve, and a 2–3 valve.

There are two pressures which effect the operation of these valves. One is the governor pressure which is affected by vehicle speed. The other is the modulator pressure which is affected by intake manifold vacuum or throttle position. Governor pressure rises with an increase in vehicle speed, and modulator pressure rises as the throttle is opened wider. By responding to these two pressures, the shift valves cause the upshift points to be delayed with increased throttle opening to make the best use of the engine's power output.

Most transmissions also make use of an auxiliary circuit for downshifting. This circuit may be actuated by the throttle linkage or the vacuum line which actuates the modulator, or by a cable or solenoid. It applies pressure to a special downshift surface on the shift valve or valves.

The transmission modulator also governs the line pressure, used to actuate the servos. In this way, the clutches and bands will be actuated with a force matching the torque output of the engine.

Transmission Application

All Mark II, all Crown and 1970–73 (early Corona, use the 3-speed Toyoglide transmissions (A30).

Starting in the spring of 1973, Corona models came equipped with a 3-speed Aisin-Warner automatic transmission (A40). The 1981 Corona and Cressida use the A40D overdrive automatic. 1982 and later Cressida models use the A43DE. The Van uses an A44DL unit.

Replenish the fluid through the filler tube with type F fluid for all models built until July, 1983; Dexron®II for all models built beginning July 1983. Models using Dexron®II have a DII stamped on the pan or drain plug. Add fluid to the top of the COLD or HOT range, depending upon engine temperature.

This section covers routine service and basic adjustments, which may be performed by the owner. More complex service is best left to an authorized service facility, as special tools and service procedures are required.

Transmission

REMOVAL AND INSTALLATION

3-Speed Toyoglide (A-30)

1. Disconnect the battery.
2. Remove the air cleaner and disconnect the accelerator torque link or the cable.
3. Disconnect the throttle link rod at the carburetor side, then disconnect the backup light wiring at the firewall (on early models).
4. Jack up the car and support it on stands, then drain the transmission (use a clean receptacle so that the fluid can be checked for color, smell and foreign matter).
5. Disconnect all shift linkage.
6. On early models, remove the cross shaft from the frame.
7. Disconnect the throttle link rod at the transmission side and remove the speedometer cable, cooler lines and parking brake equalizer brake.
8. Loosen the exhaust flange nuts and remove the exhaust pipe clamp and bracket.
9. Remove the driveshaft and the rear mounting bracket, then lower the rear end of the transmission carefully.
10. Unbolt the torque converter from the drive plate. Support the engine with a suitable jack stand and remove the seven bolts that hold the transmission to the engine.
11. Reverse the order of the removal procedures with the following precautions:
   a. Install the drive plate and ring gear, tighten the attaching bolts to 37–43 ft.lb.
   b. After assembling the torque converter to the transmission, check the clearance, it should be about 15mm.
   c. Before installing the transmission, install the oil pump locator pin on the torque converter to facilitate installation.
   d. While rotating the crankshaft, tighten the converter attaching bolts, a little at a time.
   e. After installing the throttle connecting second rod, make sure the throttle valve lever indicator aligns with the mark on the transmission with the carburetor throttle valve fully opened. If required, adjust the rod.
   f. To install the transmission control rod correctly, move the transmission lever to N (Neutral), and the selector lever to Neutral. Fill the transmission. Run the engine at idle speed and apply the brakes while moving the selector lever through all positions, then return it to Neutral.
   g. After warming the engine, move the selector lever through all positions, then back to Neutral, and check the fluid level. Fill as necessary.
   h. Adjust the engine idle to 550–650 rpm with the selector lever at Drive. Road test the vehicle.
   i. With the selector lever at 2 or Drive, check the point at which the transmission shifts. Check for shock, noise and slipping with the selector lever in all positions. Check for leaks from the transmission.

A-40, A-40D, and A-43DE

1. Perform Steps 1–3 of the 3-speed Toyoglide removal procedure.
2. Remove the upper starter mounting nuts.
3. Raise the car and support it securely with jack stands. Drain the transmission.
4. Remove the lower starter mounting bolt and lay the starter along side of the engine. Don't let it hang by the wires.
5. Unbolt the parking brake equalizer support.
6. Matchmark the driveshaft and the companion flange, to ensure correct installation. Remove the bolts securing the driveshaft to the companion flange.
7. Slide the driveshaft straight back and out of the transmission. Use a spare U-joint yoke or tie a plastic bag over the end of the transmission to keep any fluid from dripping out.
8. Remove the bolts from the cross-shaft body bracket, the cotter pin from the manual lever, and the cross-shaft socket from the transmission.
9. Remove the exhaust pipe bracket from the torque converter bell housing.
10. Disconnect the oil cooler lines from the transmission and remove the line bracket from the bell housing.
11. Disconnect the speedometer cable from the transmission.
12. Unbolt both support braces from the bell housing.
13. Use a transmission jack to raise the transmission slightly.
14. Unbolt the rear crossmember and lower the transmission about 76mm.
15. Pry the two rubber torque converter access plugs out of their holes at the back of the engine.
16. Remove the six torque converter mounting bolts through the access hole. Rotate the engine with the crankshaft pulley.
17. Cut the head off a bolt to make a guide pin for the torque converter. Install the pin on the converter.
18. Remove the converter bell housing-to-engine bolts.
19. Push on the end of the guide pin in order

to remove the converter with the transmission. Remove the transmission rearward and then bring it out from under the car.

CAUTION: *Don't catch the throttle cable during removal.*

20. Installation is the reverse of removal. Be sure to note the following, however:

    a. Install the two long bolts on the upper converter housing and tighten them to 36–58 ft.lb.

    b. Tighten the converter-to-flex plate bolts finger tight, and then tighten them with a torque wrench to 11–16 ft.lb.

    c. When installing the speedometer cable, make sure that the felt dust protector and washer are on the cable end.

    d. Tighten the cooling line and exhaust pipe bracket mounting bolts to 37–58 ft.lb. Tighten the cooling lines to 14–22 ft.lb.

    e. Align the matchmarks made on the driveshaft and the companion flange during removal. Tighten the driveshaft mounting bolts to 11–16 ft.lb.

    f. Be sure to install the oil pan drain plug. Tighten it to 11–14 ft.lb.

    g. Adjust the throttle cable.

    h. Fill the transmission to the proper capacity.

    i. Road test the car and check for leaks.

Van

1. Disconnect the battery ground.
2. Disconnect the throttle cable.
3. Disconnect all wires attached to the transmission.
4. Raise and support the vehicle on jackstands.
5. Drain the fluid.
6. Matchmark and remove the driveshaft.
7. Disconnect the exhaust pipe from the case.
8. Disconnect the shift cable.
9. Disconnect the speedometer cable.
10. Disconnect the oil cooler lines.
11. Remove the starter.
12. Support the transmission with a floor jack.
13. Support the fuel tank on jackstands, remove the fuel tank mounting bolts, and, remove the rear transmission support bolt.
14. Remove the two stiffener plates from the transmission.
15. Pry out the service hole cover at the torque converter housing and remove the six torque converter bolts.
16. Remove the transmission-to-engine bolts and slowly and carefully guide the transmission away from the engine.
17. Installation is the reverse of removal. Observe the following torques:

•Transmission-to-engine: 47 ft.lb.
•Torque converter: 14 ft.lb.
•Stiffener plates: 27 ft.lb.
•Starter: 27 ft.lb.
•Rear support bolt: 36 ft.lb.

Fill the unit with Dexron®II ATF.

PAN REMOVAL

1. Unfasten the oil plug and drain the fluid from the transmission.
2. Unfasten the pan securing bolts.
3. Withdraw the pan.
4. Installation is performed in the reverse order of removal. Torque the pan securing bolts to 4–6 ft.lb. (17–20 ft.lb. A40 and A43). Refill the transmission with fluid as outlined in Chapter 1.

FRONT BAND ADJUSTMENT

3-Speed Toyoglide

1. Remove the oil pan as previously outlined.
2. Pry the band engagement lever toward band with a screwdriver.
3. The gap between end of the piston rod and the engagement bolt should be 3.5mm.
4. If the gap does not meet the specification, adjust it by turning the engagement bolt.
5. Install the oil pan and refill the transmission as previously outlined.

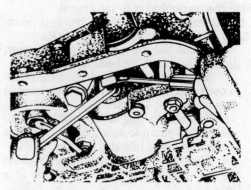

Adjusting the three-speed Toyoglide front band

REAR BAND ADJUSTMENT

3-Speed Toyoglide

The read band adjusting bolt is located on the outside of the case, so it is not necessary to remove the oil pan in order to adjust the band.

1. Loosen the adjusting bolt locknut and fully screw in the adjusting bolt.
2. Loosen the adjusting bolt one turn.
3. Tighten the locknut while holding the bolt so that it cannot turn.

BAND ADJUSTMENTS

3-Speed A-40

The A-40 transmission has no bands, and therefore no band adjustments are possible. The only external adjustments are throttle and shift linkages.

NEUTRAL SAFETY SWITCH ADJUSTMENT

3-Speed Column Selector

The neutral safety switch/reverse lamp switch on the Toyoglide transmission with a column mounted selector is located under the hood on the shift linkage. If the switch is not functioning properly, adjust as follows:

1. Loosen the switch securing bolt.
2. Move the switch so that its arm just contacts the control shaft lever when the gear selector is in Drive (D) position.
3. Tighten the switch securing bolt.
4. Check the operation of the switch. The car should start only in Park (P) or Neutral (N) and the back-up lamps should come on only when Reverse (R) is selected.
5. If the switch cannot be adjusted so that it functions properly, replace it with a new one. Perform the adjustment as previously outlined.

3-Speed Console Shift

Models with a console mounted selector have the neutral safety switch on the linkage located beneath the console.

To adjust it, proceed in the following manner:

1. Remove the screws securing the center console.
2. Unfasten the console multiconnector, if so equipped, and completely remove the console.
3. Adjust the switch in the manner outlined in the preceding column selector section.
4. Install the console in the reverse order of removal after completion of the switch adjustment.

Loosening the column shift swivel locknut

SHIFT LINKAGE ADJUSTMENT

3-Speed Toyoglide

The transmission should be engaged, in the gear selected as indicated on the shift quadrant. If it is not, then adjust the linkage as follows:

1. Check all of the shift linkage bushings for wear. Replace any worn bushings.
2. Loosen the connecting rod swivel locknut.
3. Move the selector lever and check movement of the pointer in the shift quadrant.
4. When the control shaft is set in the neutral position the quadrant pointer should indicate N as well.

Steps 5–7 apply only to cars equipped with column mounted gear selectors.

5. If the pointer does not indicate Neutral (N), then check the drive cord adjustment.
6. Remove the steering column shroud.
7. Turn the drive cord adjuster with a phillips screwdriver until the pointer indicates Neutral (N).

Steps 8–10 apply to both column mounted and floor mounted selectors:

8. Position the manual valve lever on the transmission so that it is in the Neutral position.

Adjusting the neutral safety switch on cars with three-speed automatic and floorshift

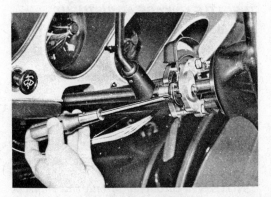

Adjusting the column shift indicator drive cord

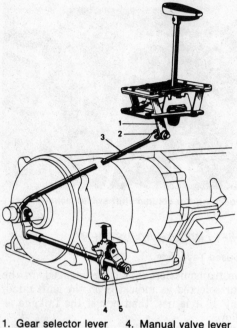

1. Gear selector lever
2. Intermediate rod
3. Control rod
4. Manual valve lever
5. Shaft

Toyoglide floorshift components

9. Lock the connecting rod swivel with the locknut so that the pointer, selector, and manual valve lever are all positioned in Neutral.

10. Check the operation of the gear selector by moving it through all ranges.

3-Speed A-40

1. Loosen the adjusting nut on the linkage and check the linkage for freedom of movement.

2. Push the manual valve lever toward the front of the car, as far as it will go.

3. Bring the lever back to its third notch (Neutral).

4. Have an assistant hold the shift lever in Neutral, while you tighten the linkage adjusting nut so that it can't slip.

THROTTLE LINKAGE ADJUSTMENT

3-Speed Toyoglide

1. Loosen the locknut at each end of the linkage adjusting turnbuckle.

2. Detach the throttle linkage connecting rod from the carburetor.

3. Align the pointer on the throttle valve lever with the mark stamped on the transmission case.

4. Rotate the turnbuckle so that the end of the throttle linkage rod and the carburetor throttle lever are aligned.

NOTE: *The carburetor throttle valve must be fully opened during this adjustment.*

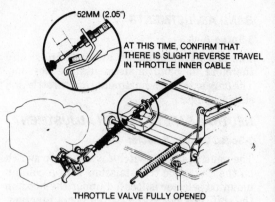

52MM (2.05")

AT THIS TIME, CONFIRM THAT THERE IS SLIGHT REVERSE TRAVEL IN THROTTLE INNER CABLE

THROTTLE VALVE FULLY OPENED

A-40 throttle linkage adjustment

5. Tighten the turnbuckle locknuts and reconnect the throttle rod to the carburetor.

6. Open the throttle valve and check the pointer alignment with the mark on the transmission case.

7. Road test the car. If the transmission hunts, i.e., keeps shifting rapidly back and forth between gears at certain speeds or if it fails to downshift properly when going up hills, repeat the throttle linkage adjustment.

3-Speed A-40 and A-40D

1. Remove the air cleaner.

2. Confirm that the accelerator linkage opens the throttle fully. Adjust the link as necessary.

3. Peel the rubber dust boot back from the throttle cable.

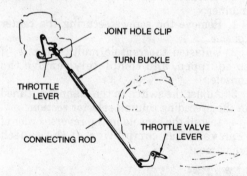

JOINT HOLE CLIP

TURN BUCKLE

THROTTLE LEVER

THROTTLE VALVE LEVER

CONNECTING ROD

Toyoglide throttle linkage components

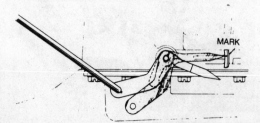

MARK

Toyoglide throttle linkage aligning marks

4. Loosen the adjustment nuts on the throttle cable bracket (rocker cover) just enough to allow cable housing movement.

5. Have an assistant depress the accelerator pedal fully.

6. Adjust the cable housing so that the distance between its end and the cable stop collar is 52mm.

7. Tighten the adjustment nuts. Make sure that the adjustment hasn't changed. Install the dust boot and the air cleaner.

Drive Train

+7

DRIVELINE

Driveshaft and U-Joints

REMOVAL AND INSTALLATION

1. Raise the rear of the car with jacks and support the rear axle housing with jackstands.
CAUTION: *Be sure that the car is securely supported. Remember, you will be working underneath it.*
2. Unfasten the bolts which attach the driveshaft universal joint yoke flange to the mounting flange on the differential drive pinion.
3. On models equipped with three universal joints, perform the following:
   a. Withdraw the driveshaft subassembly from the U-joint sleeve yoke.
   b. Unfasten the center support bearing from its bracket.
4. Remove the driveshaft end from the transmission.
5. Install an old U-joint yoke in the transmission or, if none is available, use a plastic bag secured with a rubber band over the hole to keep the transmission oil from running out.
6. Withdraw the driveshaft from beneath the vehicle.
Installation is performed in the following order:

1. Apply multipurpose grease on the section of the U-joint sleeve which is to be inserted into the transmission.
2. Insert the driveshaft sleeve into the transmission.
CAUTION: *Be careful not to damage any of the seals.*
3. For models equipped with three U-joints and center bearings, perform the following:
   a. Adjust the center bearing clearance with no load placed on the driveline components. The top of the rubber center cushion should be 1mm behind the center of the elongated bolt hole.
   b. Install the center bearing assembly.
NOTE: *Use the same number of washers on the center bearing bracket as were removed.*
4. Secure the U-joint flange to the differential pinion flange with the mounting bolts.
CAUTION: *Be sure that the bolts are of the same type as those removed and that they are tightened securely.*

U-JOINT OVERHAUL

1. Matchmark the yoke and the driveshaft.
2. Remove the lockrings from the bearings.
3. Position the yoke on vise jaws. Using a bearing remover and a hammer, gently tap the remover until the bearing is driven out of the yoke about 12mm.

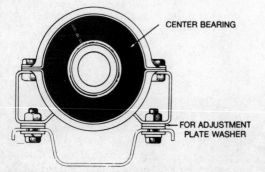

CENTER BEARING

FOR ADJUSTMENT PLATE WASHER

Center bearing adjustment

Press the bearing into place with a vise

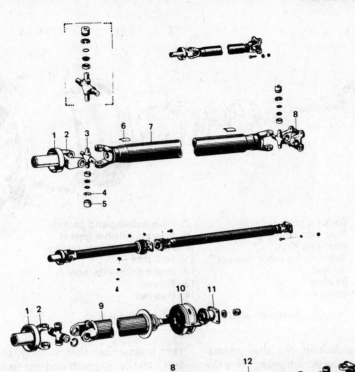

1. Transmission end of driveshaft
2. U-joint yoke and sleeve
3. U-joint spider
4. Snap-ring
5. U-joint spider bearing
6. Balancing weight
7. Driveshaft
8. U-joint yoke flange
9. Intermediate driveshaft assembly
10. Center bearing support
11. U-joint flange assembly
12. Driveshaft

Two-piece driveshaft only

Driveshaft components—upper illustration shows a single-piece driveshaft; lower, a two-piece driveshaft

4. Place the tool in the vise and drive the yoke away from the tool until the bearing is removed.

5. Repeat Steps 3 and 4 for the other bearings.

6. Check for worn or damaged parts. Inspect the bearing journal surfaces for wear.

U-joint assembly is performed in the following order:

1. Install the bearing cups, seals, and O-rings in the spider.

2. Grease the spider and the bearings.

3. Position the spider in the yoke.

4. Start the bearings in the yoke and then press them into pace, using a vise.

5. Repeat Step 4 for the other bearings.

6. If the axial play of the spider is greater than 0.05mm, select lockrings which will provide the correct play. Be sure that the lockrings are the same size on both sides or driveshaft noise and vibration will result.

7. Check the U-joint assembly for smooth operation.

REAR AXLE

Understanding Rear Axles

The rear axle is a special type of transmission that reduces the speed of the drive from the engine and transmission and divides the power to the rear wheels. Power enters the rear axle from the driveshaft via the companion flange. The flange is mounted on the drive pinion shaft. The drive pinion shaft and gear which carry the power into the differential turn at engine speed. The gear on the end of the pinion shaft drives a large ring gear the axis of rotation of which is 90 degrees away from the of the pinion. The pinion and gear reduce the gear ratio of the axle, and change the direction of rotation to turn the axle shafts which drive both wheels. The rear axle gear ratio is found by dividing the number of pinion gear teeth into the number of ring gear teeth.

The ring gear drives the differential case. The case provides the two mounting points for

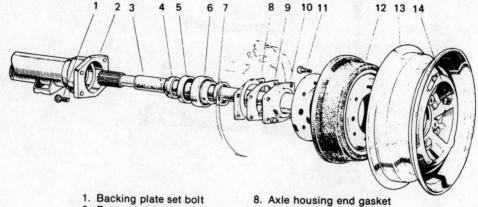

1. Backing plate set bolt
2. Rear axle housing
3. Rear axle shaft
4. Axle bearing inner retainer
5. Oil seal
6. Bearing
7. Spacer
8. Axle housing end gasket
9. Bearing retainer gasket
10. Axle bearing inner retainer
11. Hub bolt
12. Brake drum assembly
13. Wheel
14. Hub nut

Rear axle shaft and related components

the ends of a pinion shaft on which are mounted two pinion gears. The pinion gears drive the two side gears, one of which is located on the inner end of each axle shaft.

By driving the axle shafts through the arrangement, the differential allows the outer drive wheel to turn faster than the inner drive wheel in a turn.

The main drive pinion and the side bearings, which bear the weight of the differential case, are shimmed to provide proper bearing preload, and to position the pinion and ring gears properly.

NOTE: *The proper adjustment of the relationship of the ring and pinion gears is critical. It should be attempted only by those with extensive equipment and/or experience.*

Limited slip differentials include clutches which tend to link each axle shaft to the differential case. Clutches may be engaged either by spring action or by pressure produced by the torque on the axles during a turn. During turning on a dry pavement, the effects of the clutches are overcome, and each wheel turns at the required speed. When slippage occurs at either wheel, however, the clutches will transmit some of the power to the wheel which has the greater amount of traction. Because of the presence of clutches, limited slip units require a special lubricant.

Determining Axle Ratio

The drive axle of a car is said to have a certain axle ratio. This number (usually a whole number and a decimal fraction) is actually a comparison of the number of gear teeth on the ring gear and the pinion gear. For example, a 4.11

rear means that theoretically, there are 4.11 teeth on the ring gear and one tooth on the pinion gear or, put another way, the driveshaft must turn 4.11 times to turn the wheels once. Actually, on a 4.11 rear, there might be 37 teeth on the ring gear and 9 teeth on the pinion gear. By dividing the number of teeth on the pinion gear into the number of teeth on the ring gear, the numerical axle ratio (4.11) is obtained. This also provides a good method of ascertaining exactly what axle ratio one is dealing with.

Another method of determining gear ratio is to jack up and support the car so that both rear wheels are off the ground. Make a chalk mark on the rear wheel and the driveshaft. Put the transmission in neutral. Turn the rear wheel one complete turn and count the number of turns that the driveshaft makes. The number of turns that the driveshaft makes in one complete revolution of the rear wheel is an approximation of the rear axle ratio.

Axle Shaft

REMOVAL AND INSTALLATION

1. Raise the rear of the car and support it securely by using jackstands.

CAUTION: *Be sure that the vehicle is securely supported. Remember, you will be working underneath it.*

2. Drain the oil from the axle housing.

3. Remove the wheel disc, unfasten the lug nuts, and remove the wheel.

4. Punch matchmarks on the brake drum and the axle shaft to maintain rotational balance.

Axle Bearing Retaining Nut Specifications

Model	Torque Range (ft. lbs.)
Corona ('70–'73)	29–36
Corona ('74–'79)	43–53
Mark II/4	20–26
Mark II/6	43–52
Crown	29–40
Cressida	43–52

Using a slide hammer to remove the axle shaft

5. Remove the brake drum and related components, as detailed in Chapter 9.

6. Remove the rear bearing retaining nut.

7. Remove the backing plate attachment nuts through the access holes in the rear axle shaft flange.

8. Use a slide hammer with a suitable adapter to withdraw the axle shaft from its housing.

CAUTION: *Use care not to damage the oil seal when removing the axle shaft.*

9. Repeat the procedure for the axle shaft on the opposite side. Be careful not to mix the components of the two sides.

10. Installation is performed in the reverse order of removal. Coat the lips of the rear housing oil seal with multipurpose grease prior to installation of the rear axle shaft. Torque the bearing retaining nut to the specifications given in the chart below.

NOTE: *Always use new nuts, as they are of the self-locking type.*

Suspension and Steering

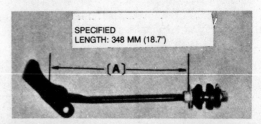

FRONT SUSPENSION

Springs

REMOVAL AND INSTALLATION

Corona, except MacPherson Strut

1. Remove the hubcap and loosen the nuts.
2. Raise the front of the car and support it by using jackstands.
   CAUTION: *Be sure that the car is securely supported. Remember, you will be working underneath it.*
3. Remove the lug nuts and the wheel.
4. Remove the shock absorber as detailed in the appropriate following section. Unfasten the stabilizer bar from the lower control arm (if equipped).
5. Remove the dust cover.
6. Install a coil spring compressor and compress the spring until there is no load on it. Place a jack under the spring seat for safety.
7. Unfasten the lower ball joint retaining bolts and withdraw the ball joint, complete with the steering knuckle, from the lower control arm.
8. Slowly and carefully loosen the spring compressor and remove the spring. (Lower the jack under the spring seat first).
9. Inspect the spring, ball joint, and related components for wear or damage. Replace any parts necessary.
10. Installation is performed in the reverse order of removal. If the spring is being replaced with a new one, be sure to purchase one of the correct load tolerance for your Corona. The ball joint/steering knuckle assembly securing bolts should be tightened to the following specifications:
   1970-73
   - 12mm bolts: 58–83 ft.lb.
   - 8mm bolts: 11–16 ft.lb.
   1974 and Later
   - Steering knuckle bolts: 51–65 ft.lb.

After completing installation of the coil spring, check to ensure that it is properly seated in the lower suspension arm. Check front end alignment.

NOTE: *The coil springs are not interchangeable from the right side to the left side.*

Mark II and Crown

1. Perform Steps 1–3 of the Corona Coil Spring Removal and Installation procedure. Be sure to observe the Caution.
2. Unfasten the stabilizer bar.
3. Measure the distance between the serrated bolt holes on the front side of the torque strut and the attachment nut on the rear side to aid in installation. Remove the strut.

Use a spring compressor to remove the load from the coil spring

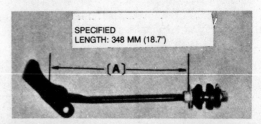

SPECIFIED LENGTH: 348 MM (18.7")

(A)

Measure the distance (A) before removing the strut

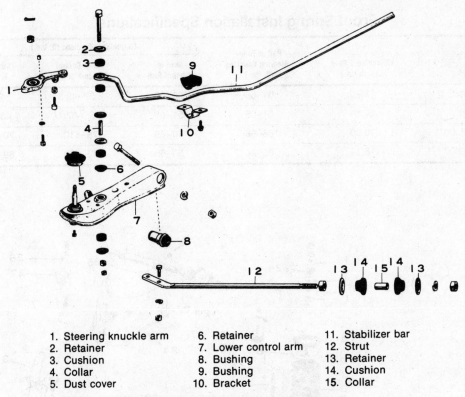

1. Steering knuckle arm
2. Retainer
3. Cushion
4. Collar
5. Dust cover
6. Retainer
7. Lower control arm
8. Bushing
9. Bushing
10. Bracket
11. Stabilizer bar
12. Strut
13. Retainer
14. Cushion
15. Collar

Components of the front suspension (typical)

4. On Crown models, disconnect the brake line.

5. Remove the shock absorber, as detailed in the appropriate following section.

6. Install the coil spring compressor on the third coil from the bottom. Tighten the compressor until the load is removed from the spring.

7. Remove the lower ball joint with a ball joint puller.

8. Unbolt and remove the lower control arm.

9. Carefully and slowly remove the spring compressor and withdraw the spring.

10. Inspect the components of the suspension which were removed for signs of wear or damage. Replace parts as required.

Installation is performed in the following order:

1. Install the lower control arm but do not fully tighten the mounting bolts.

2. Compress the spring with the spring compressor and install the spring.

NOTE: *Keep the spring compressed after installation.*

3. Install the lower ball joint on the steering knuckle and tighten it to the specifications given in the Front Spring Installation Specifications chart.

4. Install the strut on the lower control arm and temporarily install the other end on the frame.

a. The distance between the serrations and the nut should be the same as that measured during removal.

b. If a new strut is used, check the chart specifications for the proper installation distance.

c. Carefully install the rear side of the strut to the control arm and tighten the mounting nut to the specifications in the chart.

5. Slowly remove the spring compressor from the coil spring.

6. Install the shock absorber.

7. Install the stabilizer bar bracket and the bar.

NOTE: *Be sure to assemble the parts of the bracket in the order in which they were removed.*

8. Install the wheel, remove the jackstands, and lower the car.

9. Tighten the lower control arm and strut front mount to the specifications given in the chart.

NOTE: *These parts should be tightened with the equivalent of passenger weight in the car.*

10. Check the wheel alignment, after completing installation.

Front Spring Installation Specifications

Model	Replacment Strut Length (in.)	Ball Joint-to-Steering Knuckle (ft. lbs.)	Torque Specifications (ft. lbs.)		
			Strut-to-Control Arm	Lower Control Arm-to-Member	Strut-to-Frame
Mark II/4	18.70	51–65	50–65	32–43	54–80
Mark II/6	14.16	51–65	51–65	65–87	43–54
Crown 2300	16.00	66–96	50–65	75–110	70–110
Crown 2600	16.14	65–94	50–65	72–108	69–108

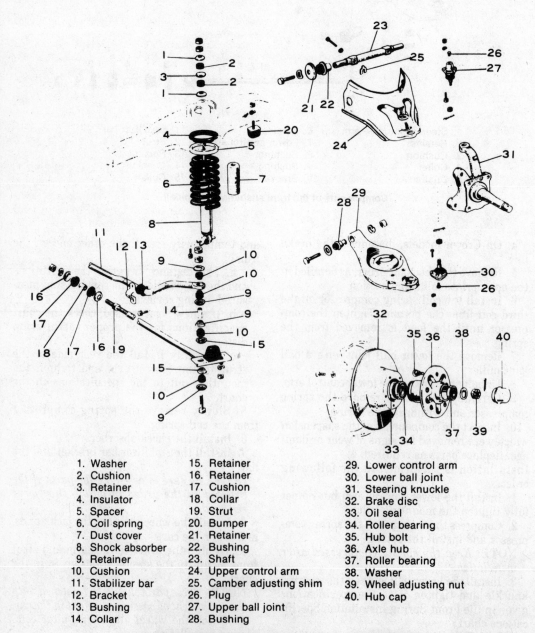

1. Washer	15. Retainer	29. Lower control arm
2. Cushion	16. Retainer	30. Lower ball joint
3. Retainer	17. Cushion	31. Steering knuckle
4. Insulator	18. Collar	32. Brake disc
5. Spacer	19. Strut	33. Oil seal
6. Coil spring	20. Bumper	34. Roller bearing
7. Dust cover	21. Retainer	35. Hub bolt
8. Shock absorber	22. Bushing	36. Axle hub
9. Retainer	23. Shaft	37. Roller bearing
10. Cushion	24. Upper control arm	38. Washer
11. Stabilizer bar	25. Camber adjusting shim	39. Wheel adjusting nut
12. Bracket	26. Plug	40. Hub cap
13. Bushing	27. Upper ball joint	
14. Collar	28. Bushing	

Components of the Crown front suspension—Mark II similar

Front Shock Absorber

REMOVAL AND INSTALLATION

1. Remove the hub cap and loosen the lug nuts.
2. Raise the front of the car and support it with jackstands.

CAUTION: *Be sure that the vehicle is supported securely. Remember, you will be working underneath it.*

3. Remove the lug nuts and the wheel.
4. Unfasten the double nuts at the top end of the shock absorber. Remove the cushions and cushion retainers.
5. Remove the two bolts which secure the lower end of the shock absorber to the lower control arm.
6. Remove the shock absorber.
7. Inspect and test the shock as detailed below.
8. Installation of the shock is performed in the reverse order of removal. Tighten the securing nuts and bolts to the following specifications:
   - Upper securing nuts: 14–22 ft.lb.
   - Lower mounting bolts: 11–16 ft.lb.

SHOCK ABSORBER INSPECTION

With the shock absorber removed from the vehicle, examine it for the following:

1. Fluid leaks.
2. Damaged housing.
3. Weakness.
4. Wear.
5. Bent or cracked studs.

Test shock absorber operation by placing it in an upright position. Push and pull on the shock. If the shock presents little resistance or binds, replace it with a new one.

MacPherson Struts

REMOVAL AND INSTALLATION

1. Disconnect the brake tube and flexible hose.
2. Remove the three nuts and lockwashers

Early Corona and Mark II shock removal

from the top of the strut inside the engine compartment.

3. Remove the two bolts and lockwashers attaching the MacPherson strut to the lower control arm. Push the arm downward slightly, and then remove the strut assembly.
4. The strut must be mounted in a vise for further disassembly. It must not be mounted by the shock absorber shell as this part is machined perfectly round and can easily be distorted. A special tool is available from Toyota for this purpose, or you can make some sort of flange that will bolt to the bottom (where the control arm attaches).
5. Using a special tool designed for this purpose, the spring must be compressed so there is no tension on the upper seat.

NOTE: *Failure to fully compress the spring and hold it securely before performing the next step is extremely hazardous.*

6. Hold the shock absorber seat (at top) with a large spanner wrench, and remove the nut from the top of the shock absorber.
7. Remove upper support, upper seat, dust cover, and spring.
8. Install in reverse order. Inspect all parts carefully for wear or distortion, and replace as necessary. Torque the top shock absorber nut to 32.6–39.8 ft.lb. on Cressida. Pack multipurpose grease into the bearing on the suspension support. Torque upper support nuts to 21.7–38.6 ft.lb. Lower control arm nuts are torqued to 57.9–86.8 ft.lb.

Torsion Bars

REMOVAL AND INSTALLATION

Van

1. Raise and support the front end on jackstands under the frame.
2. Paint match marks on the torsion bar, anchor arm and torque arm.
3. Remove the locknut and measure the threaded end A as shown. Use this figure for an installation reference.
4. Loosen the adjusting nut and remove the anchor arm and torsion bar.
5. Installation is the reverse of removal. Apply a light coating of molybdenum disulphide lithium grease to the splined end of the torsion bar. Align all matchmarks. Tighten the adjusting nut so that the exact length of thread appears as before. The proper length should be 70mm.

Lower Ball Joints

INSPECTION

Jack up the lower suspension arm. Check the front wheel play. Replace the lower ball joint if

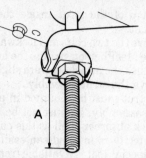

Torsion bar thread length measurement at A

the play at the wheel rim exceeds 1mm vertical motion or 2mm horizontal motion. Be sure that the dust covers are not torn and they are securely glued to the ball joints.

REMOVAL AND INSTALLATION

NOTE: *On models equipped with upper and lower ball joints-if both ball joints are to be removed, always remove the lower and then the upper ball joint.*

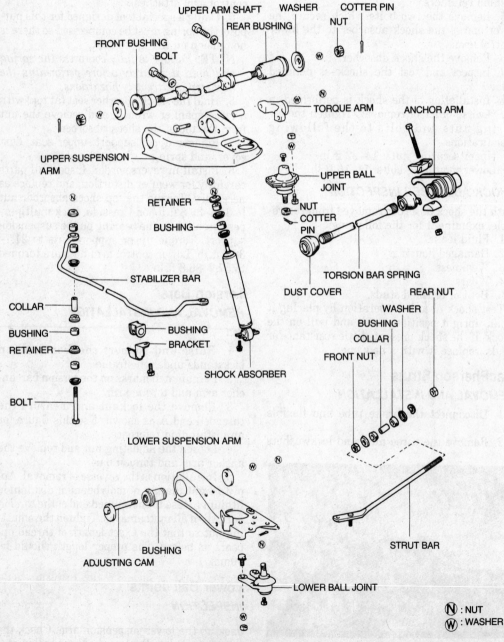

Van front suspension

Ⓝ : NUT
Ⓦ : WASHER

Torque Specifications

Part(s)	Torque (ft. lbs.)
Ball joint-to-control arm 12 mm bolt	58–83
8 mm bolt	11–16
Ball joint-to-steering knuckle	51–65

Corona lower ball joint removal

Corona, except MacPherson Strut

1. Remove the hubcap and loosen the lug nuts.

2. Raise the front of the car and support it with jackstands.

CAUTION: *Be sure that the car is securely supported. Remember, you will be working underneath it.*

3. Remove the lug nuts and the wheel. Place a jack under the spring seat on 1974–76 models, and compress the spring by raising the jack.

NOTE: *On models with ESP, unfasten the wiring from the brake sensor, and remove the clamp from the lever control arm.*

4. Remove the cotter pin and the castellated nut from the ball joint.

5. Use a ball joint puller to detach the lower ball joint from the steering knuckle.

6. Remove the securing bolt and withdraw the ball joint as detailed in Chapter 1 and check alignment.

Mark II and Crown

Perform steps 1–3 of the Mark II and Crown Coil Spring Removal procedure. When step 3 is completed, go on to steps 5–10. Lubricate the ball joints (Chapter 1) and check alignment.

Corona, with MacPherson Strut

1. Support the vehicle securely by the front suspension cross member.

2. Remove the engine lower cover. Disconnect the stabilizer bar at the lower arm and strut bar at the lower arm. Note the order of disassembly of all rubber bushings and collars!

3. Remove bolts attaching the lower arm to the bottom of the strut.

4. Using a tool designed for the purpose, press the tie rod end out of the steering knuckle arm.

5. Remove the bolt running through the crossmember and remove the control arm from the crossmember.

6. Remove cotter pin and castle nut, and then press the steering knuckle arm off the lower control arm with an appropriate tool. The lower arm and ball joint must be replaced as an assembly if either is defective.

7. In installation, torque parts as follows:

• Control arm-to-crossmember bolt (do not torque until after suspension is assembled and weight is put on it so normal ride height is achieved) 65.1–94 ft.lb.

• Steering knuckle castle nut: 50.6–65.1 ft.lb.

• Strut to knuckle arm: 57.9–86.8 ft.lb.

• Strut bar to lower arm: 43.4–53.2 ft.lb.

• Stabilizer bar to lower arm: 10.1–15.9 ft.lb.

Cressida

The ball joint and control arm cannot be separated from each other. If one fails, then both must be replaced as an assembly, in the following manner:

1. Perform Steps 1–7 of the first Front Spring Removal and Installation procedure. Skip Step 6.

2. Remove the stabilizer bar securing bolts.

3. Unfasten the torque strut mounting bolts.

4. Remove the control arm mounting bolt and detach the arm from the front suspension member.

5. Remove the steering knuckle arm from the control arm with a ball joint puller.

6. Installation is the reverse of removal. Note the following, however:

  a. When installing the control arm on the suspension member, tighten the bolts partially at first.

  b. Complete the assembly procedure and lower the car to the ground.

  c. Bounce the front of the car several times. Allow the suspension to settle, then tighten the lower control arm bolts to 51–65 ft.lb.

CAUTION: *Use only the bolt which was designed to fit the lower control arm. If a replacement is necessary, see an authorized dealer for the proper part.*

4. Remember to lubricate the ball joint. Check front end alignment.

Van

1. Raise and support the front end on jackstands under the frame.
2. Remove the hub and caliper.
3. Remove the steering knuckle dust cover.
4. Support the lower arm with a floor jack.
5. Remove the two cotter pins and nuts and disconnect the steering knuckle from the lower ball joint.
6. Disconnect the upper ball joint from the knuckle.
7. Using a ball joint removal tool, remove the ball joint from the arm.
8. Installation is the reverse of removal. Torque the ball joint nut to 50 ft.lb.

Upper Ball Joint

INSPECTION

Disconnect the ball joint from the steering knuckle and check free play by hand. Replace the ball joint, if it is noticeably loose.

REMOVAL AND INSTALLATION

NOTE: *On models equipped with both upper and lower ball joints, if both are to be removed, always remove the lower one first.*

Corona, except MacPherson Strut, and Van

1. Perform Steps 1–5 of the Corona Lower Ball Joint Removal procedure.

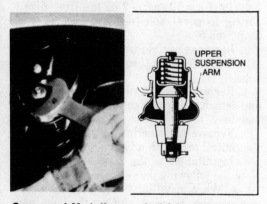

Crown and Mark II upper ball joint removal and installation

Torque Specifications (ft. lbs.)

| Model | Upper Ball Joint-to- | |
	Knuckle	Arm
Mark II/4	40–50	15–22
Mark II/6	40–51	15–22
Crown 2300	66–96	11–16
Crown 2600	65–94	11–16

2. Suspend the steering knuckle with a wire.
3. Use an open-end wrench to remove the upper ball joint.
4. Installation is performed in the reverse order of removal. Note the following:
   a. Install the upper ball joint dust cover with the escape valve toward the rear.
   b. Use sealer on the dust cover before installing it.
   c. Tighten the upper ball joint-to-steering knuckle bolt to 29–40 ft.lb. (1970–73) or to 40–51 ft.lb. (1974 and Later).

Mark II and Crown

1. Remove the wheel cover and loosen the lug nuts.
2. Raise the front of the car and support it with jackstands.
CAUTION: *Be sure that the car is securely supported. Remember, you will be working underneath it.*
3. Remove the lug nuts and the wheel.
4. Place a jack beneath the lower control arm spring seat. Raise the jack until the spring bumper separates from the frame.
5. Detach the flexible hose from the dust cover.
6. Using a ball joint puller, remove the upper ball joint from the steering knuckle.
7. Use an open end wrench to remove the ball joint from the upper control arm.
8. Installation is performed in the reverse order of removal. Tighten the components to the specifications given in the following Torque Specifications chart. Lubricate the ball joint as outlined in Chapter 1. Check front wheel alignment. Remember to bleed the air from the flexible hose.

Lower Control Arm

REMOVAL AND INSTALLATION

Cressida

1. Raise and support the front end.
2. Remove the wheel.
3. Disconnect the steering knuckle from the control arm.
4. Disconnect the tie rod stabilizer bar and strut bar from the control arm.
5. Remove the control arm mounting bolts, and remove the arm.
6. Install in reverse of above. Tighten, but do not torque fasteners until car is on ground.
7. Lower car to ground, rock it from side-to-side several times and torque control arm mounting bolts to 51–65 ft.lb., stabilizer bar to 16 ft.lb., strut bar to 40 ft.lb., and shock absorber to 65 ft.lb.

Corona

1. Raise and support the vehicle.
2. Remove the front wheel.
3. Remove the shock absorber and disconnect the stabilizer from the lower arm.
4. Install a spring compressor and fully tighten it.
5. Place a jack under the lower arm seat.
6. Disconnect the lower ball joint from the knuckle and lower the jack.
7. Remove the ball joint from the arm, remove the cam plates and bolts and take off the arm.
8. Install in reverse of above. Tighten all fasteners, but do not torque them to specification until vehicle is on ground.
9. Lower vehicle and rock it from side-to-side several times.
10. With no load in vehicle, torque the lower arm mounting bolts to 94–130 ft.lb.

Van

1. Raise and support the front end on jackstands under the frame.
2. Remove the shock absorber.
3. Disconnect the stabilizer bar from the arm.
4. Disconnect the strut bar from the arm.
5. Remove the ball joint nut and disconnect the ball joint from the knuckle. A ball joint separator is necessary.
6. Place a matchmark on the adjusting cam.
7. Remove the adjusting cam and nut and remove the lower arm.
8. Installation is the reverse of removal. Observe the following torques:
• Ball joint nut: 50 ft.lb.
• Ball joint-to-knuckle: 76 ft.lb.
• Shock absorber upper nut: 19 ft.lb.
• Shock absorber lower bolts: 13 ft.lb.
• Strut bar-to-arm: 50 ft.lb.
• Adjusting cam nut: 112 ft.lb.

Upper Control Arm
REMOVAL AND INSTALLATION
Corona

1. Remove the upper arm mounting nuts from inside the engine compartment, but do not remove the bolts.
2. Raise the vehicle, support the lower arm and remove the wheel.
3. On vehicles equipped with a ball joint wear sensor, remove the wiring from the clamp on the arm.
4. Remove the upper ball joint.
5. Remove the control arm mounting bolts.
6. Pry out the arm with a pry bar.
7. Install in reverse of removal. Do not

tighten fasteners until vehicle is on ground.
8. Lower vehicle and torque the control arm mounting bolts to 95–130 ft.lb.

Van

1. Raise and support the front end with jackstands under the frame.
2. Remove the torsion bar.
3. Remove the air duct.
4. Remove the upper ball joint nut and disconnect the ball joint from the knuckle using a separator.
5. Unbolt and remove the arm.
6. Installation is the reverse of removal. Observe the following torques:
• Upper arm front bolt: 65 ft.lb.
• Upper arm rear bolt: 112 ft.lb.
• Ball joint-to-arm nut: 22 ft.lb.
• Ball joint-to-knuckle: 58 ft.lb.

Front End Alignment

Front end alignment measurements require the use of special equipment. Before measuring alignment or attempting to adjust it, always check the following points:
1. Be sure that the tires are properly inflated.
2. Ensure that the wheels are properly balanced.
3. Check the ball joints to determine if they are worn or loose.
4. Check front wheel bearing adjustment.
5. Be sure that the car is on a level surface.
6. Check all suspension parts for tightness.

CASTER AND CAMBER ADJUSTMENTS

NOTE: *Caster and camber adjustments do not apply to vehicles with MacPherson strut front suspension. If measurements are incorrect, there is distortion or severe wear in the system and part(s) must be replaced. Toe-in is adjusted as described below.*

All Except 1974–77 Corona

NOTE: *The MacPherson strut front suspension cannot be adjusted for caster or camber. If measurements indicate that the suspension*

Removing camber adjusting shims

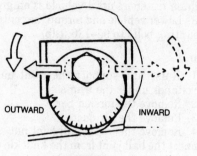
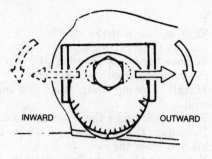

OUTWARD   INWARD   INWARD   OUTWARD

LEFT SIDE   RIGHT SIDE

As seen from rear

Front end alignment adjusting cams—1974–77 Corona

is out of alignment, the damaged part must be found and replaced.

Measure the caster and camber angles. Check them against the specifications given in the Wheel Alignment chart. If they are not within specifications, adjust them by adding or subtracting the shims on the mounting bolts between the upper control arm and the suspension member.

1. To increase camber, remove shims equally from both of the control shaft mounting bolts. Do the reverse to decrease camber.
2. To increase caster, add camber adjusting shims to the rear mounting bolt, or remove them from the front mounting bolts. Do the reverse to decrease caster.

NOTE: *Caster and camber adjustments should always be performed in a single operation.*

1974 and Later Corona, except MacPherson Strut

Caster and camber angles are measured in the same way and with the same equipment as for all the other models. However, the method of adjustment is different:

1. Measure the camber and adjust it with the rear adjusting cam.
2. Measure the caster and adjust it with the front adjusting cam.
3. Check the caster and camber again to ensure that they fall within the specifications given in the Wheel Alignment chart.
4. Tighten the control arm mounting bolts to 94–130 ft.lb.

NOTE: *There should be no more than six graduations difference between the front and rear cams. Inspect for damaged suspension parts if there is.*

TOE-IN ADJUSTMENT

Measure the toe-in. Adjust it, if necessary, by loosening the tie rod end clamping bolts and

Toe-in (tie-rod) adjustment

rotating the tie rod adjusting tubes. Tighten the clamping bolts when finished.

NOTE: *Both tie rods should be the same length. If they are not, perform the adjustment until the toe-in is within specifications and the tie rod ends are equal in length.*

REAR SUSPENSION

Leaf Springs

REMOVAL AND INSTALLATION

1. Loosen the rear wheel lug nuts.
2. Raise the rear of the vehicle. Support the frame and rear axle housing with stands.

CAUTION: *Be sure that the vehicle is securely supported.*

3. Remove the lug nuts and the wheel.
4. Remove the cotter pin, nut, and washer from the lower end of the shock absorber.
5. Detach the shock absorber from the spring seat pivot pin.
6. Remove the parking brake cable clamp.

NOTE: *Remove the parking brake equalizer, if necessary.*

7. Unfasten the U-bolt nuts and remove the spring seat assemblies.
8. Adjust the height of the rear axle housing

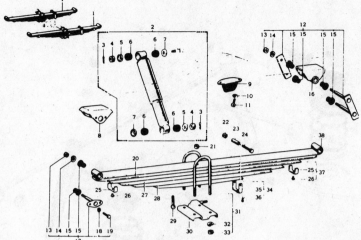

1. Rear spring
2. Rear shock absorber
3. Cotter pin
4. Castle nut
5. Shock absorber cushion washer
6. Bushing
7. Shock absorber cushion washer
8. Spring bracket
9. Rear spring bumper
10. Spring washer
11. Bolt
12. Rear spring shackle
13. Nut
14. Spring washer
15. Bushing
16. Spring bracket
17. Rear spring hanger pin
18. Spring washer
19. Bolt
20. Rear spring leaf
21. Nut
22. Nut
23. Rear spring clip bolt
24. Clip bolt
25. Rear spring clip
26. Round rivet
27. Rear spring leaf
28. Rear spring leaf
29. Rear spring center bolt
30. U-bolt seat
31. U-bolt
32. Spring washer
33. Nut
34. Rear spring leaf
35. Rear spring clip
36. Round rivet
37. Rear spring leaf
38. Rear spring leaf

Leaf spring suspension (typical)

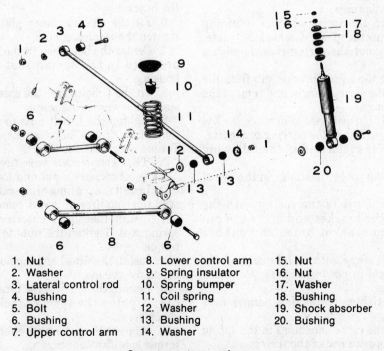

1. Nut
2. Washer
3. Lateral control rod
4. Bushing
5. Bolt
6. Bushing
7. Upper control arm
8. Lower control arm
9. Spring insulator
10. Spring bumper
11. Coil spring
12. Washer
13. Bushing
14. Washer
15. Nut
16. Nut
17. Washer
18. Bushing
19. Shock absorber
20. Bushing

Crown rear suspension

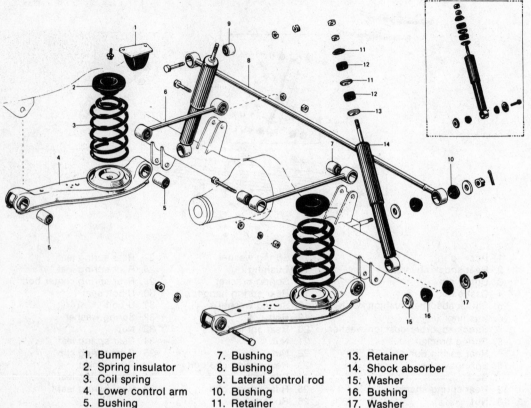

1. Bumper
2. Spring insulator
3. Coil spring
4. Lower control arm
5. Bushing
6. Upper control arm
7. Bushing
8. Bushing
9. Lateral control rod
10. Bushing
11. Retainer
12. Cushion
13. Retainer
14. Shock absorber
15. Washer
16. Bushing
17. Washer

Mark II/6 rear suspension

so that the weight of the rear axle is removed from the rear springs.

9. Unfasten the spring shackle retaining nuts. Withdraw the spring shackle inner plate. Carefully pry out the spring shackle with a bar.

10. Remove the spring bracket pin from the front end of the spring hanger and remove the rubber bushings.

CAUTION: *Use care not to damage the hydraulic brake line or the parking brake line.*

Installation is performed in the following order:

1. Install the rubber bushings in the eye of the spring.

2. Align the eye of the spring with the spring hanger bracket and drive the pin through the bracket holes and rubber bushings.

NOTE: *Use soapy water as lubricant, if necessary, to aid in pin installation. Never use oil or grease.*

3. Finger tighten the spring hanger nuts and/or bolts.

4. Install the rubber bushings in the spring eye at the opposite end of the spring.

5. Raise the free end of the spring. Install

the spring shackle through the bushings and the bracket.

6. Fit the shackle inner plate and finger tighten the retaining nuts.

7. Center the bolt head in the hole which is provided in the spring seat on the axle housing.

8. Fit the U-bolts over the axle housing. Install the lower spring seat.

9. Tighten the U-bolt nuts to the specifications listed in the following Rear Suspension Torque Specifications Chart.

NOTE: *Some models have two sets of nuts, while others have a nut and lockwasher.*

10. Install the parking brake cable clamp. Install the equalizer, if it was removed.

11. Install the shock absorber end at the spring seat. Tighten the nuts to the specified torque.

12. Install the wheel and lug nuts. Lower the car to the ground.

13. Bounce the car several times.

14. Tighten the spring bracket pins and shackles.

15. Repeat Step 13 and check all of the torque specifications again.

Coil Springs
REMOVAL AND INSTALLATION

1. Remove the hubcap and loosen the lug nuts.

2. Jack up the rear axle housing and support the frame with jackstands. Leave the jack in place under the rear axle housing.

CAUTION: *Support the car securely. Remember, you will be working underneath it.*

3. Remove the lug nuts and wheel.

4. Unfasten the lower shock absorber end. On the Van, disconnect the lateral control rod at the axle.

5. Slowly lower the jack under the rear axle housing until the axle is at the bottom of its travel.

6. Withdraw the coil spring, complete with its insulator.

7. Inspect the coil spring and insulator for wear, cracks, or weakness. Replace either or both, as necessary.

8. Installation is performed in the reverse order of removal. Tighten the lower shock absorber mounting to the specifications listed in the Shock Absorber Tightening Torque chart at the end of the Rear Shock Absorber Removal and Installation section.

Rear Shock Absorbers
REMOVAL AND INSTALLATION

1. Jack up the rear end of the vehicle.

CAUTION: *Be sure that the vehicle is securely supported. Remember, you will be working underneath it.*

2. Support the rear axle housing with jackstands.

3. Unfasten the upper shock absorber retaining nuts and/or bolts from the upper frame member.

4. Depending upon the type of rear springs used, either disconnect the lower end of the shock absorber from the spring seat or the rear

axle housing by removing its cotter pins, nuts, and/or bolts.

5. Remove the shock absorber.

6. Inspect the shock for wear, leaks, or other signs of damage. Test it as outlined in the Front Suspension Shock Absorber section.

7. Installation is performed in the reverse order of removal. Tighten the shock absorber securing nuts and bolts to the specifications given in the following chart.

STEERING

Steering Wheel
REMOVAL AND INSTALLATION

Three-Spoke

CAUTION: *Do not attempt to remove or install the steering wheel by hammering on it. Damage to the energy absorbing steering column could result.*

1. Unfasten the horn and turn signal multiconnector(s) at the base of the steering column shroud.

2. Loosen the trim pad retaining screws from the back side of the steering wheel.

3. Lift the trim pad and horn button assembly(ies) from the wheel.

4. Remove the steering wheel hub retaining nut.

5. Scratch matchmarks on the hub and shaft to aid in correct installation.

6. Use a steering wheel puller to remove the steering wheel.

7. Installation is performed in the reverse order of removal. Tighten the wheel retaining nut to 15–22 ft.lb., except for the Mark II/6 and 1974–77 Corona, which should be tightened to 22–29 ft.lb.

Two-Spoke

The two-spoke steering wheel is removed in the same manner as the three-spoke, except that the trim pad should be pried off with a screwdriver. Remove the pad by lifting it toward the top of the wheel.

Shock Absorber Tightening Torque (ft. lbs.)

Model	Upper Mounting	Lower Mounting
Corona	—	25–40
Mark II/4	—	25–40
Mark II/6 Sedan and Coupe	14–22	26–33
Station Wagon	36–58	14–22
Crown 2300	11–16	22–23
Crown 2600 Sedan and Coupe	11–16	22–33

Remove the pad on the two-spoke steering wheel the direction of arrow

Removing the four-spoke wheel with a puller

Four-Spoke

CAUTION: *Do not attempt to remove or install the steering wheel by hammering on it. Damage to the energy absorbing steering column could result.*

1. Unfasten the horn and turn signal multiconnectors at the base of the steering column shroud (underneath the instrument panel).

2. Gently pry the center emblem off the front of the steering wheel.

3. Insert a wrench through the hole and remove the steering wheel retaining nut.

4. Scratch matchmarks on the hub and shaft to aid installation.

5. Use a steering wheel puller to remove the steering wheel.

6. Installation is the reverse of removal. Tighten the steering wheel retaining nut to 15–22 lbs.

Turn Signal Switch

REMOVAL AND INSTALLATION

All models Except 1970–72 Mark II/4

1. Disconnect the negative (–) battery cable.

2. Remove the steering wheel, as outlined in the appropriate preceding section.

3. Unfasten the screws which secure the upper and lower steering column shroud halves. On 1974–76 Corona models, remove the lower instrument panel garnish first.

4. Unfasten the screws which retain the turn signal switch and remove the switch from the column. On later Coronas the hazard warning and windshield wiper switches are part of the assembly, and will be removed as well.

5. Installation is performed in the reverse order of removal.

1970–72 Mark II/4

1. Disconnect the negative battery cable.

2. Remove the steering wheel as outlined in the appropriate preceding section.

3. Remove the turn signal switch housing and the turn signal switch.

4. Installation is performed in the reverse order of removal.

Ignition Lock/Switch

REMOVAL AND INSTALLATION

All models Except 1970–72 Mark II/4

1. Disconnect the negative battery cable.

2. Unfasten the ignition switch multiconnector underneath the instrument panel.

3. Remove the screws which secure the upper and lower halves of the steering column cover. Remove the lower instrument panel garnish on 1974–77 Corona models first.

4. Turn the lock cylinder to the ACC position with the ignition key.

5. Push the lock cylinder stop in with a small, round object (cotter pin, punch, etc).

NOTE: *On some models it may be necessary to remove the steering wheel and turn signal switch first.*

6. Withdraw the lock cylinder from the lock housing while depressing the stop tab.

7. To remove the ignition switch, unfasten its securing screws and withdraw the switch from the lock housing.

Installation is performed in the following order:

1. Align the locking cam with the hole in the ignition switch and insert the switch in the lock housing.

2. Secure the switch with its screw(s).

3. Make sure that both the lock cylinder and the column lock are in the ACC position. Slide the cylinder into the lock housing until the stop tab engages the hole in the lock.

4. The rest of installation is performed in the reverse order of removal.

1970–72 Mark II/4

NOTE: *Disconnect the negative battery cable.*

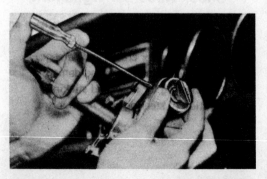

Depress the stop in order to remove the lock cylinder

1. Remove the steering wheel, turn signal switch housing, and turn signal switch as previously outlined.

2. Remove the lock assembly retaining screw.

3. Withdraw the switch assembly from the column by pulling it out with the ignition key.

4. Installation is performed in the reverse order of removal.

Manual Steering Gear

REMOVAL AND INSTALLATION

Corona

1. Remove the bolt attaching the coupling yoke to the steering worm.

2. Disconnect the relay rod from the pitman arm.

3. Remove the steering gear housing down and to the left.

4. Install in reverse of removal. Torque the housing-to-frame bolts to 25–36 ft.lb.; the coupling yoke bolt to 15–20 ft.lb.; the relay rod to 36–50 ft.lb.

Cressida

1. Open the hood, and find the steering gearbox. Place matchmarks on the coupling and steering column shaft.

2. Disconnect the pitman arm from the relay rod using a tie rod puller on the pitman arm set nut.

3. Disconnect the steering gearbox at the coupling. Unbolt the gearbox from the chassis and remove.

4. Installation is in the reverse order of removal, with the exception of first aligning the matchmarks and connecting the steering shaft to the coupling before you bolt the gearbox into the car permanently.

Van

1. Raise and support the front end on jackstands.

2. Remove the steering shaft coupling bolt. Disconnect the fluid lines.

3. Remove the Pitman arm nut. Loosen the drag link set nut.

4. Using a puller, remove the Pitman arm.

5. Unbolt and remove the gear housing.

6. Installation is the reverse of removal. Torque the gear housing bolts to 70 ft.lb.; the Pitman arm nut to 90 ft.lb.; the coupling bolt to 18 ft.lb.

Power Steering Pump

REMOVAL AND INSTALLATION

1. Remove the fan shroud.

2. Unfasten the nut from the center of the pump pulley.

NOTE: *Use the drive belt as a brake to keep the pulley from rotating.*

3. Withdraw the drive belt.

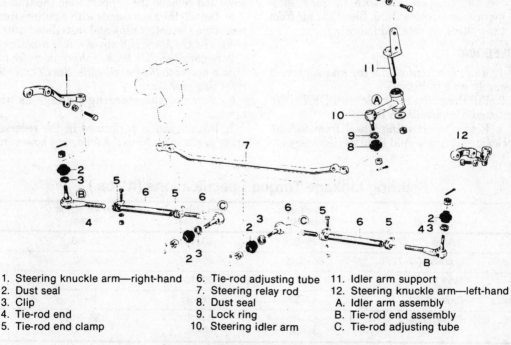

1. Steering knuckle arm—right-hand
2. Dust seal
3. Clip
4. Tie-rod end
5. Tie-rod end clamp
6. Tie-rod adjusting tube
7. Steering relay rod
8. Dust seal
9. Lock ring
10. Steering idler arm
11. Idler arm support
12. Steering knuckle arm—left-hand
A. Idler arm assembly
B. Tie-rod end assembly
C. Tie-rod adjusting tube

Steering linkage components (typical)

Power steering pump removal showing (1) front mounting bolts and (2) pump

4. Remove the pulley and the woodruff key from the pump shaft.

5. Detach the intake and outlet hoses from the pump reservoir.

NOTE: *Tie the hose ends up high, so that the fluid cannot flow out of them. Drain or plug the pump to prevent fluid leakage.*

6. Remove the bolt from the rear mounting brace.

7. Remove the front bracket bolts and withdraw the pump.

8. Installation is performed in the reverse order of removal. Note the following, however:

a. Tighten the pump pulley mounting bolt to 25–39 ft.lb.

b. Adjust the pump drive belt tension. The belt should deflect 8–10mm when 22 lbs. pressure is applied midway between the air pump and the power steering pump.

c. Fill the reservoir with Dexron® automatic transmission fluid. Bleed the air from the system, as detailed following.

BLEEDING

1. Raise the front of the car and support it securely with jackstands.

2. Fill the pump reservoir with DEXRON® automatic transmission fluid.

3. Rotate the steering wheel from lock-to-lock several times. Add fluid as necessary.

4. With the steering wheel turned fully to one lock, crank the starter while watching the fluid level in the reservoir.

NOTE: *Disconnect the high tension lead from the coil. Do not start the engine. Operate the starter with a remote starter switch or have an assistant do it from inside of the car. Do not run the starter for prolonged periods.*

5. Repeat Step 4 with the steering wheel turned to the opposite lock.

6. Start the engine. With the engine idling, turn the steering wheel from lock-to-lock two or three times.

7. Lower the front of the car and repeat Step 6.

8. Center the wheel at the midpoint of its travel. Stop the engine.

9. The fluid level should not have risen more than 5mm. If it does, repeat Step 7 again.

10. Check for fluid leakage.

Steering Linkage
REMOVAL AND INSTALLATION

1. Raise the front of the vehicle and support it with jackstands.

CAUTION: *Be sure that the vehicle is securely supported. Do not support it by the lower control arms.*

2. Remove the gravel shields if they prevent access to the steering linkage.

3. Unfasten the nut and, using a puller, disconnect the pitman arm from the sector shaft.

4. Unfasten the idler arm support securing bolts and remove the support from the frame.

5. Detach the tie rod ends with a puller after removing the cotter pins and castellated nuts.

NOTE: *On Mark II/6 models, it is necessary to remove the disc brake caliper in order to gain access to the tie rod ends. See Chapter 9 for this procedure.*

6. Remove the steering linkage as an assembly.

7. Installation is performed in the reverse order of removal. Note the following however:

Steering Linkage Torque Specifications (ft. lbs.)

Model	Tie-Rod Ends-to-Knuckle Arms	Pitman Arm-to-Sector Shaft	Idler Arm-Support-to-Frame
Corona ('70–'73)	36–51	80–101	25–36
Corona ('74–'77)	36–51 ①	80–101	36–51
Mark II	36–51	80–101	29–40
Crown 2300	37–52	80–90	36–51
Crown 2600	54–80 32–50	80–101 80–101	36–51 32–50

① 1976-77—36–65

Wheel Alignment Specifications

Model/Year	Caster		Camber		Toe-in (in.)	Steering Axis Inclination	Wheel Pivot Ratio (deg)	
	Range (deg)	Pref Setting (deg)	Range (deg)	Pref Setting (deg)			Inner Wheel	Outer Wheel
Corona 1970–73	0–1P	½P	1P–2P	1½P	0.16–0.24	7P	38½	31
Corona 1974–75	½P–1½P	1P	0–1P	½P	0.06–0.12	7P	—	—
Corona 1976	½P–1½P	1P	0–1P	½P	0.04–0.12	7P	36½–38½	31
Corona 1977	⅓–1⅓	1P	0–1P	½P	0.04–0.12	7P	36½–38½	31
Corona 1978–79	⅓P–1⅓P	⅘P	1/12P–1⅙P	⅗P	0.04–0.12	7P	37½	31
Corona 1980–82	1¼P–2¼P	1¾P	½P–1½P	1P	0–.08	7⅔P	36–38	28–32
Cressida 1978–80	½P–1½P	1P	⅓P–1⅓P	⅚P	0.08–0.16 out	7½P	36–39	30–34
Cressida 1981–83	1P–2P	1½P	⅓P–1⅓P	⅚P	0.08–0.16 out	9P	35–39	30–32
Cressida 1984–86 Sedan	2P–3P	2½P	¼P–1¼P	¾P	0.08–0.16	9P	35–39	30–32
Cressida 1984–86 sta. wgn.	1⅔P–2⅔P	2⅙P	⅔P–1⅓P	⅚P	0.08–0.16	9P	35–39	30–32
Mark II/4 All	1P–2P	1½P	1P–2P	1P	0.16–0.24	7P	40	32½
Mark II/6 1972–75	0–1P	½P	½P–1½P	1P	0.16–0.24	7P	36½	32½
Mark II/6 1976	1½P–2½P	2P	½P–1½P	1P	0.16–0.24	7P	36½–38½	31–32
Crown 2300	1N–0	½N	0–1P	½P	0.12–0.20	7½P	38	29½
Crown 2600	1N–½P	½N	0–1P	½P	0.12–0.20	7½P	38	29
Camry 1983–85	①	②	0–1P	½P	③	—	—	—
Van 1984–86	1½P–2½P	2P	0–1P	½P	0.040 out–0.04 in	—	—	—

P Positive
N Negative
① Man. str.: ½P–1½P
Pwr. Str.: 2P–3P
② Man. str.: 1P
Pwr. str.: 2½P
③ Man. str.: 0
Pwr. str.: 0.08

a. Tighten the linkage parts to the torque figures given in the Steering Linkage Torque Specifications chart.

b. Align the marks on pitman arm and sector shaft before installing the pitman arm.

c. The self locking nut used on some models, on the idler arm, may be reused if it cannot be turned by hand when fitted to the bolt.

d. Adjust the toe-in to specifications after completing the steering linkage installation procedure.

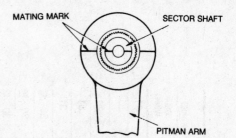

Align the marks on the pitman arm and the sector shaft

BRAKE SYSTEM

Understanding the Brakes

HYDRAULIC SYSTEM

Basic Operating Principles

Hydraulic systems are used to actuate the brakes of all modern automobiles. The system transports the power required to force the frictional surfaces of the braking system together from the pedal to the individual brake units at each wheel. A hydraulic system is used for two reasons. First, fluid under pressure can be carried to all parts of an automobile by small hoses, some of which are flexible, without taking up a significant amount of room or posing routing problems. Second, a great mechanical advantage can be given to the brake pedal end of the system, and the foot pressure required to actuate the brakes can be reduced by making the surface area of the master cylinder pistons smaller than that of any of the pistons in the wheel cylinders or calipers.

The master cylinder consists of a fluid reservoir and either a single or double cylinder and piston assembly. Double type master cylinders are designed to separate the front and rear braking systems hydraulically in case of a leak.

Steel lines carry the brake fluid to a point on the vehicle's frame near each of the vehicle's wheels. The fluid is then carried to the wheel cylinders by flexible tubes in order to allow for suspension and steering movements.

Each wheel cylinder contains two pistons, one at either end, which push outward in opposite directions. In disc brake systems, the cylinders are part of the calipers. One or four cylinders are used to force the brake pads against the disc, but all cylinders contain one piston only. All pistons employ some type of seal, usually made of rubber, to minimize fluid leakage. A rubber dust boot seals the outer end of the cylinder against dust and dirt. The boot fits around the outer end of the piston on disc brake calipers, and around the brake actuating rod on wheel cylinders.

The hydraulic system operates as follows: When at rest, the entire system, from the piston(s) in the master cylinder to those in the wheel cylinders or calipers, is full of brake fluid. Upon application of the brake pedal, fluid trapped in front of the master cylinder piston(s) is forced through the lines to the wheel cylinders. Here, it forces the pistons outward, in the case of drum brakes, and inward toward the disc, in the case of disc brakes. The motion of the pistons is opposed by return springs mounted outside the cylinders in drum brakes, and by internal springs or spring seals, in disc brakes.

Upon release of the brake pedal, a spring located inside the master cylinder immediately returns the master cylinder pistons to the normal position. The pistons contain check valves and the master cylinder has compensating ports drilled in it. These are uncovered as the pistons reach their normal position. The piston check valves allow fluid to flow toward the wheel cylinders or calipers as the pistons withdraw. Then, as the return springs force the brake pads or shoes into the released position, the excess fluid reservoir through the compensating ports. It is during the time the pedal is in the released position that any fluid that has leaked out of the system will be replaced through the compensating ports.

Dual circuit master cylinders employ two pistons, located one behind the other, in the same cylinder. The primary piston is actuated directly by mechanical linkage from the brake pedal. The secondary piston is actuated by fluid trapped between the two pistons. If a leak develops in front of the secondary piston, it moves forward until it bottoms against the front of the master cylinder, and the fluid trapped between the pistons will operate the rear brakes. If the rear brakes develop a leak, the primary piston will move forward until direct contact with the secondary piston takes place, and it will force the secondary piston to actuate the front brakes. In either case, the brake pedal moves farther when the brakes are applied, and less braking power is available.

All dual circuit systems use a switch to warn the driver when only half of the brake system is operational. This switch is located in a valve body which is mounted on the firewall or the frame below the master cylinder. A hydraulic piston receives pressure from both circuits, each circuit's pressure being applied to one end of the piston. When the pressures are in balance, the piston remains stationary. When one circuit has a leak, however, the greater pressure in that circuit during application of the brakes will push the piston to one side, closing the switch and activating the brake warning light.

In disc brake systems, this valve body also contains a metering valve and, in some cases, a proportioning valve. The metering valve keeps pressure from traveling to the disc brakes on the front wheels until the brake shoes on the rear wheels have contacted the drums, ensuring that the front brakes will never be used alone. The proportioning valve controls the pressure to the rear brakes to avoid rear wheel lock-up during very hard braking.

Warning lights may be tested by depressing the brake pedal and holding it while opening one of the wheel cylinder bleeder screws. If this does not cause the light to go on, substitute a new lamp, make continuity checks, and, finally, replace the switch as necessary.

The hydraulic system may be checked for leaks by applying pressure to the pedal gradually and steadily. If the pedal sinks very slowly to the floor, the system has a leak. This is not to be confused with a springy or spongy feel due to the compression of air within the lines. If the system leaks, there will be a gradual change in the position of the pedal with a constant pressure.

Check for leaks along all lines and at wheel cylinders. If no external leaks are apparent, the problem is inside the master cylinder.

DISC BRAKES

Basic Operating Principles

Instead of the traditional expanding brakes that press outward against a circular drum, disc brake systems utilize a disc (rotor) with brake pads positioned on either side of it.

Braking effect is achieved in a manner similar to the way you would squeeze a spinning phonograph record between your fingers. The disc (rotor) is a casting with cooling fins between the two braking surfaces. This enables air to circulate between the braking surfaces making them less sensitive to heat buildup and more resistant to fade. Dirt and water do not affect braking action since contaminants are thrown off by the centrifugal action of the rotor or scraped off the by the pads. Also, the equal clamping action of the two brake pads tends to ensure uniform, straight line stops. Disc brakes are inherently self-adjusting.

There are three general types of disc brake:
1. A fixed caliper.
2. A floating caliper.
3. A sliding caliper.

The fixed caliper design uses two pistons mounted on either side of the rotor (in each side of the caliper). The caliper is mounted rigidly and does not move.

The sliding and floating designs are quite similar. In fact, these two types are often lumped together. In both designs, the pad on the inside of the rotor is moved into contact with the rotor by hydraulic force. The caliper, which is not held in a fixed position, moves slightly, bringing the outside pad into contact with the rotor. There are various methods of attaching floating calipers. Some pivot at the bottom or top, and some slide on mounting bolts. In any event, the end result is the same.

DRUM BRAKES

Basic Operating Principles

Drum brakes employ two brake shoes mounted on a stationary backing plate. These shoes are positioned inside a circular drum which rotates with the wheel assembly. The shoes are held in place by springs. This allows them to slide toward the drums (when they are applied) while keeping the linings and drums in alignment. The shoes are actuated by a wheel cylinder which is mounted at the top of the backing plate. When the brakes are applied, hydraulic pressure forces the wheel cylinder's actuating links outward. Since these links bear directly against the top of the brake shoes, the tops of the shoes are then forced against the inner side of the drum. This action forces the bottoms of the two shoes to contact the brake drum by rotating the entire assembly slightly (known as servo action). When pressure within the wheel cylinder is relaxed, return springs pull the shoes back away from the drum.

Most modern drum brakes are designed to

adjust themselves during application when the vehicle is moving in reverse. This motion causes both shoes to rotate very slightly with the drum, rocking an adjusting lever, thereby causing rotation of the adjusting screw.

POWER BRAKE BOOSTERS

Power brakes operate just as standard brake systems except in the actuation of the master cylinder pistons. A vacuum diaphragm is located on the front of the master cylinder and assists the driver in applying the brakes, reducing both the effort and travel he must put into moving the brake pedal.

The vacuum diaphragm housing is connected to the intake manifold by a vacuum hose. A check valve is placed at the point where the hose enters the diaphragm housing, so that during periods of low manifold vacuum brake assist vacuum will not be lost.

Depressing the brake pedal closes off the vacuum source and allows atmospheric pressure to enter on one side of the diaphragm. This causes the master cylinder pistons to move and apply the brakes. When the brake pedal is released, vacuum is applied to both sides of the diaphragm, and return springs return the diaphragm and master cylinder pistons to the released position. If the vacuum fails, the brake pedal rod will butt against the end of the master cylinder actuating rod, and direct mechanical application will occur as the pedal is depressed.

The hydraulic and mechanical problems that apply to conventional brake systems also apply to power brakes, and should be checked for if the tests below do not reveal the problem.

Test for a system vacuum leak as described below:

1. Operate the engine at idle without touching the brake pedal for at least one minute.
2. Turn off the engine, and wait one minute.
3. Test for the presence of assist vacuum by depressing the brake pedal and releasing it several times. Light application will produce less and less pedal travel, if vacuum was present. If there is no vacuum, air is leaking into the system somewhere.

Test for system operation as follows:

1. Pump the brake pedal (with engine off) until the supply vacuum is entirely gone.
2. Put a light, steady pressure on the pedal.
3. Start the engine, and operate it at idle. If the system is operating, the brake pedal should fall toward the floor if constant pressure is maintained on the pedal.

Power brake systems may be tested for hydraulic leaks just as ordinary systems are tested.

Adjustments
REAR DRUM BRAKES
All Models

These models are equipped with self-adjusting rear drum brakes. No adjustment is possible or necessary.

FRONT DISC BRAKES

Front disc brakes require no adjustment, as hydraulic pressure maintains the proper brake pad-to-disc contact at all times.

NOTE: *The brake fluid level should be checked regularly. (See Chapter 1).*

Master Cylinder
REMOVAL AND INSTALLATION
All Except Van

CAUTION: *Be careful not to spill brake fluid on the painted surfaces of the vehicle. It will damage the paint.*

1. Unfasten the hydraulic lines from the master cylinder.
2. Detach the hydraulic fluid pressure differential switch wiring connectors. On models with ESP (brake fluid level warning device), disconnect the fluid level sensor wiring connectors, as well.
3a. On models with manual brakes and on the Crown 2300, remove the master cylinder securing bolts and the clevis pin from the brake pedal. Remove the master cylinder.
3b. On the other models with power brakes, unfasten the nuts and remove the master cylinder assembly from the power brake unit.
4. Installation is performed in the reverse order of removal. Note the following, however:

    a. Before tightening the master cylinder mounting nuts or bolts, screw the hydraulic line into the cylinder body, a few turns.

    b. After installation is completed, bleed the master cylinder and the brake system.

Van

1. Disconnect the battery ground.
2. Remove the instrument cluster face panel, cluster and lower cluster panel.
3. Remove the defroster ducts.
4. Syphon off the fluid from the master cylinder with a syringe.
5. Disconnect the brake lines from the master cylinder.
6. Unbolt and remove the master cylinder. Installation is the reverse of removal. Torque the nuts to 9 ft.lb.

OVERHAUL

1. Remove the reservoir caps and floats. Unscrew the bolts and secure the reservoirs to the main body.

2. Remove the pressure differential warning switch assembly (if equipped). Then, working from the rear of the cylinder, remove the boot, snapping, stop washer, piston No. 1, spacer, cylinder cup, spring retainer, and spring, in that order.

NOTE: *Depending on the model, it may be necessary to remove the side mounted stop bolt before the pistons can be removed.*

3. Remove the endplug and gasket from the front of the cylinder, then remove the front piston stop-bolt from underneath. Pull out the spring, retainer, piston No. 2, spacer, and the cylinder cup.

4. Remove the two outlet fittings, washers, check valves and springs.

5. Remove the piston cups from their seats only if they are to be replaced.

6. After washing all parts in clean brake fluid, dry them with compressed air (if available). Inspect the cylinder bore for wear, scuff marks, or nicks. Cylinders may be honed slightly, but the limit is 0.15mm. In view of the importance of the master cylinder, it is recommended that it is replaced rather than overhauled if worn or damaged.

7. Assembly is performed in the reverse order of disassembly. Absolute cleanliness is important. Coat all parts with clean brake fluid prior to assembly.

Bleed the hydraulic system after the master cylinder is installed, as detailed following.

Proportioning Valve

A proportioning valve is used to reduce the hydraulic pressure to the rear brakes because of weight transfer during high speed stops. This helps to keep the rear brakes from locking up by improving front-to-rear brake balance.

On 1970–71 Crown models, the proportioning valve is attached to the side frame side rail, about halfway between the front and rear wheels. On all other models, it is located in the engine compartment, near the master cylinder.

REMOVAL AND INSTALLATION

1. Disconnect the brake lines from the valve unions.

2. Unfasten the valve mounting bolt, if used.

3. Remove the proportioning valve assembly.

NOTE: *If the proportioning valve is defec-tive, it must be replaced as an assembly. It cannot be rebuilt.*

4. Installation is the reverse of removal. Bleed the brake system after it is completed.

Bleeding

CAUTION: *Do not reuse brake fluid which has been bled from the brake system.*

1. Insert a clear vinyl tube into the bleeder plug on the master cylinder or the wheel cylinders.

NOTE: *If the master cylinder has been over-hauled or if air is present in it, start the bleeding procedure with the master cylinder. Otherwise (and after bleeding the master cylinder), start with the wheel cylinder which is farthest from the master cylinder.*

2. Insert the other end of the tube into a jar which is half filled with brake fluid.

3. Slowly depress the brake pedal (have an assistant do it) and turn the bleeder plug 1/3–1/2 of a turn at the same time.

NOTE: *If the brake pedal is depressed too fast, small air bubbles will form in the brake fluid which will be very difficult to remove.*

4. Bleed the cylinder before hydraulic pressure decreases in the cylinder.

5. Repeat this procedure until the air bubbles are removed and then go on to the next wheel cylinder.

CAUTION: *Add brake fluid to the master cylinder reservoir, so that it does not completely drain during bleeding.*

Bleeding the disc brake caliper

FRONT DISC BRAKES

INSPECTION

An inspection slot is provided, in most cases, in the top of the caliper for checking the brake pad thickness. However, if the thickness seems marginal, the pads should be removed from the caliper and checked.

NOTE: *Always replace the pads on both front wheels. When inspecting or replacing the brake pads, check the surface of the disc*

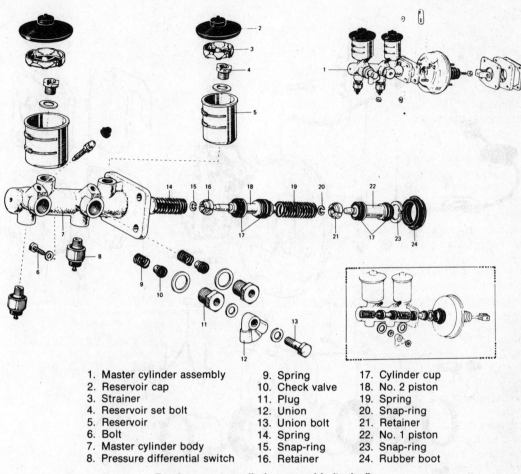

1. Master cylinder assembly
2. Reservoir cap
3. Strainer
4. Reservoir set bolt
5. Reservoir
6. Bolt
7. Master cylinder body
8. Pressure differential switch
9. Spring
10. Check valve
11. Plug
12. Union
13. Union bolt
14. Spring
15. Snap-ring
16. Retainer
17. Cylinder cup
18. No. 2 piston
19. Spring
20. Snap-ring
21. Retainer
22. No. 1 piston
23. Snap-ring
24. Rubber boot

Tandem master cylinder assembly (typical)

rotors for scoring, wear and runout. The rotors should be resurfaced if badly scored or replaced if badly worn.

Fixed Caliper Type Disc Brakes

The fixed caliper design uses two pistons mounted on either side of the disc rotor. The caliper is rigidly mounted and does not move.

Sliding Caliper Type Disc Brake

The sliding caliper design uses one piston mounted on the inboard side of the disc rotor. The caliper, which is not held in a fixed position, moves slightly when the brake is applied. The movement of the caliper brings the outside brake pad into contact with the disc rotor.

Disc Brake Pads

REMOVAL AND INSTALLATION

Fixed Caliper

1. Loosen the front wheel lugs slightly, then raise and safely support the front of the car. Remove the front wheel(s).

2. Remove the center spring, the retaining clips and the mounting pins from the caliper.

3. Remove the brake pads and antisqueal shims. A pair of locking pliers will help when you are pulling the pads from the caliper.

4. Remove the master cylinder cap and take a small amount of brake fluid from the reservoir. Force the pistons back into their bores to accommodate the greater thickness of the new brake pads.

5. Clean all caliper and pad locating parts.

6. Check the disc rotor for excessive runout. (See following section on disc rotors).

7. Apply a light coating of grease on the shims and on the metal backing of the pad.

8. Install the brake pads with the antisqueal shims (be sure the arrows are pointed in the right direction), the retaining pins and clips and the center spring in the reverse order of removal.

9. Pump the brake pedal several times to adjust the caliper pistons. Road test the car. If the brake pedal feels soft, it may be necessary to bleed the system.

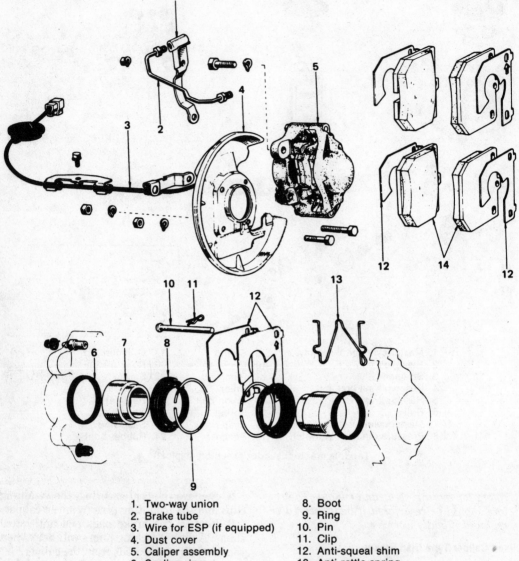

1. Two-way union
2. Brake tube
3. Wire for ESP (if equipped)
4. Dust cover
5. Caliper assembly
6. Sealing ring
7. Piston
8. Boot
9. Ring
10. Pin
11. Clip
12. Anti-squeal shim
13. Anti-rattle spring
14. Pad

Fixed caliper disc brake (typical)

Sliding Caliper

1. Loosen the front wheel lugs slightly, then raise and safely support the front of the car. Remove the front wheel(s).

2. Remove the guide key retainers. Apply light pressure to the caliper housing and slide the guide keys from (between) the caliper housing and the pad support.

3. Remove the caliper housing. Suspend the housing (with wire) so there is no strain on the brake hose.

4. Remove the brake pads and the support springs. Note the various positions of the parts removed.

5. Clean all of the parts that will be used over again. Remove the master cylinder cap and take a small amount of brake fluid from the reservoir. Force the piston back into the caliper bore to accommodate the greater thickness of the new brake pads.

6. Install the support springs, the brake pads, and the antirattle clips into the pad support.

7. Position the caliper housing on the support and install the guide keys and retainers.

8. Pump the brake pedal several times to adjust the caliper piston. Road test the car. If the brake pedal feels soft, it may be necessary to bleed the system.

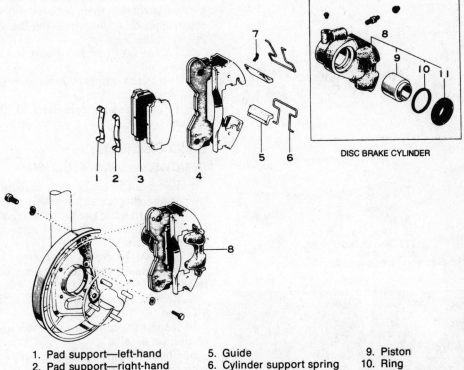

1. Pad support—left-hand
2. Pad support—right-hand
3. Disc brake pad
4. Disc brake caliper mounting
5. Guide
6. Cylinder support spring
7. Clip
8. Caliper assembly
9. Piston
10. Ring
11. Cylinder boot

Sliding caliper disc brake (typical)

Disc Brake Caliper

REMOVAL AND INSTALLATION

1. Remove the disc brake pads as previously described.

2. Disconnect the brake hose from the caliper. The fixed caliper is mounted by two bolts, cut the safety wire and remove the bolts. Remove the caliper. The sliding caliper support is held on by two mounting bolts, cut the safety wire and remove the bolts. Remove the caliper support.

3. Installation is the reverse of removal. Be sure to safety wire the mounting bolts.

OVERHAUL

Fixed Caliper

1. Remove the caliper as previously described.

CAUTION: *The caliper halves must not be separated. If brake fluid leaks from the bridge seal, replace the caliper assembly.*

2. Clean the caliper assembly of all accumulated mud and dust.

3. Remove the retaining rings. Remove the dust covers.

4. Hold one piston with a finger so that it will not come out and gradually apply air pressure to the brake line fitting. This should cause the other piston to come out, but if the piston you are holding begins moving before the other, switch your finger over and remove the more movable one first.

5. Carefully remove the other piston.

6. With a finger, carefully remove both piston seals.

7. Thoroughly clean all parts in brake fluid.

8. Inspect, as follows:

a. Check cylinder walls for damage or excessive wear. Light rust, etc. should be removed with fine emery paper. If the wall is heavily rusted, replace the caliper assembly.

b. Inspect the pad, as previously described.

c. Inspect the piston for uneven wear, damage or any rust. Replace the piston if there is any rust, as it is chrome plated and cannot be cleaned.

d. Replace piston seals and dust covers.

9. Coat the piston seal with brake fluid and carefully install the piston seal.

10. Install the dust seal onto the piston. Coat

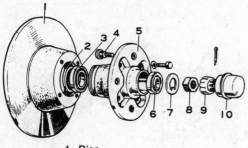

1. Disc
2. Oil seal
3. Tapered roller bearing
4. Hub bolt
5. Hub
6. Tapered roller bearing
7. Washer
8. Nut
9. Adjusting lock cap
10. Grease cap

Brake disc and hub assembly

Checking disc run-out

the piston with brake fluid. Install the piston and seal assembly and install the retaining ring.

11. Repeat Steps 9 and 10 for the other piston.

12. Install the caliper assembly. Fill the master cylinder and bleed the system.

Sliding Caliper

1. Remove the caliper cylinder from the car. (See the appropriate preceding Brake Pad Removal procedure).

2. Carefully remove the dust boot from around the cylinder bore.

3. Place a folded towel between the piston and housing. Apply compressed air to the brake line union to force the piston out of its bore. Be careful, the piston may come out forcefully.

4. Remove the seal from the piston. Check the piston and cylinder bore for wear and/or corrosion. Replace components as necessary. Assembly is performed in the following order:

1. Coat all components with clean brake fluid.

2. Install the seal and piston in the cylinder bore, after coating them with the rubber lubricant supplied in the rebuilding kit. Seat the piston in the bore.

3. Fit the boot into the groove in the cylinder bore.

4. Install the caliper cylinder assembly on to the support.

5. Fill the master cylinder and bleed the system.

Brake Disc (Rotor)

REMOVAL AND INSTALLATION

1. Remove the brake pads and caliper, or caliper and support as previously described.

2. Check the disc runout with a dial indicator, if available. See the rotor inspection section for details.

3. Remove the grease cap from the center of the hub. Remove the cotter pin and the castellated nut.

4. Remove the wheel hub with the disc rotor attached.

5. Inspect the rotor. See the rotor inspection section for details.

6. Check the wheel bearings, repack them with grease if necessary.

7. Installation is the reverse of removal. Before installation, coat the hub oil seal with multipurpose grease. Install the hub and disc rotor. Adjust the wheel bearing preload. See the wheel bearing section.

INSPECTION

Examine the disc. If it is worn, warped or scored, it must be replaced. Check the thickness of the disc against the specifications given in the Disc and Pad Specifications chart. If it is below specifications, replace it. Use a micrometer to measure the thickness.

The disc run-out should be measured before the disc is removed and again, after the disc is installed. Use a dial indicator mounted on a stand to determine run-out. If run-out exceeds 0.15mm (all models), replace the disc.

NOTE: *Be sure that the wheel bearing nut is properly tightened. If it is not, an inaccurate run-out reading may be obtained. If different run-out readings are obtained with the same disc, between removal and installation, this is probably the cause.*

Wheel Bearings

REMOVAL AND INSTALLATION

Rear Wheel Drive

1. Remove the caliper and the disc/hub assembly, as previously detailed.

2. If either the disc or the entire hub assem-

bly is to be replaced, unbolt the hub from the disc.

NOTE: *If only the bearings are to be replaced, do not separate the disc and hub.*

3. Using a brass rod as a drift, tap the inner bearing cone out. Remove the oil seal and the inner bearing.

NOTE: *Throw the old oil seal away.*

4. Drift out the inner bearing cup.

5. Drift out the outer bearing cup.

6. Inspect the bearings and the hub for signs of wear or damage. Replace components, as necessary.

Installation is performed in the following order:

1. Install the inner bearing cup and then the outer bearing cup, by drifting them into place.

CAUTION: *Use care not to cock the bearing cups in the hub.*

2. Pack the bearings, hub inner well and grease cap with multipurpose grease.

3. Install the inner bearing into the hub.

4. Carefully install a new oil seal with a soft drift.

5. Install the hub on the spindle. Be sure to install all of the washers and nuts which were removed.

6. Adjust the bearing preload, as detailed following.

7. Install the caliper assembly, as previously detailed.

PRELOAD ADJUSTMENT

Rear Wheel Drive

1. With the front hub/disc assembly installed, tighten the castellated nut to the torque figure specified in the Preload Specifications chart.

2. Rotate the disc back and forth, two or three times, to allow the bearing to seat properly.

3. Loosen the castellated nut until it is only finger tight.

4. Tighten the nut firmly, using a box wrench.

5. Measure the bearing preload with a spring scale attached to a wheel mounting

Preload Specifications—1970–77

Model	Initial Torque Setting (ft. lbs.)	Preload (oz)
Corona ('70–'73)	19–26	10–22
Corona ('74–'77)	22	12–31
Mark II	19–23	10–22
Crown 2300	22	12–38
Crown 2600	22	12–30

Preload Specifications—1978–86

Model	Initial Torque Setting (ft. lbs.)	Preload (oz)
Corona ('70–'77)	19–26	10–22
Corona ('78–'82)	19–26	12–31
Cressida	22	37–56
Van ('84–'86)	21	12.8–30.4

stud. Check it against the specifications given in the Preload Specifications chart.

6. Install the cotter pin.

NOTE: *If the hole does not align with the nut (or cap) holes, tighten the nut slightly until it does.*

7. Finish installing the brake components and the wheel.

Front Wheel Drive

1. Raise and support the front end.

2. Remove the caliper and wire it out of the way.

3. Remove the bearing cap, cotter pin, locknut and nut.

4. Remove the hub, rotor and outer bearing.

5. Installation is the reverse of removal. Torque the caliper bolts to 65 ft.lb.; the bearing locknut to 137 ft.lb.

REAR DRUM BRAKES

Brake Drums

REMOVAL AND INSTALLATION

All Models

1. Remove the hub cap (if used) and loosen the lug nuts. Release the parking brake.

2. Block the front wheels, raise the rear of the car, and support it with jackstands.

CAUTION: *Support the car securely.*

3. Remove the lug nuts and the wheel.

4. Unfasten the brake drum retaining screws.

5. Tap the drum lightly with a mallet in order to free it. If the drum is difficult to remove use a puller. But first be sure that the parking brake is released.

CAUTION: *Don't depress the brake pedal once the drum has been removed.*

Model	Inside Diameter Limit (in.)
Corona	9.08
Corona (1977 and later)	9.0
Mark II (all)	9.08
Crown 2300	9.13
Crown 2600	10.08

Disc and Pad Specifications (in.)

Model	New Disc Thickness	Disc Service Limit Thickness	Run-Out Limit	Pad Thickness Limit
Corona ('70–'73)	0.39	0.35	0.006	0.35
Corona ('74–'84)	0.49	0.45	0.006	0.04 ①
Mark II/4	0.39	0.37	0.006	0.08
Mark II/6	0.49	0.45	0.006	0.28 ②
Crown 2300	0.46	0.40	0.006	0.40
Crown 2600	0.50	0.45	0.006	0.27
Cressida	③	④	0.006	0.040
Camry	0.85	0.83	0.006	0.040
Van	0.80	0.75	0.006	0.040

① 1976—0.08 in.   ③ 1978–80: 0.50   ④ 1978–80: 0.45
② 1976—0.45 in.   1981–84: 0.70   1981–84: 0.67
                  1985–86: 0.87   1985–86: 0.83

6. Inspect the brake drum as detailed following.

7. Brake drum installation is performed in the reverse order of removal.

INSPECTION

1. Clean the drum.

2. Inspect the drum for scoring, cracks, grooves and out-of-roundness. Replace or turn the drum, as required.

3. Light scoring may be removed by dressing the drum with fine emery cloth.

4. Heavy scoring will require the use of a brake drum lathe to turn the drum. The service limits of the drum inside diameter are as follows:

Brake Shoes

REMOVAL AND INSTALLATION

Corona (1974–82), Crown, Cressida, Van

1. Perform the Brake Drum Removal procedure as previously detailed.

2. Unhook the shoe tension springs from the shoes with the aid of a brake spring removing tool.

3. Remove the brake shoe securing springs.

4. Disconnect the parking brake cable at the parking brake shoe lever.

5. Withdraw the shoes, complete with the parking brake shoe lever.

6. Unfasten the C-clip and remove the adjuster assembly from the shoes.

7. Inspect the shoes for wear and scoring. Have the linings replaced if their thickness is less than 1mm (1.5mm on the Crown).

8. Check the tension springs to see if they are weak, distorted or rusted.

9. Inspect the teeth on the automatic adjuster wheel for chipping or other damage.

NOTE: *Grease the point of the shoe which slides against the backing plate. Do not get grease on the linings.*

10. Installation is performed in the following order:

a. Attach the parking brake shoe lever and the automatic adjuster lever to the rear side of the shoe.

b. Fasten the parking brake cable to the lever on the brake shoe.

c. Install the automatic adjuster and fit the tension spring on the adjuster lever.

d. Install the securing spring on the rear shoe and then install the securing spring on the front shoe.

NOTE: *The tension spring should be installed on the anchor, before performing Step d.*

e. Hook one end of the tension spring over the rear shoe with the tool used during removal. Hook the other end over the front shoe.

CAUTION: *Be sure that the wheel cylinder boots are not being pinched in the ends of the shoes.*

f. Test the automatic adjuster by operating the parking brake shoe lever.

g. Install the drum and adjust the brakes as previously detailed.

Corona (1970–73) and Mark II (All)

1. Remove the rear brake drum by performing the procedure previously detailed.

2. Remove the tension springs from the trailing (rear) shoe with the aid of a brake return spring removal tool.

3. Press down on the brake adjuster ratchet and move the shoe adjusting lever forward, to the center of the drum.

4. Remove the securing spring and remove

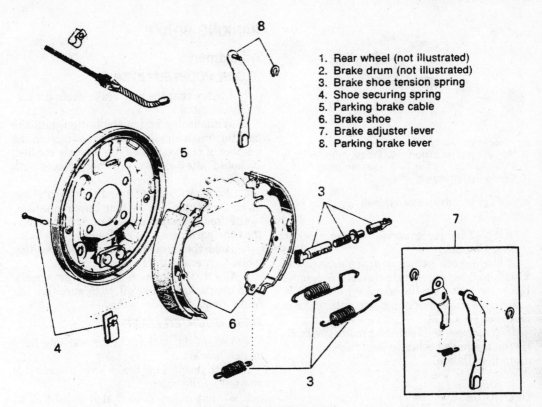

1. Rear wheel (not illustrated)
2. Brake drum (not illustrated)
3. Brake shoe tension spring
4. Shoe securing spring
5. Parking brake cable
6. Brake shoe
7. Brake adjuster lever
8. Parking brake lever

Rear brake shoes (typical)

the leading (front) shoe with the tension spring attached.

5. Disconnect the trailing shoe from the parking brake cable and remove the shoe retaining spring. Withdraw the shoe.

CAUTION: *Use care not to get grease on the lining surface.*

6. Inspect all of the parts removed for wear or damage. Check the lining thickness. It should be no less than 1.5mm. If it is less than this have the brakes relined.

Installation is performed in the following order:

1. Install the adjusting lever and ratchet on to the leading shoe. Attach the parking brake cable to the trailing shoe.

NOTE: *Use a new retaining clip.*

2. Apply non-melting lubricant to the shoe parts which contact other components of the brake.

CAUTION: *Do not allow lubricant to get on the surface of the brake lining.*

3. Install the parking brake strut on the trailing shoe with its retaining spring.

4. Attach the parking brake cable to the lever.

5. Fasten the trailing shoe with its security spring.

6. Push the adjusting lever toward the center of the brake and install it with the tension spring. Fasten the shoe retaining spring.

NOTE: *The longer hook of the tension spring attaches to the leading shoe.*

7. Push the adjusting ratchet downward, while returning the lever, so that it contacts the rim of the shoe.

8. Install the retaining spring.

9. Attach the tension spring to the shoes with the tool used during removal. Install the brake drum.

Wheel Cylinders

REMOVAL AND INSTALLATION

1. Plug the master cylinder inlet to prevent hydraulic fluid from leaking.

2. Remove the brake drums and shoes as detailed in the appropriate preceding section.

3. Working from behind the backing plate, disconnect the hydraulic line from the wheel cylinder.

4. Unfasten the screws retaining the wheel cylinder and withdraw the cylinder.

5. Installation is performed in the reverse order of removal. However, once the hydraulic line has been disconnected from the wheel cylinder, the union seat must be replaced.

To replace the seat, proceed in the following manner:

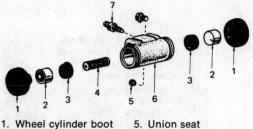

1. Wheel cylinder boot
2. Wheel cylinder piston
3. Cylinder cup
4. Compression spring
5. Union seat
6. Wheel cylinder body
7. Bleeder plug

Wheel cylinder assembly (typical)

NOTE: *This procedure is not required on Crown models.*

1. Use a screw extractor with a diameter of 2.5mm and having reverse threads, to remove the union seat from the wheel cylinder.
2. Drive in the new union seat with an 8mm bar, used as a drift.
3. Remember to bleed the brake system after completing wheel cylinder, brake shoe and drum installation.

OVERHAUL

It is not necessary to remove the wheel cylinder from the backing plate if it is only to be inspected or rebuilt.

1. Remove the brake drum and shoes. Remove the wheel cylinder only if it is going to be replaced.
2. Remove the rubber boots from either end of the wheel cylinder.
3. Withdraw the piston and cup assemblies.
4. Take the compression spring out of the wheel cylinder body, except on Crown models.
5. Remove the bleeder plug (and ball), if necessary.
6. Check all components for wear or damage. Inspect the bore for signs of wear, scoring, and/or scuffing. If in doubt, replace or hone the wheel cylinder (with a special hone). The limit for honing a cylinder is 0.127mm oversize. Wash all the residue from the cylinder bore with clean brake fluid and blow dry.

Assembly is performed in the following order:

1. Soak all components in clean brake fluid, or coat them with the rubber grease supplied in the wheel cylinder rebuilding kit.
2. Install the spring, cups (recesses toward the center), and pistons in the cylinder body, in that order.
3. Insert the boots over the ends of the cylinder.
4. Install the bleeder plug (and ball), if removed.
5. Assemble the brake shoes and install the drum.

PARKING BRAKE

Adjustments

FLOOR MOUNTED LEVER

1. Ensure that the rear brake shoes are correctly adjusted.
2. Without depressing the button, pull the parking brake handle up slowly, and count the number of notches before the brake is applied. It should take 3–6 notches. If not, proceed with Step 3.
3. Working from underneath of the car, loosen the locknut on the parking brake equalizer.
4. Screw the adjusting nut in, just enough so that the parking brake cables have no slack.
5. Hold the adjusting nut in this position while tightening the locknut.
6. Check the rotation of the rear wheels, with the parking brake off, to be sure that the brake shoes aren't dragging.

DASH MOUNTED LEVER

1. Loosen the parking brake warning light switch bracket.
2. Push the parking brake lever in until it is stopped by the pawl.
3. Move the switch so that it will be off at this position, but on when the handle is pulled out.
4. Tighten the switch bracket and push the brake lever in again.
5. Working from underneath the vehicle, loosen the locknut on the parking brake cable equalizer.
6. Screw the adjusting nut in, just enough so that the brake cables have no slack.
7. Hold the adjusting nut in this position while tightening the locknut.
8. Check the rotation of the rear wheels to make sure that the brakes are not dragging.
9. Pull out on the parking brake lever, and count the number of notches needed to apply the parking brake. Adjust cable if necessary.

Parking Brake Adjustment

Model	Adjusting Range (Notches)
Corona	7–12 ①
Mark II/4 ('70–'72)	5–9
Mark II/6 ('72–'76)	8–10 ②
Crown 2300 ('70–'71)	5–9
Crown 2600 ('72)	8–11
Cressida	5–8
Camry	4–7
Van	7–9

① 1976 and later—3–6   ② 1976—8–12

Troubleshooting

10

This section is designed to aid in the quick, accurate diagnosis of automotive problems. While automotive repairs can be made by many people, accurate troubleshooting is a rare skill for the amateur and professional alike.

In its simplest state, troubleshooting is an exercise in logic. It is essential to realize that an automobile is really composed of a series of systems. Some of these systems are interrelated; others are not. Automobiles operate within a framework of logical rules and physical laws, and the key to troubleshooting is a good understanding of all the automotive systems.

This section breaks the car or truck down into its component systems, allowing the problem to be isolated. The charts and diagnostic road maps list the most common problems and the most probable causes of trouble. Obviously it would be impossible to list every possible problem that could happen along with every possible cause, but it will locate MOST problems and eliminate a lot of unnecessary guesswork. The systematic format will locate problems within a given system, but, because many automotive systems are interrelated, the solution to your particular problem may be found in a number of systems on the car or truck.

USING THE TROUBLESHOOTING CHARTS

This book contains all of the specific information that the average do-it-yourself mechanic needs to repair and maintain his or her car or truck. The troubleshooting charts are designed to be used in conjunction with the specific procedures and information in the text. For instance, troubleshooting a point-type ignition system is fairly standard for all models, but you may be directed to the text to find procedures for troubleshooting an individual type of electronic ignition. You will also have to refer to the specification charts throughout the book for specifications applicable to your car or truck.

TOOLS AND EQUIPMENT

The tools illustrated in Chapter 1 (plus two more diagnostic pieces) will be adequate to troubleshoot most problems. The two other tools needed are a voltmeter and an ohmmeter. These can be purchased separately or in combination, known as a VOM meter.

In the event that other tools are required, they will be noted in the procedures.

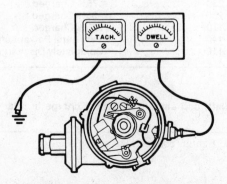

Tach-dwell hooked-up to distributor

Specific Diagnosis

This section is arranged so that following each test, instructions are given to proceed to another, until a problem is diagnosed.

Section 1—Battery

Test and Procedure	Results and Indications	Proceed to
1.1—Inspect the battery visually for case condition (corrosion, cracks) and water level.	If case is cracked, replace battery:	**1.4**
	If the case is intact, remove corrosion with a solution of baking soda and water (**CAUTION:** *do not get the solution into the battery*), and fill with water:	**1.2**

DIRT ON TOP OF BATTERY
CORROSION
PLUGGED VENT
LOOSE CABLE OR POSTS
CRACKS
LOW WATER LEVEL

Inspect the battery case

Test and Procedure	Results and Indications	Proceed to
1.2—Check the battery cable connections: Insert a screwdriver between the battery post and the cable clamp. Turn the headlights on high beam, and observe them as the screwdriver is gently twisted to ensure good metal to metal contact.	If the lights brighten, remove and clean the clamp and post; coat the post with petroleum jelly, install and tighten the clamp:	**1.4**
	If no improvement is noted:	**1.3**

TESTING BATTERY CABLE CONNECTIONS USING A SCREWDRIVER

Test and Procedure	Results and Indications	Proceed to
1.3—Test the state of charge of the battery using an individual cell tester or hydrometer.	If indicated, charge the battery. **NOTE:** *If no obvious reason exists for the low state of charge (i.e., battery age, prolonged storage), proceed to:*	**1.4**

°F

ADD THIS NUMBER TO THE HYDROMETER READING TO OBTAIN THE CORRECTED SPECIFIC GRAVITY

SUBTRACT THIS NUMBER FROM THE HYDROMETER READING TO OBTAIN THE CORRECTED SPECIFIC GRAVITY

Specific Gravity (@ 80° F.)

Minimum		Battery Charge
1.260	....	100% Charged
1.230	....	75% Charged
1.200	....	50% Charged
1.170	....	25% Charged
1.140	....	Very Little Power Left
1.110	....	Completely Discharged

The effects of temperature on battery specific gravity (left) and amount of battery charge in relation to specific gravity (right)

Test and Procedure	Results and Indications	Proceed to
1.4—Visually inspect battery cables for cracking, bad connection to ground, or bad connection to starter.	If necessary, tighten connections or replace the cables:	**2.1**

Section 2—Starting System
See Chapter 3 for service procedures

Test and Procedure	Results and Indications	Proceed to
Note: Tests in Group 2 are performed with coil high tension lead disconnected to prevent accidental starting.		
2.1—Test the starter motor and solenoid: Connect a jumper from the battery post of the solenoid (or relay) to the starter post of the solenoid (or relay).	If starter turns the engine normally:	**2.2**
	If the starter buzzes, or turns the engine very slowly:	**2.4**
	If no response, replace the solenoid (or relay).	**3.1**
	If the starter turns, but the engine doesn't, ensure that the flywheel ring gear is intact. If the gear is undamaged, replace the starter drive.	**3.1**
2.2—Determine whether ignition override switches are functioning properly (clutch start switch, neutral safety switch), by connecting a jumper across the switch(es), and turning the ignition switch to "start".	If starter operates, adjust or replace switch:	**3.1**
	If the starter doesn't operate:	**2.3**
2.3—Check the ignition switch "start" position: Connect a 12V test lamp or voltmeter between the starter post of the solenoid (or relay) and ground. Turn the ignition switch to the "start" position, and jiggle the key.	If the lamp doesn't light or the meter needle doesn't move when the switch is turned, check the ignition switch for loose connections, cracked insulation, or broken wires. Repair or replace as necessary:	**3.1**
	If the lamp flickers or needle moves when the key is jiggled, replace the ignition switch.	**3.3**

Checking the ignition switch "start" position   STARTER RELAY (IF EQUIPPED)

Test and Procedure	Results and Indications	Proceed to
2.4—Remove and bench test the starter, according to specifications in the engine electrical section.	If the starter does not meet specifications, repair or replace as needed:	**3.1**
	If the starter is operating properly:	**2.5**
2.5—Determine whether the engine can turn freely: Remove the spark plugs, and check for water in the cylinders. Check for water on the dipstick, or oil in the radiator. Attempt to turn the engine using an 18" flex drive and socket on the crankshaft pulley nut or bolt.	If the engine will turn freely only with the spark plugs out, and hydrostatic lock (water in the cylinders) is ruled out, check valve timing:	**9.2**
	If engine will not turn freely, and it is known that the clutch and transmission are free, the engine must be disassembled for further evaluation:	**Chapter 3**

Section 3—Primary Electrical System

Test and Procedure	Results and Indications	Proceed to
3.1—Check the ignition switch "on" position: Connect a jumper wire between the distributor side of the coil and ground, and a 12V test lamp between the switch side of the coil and ground. Remove the high tension lead from the coil. Turn the ignition switch on and jiggle the key.	If the lamp lights:	3.2
	If the lamp flickers when the key is jiggled, replace the ignition switch:	3.3
	If the lamp doesn't light, check for loose or open connections. If none are found, remove the ignition switch and check for continuity. If the switch is faulty, replace it:	3.3

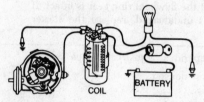

Checking the ignition switch "on" position

3.2—Check the ballast resistor or resistance wire for an open circuit, using an ohmmeter. See Chapter 3 for specific tests.	Replace the resistor or resistance wire if the resistance is zero. **NOTE: Some ignition systems have no ballast resistor.**	3.3

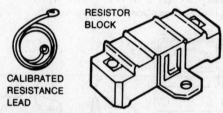

Two types of resistors

3.3—On point-type ignition systems, visually inspect the breaker points for burning, pitting or excessive wear. Gray coloring of the point contact surfaces is normal. Rotate the crankshaft until the contact heel rests on a high point of the distributor cam and adjust the point gap to specifications. On electronic ignition models, remove the distributor cap and visually inspect the armature. Ensure that the armature pin is in place, and that the armature is on tight and rotates when the engine is cranked. Make sure there are no cracks, chips or rounded edges on the armature.	If the breaker points are intact, clean the contact surfaces with fine emery cloth, and adjust the point gap to specifications. If the points are worn, replace them. On electronic systems, replace any parts which appear defective. If condition persists:	3.4

Test and Procedure	Results and Indications	Proceed to
3.4—On point-type ignition systems, connect a dwell-meter between the distributor primary lead and ground. Crank the engine and observe the point dwell angle. On electronic ignition systems, conduct a stator (magnetic pickup assembly) test. See Chapter 3.	On point-type systems, adjust the dwell angle if necessary. **NOTE:** *Increasing the point gap decreases the dwell angle and vice-versa.*	**3.6**
	If the dwell meter shows little or no reading;	**3.5**
	On electronic ignition systems, if the stator is bad, replace the stator. If the stator is good, proceed to the other tests in Chapter 3.	

Dwell is a function of point gap

3.5—On the point-type ignition systems, check the condenser for short: connect an ohmeter across the condenser body and the pigtail lead.	If any reading other than infinite is noted, replace the condenser	**3.6**

Checking the condenser for short

3.6—Test the coil primary resistance: On point-type ignition systems, connect an ohmmeter across the coil primary terminals, and read the resistance on the low scale. Note whether an external ballast resistor or resistance wire is used. On electronic ignition systems, test the coil primary resistance as in Chapter 3.	Point-type ignition coils utilizing ballast resistors or resistance wires should have approximately 1.0 ohms resistance. Coils with internal resistors should have approximately 4.0 ohms resistance. If values far from the above are noted, replace the coil.	**4.1**

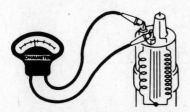

Check the coil primary resistance

Section 4—Secondary Electrical System

See Chapters 2–3 for service procedures

Test and Procedure	Results and Indications	Proceed to
4.1—Check for spark: Hold each spark plug wire approximately ¼″ from ground with gloves or a heavy, dry rag. Crank the engine, and observe the spark.	If no spark is evident:	4.2
	If spark is good in some cylinders:	4.3
	If spark is good in all cylinders:	4.6

Check for spark at the plugs

Test and Procedure	Results and Indications	Proceed to
4.2—Check for spark at the coil high tension lead: Remove the coil high tension lead from the distributor and position it approximately ¼″ from ground. Crank the engine and observe spark. **CAUTION: *This test should not be performed on engines equipped with electronic ignition.***	If the spark is good and consistent:	4.3
	If the spark is good but intermittent, test the primary electrical system starting at 3.3:	3.3
	If the spark is weak or non-existent, replace the coil high tension lead, clean and tighten all connections and retest. If no improvement is noted:	4.4
4.3—Visually inspect the distributor cap and rotor for burned or corroded contacts, cracks, carbon tracks, or moisture. Also check the fit of the rotor on the distributor shaft (where applicable).	If moisture is present, dry thoroughly, and retest per 4.1:	4.1
	If burned or excessively corroded contacts, cracks, or carbon tracks are noted, replace the defective part(s) and retest per 4.1:	4.1
	If the rotor and cap appear intact, or are only slightly corroded, clean the contacts thoroughly (including the cap towers and spark plug wire ends) and retest per 4.1:	
	If the spark is good in all cases:	4.6
	If the spark is poor in all cases:	4.5

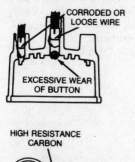

CORRODED OR LOOSE WIRE

EXCESSIVE WEAR OF BUTTON

HIGH RESISTANCE CARBON

ROTOR TIP BURNED AWAY

Inspect the distributor cap and rotor

Test and Procedure	Results and Indications	Proceed to
4.4—Check the coil secondary resistance: On point-type systems connect an ohmmeter across the distributor side of the coil and the coil tower. Read the resistance on the high scale of the ohmmeter. On electronic ignition systems, see Chapter 3 for specific tests.	The resistance of a satisfactory coil should be between 4,000 and 10,000 ohms. If resistance is considerably higher (i.e., 40,000 ohms) replace the coil and retest per 4.1. **NOTE:** *This does not apply to high performance coils.*	

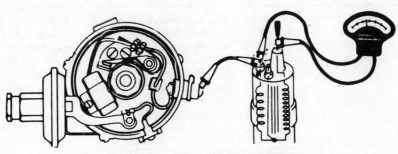

Testing the coil secondary resistance

4.5—Visually inspect the spark plug wires for cracking or brittleness. Ensure that no two wires are positioned so as to cause induction firing (adjacent and parallel). Remove each wire, one by one, and check resistance with an ohmmeter.	Replace any cracked or brittle wires. If any of the wires are defective, replace the entire set. Replace any wires with excessive resistance (over $8000\,\Omega$ per foot for suppression wire), and separate any wires that might cause induction firing.	4.6

Misfiring can be the result of spark plug leads to adjacent, consecutively firing cylinders running parallel and too close together

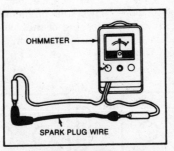

On point-type ignition systems, check the spark plug wires as shown. On electronic ignitions, do not remove the wire from the distributor cap terminal; instead, test through the cap

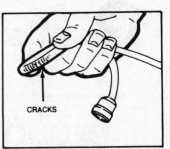

Spark plug wires can be checked visually by bending them in a loop over your finger. This will reveal any cracks, burned or broken insulation. Any wire with cracked insulation should be replaced

4.6—Remove the spark plugs, noting the cylinders from which they were removed, and evaluate according to the color photos in the middle of this book.	See following.	**See following.**

Test and Procedure	Results and Indications	Proceed to
4.7—Examine the location of all the plugs.	The following diagrams illustrate some of the conditions that the location of plugs will reveal.	4.8

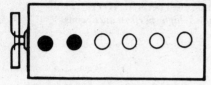

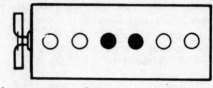

Two adjacent plugs are fouled in a 6-cylinder engine, 4-cylinder engine or either bank of a V-8. This is probably due to a blown head gasket between the two cylinders

The two center plugs in a 6-cylinder engine are fouled. Raw fuel may be "boiled" out of the carburetor into the intake manifold after the engine is shut-off. Stop-start driving can also foul the center plugs, due to overly rich mixture. Proper float level, a new float needle and seat or use of an insulating spacer may help this problem

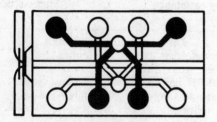

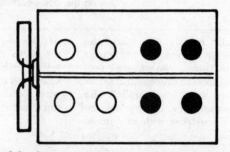

An unbalanced carburetor is indicated. Following the fuel flow on this particular design shows that the cylinders fed by the right-hand barrel are fouled from overly rich mixture, while the cylinders fed by the left-hand barrel are normal

If the four rear plugs are overheated, a cooling system problem is suggested. A thorough cleaning of the cooling system may restore coolant circulation and cure the problem

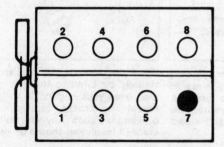

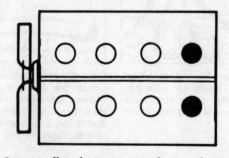

Finding one plug overheated may indicate an intake manifold leak near the affected cylinder. If the overheated plug is the second of two adjacent, consecutively firing plugs, it could be the result of ignition cross-firing. Separating the leads to these two plugs will eliminate cross-fire

Occasionally, the two rear plugs in large, lightly used V-8's will become oil fouled. High oil consumption and smoky exhaust may also be noticed. It is probably due to plugged oil drain holes in the rear of the cylinder head, causing oil to be sucked in around the valve stems. This usually occurs in the rear cylinders first, because the engine slants that way

Test and Procedure	Results and Indications	Proceed to
4.8—Determine the static ignition timing. Using the crankshaft pulley timing marks as a guide, locate top dead center on the compression stroke of the number one cylinder.	The rotor should be pointing toward the No. 1 tower in the distributor cap, and, on electronic ignitions, the armature spoke for that cylinder should be lined up with the stator.	4.8
4.9—Check coil polarity: Connect a voltmeter negative lead to the coil high tension lead, and the positive lead to ground (**NOTE**: *Reverse the hook-up for positive ground systems*). Crank the engine momentarily. **Checking coil polarity**	If the voltmeter reads up-scale, the polarity is correct: If the voltmeter reads down-scale, reverse the coil polarity (switch the primary leads):	5.1 5.1

Section 5—Fuel System
See Chapter 4 for service procedures

Test and Procedure	Results and Indications	Proceed to
5.1—Determine that the air filter is functioning efficiently: Hold paper elements up to a strong light, and attempt to see light through the filter.	Clean permanent air filters in solvent (or manufacturer's recommendation), and allow to dry. Replace paper elements through which light cannot be seen:	5.2
5.2—Determine whether a flooding condition exists: Flooding is identified by a strong gasoline odor, and excessive gasoline present in the throttle bore(s) of the carburetor.	If flooding is not evident: If flooding is evident, permit the gasoline to dry for a few moments and restart. If flooding doesn't recur: If flooding is persistent:	5.3 5.7 5.5

If the engine floods repeatedly, check the choke butterfly flap

5.3—Check that fuel is reaching the carburetor: Detach the fuel line at the carburetor inlet. Hold the end of the line in a cup (not styrofoam), and crank the engine.	If fuel flows smoothly: If fuel doesn't flow (**NOTE**: *Make sure that there is fuel in the tank*), or flows erratically:	5.7 5.4

Check the fuel pump by disconnecting the output line (fuel pump-to-carburetor) at the carburetor and operating the starter briefly

Test and Procedure	Results and Indications	Proceed to
5.4—Test the fuel pump: Disconnect all fuel lines from the fuel pump. Hold a finger over the input fitting, crank the engine (with electric pump, turn the ignition or pump on); and feel for suction.	If suction is evident, blow out the fuel line to the tank with low pressure compressed air until bubbling is heard from the fuel filler neck. Also blow out the carburetor fuel line (both ends disconnected):	**5.7**
	If no suction is evident, replace or repair the fuel pump: NOTE: *Repeated oil fouling of the spark plugs, or a no-start condition, could be the result of a ruptured vacuum booster pump diaphragm, through which oil or gasoline is being drawn into the intake manifold (where applicable).*	**5.7**
5.5—Occasionally, small specks of dirt will clog the small jets and orifices in the carburetor. With the engine cold, hold a flat piece of wood or similar material over the carburetor, where possible, and crank the engine.	If the engine starts, but runs roughly the engine is probably not run enough. If the engine won't start:	**5.9**
5.6—Check the needle and seat: Tap the carburetor in the area of the needle and seat.	If flooding stops, a gasoline additive (e.g., Gumout) will often cure the problem:	**5.7**
	If flooding continues, check the fuel pump for excessive pressure at the carburetor (according to specifications). If the pressure is normal, the needle and seat must be removed and checked, and/or the float level adjusted:	**5.7**
5.7—Test the accelerator pump by looking into the throttle bores while operating the throttle.	If the accelerator pump appears to be operating normally:	**5.8**
	If the accelerator pump is not operating, the pump must be reconditioned. Where possible, service the pump with the carburetor(s) installed on the engine. If necessary, remove the carburetor. Prior to removal:	**5.8**

Check for gas at the carburetor by looking down the carburetor throat while someone moves the accelerator

5.8—Determine whether the carburetor main fuel system is functioning: Spray a commercial starting fluid into the carburetor while attempting to start the engine.	If the engine starts, runs for a few seconds, and dies:	**5.9**
	If the engine doesn't start:	**6.1**

Test and Procedure	Results and Indications	Proceed to
5.9—Uncommon fuel system malfunctions: See below:	If the problem is solved:	6.1
	If the problem remains, remove and recondition the carburetor.	

Condition	Indication	Test	Prevailing Weather Conditions	Remedy
Vapor lock	Engine will not restart shortly after running.	Cool the components of the fuel system until the engine starts. Vapor lock can be cured faster by draping a wet cloth over a mechanical fuel pump.	Hot to very hot	Ensure that the exhaust manifold heat control valve is operating. Check with the vehicle manufacturer for the recommended solution to vapor lock on the model in question.
Carburetor icing	Engine will not idle, stalls at low speeds.	Visually inspect the throttle plate area of the throttle bores for frost.	High humidity, 32–40° F.	Ensure that the exhaust manifold heat control valve is operating, and that the intake manifold heat riser is not blocked.
Water in the fuel	Engine sputters and stalls; may not start.	Pump a small amount of fuel into a glass jar. Allow to stand, and inspect for droplets or a layer of water.	High humidity, extreme temperature changes.	For droplets, use one or two cans of commercial gas line anti-freeze. For a layer of water, the tank must be drained, and the fuel lines blown out with compressed air.

Section 6—Engine Compression
See Chapter 3 for service procedures

6.1—Test engine compression: Remove all spark plugs. Block the throttle wide open. Insert a compression gauge into a spark plug port, crank the engine to obtain the maximum reading, and record.	If compression is within limits on all cylinders:	7.1
	If gauge reading is extremely low on all cylinders:	6.2
	If gauge reading is low on one or two cylinders: (If gauge readings are identical and low on two or more adjacent cylinders, the head gasket must be replaced.)	6.2

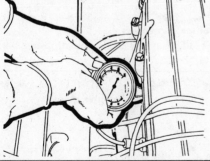

Checking compression

6.2—Test engine compression (wet): Squirt approximately 30 cc. of engine oil into each cylinder, and retest per 6.1.	If the readings improve, worn or cracked rings or broken pistons are indicated:	See Chapter 3
	If the readings do not improve, burned or excessively carboned valves or a jumped timing chain are indicated: NOTE: *A jumped timing chain is often indicated by difficult cranking.*	7.1

Section 7—Engine Vacuum
See Chapter 3 for service procedures

Test and Procedure	Results and Indications	Proceed to
7.1—Attach a vacuum gauge to the intake manifold beyond the throttle plate. Start the engine, and observe the action of the needle over the range of engine speeds.	See below.	**See below**

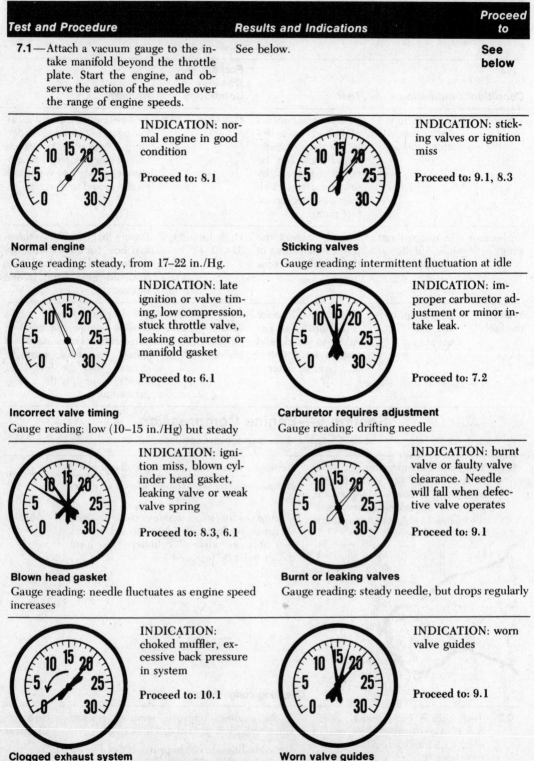

INDICATION: normal engine in good condition

Proceed to: 8.1

Normal engine
Gauge reading: steady, from 17–22 in./Hg.

INDICATION: sticking valves or ignition miss

Proceed to: 9.1, 8.3

Sticking valves
Gauge reading: intermittent fluctuation at idle

INDICATION: late ignition or valve timing, low compression, stuck throttle valve, leaking carburetor or manifold gasket

Proceed to: 6.1

Incorrect valve timing
Gauge reading: low (10–15 in./Hg) but steady

INDICATION: improper carburetor adjustment or minor intake leak.

Proceed to: 7.2

Carburetor requires adjustment
Gauge reading: drifting needle

INDICATION: ignition miss, blown cylinder head gasket, leaking valve or weak valve spring

Proceed to: 8.3, 6.1

Blown head gasket
Gauge reading: needle fluctuates as engine speed increases

INDICATION: burnt valve or faulty valve clearance. Needle will fall when defective valve operates

Proceed to: 9.1

Burnt or leaking valves
Gauge reading: steady needle, but drops regularly

INDICATION: choked muffler, excessive back pressure in system

Proceed to: 10.1

Clogged exhaust system
Gauge reading: gradual drop in reading at idle

INDICATION: worn valve guides

Proceed to: 9.1

Worn valve guides
Gauge reading: needle vibrates excessively at idle, but steadies as engine speed increases

---

White pointer = steady gauge hand   Black pointer = fluctuating gauge hand

Test and Procedure	Results and Indications	Proceed to
7.2—Attach a vacuum gauge per 7.1, and test for an intake manifold leak. Squirt a small amount of oil around the intake manifold gaskets, carburetor gaskets, plugs and fittings. Observe the action of the vacuum gauge.	If the reading improves, replace the indicated gasket, or seal the indicated fitting or plug: If the reading remains low:	**8.1** **7.3**
7.3—Test all vacuum hoses and accessories for leaks as described in 7.2. Also check the carburetor body (dashpots, automatic choke mechanism, throttle shafts) for leaks in the same manner.	If the reading improves, service or replace the offending part(s): If the reading remains low:	**8.1** **6.1**

Section 8—Secondary Electrical System
See Chapter 2 for service procedures

Test and Procedure	Results and Indications	Proceed to
8.1—Remove the distributor cap and check to make sure that the rotor turns when the engine is cranked. Visually inspect the distributor components.	Clean, tighten or replace any components which appear defective.	**8.2**
8.2—Connect a timing light (per manufacturer's recommendation) and check the dynamic ignition timing. Disconnect and plug the vacuum hose(s) to the distributor if specified, start the engine, and observe the timing marks at the specified engine speed.	If the timing is not correct, adjust to specifications by rotating the distributor in the engine: (Advance timing by rotating distributor opposite normal direction of rotor rotation, retard timing by rotating distributor in same direction as rotor rotation.)	**8.3**
8.3—Check the operation of the distributor advance mechanism(s): To test the mechanical advance, disconnect the vacuum lines from the distributor advance unit and observe the timing marks with a timing light as the engine speed is increased from idle. If the mark moves smoothly, without hesitation, it may be assumed that the mechanical advance is functioning properly. To test vacuum advance and/or retard systems, alternately crimp and release the vacuum line, and observe the timing mark for movement. If movement is noted, the system is operating.	If the systems are functioning: If the systems are not functioning, remove the distributor, and test on a distributor tester:	**8.4** **8.4**
8.4—Locate an ignition miss: With the engine running, remove each spark plug wire, one at a time, until one is found that doesn't cause the engine to roughen and slow down.	When the missing cylinder is identified:	**4.1**

Section 9—Valve Train
See Chapter 3 for service procedures

Test and Procedure	Results and Indications	Proceed to
9.1—Evaluate the valve train: Remove the valve cover, and ensure that the valves are adjusted to specifications. A mechanic's stethoscope may be used to aid in the diagnosis of the valve train. By pushing the probe on or near push rods or rockers, valve noise often can be isolated. A timing light also may be used to diagnose valve problems. Connect the light according to manufacturer's recommendations, and start the engine. Vary the firing moment of the light by increasing the engine speed (and therefore the ignition advance), and moving the trigger from cylinder to cylinder. Observe the movement of each valve.	Sticking valves or erratic valve train motion can be observed with the timing light. The cylinder head must be disassembled for repairs.	**See Chapter 3**
9.2—Check the valve timing: Locate top dead center of the No. 1 piston, and install a degree wheel or tape on the crankshaft pulley or damper with zero corresponding to an index mark on the engine. Rotate the crankshaft in its direction of rotation, and observe the opening of the No. 1 cylinder intake valve. The opening should correspond with the correct mark on the degree wheel according to specifications.	If the timing is not correct, the timing cover must be removed for further investigation.	**See Chapter 3**

Section 10—Exhaust System

Test and Procedure	Results and Indications	Proceed to
10.1—Determine whether the exhaust manifold heat control valve is operating: Operate the valve by hand to determine whether it is free to move. If the valve is free, run the engine to operating temperature and observe the action of the valve, to ensure that it is opening.	If the valve sticks, spray it with a suitable solvent, open and close the valve to free it, and retest. If the valve functions properly:	**10.2**
	If the valve does not free, or does not operate, replace the valve:	**10.2**
10.2—Ensure that there are no exhaust restrictions: Visually inspect the exhaust system for kinks, dents, or crushing. Also note that gases are flowing freely from the tailpipe at all engine speeds, indicating no restriction in the muffler or resonator.	Replace any damaged portion of the system:	**11.1**

CHILTON'S
AUTO BODY
REPAIR TIPS

Tools and Materials • Step-by-Step Illustrated Procedures
How To Repair Dents, Scratches and Rust Holes
Spray Painting and Refinishing Tips

With a little practice, basic body repair procedures can be mastered by any do-it-yourself mechanic. The step-by-step repairs shown here can be applied to almost any type of auto body repair.

TOOLS & MATERIALS

You may already have basic tools, such as hammers and electric drills. Other tools unique to body repair — body hammers, grinding attachments, sanding blocks, dent puller, half-round plastic file and plastic spreaders — are relatively inexpensive and can be obtained wherever auto parts or auto body repair parts are sold. Portable air compressors and paint spray guns can be purchased or rented.

Auto Body Repair Kits

The best and most often used products are available to the do-it-yourselfer in kit form, from major manufacturers of auto body repair products. The same manufacturers also merchandise the individual products for use by pros.

Kits are available to make a wide variety of repairs, including holes, dents and scratches and fiberglass, and offer the advantage of buying the materials you'll need for the job. There is little waste or chance of materials going bad from not being used. Many kits may also contain basic body-working tools such as body files, sanding blocks and spreaders. Check the contents of the kit before buying your tools.

BODY REPAIR TIPS

Safety

Many of the products associated with auto body repair and refinishing contain toxic chemicals. Read all labels before opening containers and store them in a safe place and manner.

• Wear eye protection (safety goggles) when using power tools or when performing any operation that involves the removal of any type of material.

• Wear lung protection (disposable mask or respirator) when grinding, sanding or painting.

Sanding

1 Sand off paint before using a dent puller. When using a non-adhesive sanding disc, cover the back of the disc with an overlapping layer or two of masking tape and trim the edges. The disc will last considerably longer.

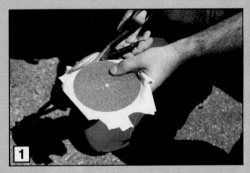

2 Use the circular motion of the sanding disc to grind *into* the edge of the repair. Grinding or sanding away from the jagged edge will only tear the sandpaper.

3 Use the palm of your hand flat on the panel to detect high and low spots. Do not use your fingertips. Slide your hand slowly back and forth.

WORKING WITH BODY FILLER

Mixing The Filler

Cleanliness and proper mixing and application are extremely important. Use a clean piece of plastic or glass or a disposable artist's palette to mix body filler.

1 Allow plenty of time and follow directions. No useful purpose will be served by adding more hardener to make it cure (set-up) faster. Less hardener means more curing time, but the mixture dries harder; more hardener means less curing time but a softer mixture.

2 Both the hardener and the filler should be thoroughly kneaded or stirred before mixing. Hardener should be a solid paste and dispense like thin toothpaste. Body filler should be smooth, and free of lumps or thick spots.

Getting the proper amount of hardener in the filler is the trickiest part of preparing the filler. Use the same amount of hardener in cold or warm weather. For contour filler (thick coats), a bead of hardener twice the diameter of the filler is about right. There's about a 15% margin on either side, but, if in doubt use less hardener.

3 Mix the body filler and hardener by wiping across the mixing surface, picking the mixture up and wiping it again. Colder weather requires longer mixing times. Do not mix in a circular motion; this will trap air bubbles which will become holes in the cured filler.

Applying The Filler

1 For best results, filler should not be applied over ¼" thick.

Apply the filler in several coats. Build it up to above the level of the repair surface so that it can be sanded or grated down.

The first coat of filler must be pressed on with a firm wiping motion.

Apply the filler in one direction only. Working the filler back and forth will either pull it off the metal or trap air bubbles.

REPAIRING DENTS

Before you start, take a few minutes to study the damaged area. Try to visualize the shape of the panel before it was damaged. If the damage is on the left fender, look at the right fender and use it as a guide. If there is access to the panel from behind, you can reshape it with a body hammer. If not, you'll have to use a dent puller. Go slowly and work the metal a little at a time. Get the panel as straight as possible before applying filler.

1 This dent is typical of one that can be pulled out or hammered out from behind. Remove the headlight cover, headlight assembly and turn signal housing.

2 Drill a series of holes ½ the size of the end of the dent puller along the stress line. Make some trial pulls and assess the results. If necessary, drill more holes and try again. Do not hurry.

3 If possible, use a body hammer and block to shape the metal back to its original contours. Get the metal back as close to its original shape as possible. Don't depend on body filler to fill dents.

4 Using an 80-grit grinding disc on an electric drill, grind the paint from the surrounding area down to bare metal. Use a new grinding pad to prevent heat buildup that will warp metal.

5 The area should look like this when you're finished grinding. Knock the drill holes in and tape over small openings to keep plastic filler out.

6 Mix the body filler (see Body Repair Tips). Spread the body filler evenly over the entire area (see Body Repair Tips). Be sure to cover the area completely.

7 Let the body filler dry until the surface can just be scratched with your fingernail. Knock the high spots from the body filler with a body file ("Cheesegrater"). Check frequently with the palm of your hand for high and low spots.

8 Check to be sure that trim pieces that will be installed later will fit exactly. Sand the area with 40-grit paper.

9 If you wind up with low spots, you may have to apply another layer of filler.

10 Knock the high spots off with 40-grit paper. When you are satisfied with the contours of the repair, apply a thin coat of filler to cover pin holes and scratches.

11 Block sand the area with 40-grit paper to a smooth finish. Pay particular attention to body lines and ridges that must be well-defined.

12 Sand the area with 400 paper and then finish with a scuff pad. The finished repair is ready for priming and painting (see Painting Tips).

Materials and photos courtesy of Ritt Jones Auto Body, Prospect Park, PA.

REPAIRING RUST HOLES

There are many ways to repair rust holes. The fiberglass cloth kit shown here is one of the most cost efficient for the owner because it provides a strong repair that resists cracking and moisture and is relatively easy to use. It can be used on large and small holes (with or without backing) and can be applied over contoured areas. Remember, however, that short of replacing an entire panel, no repair is a guarantee that the rust will not return.

1 Remove any trim that will be in the way. Clean away all loose debris. Cut away all the rusted metal. But be sure to leave enough metal to retain the contour or body shape.

2 Grind away all traces of rust with a 24-grit grinding disc. Be sure to grind back 3-4 inches from the edge of the hole down to bare metal and be sure all traces of paint, primer and rust are removed.

3 Block sand the area with 80 or 100 grit sandpaper to get a clear, shiny surface and feathered paint edge. Tap the edges of the hole inward with a ball peen hammer.

4 If you are going to use release film, cut a piece about 2-3″ larger than the area you have sanded. Place the film over the repair and mark the sanded area on the film. Avoid any unnecessary wrinkling of the film.

5 Cut 2 pieces of fiberglass matte to match the shape of the repair. One piece should be about 1″ smaller than the sanded area and the second piece should be 1″ smaller than the first. Mix enough filler and hardener to saturate the fiberglass material (see Body Repair Tips).

6 Lay the release sheet on a flat surface and spread an even layer of filler, large enough to cover the repair. Lay the smaller piece of fiberglass cloth in the center of the sheet and spread another layer of filler over the fiberglass cloth. Repeat the operation for the larger piece of cloth.

7 Place the repair material over the repair area, with the release film facing outward. Use a spreader and work from the center outward to smooth the material, following the body contours. Be sure to remove all air bubbles.

8 Wait until the repair has dried tack-free and peel off the release sheet. The ideal working temperature is 60°-90° F. Cooler or warmer temperatures or high humidity may require additional curing time. Wait longer, if in doubt.

9 Sand and feather-edge the entire area. The initial sanding can be done with a sanding disc on an electric drill if care is used. Finish the sanding with a block sander. Low spots can be filled with body filler; this may require several applications.

10 When the filler can just be scratched with a fingernail, knock the high spots down with a body file and smooth the entire area with 80-grit. Feather the filled areas into the surrounding areas.

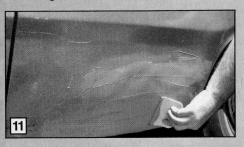

11 When the area is sanded smooth, mix some topcoat and hardener and apply it directly with a spreader. This will give a smooth finish and prevent the glass matte from showing through the paint.

12 Block sand the topcoat smooth with finishing sandpaper (200 grit), and 400 grit. The repair is ready for masking, priming and painting (see Painting Tips).

Materials and photos courtesy Marson Corporation, Chelsea, Massachusetts

PAINTING TIPS

Preparation

1 SANDING — Use a 400 or 600 grit wet or dry sandpaper. Wet-sand the area with a ¼ sheet of sandpaper soaked in clean water. Keep the paper wet while sanding. Sand the area until the repaired area tapers into the original finish.

2 CLEANING — Wash the area to be painted thoroughly with water and a clean rag. Rinse it thoroughly and wipe the surface dry until you're sure it's completely free of dirt, dust, fingerprints, wax, detergent or other foreign matter.

3 MASKING — Protect any areas you don't want to overspray by covering them with masking tape and newspaper. Be careful not get fingerprints on the area to be painted.

4 PRIMING — All exposed metal should be primed before painting. Primer protects the metal and provides an excellent surface for paint adhesion. When the primer is dry, wet-sand the area again with 600 grit wet-sandpaper. Clean the area again after sanding.

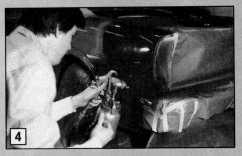

Painting Techniques

P aint applied from either a spray gun or a spray can (for small areas) will provide good results. Experiment on an old piece of metal to get the right combination before you begin painting.

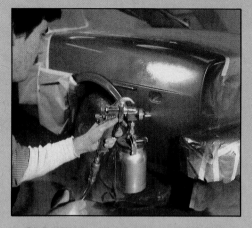

SPRAYING VISCOSITY (SPRAY GUN ONLY) — Paint should be thinned to spraying viscosity according to the directions on the can. Use only the recommended thinner or reducer and the same amount of reduction regardless of temperature.

AIR PRESSURE (SPRAY GUN ONLY) — This is extremely important. Be sure you are using the proper recommended pressure.

TEMPERATURE — The surface to be painted should be approximately the same temperature as the surrounding air. Applying warm paint to a cold surface, or vice versa, will completely upset the paint characteristics.

THICKNESS — Spray with smooth strokes. In general, the thicker the coat of paint, the longer the drying time. Apply several thin coats about 30 seconds apart. The paint should remain wet long enough to flow out and no longer; heavier coats will only produce sags or wrinkles. Spray a light (fog) coat, followed by heavier color coats.

DISTANCE — The ideal spraying distance is 8″-12″ from the gun or can to the surface. Shorter distances will produce ripples, while greater distances will result in orange peel, dry film and poor color match and loss of material due to overspray.

OVERLAPPING — The gun or can should be kept at right angles to the surface at all times. Work to a wet edge at an even speed, using a 50% overlap and direct the center of the spray at the lower or nearest edge of the previous stroke.

RUBBING OUT (BLENDING) FRESH PAINT — Let the paint dry thoroughly. Runs or imperfections can be sanded out, primed and repainted.

Don't be in too big a hurry to remove the masking. This only produces paint ridges. When the finish has dried for at least a week, apply a small amount of fine grade rubbing compound with a clean, wet cloth. Use lots of water and blend the new paint with the surrounding area.

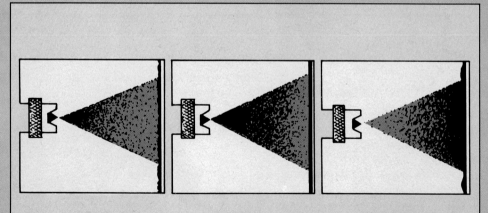

WRONG	CORRECT	WRONG
Thin coat. Stroke too fast, not enough overlap, gun too far away.	*Medium coat. Proper distance, good stroke, proper overlap.*	*Heavy coat. Stroke too slow, too much overlap, gun too close.*

Section 11—Cooling System
See Chapter 3 for service procedures

Test and Procedure	Results and Indications	Proceed to
11.1—Visually inspect the fan belt for glazing, cracks, and fraying, and replace if necessary. Tighten the belt so that the longest span has approximately ½″ play at its midpoint under thumb pressure (see Chapter 1).	Replace or tighten the fan belt as necessary: 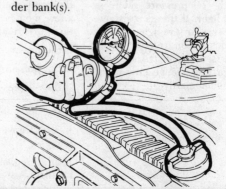 **Checking belt tension**	**11.2**
11.2—Check the fluid level of the cooling system.	If full or slightly low, fill as necessary:	**11.5**
	If extremely low:	**11.3**
11.3—Visually inspect the external portions of the cooling system (radiator, radiator hoses, thermostat elbow, water pump seals, heater hoses, etc.) for leaks. If none are found, pressurize the cooling system to 14–15 psi.	If cooling system holds the pressure:	**11.5**
	If cooling system loses pressure rapidly, reinspect external parts of the system for leaks under pressure. If none are found, check dipstick for coolant in crankcase. If no coolant is present, but pressure loss continues:	**11.4**
	If coolant is evident in crankcase, remove cylinder head(s), and check gasket(s). If gaskets are intact, block and cylinder head(s) should be checked for cracks or holes.	
	If the gasket(s) is blown, replace, and purge the crankcase of coolant:	**12.6**
	NOTE: *Occasionally, due to atmospheric and driving conditions, condensation of water can occur in the crankcase. This causes the oil to appear milky white. To remedy, run the engine until hot, and change the oil and oil filter.*	
11.4—Check for combustion leaks into the cooling system: Pressurize the cooling system as above. Start the engine, and observe the pressure gauge. If the needle fluctuates, remove each spark plug wire, one at a time, noting which cylinder(s) reduce or eliminate the fluctuation.	Cylinders which reduce or eliminate the fluctuation, when the spark plug wire is removed, are leaking into the cooling system. Replace the head gasket on the affected cylinder bank(s).	

Pressurizing the cooling system

Test and Procedure	Results and Indications	Proceed to
11.5—Check the radiator pressure cap: Attach a radiator pressure tester to the radiator cap (wet the seal prior to installation). Quickly pump up the pressure, noting the point at which the cap releases.	If the cap releases within ± 1 psi of the specified rating, it is operating properly:	**11.6**
	If the cap releases at more than ± 1 psi of the specified rating, it should be replaced:	**11.6**

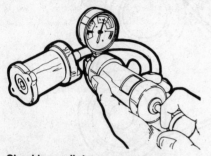

Checking radiator pressure cap

Test and Procedure	Results and Indications	Proceed to
11.6—Test the thermostat: Start the engine cold, remove the radiator cap, and insert a thermometer into the radiator. Allow the engine to idle. After a short while, there will be a sudden, rapid increase in coolant temperature. The temperature at which this sharp rise stops is the thermostat opening temperature.	If the thermostat opens at or about the specified temperature:	**11.7**
	If the temperature doesn't increase: (If the temperature increases slowly and gradually, replace the thermostat.)	**11.7**
11.7—Check the water pump: Remove the thermostat elbow and the thermostat, disconnect the coil high tension lead (to prevent starting), and crank the engine momentarily.	If coolant flows, replace the thermostat and retest per 11.6:	**11.6**
	If coolant doesn't flow, reverse flush the cooling system to alleviate any blockage that might exist. If system is not blocked, and coolant will not flow, replace the water pump.	

Section 12—Lubrication
See Chapter 3 for service procedures

Test and Procedure	Results and Indications	Proceed to
12.1—Check the oil pressure gauge or warning light: If the gauge shows low pressure, or the light is on for no obvious reason, remove the oil pressure sender. Install an accurate oil pressure gauge and run the engine momentarily.	If oil pressure builds normally, run engine for a few moments to determine that it is functioning normally, and replace the sender.	—
	If the pressure remains low:	**12.2**
	If the pressure surges:	**12.3**
	If the oil pressure is zero:	**12.3**
12.2—Visually inspect the oil: If the oil is watery or very thin, milky, or foamy, replace the oil and oil filter.	If the oil is normal:	**12.3**
	If after replacing oil the pressure remains low:	**12.3**
	If after replacing oil the pressure becomes normal:	—

Test and Procedure	Results and Indications	Proceed to
12.3—Inspect the oil pressure relief valve and spring, to ensure that it is not sticking or stuck. Remove and thoroughly clean the valve, spring, and the valve body.	If the oil pressure improves: If no improvement is noted:	— **12.4**
12.4—Check to ensure that the oil pump is not cavitating (sucking air instead of oil): See that the crankcase is neither over nor underfull, and that the pickup in the sump is in the proper position and free from sludge.	Fill or drain the crankcase to the proper capacity, and clean the pickup screen in solvent if necessary. If no improvement is noted:	**12.5**
12.5—Inspect the oil pump drive and the oil pump:	If the pump drive or the oil pump appear to be defective, service as necessary and retest per 12.1: If the pump drive and pump appear to be operating normally, the engine should be disassembled to determine where blockage exists:	**12.1** **See Chapter 3**
12.6—Purge the engine of ethylene glycol coolant: Completely drain the crankcase and the oil filter. Obtain a commercial butyl cellosolve base solvent, designated for this purpose, and follow the instructions precisely. Following this, install a new oil filter and refill the crankcase with the proper weight oil. The next oil and filter change should follow shortly thereafter (1000 miles).		

TROUBLESHOOTING EMISSION CONTROL SYSTEMS

See Chapter 4 for procedures applicable to individual emission control systems used on specific combinations of engine/transmission/model.

TROUBLESHOOTING THE CARBURETOR
See Chapter 4 for service procedures

Carburetor problems cannot be effectively isolated unless all other engine systems (particularly ignition and emission) are functioning properly and the engine is properly tuned.

Condition	Possible Cause
Engine cranks, but does not start	1. Improper starting procedure 2. No fuel in tank 3. Clogged fuel line or filter 4. Defective fuel pump 5. Choke valve not closing properly 6. Engine flooded 7. Choke valve not unloading 8. Throttle linkage not making full travel 9. Stuck needle or float 10. Leaking float needle or seat 11. Improper float adjustment
Engine stalls	1. Improperly adjusted idle speed or mixture **Engine hot** 2. Improperly adjusted dashpot 3. Defective or improperly adjusted solenoid 4. Incorrect fuel level in fuel bowl 5. Fuel pump pressure too high 6. Leaking float needle seat 7. Secondary throttle valve stuck open 8. Air or fuel leaks 9. Idle air bleeds plugged or missing 10. Idle passages plugged **Engine Cold** 11. Incorrectly adjusted choke 12. Improperly adjusted fast idle speed 13. Air leaks 14. Plugged idle or idle air passages 15. Stuck choke valve or binding linkage 16. Stuck secondary throttle valves 17. Engine flooding—high fuel level 18. Leaking or misaligned float
Engine hesitates on acceleration	1. Clogged fuel filter 2. Leaking fuel pump diaphragm 3. Low fuel pump pressure 4. Secondary throttle valves stuck, bent or misadjusted 5. Sticking or binding air valve 6. Defective accelerator pump 7. Vacuum leaks 8. Clogged air filter 9. Incorrect choke adjustment (engine cold)
Engine feels sluggish or flat on acceleration	1. Improperly adjusted idle speed or mixture 2. Clogged fuel filter 3. Defective accelerator pump 4. Dirty, plugged or incorrect main metering jets 5. Bent or sticking main metering rods 6. Sticking throttle valves 7. Stuck heat riser 8. Binding or stuck air valve 9. Dirty, plugged or incorrect secondary jets 10. Bent or sticking secondary metering rods. 11. Throttle body or manifold heat passages plugged 12. Improperly adjusted choke or choke vacuum break.
Carburetor floods	1. Defective fuel pump. Pressure too high. 2. Stuck choke valve 3. Dirty, worn or damaged float or needle valve/seat 4. Incorrect float/fuel level 5. Leaking float bowl

Condition	Possible Cause
Engine idles roughly and stalls	1. Incorrect idle speed 2. Clogged fuel filter 3. Dirt in fuel system or carburetor 4. Loose carburetor screws or attaching bolts 5. Broken carburetor gaskets 6. Air leaks 7. Dirty carburetor 8. Worn idle mixture needles 9. Throttle valves stuck open 10. Incorrectly adjusted float or fuel level 11. Clogged air filter
Engine runs unevenly or surges	1. Defective fuel pump 2. Dirty or clogged fuel filter 3. Plugged, loose or incorrect main metering jets or rods 4. Air leaks 5. Bent or sticking main metering rods 6. Stuck power piston 7. Incorrect float adjustment 8. Incorrect idle speed or mixture 9. Dirty or plugged idle system passages 10. Hard, brittle or broken gaskets 11. Loose attaching or mounting screws 12. Stuck or misaligned secondary throttle valves
Poor fuel economy	1. Poor driving habits 2. Stuck choke valve 3. Binding choke linkage 4. Stuck heat riser 5. Incorrect idle mixture 6. Defective accelerator pump 7. Air leaks 8. Plugged, loose or incorrect main metering jets 9. Improperly adjusted float or fuel level 10. Bent, misaligned or fuel-clogged float 11. Leaking float needle seat 12. Fuel leak 13. Accelerator pump discharge ball not seating properly 14. Incorrect main jets
Engine lacks high speed performance or power	1. Incorrect throttle linkage adjustment 2. Stuck or binding power piston 3. Defective accelerator pump 4. Air leaks 5. Incorrect float setting or fuel level 6. Dirty, plugged, worn or incorrect main metering jets or rods 7. Binding or sticking air valve 8. Brittle or cracked gaskets 9. Bent, incorrect or improperly adjusted secondary metering rods 10. Clogged fuel filter 11. Clogged air filter 12. Defective fuel pump

TROUBLESHOOTING FUEL INJECTION PROBLEMS

Each fuel injection system has its own unique components and test procedures, for which it is impossible to generalize. Refer to Chapter 4 of this Repair & Tune-Up Guide for specific test and repair procedures, if the vehicle is equipped with fuel injection.

TROUBLESHOOTING ELECTRICAL PROBLEMS

See Chapter 5 for service procedures

For any electrical system to operate, it must make a complete circuit. This simply means that the power flow from the battery must make a complete circle. When an electrical component is operating, power flows from the battery to the component, passes through the component causing it to perform its function (lighting a light bulb), and then returns to the battery through the ground of the circuit. This ground is usually (but not always) the metal part of the car or truck on which the electrical component is mounted.

Perhaps the easiest way to visualize this is to think of connecting a light bulb with two wires attached to it to the battery. If one of the two wires attached to the light bulb were attached to the negative post of the battery and the other were attached to the positive post of the battery, you would have a complete circuit. Current from the battery would flow to the light bulb, causing it to light, and return to the negative post of the battery.

The normal automotive circuit differs from this simple example in two ways. First, instead of having a return wire from the bulb to the battery, the light bulb returns the current to the battery through the chassis of the vehicle. Since the negative battery cable is attached to the chassis and the chassis is made of electrically conductive metal, the chassis of the vehicle can serve as a ground wire to complete the circuit. Secondly, most automotive circuits contain switches to turn components on and off as required.

Every complete circuit from a power source must include a component which is using the power from the power source. If you were to disconnect the light bulb from the wires and touch the two wires together (don't do this) the power supply wire to the component would be grounded before the normal ground connection for the circuit.

Because grounding a wire from a power source makes a complete circuit—less the required component to use the power—this phenomenon is called a short circuit. Common causes are: broken insulation (exposing the metal wire to a metal part of the car or truck), or a shorted switch.

Some electrical components which require a large amount of current to operate also have a relay in their circuit. Since these circuits carry a large amount of current, the thickness of the wire in the circuit (gauge size) is also greater. If this large wire were connected from the component to the control switch on the instrument panel, and then back to the component, a voltage drop would occur in the circuit. To prevent this potential drop in voltage, an electromagnetic switch (relay) is used. The large wires in the circuit are connected from the battery to one side of the relay, and from the opposite side of the relay to the component. The relay is normally open, preventing current from passing through the circuit. An additional, smaller, wire is connected from the relay to the control switch for the circuit. When the control switch is turned on, it grounds the smaller wire from the relay and completes the circuit. This closes the relay and allows current to flow from the battery to the component. The horn, headlight, and starter circuits are three which use relays.

It is possible for larger surges of current to pass through the electrical system of your car or truck. If this surge of current were to reach an electrical component, it could burn it out. To prevent this, fuses, circuit breakers or fusible links are connected into the current supply wires of most of the major electrical systems. When an electrical current of excessive power passes through the component's fuse, the fuse blows out and breaks the circuit, saving the component from destruction.

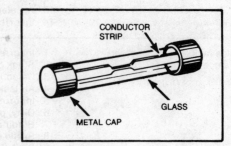

CONDUCTOR STRIP

GLASS

METAL CAP

Typical automotive fuse

A circuit breaker is basically a self-repairing fuse. The circuit breaker opens the circuit the same way a fuse does. However, when either the short is removed from the circuit or the surge subsides, the circuit breaker resets itself and does not have to be replaced as a fuse does.

A fuse link is a wire that acts as a fuse. It is normally connected between the starter relay and the main wiring harness. This connection is usually under the hood. The fuse link (if installed) protects all the

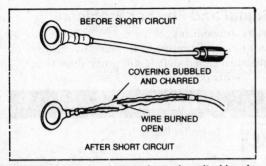

Most fusible links show a charred, melted insulation when they burn out

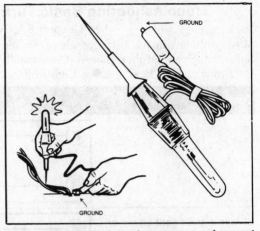

The test light will show the presence of current when touched to a hot wire and grounded at the other end

chassis electrical components, and is the probable cause of trouble when none of the electrical components function, unless the battery is disconnected or dead.

Electrical problems generally fall into one of three areas:

1. The component that is not functioning is not receiving current.

2. The component itself is not functioning.

3. The component is not properly grounded.

The electrical system can be checked with a test light and a jumper wire. A test light is a device that looks like a pointed screwdriver with a wire attached to it and has a light bulb in its handle. A jumper wire is a piece of insulated wire with an alligator clip attached to each end.

If a component is not working, you must follow a systematic plan to determine which of the three causes is the villain.

1. Turn on the switch that controls the inoperable component.

2. Disconnect the power supply wire from the component.

3. Attach the ground wire on the test light to a good metal ground.

4. Touch the probe end of the test light to the end of the power supply wire that was disconnected from the component. If the component is receiving current, the test light will go on.

NOTE: *Some components work only when the ignition switch is turned on.*

If the test light does not go on, then the problem is in the circuit between the battery and the component. This includes all the switches, fuses, and relays in the system. Follow the wire that runs back to the battery. The problem is an open circuit between the

battery and the component. If the fuse is blown and, when replaced, immediately blows again, there is a short circuit in the system which must be located and repaired. If there is a switch in the system, bypass it with a jumper wire. This is done by connecting one end of the jumper wire to the power supply wire into the switch and the other end of the jumper wire to the wire coming out of the switch. If the test light lights with the jumper wire installed, the switch or whatever was bypassed is defective.

NOTE: *Never substitute the jumper wire for the component, since it is required to use the power from the power source.*

5. If the bulb in the test light goes on, then the current is getting to the component that is not working. This eliminates the first of the three possible causes. Connect the power supply wire and connect a jumper wire from the component to a good metal ground. Do this with the switch which controls the component turned on, and also the ignition switch turned on if it is required for the component to work. If the component works with the jumper wire installed, then it has a bad ground. This is usually caused by the metal area on which the component mounts to the chassis being coated with some type of foreign matter.

6. If neither test located the source of the trouble, then the component itself is defective. Remember that for any electrical system to work, all connections must be clean and tight.

Troubleshooting Basic Turn Signal and Flasher Problems
See Chapter 5 for service procedures

Most problems in the turn signals or flasher system can be reduced to defective flashers or bulbs, which are easily replaced. Occasionally, the turn signal switch will prove defective.

F = Front   R = Rear   ● = Lights off   ○ = Lights on

Condition	Possible Cause
Turn signals light, but do not flash	Defective flasher
No turn signals light on either side	Blown fuse. Replace if defective. Defective flasher. Check by substitution. Open circuit, short circuit or poor ground.
Both turn signals on one side don't work	Bad bulbs. Bad ground in both (or either) housings.
One turn signal light on one side doesn't work	Defective bulb. Corrosion in socket. Clean contacts. Poor ground at socket.
Turn signal flashes too fast or too slowly	Check any bulb on the side flashing too fast. A heavy-duty bulb is probably installed in place of a regular bulb. Check the bulb flashing too slowly. A standard bulb was probably installed in place of a heavy-duty bulb. Loose connections or corrosion at the bulb socket.
Indicator lights don't work in either direction	Check if the turn signals are working. Check the dash indicator lights. Check the flasher by substitution.
One indicator light doesn't light	On systems with one dash indicator: See if the lights work on the same side. Often the filaments have been reversed in systems combining stoplights with taillights and turn signals. Check the flasher by substitution. On systems with two indicators: Check the bulbs on the same side. Check the indicator light bulb. Check the flasher by substitution.

Troubleshooting Lighting Problems
See Chapter 5 for service procedures

Condition	Possible Cause
One or more lights don't work, but others do	1. Defective bulb(s) 2. Blown fuse(s) 3. Dirty fuse clips or light sockets 4. Poor ground circuit
Lights burn out quickly	1. Incorrect voltage regulator setting or defective regulator 2. Poor battery/alternator connections
Lights go dim	1. Low/discharged battery 2. Alternator not charging 3. Corroded sockets or connections 4. Low voltage output
Lights flicker	1. Loose connection 2. Poor ground. (Run ground wire from light housing to frame) 3. Circuit breaker operating (short circuit)
Lights "flare"—Some flare is normal on acceleration—If excessive, see "Lights Burn Out Quickly"	High voltage setting
Lights glare—approaching drivers are blinded	1. Lights adjusted too high 2. Rear springs or shocks sagging 3. Rear tires soft

Troubleshooting Dash Gauge Problems

Most problems can be traced to a defective sending unit or faulty wiring. Occasionally, the gauge itself is at fault. See Chapter 5 for service procedures.

Condition	Possible Cause
COOLANT TEMPERATURE GAUGE	
Gauge reads erratically or not at all	1. Loose or dirty connections 2. Defective sending unit. 3. Defective gauge. To test a bi-metal gauge, remove the wire from the sending unit. Ground the wire for an instant. If the gauge registers, replace the sending unit. To test a magnetic gauge, disconnect the wire at the sending unit. With ignition ON gauge should register COLD. Ground the wire; gauge should register HOT.
AMMETER GAUGE—TURN HEADLIGHTS ON (DO NOT START ENGINE). NOTE REACTION	
Ammeter shows charge Ammeter shows discharge Ammeter does not move	1. Connections reversed on gauge 2. Ammeter is OK 3. Loose connections or faulty wiring 4. Defective gauge

Condition	Possible Cause

OIL PRESSURE GAUGE

Gauge does not register or is inaccurate	1. On mechanical gauge, Bourdon tube may be bent or kinked. 2. Low oil pressure. Remove sending unit. Idle the engine briefly. If no oil flows from sending unit hole, problem is in engine. 3. Defective gauge. Remove the wire from the sending unit and ground it for an instant with the ignition ON. A good gauge will go to the top of the scale. 4. Defective wiring. Check the wiring to the gauge. If it's OK and the gauge doesn't register when grounded, replace the gauge. 5. Defective sending unit.

ALL GAUGES

All gauges do not operate All gauges read low or erratically All gauges pegged	1. Blown fuse 2. Defective instrument regulator 3. Defective or dirty instrument voltage regulator 4. Loss of ground between instrument voltage regulator and frame 5. Defective instrument regulator

WARNING LIGHTS

Light(s) do not come on when ignition is ON, but engine is not started Light comes on with engine running	1. Defective bulb 2. Defective wire 3. Defective sending unit. Disconnect the wire from the sending unit and ground it. Replace the sending unit if the light comes on with the ignition ON. 4. Problem in individual system 5. Defective sending unit

Troubleshooting Clutch Problems

It is false economy to replace individual clutch components. The pressure plate, clutch plate and throwout bearing should be replaced as a set, and the flywheel face inspected, whenever the clutch is overhauled. See Chapter 6 for service procedures.

Condition	Possible Cause
Clutch chatter	1. Grease on driven plate (disc) facing 2. Binding clutch linkage or cable 3. Loose, damaged facings on driven plate (disc) 4. Engine mounts loose 5. Incorrect height adjustment of pressure plate release levers 6. Clutch housing or housing to transmission adapter misalignment 7. Loose driven plate hub
Clutch grabbing	1. Oil, grease on driven plate (disc) facing 2. Broken pressure plate 3. Warped or binding driven plate. Driven plate binding on clutch shaft
Clutch slips	1. Lack of lubrication in clutch linkage or cable (linkage or cable binds, causes incomplete engagement) 2. Incorrect pedal, or linkage adjustment 3. Broken pressure plate springs 4. Weak pressure plate springs 5. Grease on driven plate facings (disc)

Troubleshooting Clutch Problems (cont.)

Condition	Possible Cause
Incomplete clutch release	1. Incorrect pedal or linkage adjustment or linkage or cable binding 2. Incorrect height adjustment on pressure plate release levers 3. Loose, broken facings on driven plate (disc) 4. Bent, dished, warped driven plate caused by overheating
Grinding, whirring grating noise when pedal is depressed	1. Worn or defective throwout bearing 2. Starter drive teeth contacting flywheel ring gear teeth. Look for milled or polished teeth on ring gear.
Squeal, howl, trumpeting noise when pedal is being released (occurs during first inch to inch and one-half of pedal travel)	Pilot bushing worn or lack of lubricant. If bushing appears OK, polish bushing with emery cloth, soak lube wick in oil, lube bushing with oil, apply film of chassis grease to clutch shaft pilot hub, reassemble. NOTE: Bushing wear may be due to misalignment of clutch housing or housing to transmission adapter
Vibration or clutch pedal pulsation with clutch disengaged (pedal fully depressed)	1. Worn or defective engine transmission mounts 2. Flywheel run out. (Flywheel run out at face not to exceed 0.005″) 3. Damaged or defective clutch components

Troubleshooting Manual Transmission Problems
See Chapter 6 for service procedures

Condition	Possible Cause
Transmission jumps out of gear	1. Misalignment of transmission case or clutch housing. 2. Worn pilot bearing in crankshaft. 3. Bent transmission shaft. 4. Worn high speed sliding gear. 5. Worn teeth or end-play in clutch shaft. 6. Insufficient spring tension on shifter rail plunger. 7. Bent or loose shifter fork. 8. Gears not engaging completely. 9. Loose or worn bearings on clutch shaft or mainshaft. 10. Worn gear teeth. 11. Worn or damaged detent balls.
Transmission sticks in gear	1. Clutch not releasing fully. 2. Burred or battered teeth on clutch shaft, or sliding sleeve. 3. Burred or battered transmission mainshaft. 4. Frozen synchronizing clutch. 5. Stuck shifter rail plunger. 6. Gearshift lever twisting and binding shifter rail. 7. Battered teeth on high speed sliding gear or on sleeve. 8. Improper lubrication, or lack of lubrication. 9. Corroded transmission parts. 10. Defective mainshaft pilot bearing. 11. Locked gear bearings will give same effect as stuck in gear.
Transmission gears will not synchronize	1. Binding pilot bearing on mainshaft, will synchronize in high gear only. 2. Clutch not releasing fully. 3. Detent spring weak or broken. 4. Weak or broken springs under balls in sliding gear sleeve. 5. Binding bearing on clutch shaft, or binding countershaft. 6. Binding pilot bearing in crankshaft. 7. Badly worn gear teeth. 8. Improper lubrication. 9. Constant mesh gear not turning freely on transmission mainshaft. Will synchronize in that gear only.

Condition	Possible Cause
Gears spinning when shifting into gear from neutral	1. Clutch not releasing fully. 2. In some cases an extremely light lubricant in transmission will cause gears to continue to spin for a short time after clutch is released. 3. Binding pilot bearing in crankshaft.
Transmission noisy in all gears	1. Insufficient lubricant, or improper lubricant. 2. Worn countergear bearings. 3. Worn or damaged main drive gear or countergear. 4. Damaged main drive gear or mainshaft bearings. 5. Worn or damaged countergear anti-lash plate.
Transmission noisy in neutral only	1. Damaged main drive gear bearing. 2. Damaged or loose mainshaft pilot bearing. 3. Worn or damaged countergear anti-lash plate. 4. Worn countergear bearings.
Transmission noisy in one gear only	1. Damaged or worn constant mesh gears. 2. Worn or damaged countergear bearings. 3. Damaged or worn synchronizer.
Transmission noisy in reverse only	1. Worn or damaged reverse idler gear or idler bushing. 2. Worn or damaged mainshaft reverse gear. 3. Worn or damaged reverse countergear. 4. Damaged shift mechanism.

TROUBLESHOOTING AUTOMATIC TRANSMISSION PROBLEMS

Keeping alert to changes in the operating characteristics of the transmission (changing shift points, noises, etc.) can prevent small problems from becoming large ones. If the problem cannot be traced to loose bolts, fluid level, misadjusted linkage, clogged filters or similar problems, you should probably seek professional service.

Transmission Fluid Indications

The appearance and odor of the transmission fluid can give valuable clues to the overall condition of the transmission. Always note the appearance of the fluid when you check the fluid level or change the fluid. Rub a small amount of fluid between your fingers to feel for grit and smell the fluid on the dipstick.

If the fluid appears:	It indicates:
Clear and red colored	Normal operation
Discolored (extremely dark red or brownish) or smells burned	Band or clutch pack failure, usually caused by an overheated transmission. Hauling very heavy loads with insufficient power or failure to change the fluid often result in overheating. Do not confuse this appearance with newer fluids that have a darker red color and a strong odor (though not a burned odor).
Foamy or aerated (light in color and full of bubbles)	1. The level is too high (gear train is churning oil) 2. An internal air leak (air is mixing with the fluid). Have the transmission checked professionally.
Solid residue in the fluid	Defective bands, clutch pack or bearings. Bits of band material or metal abrasives are clinging to the dipstick. Have the transmission checked professionally.
Varnish coating on the dipstick	The transmission fluid is overheating

TROUBLESHOOTING DRIVE AXLE PROBLEMS

First, determine when the noise is most noticeable.

Drive Noise: Produced under vehicle acceleration.

Coast Noise: Produced while coasting with a closed throttle.

Float Noise: Occurs while maintaining constant speed (just enough to keep speed constant) on a level road.

External Noise Elimination

It is advisable to make a thorough road test to determine whether the noise originates in the rear axle or whether it originates from the tires, engine, transmission, wheel bearings or road surface. Noise originating from other places cannot be corrected by servicing the rear axle.

ROAD NOISE

Brick or rough surfaced concrete roads produce noises that seem to come from the rear axle. Road noise is usually identical in Drive or Coast and driving on a different type of road will tell whether the road is the problem.

TIRE NOISE

Tire noise can be mistaken as rear axle noise, even though the tires on the front are at fault. Snow tread and mud tread tires or tires worn unevenly will frequently cause vibrations which seem to originate elsewhere; *temporarily, and for test purposes only,* inflate the tires to 40–50 lbs. This will significantly alter the noise produced by the tires, but will not alter noise from the rear axle. Noises from the rear axle will normally cease at speeds below 30 mph on coast, while tire noise will continue at lower tone as speed is decreased. The rear axle noise will usually change from drive conditions to coast conditions, while tire noise will not. Do not forget to lower the tire pressure to normal after the test is complete.

ENGINE/TRANSMISSION NOISE

Determine at what speed the noise is most pronounced, then stop in a quiet place. With the transmission in Neutral, run the engine through speeds corresponding to road speeds where the noise was noticed. Noises produced with the vehicle standing still are coming from the engine or transmission.

FRONT WHEEL BEARINGS

Front wheel bearing noises, sometimes confused with rear axle noises, will not change when comparing drive and coast conditions. While holding the speed steady, lightly apply the footbrake. This will often cause wheel bearing noise to lessen, as some of the weight is taken off the bearing. Front wheel bearings are easily checked by jacking up the wheels and spinning the wheels. Shaking the wheels will also determine if the wheel bearings are excessively loose.

REAR AXLE NOISES

Eliminating other possible sources can narrow the cause to the rear axle, which normally produces noise from worn gears or bearings. Gear noises tend to peak in a narrow speed range, while bearing noises will usually vary in pitch with engine speeds.

Noise Diagnosis

The Noise Is:	Most Probably Produced By:
1. Identical under Drive or Coast	Road surface, tires or front wheel bearings
2. Different depending on road surface	Road surface or tires
3. Lower as speed is lowered	Tires
4. Similar when standing or moving	Engine or transmission
5. A vibration	Unbalanced tires, rear wheel bearing, unbalanced driveshaft or worn U-joint
6. A knock or click about every two tire revolutions	Rear wheel bearing
7. Most pronounced on turns	Damaged differential gears
8. A steady low-pitched whirring or scraping, starting at low speeds	Damaged or worn pinion bearing
9. A chattering vibration on turns	Wrong differential lubricant or worn clutch plates (limited slip rear axle)
10. Noticed only in Drive, Coast or Float conditions	Worn ring gear and/or pinion gear

Troubleshooting Steering & Suspension Problems

Condition	Possible Cause
Hard steering (wheel is hard to turn)	1. Improper tire pressure 2. Loose or glazed pump drive belt 3. Low or incorrect fluid 4. Loose, bent or poorly lubricated front end parts 5. Improper front end alignment (excessive caster) 6. Bind in steering column or linkage 7. Kinked hydraulic hose 8. Air in hydraulic system 9. Low pump output or leaks in system 10. Obstruction in lines 11. Pump valves sticking or out of adjustment 12. Incorrect wheel alignment
Loose steering (too much play in steering wheel)	1. Loose wheel bearings 2. Faulty shocks 3. Worn linkage or suspension components 4. Loose steering gear mounting or linkage points 5. Steering mechanism worn or improperly adjusted 6. Valve spool improperly adjusted 7. Worn ball joints, tie-rod ends, etc.
Veers or wanders (pulls to one side with hands off steering wheel)	1. Improper tire pressure 2. Improper front end alignment 3. Dragging or improperly adjusted brakes 4. Bent frame 5. Improper rear end alignment 6. Faulty shocks or springs 7. Loose or bent front end components 8. Play in Pitman arm 9. Steering gear mountings loose 10. Loose wheel bearings 11. Binding Pitman arm 12. Spool valve sticking or improperly adjusted 13. Worn ball joints
Wheel oscillation or vibration transmitted through steering wheel	1. Low or uneven tire pressure 2. Loose wheel bearings 3. Improper front end alignment 4. Bent spindle 5. Worn, bent or broken front end components 6. Tires out of round or out of balance 7. Excessive lateral runout in disc brake rotor 8. Loose or bent shock absorber or strut
Noises (see also "Troubleshooting Drive Axle Problems")	1. Loose belts 2. Low fluid, air in system 3. Foreign matter in system 4. Improper lubrication 5. Interference or chafing in linkage 6. Steering gear mountings loose 7. Incorrect adjustment or wear in gear box 8. Faulty valves or wear in pump 9. Kinked hydraulic lines 10. Worn wheel bearings
Poor return of steering	1. Over-inflated tires 2. Improperly aligned front end (excessive caster) 3. Binding in steering column 4. No lubrication in front end 5. Steering gear adjusted too tight
Uneven tire wear (see "How To Read Tire Wear")	1. Incorrect tire pressure 2. Improperly aligned front end 3. Tires out-of-balance 4. Bent or worn suspension parts

HOW TO READ TIRE WEAR

The way your tires wear is a good indicator of other parts of the suspension. Abnormal wear patterns are often caused by the need for simple tire maintenance, or for front end alignment.

Excessive wear at the center of the tread indicates that the air pressure in the tire is consistently too high. The tire is riding on the center of the tread and wearing it prematurely. Occasionally, this wear pattern can result from outrageously wide tires on narrow rims. The cure for this is to replace either the tires or the wheels.

This type of wear usually results from consistent under-inflation. When a tire is under-inflated, there is too much contact with the road by the outer treads, which wear prematurely. When this type of wear occurs, and the tire pressure is known to be consistently correct, a bent or worn steering component or the need for wheel alignment could be indicated.

Feathering is a condition when the edge of each tread rib develops a slightly rounded edge on one side and a sharp edge on the other. By running your hand over the tire, you can usually feel the sharper edges before you'll be able to see them. The most common causes of feathering are incorrect toe-in setting or deteriorated bushings in the front suspension.

When an inner or outer rib wears faster than the rest of the tire, the need for wheel alignment is indicated. There is excessive camber in the front suspension, causing the wheel to lean too much putting excessive load on one side of the tire. Misalignment could also be due to sagging springs, worn ball joints, or worn control arm bushings. Be sure the vehicle is loaded the way it's normally driven when you have the wheels aligned.

Cups or scalloped dips appearing around the edge of the tread almost always indicate worn (sometimes bent) suspension parts. Adjustment of wheel alignment alone will seldom cure the problem. Any worn component that connects the wheel to the suspension can cause this type of wear. Occasionally, wheels that are out of balance will wear like this, but wheel imbalance usually shows up as bald spots between the outside edges and center of the tread.

Second-rib wear is usually found only in radial tires, and appears where the steel belts end in relation to the tread. It can be kept to a minimum by paying careful attention to tire pressure and frequently rotating the tires. This is often considered normal wear but excessive amounts indicate that the tires are too wide for the wheels.

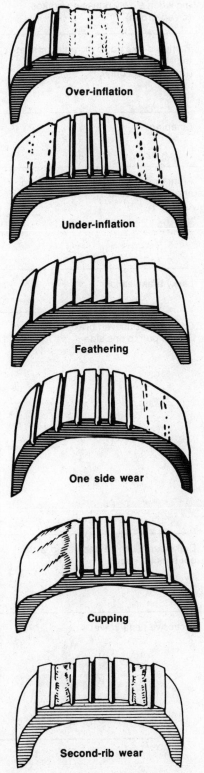

Over-inflation

Under-inflation

Feathering

One side wear

Cupping

Second-rib wear

Troubleshooting Disc Brake Problems

Condition	Possible Cause
Noise—groan—brake noise emanating when slowly releasing brakes (creep-groan)	Not detrimental to function of disc brakes—no corrective action required. (This noise may be eliminated by slightly increasing or decreasing brake pedal efforts.)
Rattle—brake noise or rattle emanating at low speeds on rough roads, (front wheels only).	1. Shoe anti-rattle spring missing or not properly positioned. 2. Excessive clearance between shoe and caliper. 3. Soft or broken caliper seals. 4. Deformed or misaligned disc. 5. Loose caliper.
Scraping	1. Mounting bolts too long. 2. Loose wheel bearings. 3. Bent, loose, or misaligned splash shield.
Front brakes heat up during driving and fail to release	1. Operator riding brake pedal. 2. Stop light switch improperly adjusted. 3. Sticking pedal linkage. 4. Frozen or seized piston. 5. Residual pressure valve in master cylinder. 6. Power brake malfunction. 7. Proportioning valve malfunction.
Leaky brake caliper	1. Damaged or worn caliper piston seal. 2. Scores or corrosion on surface of cylinder bore.
Grabbing or uneven brake action—Brakes pull to one side	1. Causes listed under "Brakes Pull". 2. Power brake malfunction. 3. Low fluid level in master cylinder. 4. Air in hydraulic system. 5. Brake fluid, oil or grease on linings. 6. Unmatched linings. 7. Distorted brake pads. 8. Frozen or seized pistons. 9. Incorrect tire pressure. 10. Front end out of alignment. 11. Broken rear spring. 12. Brake caliper pistons sticking. 13. Restricted hose or line. 14. Caliper not in proper alignment to braking disc. 15. Stuck or malfunctioning metering valve. 16. Soft or broken caliper seals. 17. Loose caliper.
Brake pedal can be depressed without braking effect	1. Air in hydraulic system or improper bleeding procedure. 2. Leak past primary cup in master cylinder. 3. Leak in system. 4. Rear brakes out of adjustment. 5. Bleeder screw open.
Excessive pedal travel	1. Air, leak, or insufficient fluid in system or caliper. 2. Warped or excessively tapered shoe and lining assembly. 3. Excessive disc runout. 4. Rear brake adjustment required. 5. Loose wheel bearing adjustment. 6. Damaged caliper piston seal. 7. Improper brake fluid (boil). 8. Power brake malfunction. 9. Weak or soft hoses.

Troubleshooting Disc Brake Problems (cont.)

Condition	Possible Cause
Brake roughness or chatter (pedal pumping)	1. Excessive thickness variation of braking disc. 2. Excessive lateral runout of braking disc. 3. Rear brake drums out-of-round. 4. Excessive front bearing clearance.
Excessive pedal effort	1. Brake fluid, oil or grease on linings. 2. Incorrect lining. 3. Frozen or seized pistons. 4. Power brake malfunction. 5. Kinked or collapsed hose or line. 6. Stuck metering valve. 7. Scored caliper or master cylinder bore. 8. Seized caliper pistons.
Brake pedal fades (pedal travel increases with foot on brake)	1. Rough master cylinder or caliper bore. 2. Loose or broken hydraulic lines/connections. 3. Air in hydraulic system. 4. Fluid level low. 5. Weak or soft hoses. 6. Inferior quality brake shoes or fluid. 7. Worn master cylinder piston cups or seals.

Troubleshooting Drum Brakes

Condition	Possible Cause
Pedal goes to floor	1. Fluid low in reservoir. 2. Air in hydraulic system. 3. Improperly adjusted brake. 4. Leaking wheel cylinders. 5. Loose or broken brake lines. 6. Leaking or worn master cylinder. 7. Excessively worn brake lining.
Spongy brake pedal	1. Air in hydraulic system. 2. Improper brake fluid (low boiling point). 3. Excessively worn or cracked brake drums. 4. Broken pedal pivot bushing.
Brakes pulling	1. Contaminated lining. 2. Front end out of alignment. 3. Incorrect brake adjustment. 4. Unmatched brake lining. 5. Brake drums out of round. 6. Brake shoes distorted. 7. Restricted brake hose or line. 8. Broken rear spring. 9. Worn brake linings. 10. Uneven lining wear. 11. Glazed brake lining. 12. Excessive brake lining dust. 13. Heat spotted brake drums. 14. Weak brake return springs. 15. Faulty automatic adjusters. 16. Low or incorrect tire pressure.

Condition	Possible Cause
Squealing brakes	1. Glazed brake lining. 2. Saturated brake lining. 3. Weak or broken brake shoe retaining spring. 4. Broken or weak brake shoe return spring. 5. Incorrect brake lining. 6. Distorted brake shoes. 7. Bent support plate. 8. Dust in brakes or scored brake drums. 9. Linings worn below limit. 10. Uneven brake lining wear. 11. Heat spotted brake drums.
Chirping brakes	1. Out of round drum or eccentric axle flange pilot.
Dragging brakes	1. Incorrect wheel or parking brake adjustment. 2. Parking brakes engaged or improperly adjusted. 3. Weak or broken brake shoe return spring. 4. Brake pedal binding. 5. Master cylinder cup sticking. 6. Obstructed master cylinder relief port. 7. Saturated brake lining. 8. Bent or out of round brake drum. 9. Contaminated or improper brake fluid. 10. Sticking wheel cylinder pistons. 11. Driver riding brake pedal. 12. Defective proportioning valve. 13. Insufficient brake shoe lubricant.
Hard pedal	1. Brake booster inoperative. 2. Incorrect brake lining. 3. Restricted brake line or hose. 4. Frozen brake pedal linkage. 5. Stuck wheel cylinder. 6. Binding pedal linkage. 7. Faulty proportioning valve.
Wheel locks	1. Contaminated brake lining. 2. Loose or torn brake lining. 3. Wheel cylinder cups sticking. 4. Incorrect wheel bearing adjustment. 5. Faulty proportioning valve.
Brakes fade (high speed)	1. Incorrect lining. 2. Overheated brake drums. 3. Incorrect brake fluid (low boiling temperature). 4. Saturated brake lining. 5. Leak in hydraulic system. 6. Faulty automatic adjusters.
Pedal pulsates	1. Bent or out of round brake drum.
Brake chatter and shoe knock	1. Out of round brake drum. 2. Loose support plate. 3. Bent support plate. 4. Distorted brake shoes. 5. Machine grooves in contact face of brake drum (Shoe Knock). 6. Contaminated brake lining. 7. Missing or loose components. 8. Incorrect lining material. 9. Out-of-round brake drums. 10. Heat spotted or scored brake drums. 11. Out-of-balance wheels.

Troubleshooting Drum Brakes (cont.)

Condition	Possible Cause
Brakes do not self adjust	1. Adjuster screw frozen in thread. 2. Adjuster screw corroded at thrust washer. 3. Adjuster lever does not engage star wheel. 4. Adjuster installed on wrong wheel.
Brake light glows	1. Leak in the hydraulic system. 2. Air in the system. 3. Improperly adjusted master cylinder pushrod. 4. Uneven lining wear. 5. Failure to center combination valve or proportioning valve.

Mechanic's Data

General Conversion Table

Multiply By	To Convert	To	
LENGTH			
2.54	Inches	Centimeters	.3937
25.4	Inches	Millimeters	.03937
30.48	Feet	Centimeters	.0328
.304	Feet	Meters	3.28
.914	Yards	Meters	1.094
1.609	Miles	Kilometers	.621
VOLUME			
.473	Pints	Liters	2.11
.946	Quarts	Liters	1.06
3.785	Gallons	Liters	.264
.016	Cubic inches	Liters	61.02
16.39	Cubic inches	Cubic cms.	.061
28.3	Cubic feet	Liters	.0353
MASS (Weight)			
28.35	Ounces	Grams	.035
.4536	Pounds	Kilograms	2.20
—	To obtain	From	Multiply by

Multiply By	To Convert	To	
AREA			
.645	Square inches	Square cms.	.155
.836	Square yds.	Square meters	1.196
FORCE			
4.448	Pounds	Newtons	.225
.138	Ft./lbs.	Kilogram/meters	7.23
1.36	Ft./lbs.	Newton-meters	.737
.112	In./lbs.	Newton-meters	8.844
PRESSURE			
.068	Psi	Atmospheres	14.7
6.89	Psi	Kilopascals	.145
OTHER			
1.104	Horsepower (DIN)	Horsepower (SAE)	.9861
.746	Horsepower (SAE)	Kilowatts (KW)	1.34
1.60	Mph	Km/h	.625
.425	Mpg	Km/1	2.35
—	To obtain	From	Multiply by

Tap Drill Sizes

National Coarse or U.S.S.

Screw & Tap Size	Threads Per Inch	Use Drill Number
No. 5	40	39
No. 6	32	36
No. 8	32	29
No. 10	24	25
No. 12	24	17
$\frac{1}{4}$	20	8
$\frac{5}{16}$	18	F
$\frac{3}{8}$	16	$\frac{5}{16}$
$\frac{7}{16}$	14	U
$\frac{1}{2}$	13	$\frac{27}{64}$
$\frac{9}{16}$	12	$\frac{31}{64}$
$\frac{5}{8}$	11	$\frac{17}{32}$
$\frac{3}{4}$	10	$\frac{21}{32}$
$\frac{7}{8}$	9	$\frac{49}{64}$

National Coarse or U.S.S.

Screw & Tap Size	Threads Per Inch	Use Drill Number
1	8	$\frac{7}{8}$
$1\frac{1}{8}$	7	$\frac{63}{64}$
$1\frac{1}{4}$	7	$1\frac{7}{64}$
$1\frac{1}{2}$	6	$1\frac{11}{32}$

National Fine or S.A.E.

Screw & Tap Size	Threads Per Inch	Use Drill Number
No. 5	44	37
No. 6	40	33
No. 8	36	29
No. 10	32	21

National Fine or S.A.E.

Screw & Tap Size	Threads Per Inch	Use Drill Number
No. 12	28	15
$\frac{1}{4}$	28	3
$\frac{6}{16}$	24	1
$\frac{3}{8}$	24	Q
$\frac{7}{16}$	20	W
$\frac{1}{2}$	20	$\frac{29}{64}$
$\frac{9}{16}$	18	$\frac{33}{64}$
$\frac{5}{8}$	18	$\frac{37}{64}$
$\frac{3}{4}$	16	$\frac{11}{16}$
$\frac{7}{8}$	14	$\frac{13}{16}$
$1\frac{1}{8}$	12	$1\frac{3}{64}$
$1\frac{1}{4}$	12	$1\frac{11}{64}$
$1\frac{1}{2}$	12	$1\frac{27}{64}$

Drill Sizes In Decimal Equivalents

Inch	Decimal	Wire	mm
1/64	.0156		.39
	.0157		.4
	.0160	78	
	.0165		.42
	.0173		.44
	.0177		.45
	.0180	77	
	.0181		.46
	.0189		.48
	.0197		.5
	.0200	76	
	.0210	75	
	.0217		.55
	.0225	74	
	.0236		.6
	.0240	73	
	.0250	72	
	.0256		.65
	.0260	71	
	.0276		.7
	.0280	70	
	.0292	69	
	.0295		.75
	.0310	68	
1/32	.0312		.79
	.0315		.8
	.0320	67	
	.0330	66	
	.0335		.85
	.0350	65	
	.0354		.9
	.0360	64	
	.0370	63	
	.0374		.95
	.0380	62	
	.0390	61	
	.0394		1.0
	.0400	60	
	.0410	59	
	.0413		1.05
	.0420	58	
	.0430	57	
	.0433		1.1
	.0453		1.15
3/64	.0465	56	
	.0469		1.19
	.0472		1.2
	.0492		1.25
	.0512		1.3
	.0520	55	
	.0531		1.35
	.0550	54	
	.0551		1.4
	.0571		1.45
	.0591		1.5
	.0595	53	
	.0610		1.55
1/16	.0625		1.59
	.0630		1.6
	.0635	52	
	.0650		1.65
	.0669		1.7
	.0670	51	
	.0689		1.75
	.0700	50	
	.0709		1.8
	.0728		1.85

Inch	Decimal	Wire	mm
	.0730	49	
	.0748		1.9
	.0760	48	
	.0768		1.95
5/64	.0781		1.98
	.0785	47	
	.0787		2.0
	.0807		2.05
	.0810	46	
	.0820	45	
	.0827		2.1
	.0846		2.15
	.0860	44	
	.0866		2.2
	.0886		2.25
	.0890	43	
	.0906		2.3
	.0925		2.35
	.0935	42	
3/32	.0938		2.38
	.0945		2.4
	.0960	41	
	.0965		2.45
	.0980	40	
	.0981		2.5
	.0995	39	
	.1015	38	
	.1024		2.6
	.1040	37	
	.1063		2.7
	.1065	36	
	.1083		2.75
7/64	.1094		2.77
	.1100	35	
	.1102		2.8
	.1110	34	
	.1130	33	
	.1142		2.9
	.1160	32	
	.1181		3.0
	.1200	31	
	.1220		3.1
1/8	.1250		3.17
	.1260		3.2
	.1280		3.25
	.1285	30	
	.1299		3.3
	.1339		3.4
	.1360	29	
	.1378		3.5
	.1405	28	
9/64	.1406		3.57
	.1417		3.6
	.1440	27	
	.1457		3.7
	.1470	26	
	.1476		3.75
	.1495	25	
	.1496		3.8
	.1520	24	
	.1535		3.9
	.1540	23	
5/32	.1562		3.96
	.1570	22	
	.1575		4.0
	.1590	21	
	.1610	20	

Inch	Decimal	Wire & Letter	mm
	.1614		4.1
	.1654		4.2
	.1660	19	
	.1673		4.25
	.1693		4.3
	.1695	18	
11/64	.1719		4.36
	.1730	17	
	.1732		4.4
	.1770	16	
	.1772		4.5
	.1800	15	
	.1811		4.6
	.1820	14	
	.1850	13	
	.1850		4.7
	.1870		4.75
3/16	.1875		4.76
	.1890		4.8
	.1890	12	
	.1910	11	
	.1929		4.9
	.1935	10	
	.1960	9	
	.1969		5.0
	.1990	8	
	.2008		5.1
	.2010	7	
13/64	.2031		5.16
	.2040	6	
	.2047		5.2
	.2055	5	
	.2067		5.25
	.2087		5.3
	.2090	4	
	.2126		5.4
	.2130	3	
	.2165		5.5
7/32	.2188		5.55
	.2205		5.6
	.2210	2	
	.2244		5.7
	.2264		5.75
	.2280	1	
	.2283		5.8
	.2323		5.9
	.2340	A	
15/64	.2344		5.95
	.2362		6.0
	.2380	B	
	.2402		6.1
	.2420	C	
	.2441		6.2
	.2460	D	
	.2461		6.25
	.2480		6.3
1/4	.2500	E	6.35
	.2520		6.
	.2559		6.5
	.2570	F	
	.2598		6.6
	.2610	G	
	.2638		6.7
17/64	.2656		6.74
	.2657		6.75
	.2660	H	
	.2677		6.8

Inch	Decimal	Letter	mm
	.2717		6.9
	.2720	I	
	.2756		7.0
	.2770	J	
	.2795		7.1
	.2810	K	
9/32	.2812		7.14
	.2835		7.2
	.2854		7.25
	.2874		7.3
	.2900	L	
	.2913		7.4
	.2950	M	
	.2953		7.5
19/64	.2969		7.54
	.2992		7.6
	.3020	N	
	.3031		7.7
	.3051		7.75
	.3071		7.8
	.3110		7.9
5/16	.3125		7.93
	.3150		8.0
	.3160	O	
	.3189		8.1
	.3228		8.2
	.3230	P	
	.3248		8.25
21/64	.3268		8.3
	.3281		8.33
	.3307		8.4
	.3320	Q	
	.3346		8.5
	.3386		8.6
	.3390	R	
	.3425		8.7
11/32	.3438		8.73
	.3445		8.75
	.3465		8.8
	.3480	S	
	.3504		8.9
	.3543		9.0
	.3580	T	
	.3583		9.1
23/64	.3594		9.12
	.3622		9.2
	.3642		9.25
	.3661		9.3
	.3680	U	
	.3701		9.4
	.3740		9.5
3/8	.3750		9.52
	.3770	V	
	.3780		9.6
	.3819		9.7
	.3839		9.75
	.3858		9.8
	.3860	W	
	.3898		9.9
25/64	.3906		9.92
	.3937		10.0
	.3970	X	
	.4040	Y	
13/32	.4062		10.31
	.4130	Z	
	.4134		10.5
27/64	.4219		10.71

Inch	Decimal	mm
	.4331	11.0
7/16	.4375	11.11
	.4528	11.5
29/64	.4531	11.51
15/32	.4688	11.90
	.4724	12.0
31/64	.4844	12.30
	.4921	12.5
1/2	.5000	12.70
	.5118	13.0
33/64	.5156	13.09
17/32	.5312	13.49
	.5315	13.5
35/64	.5469	13.89
	.5512	14.0
9/16	.5625	14.28
	.5709	14.5
37/64	.5781	14.68
	.5906	15.0
19/32	.5938	15.08
39/64	.6094	15.47
	.6102	15.5
5/8	.6250	15.87
	.6299	16.0
41/64	.6406	16.27
	.6496	16.5
21/32	.6562	16.66
	.6693	17.0
43/64	.6719	17.06
11/16	.6875	17.46
	.6890	17.5
45/64	.7031	17.85
	.7087	18.0
23/32	.7188	18.25
	.7283	18.5
47/64	.7344	18.65
	.7480	19.0
3/4	.7500	19.05
49/64	.7656	19.44
	.7677	19.5
25/32	.7812	19.84
	.7874	20.0
51/64	.7969	20.24
	.8071	20.5
13/16	.8125	20.63
	.8268	21.0
53/64	.8281	21.03
27/32	.8438	21.43
	.8465	21.5
55/64	.8594	21.82
	.8661	22.0
7/8	.8750	22.22
	.8858	22.5
57/64	.8906	22.62
	.9055	23.0
29/32	.9062	23.01
59/64	.9219	23.41
	.9252	23.5
15/16	.9375	23.81
	.9449	24.0
61/64	.9531	24.2
	.9646	24.5
31/32	.9688	24.6
	.9843	25.0
63/64	.9844	25.0
1	1.0000	25.4

GLOSSARY OF TERMS

AIR/FUEL RATIO: The ratio of air to gasoline by weight in the fuel mixture drawn into the engine.

AIR INJECTION: One method of reducing harmful exhaust emissions by injecting air into each of the exhaust ports of an engine. The fresh air entering the hot exhaust manifold causes any remaining fuel to be burned before it can exit the tailpipe.

ALTERNATOR: A device used for converting mechanical energy into electrical energy.

AMMETER: An instrument, calibrated in amperes, used to measure the flow of an electrical current in a circuit. Ammeters are always connected in series with the circuit being tested.

AMPERE: The rate of flow of electrical current present when one volt of electrical pressure is applied against one ohm of electrical resistance.

ANALOG COMPUTER: Any microprocessor that uses similar (analogous) electrical signals to make its calculations.

ARMATURE: A laminated, soft iron core wrapped by a wire that converts electrical energy to mechanical energy as in a motor or relay. When rotated in a magnetic field, it changes mechanical energy into electrical energy as in a generator.

ATMOSPHERIC PRESSURE: The pressure on the Earth's surface caused by the weight of the air in the atmosphere. At sea level, this pressure is 14.7 psi at 32°F (101 kPa at 0°C).

ATOMIZATION: The breaking down of a liquid into a fine mist that can be suspended in air.

AXIAL PLAY: Movement parallel to a shaft or bearing bore.

BACKFIRE: The sudden combustion of gases in the intake or exhaust system that results in a loud explosion.

BACKLASH: The clearance or play between two parts, such as meshed gears.

BACKPRESSURE: Restrictions in the exhaust system that slow the exit of exhaust gases from the combustion chamber.

BAKELITE: A heat resistant, plastic insulator material commonly used in printed circuit boards and transistorized components.

BALL BEARING: A bearing made up of hardened inner and outer races between which hardened steel ball roll.

BALLAST RESISTOR: A resistor in the primary ignition circuit that lowers voltage after the engine is started to reduce wear on ignition components.

BEARING: A friction reducing, supportive device usually located between a stationary part and a moving part.

BIMETAL TEMPERATURE SENSOR: Any sensor or switch made of two dissimilar types of metal that bend when heated or cooled due to the different expansion rates of the alloys. These types of sensors usually function as an on/off switch.

BLOWBY: Combustion gases, composed of water vapor and unburned fuel, that leak past the piston rings into the crankcase during normal engine operation. These gases are removed by the PCV system to prevent the build-up of harmful acids in the crankcase.

BRAKE PAD: A brake shoe and lining assembly used with disc brakes.

BRAKE SHOE: The backing for the brake lining. The term is, however, usually applied to the assembly of the brake backing and lining.

BUSHING: A liner, usually removable, for a bearing; an anti-friction liner used in place of a bearing.

BYPASS: System used to bypass ballast resistor during engine cranking to increase voltage supplied to the coil.

CALIPER: A hydraulically activated device in a disc brake system, which is mounted straddling the brake rotor (disc). The caliper contains at least one piston and two brake pads. Hydraulic pressure on the piston(s) forces the pads against the rotor.

CAMSHAFT: A shaft in the engine on which are the lobes (cams) which operate the valves. The camshaft is driven by the crankshaft, via a belt, chain or gears, at one half the crankshaft speed.

CAPACITOR: A device which stores an electrical charge.

CARBON MONOXIDE (CO): a colorless, odorless gas given off as a normal byproduct of combustion. It is poisonous and extremely dangerous in confined areas, building up slowly to toxic levels without warning if adequate ventilation is not available.

CARBURETOR: A device, usually mounted on the intake manifold of an engine, which mixes the air and fuel in the proper proportion to allow even combustion.

CATALYTIC CONVERTER: A device installed in the exhaust system, like a muffler, that converts harmful byproducts of combustion into carbon dioxide and water vapor by means of a heat-producing chemical reaction.

CENTRIFUGAL ADVANCE: A mechanical method of advancing the spark timing by using flyweights in the distributor that react to centrifugal force generated by the distributor shaft rotation.

CHECK VALVE: Any one-way valve installed to permit the flow of air, fuel or vacuum in one direction only.

CHOKE: A device, usually a moveable valve, placed in the intake path of a carburetor to restrict the flow of air.

CIRCUIT: Any unbroken path through which an electrical current can flow. Also used to describe fuel flow in some instances.

CIRCUIT BREAKER: A switch which protects an electrical circuit from overload by opening the circuit when the current flow exceeds a predetermined level. Some circuit breakers must be reset manually, while other reset automatically

COIL (IGNITION): A transformer in the ignition circuit which steps of the voltage provided to the spark plugs.

COMBINATION MANIFOLD: An assembly which includes both the intake and exhaust manifolds in one casting.

COMBINATION VALVE: A device used in some fuel systems that routes fuel vapors to a charcoal storage canister instead of venting

them into the atmosphere. The valve relieves fuel tank pressure and allows fresh air into the tank as fuel level drops to prevent a vapor lock situation.

COMPRESSION RATIO: The comparison of the total volume of the cylinder and combustion chamber with the piston at BDC and the piston at TDC.

CONDENSER: 1. An electrical device which acts to store an electrical charge, preventing voltage surges.
2. A radiator-like device in the air conditioning system in which refrigerant gas condenses into a liquid, giving off heat.

CONDUCTOR: Any material through which an electrical current can be transmitted easily.

CONTINUITY: Continuous or complete circuit. Can be checked with an ohmmeter.

COUNTERSHAFT: An intermediate shaft which is rotated by a mainshaft and transmits, in turn, that rotation to a working part.

CRANKCASE: The lower part of an engine in which the crankshaft and related parts operate.

CRANKSHAFT: The main driving shaft of an engine which receives reciprocating motion from the pistons and converts it to rotary motion.

CYLINDER: In an engine, the round hole in the engine block in which the piston(s) ride.

CYLINDER BLOCK: The main structural member of an engine in which is found the cylinders, crankshaft and other principal parts.

CYLINDER HEAD: The detachable portion of the engine, fastened, usually, to the top of the cylinder block, containing all or most of the combustion chambers. On overhead valve engines, it contains the valves and their operating parts. On overhead cam engines, it contains the camshaft as well.

DEAD CENTER: The extreme top or bottom of the piston stroke.

DETONATION: An unwanted explosion of the air fuel mixture in the combustion chamber caused by excess heat and compression, advanced timing, or an overly lean mixture. Also referred to as "ping".

DIAPHRAGM: A thin, flexible wall separating two cavities, such as in a vacuum advance unit.

DIESELING: A condition in which hot spots in the combustion chamber cause the engine to run on after the key is turned off.

DIFFERENTIAL: A geared assembly which allows the transmission of motion between drive axles, giving one axle the ability to turn faster than the other.

DIODE: An electrical device that will allow current to flow in one direction only.

DISC BRAKE: A hydraulic braking assembly consisting of a brake disc, or rotor, mounted on an axle, and a caliper assembly containing, usually two brake pads which are activated by hydraulic pressure. The pads are forced against the sides of the disc, creating friction which slows the vehicle.

DISTRIBUTOR: A mechanically driven device on an engine which is responsible for electrically firing the spark plug at a predetermined point of the piston stroke.

DOWEL PIN: A pin, inserted in mating holes in two different parts allowing those parts to maintain a fixed relationship.

DRUM BRAKE: A braking system which consists of two brake shoes and one or two wheel cylinders, mounted on a fixed backing plate, and a brake drum, mounted on an axle, which revolves around the assembly. Hydraulic action applied to the wheel cylinders forces the shoes outward against the drum, creating friction and slowing the vehicle.

DWELL: The rate, measured in degrees of shaft rotation, at which an electrical circuit cycles on and off.

ELECTRONIC CONTROL UNIT (ECU): Ignition module, module, amplifier or igniter. See Module for definition.

ELECTRONIC IGNITION: A system in which the timing and firing of the spark plugs is controlled by an electronic control unit, usually called a module. These systems have not points or condenser.

ENDPLAY: The measured amount of axial movement in a shaft.

ENGINE: A device that converts heat into mechanical energy.

EXHAUST MANIFOLD: A set of cast passages or pipes which conduct exhaust gases from the engine.

FEELER GAUGE: A blade, usually metal, of precisely predetermined thickness, used to measure the clearance between two parts. These blades usually are available in sets of assorted thicknesses.

F-Head: An engine configuration in which the intake valves are in the cylinder head, while the camshaft and exhaust valves are located in the cylinder block. The camshaft operates the intake valves via lifters and pushrods, while it operates the exhaust valves directly.

FIRING ORDER: The order in which combustion occurs in the cylinders of an engine. Also the order in which spark is distributed to the plugs by the distributor.

FLATHEAD: An engine configuration in which the camshaft and all the valves are located in the cylinder block.

FLOODING: The presence of too much fuel in the intake manifold and combustion chamber which prevents the air/fuel mixture from firing, thereby causing a no-start situation.

FLYWHEEL: A disc shaped part bolted to the rear end of the crankshaft. Around the outer perimeter is affixed the ring gear. The starter drive engages the ring gear, turning the flywheel, which rotates the crankshaft, imparting the initial starting motion to the engine.

FOOT POUND (ft.lb. or sometimes, ft. lbs.): The amount of energy or work needed to raise an item weighing one pound, a distance of one foot.

FUSE: A protective device in a circuit which prevents circuit overload by breaking the circuit when a specific amperage is present. The device is constructed around a strip or wire of a lower amperage rating than the circuit it is designed to protect. When an amperage higher than that stamped on the fuse is present in the circuit, the strip or wire melts, opening the circuit.

GEAR RATIO: The ratio between the number of teeth on meshing gears.

GENERATOR: A device which converts mechanical energy into electrical energy.

HEAT RANGE: The measure of a spark plug's ability to dissipate heat from its firing end. The higher the heat range, the hotter the plug fires.

HUB: The center part of a wheel or gear.

HYDROCARBON (HC): Any chemical compound made up of hydrogen and carbon. A major pollutant formed by the engine as a byproduct of combustion.

HYDROMETER: An instrument used to measure the specific gravity of a solution.

INCH POUND (in.lb. or sometimes, in. lbs.): One twelfth of a foot pound.

INDUCTION: A means of transferring electrical energy in the form of a magnetic field. Principle used in the ignition coil to increase voltage.

INJECTION PUMP: A device, usually mechanically operated, which meters and delivers fuel under pressure to the fuel injector.

INJECTOR: A device which receives metered fuel under relatively low pressure and is activated to inject the fuel into the engine under relatively high pressure at a predetermined time.

INPUT SHAFT: The shaft to which torque is applied, usually carrying the driving gear or gears.

INTAKE MANIFOLD: A casting of passages or pipes used to conduct air or a fuel/air mixture to the cylinders.

JOURNAL: The bearing surface within which a shaft operates.

KEY: A small block usually fitted in a notch between a shaft and a hub to prevent slippage of the two parts.

MANIFOLD: A casting of passages or set of pipes which connect the cylinders to an inlet or outlet source.

MANIFOLD VACUUM: Low pressure in an engine intake manifold formed just below the throttle plates. Manifold vacuum is highest at idle and drops under acceleration.

MASTER CYLINDER: The primary fluid pressurizing device in a hydraulic system. In automotive use, it is found in brake and hydraulic clutch systems and is pedal activated, either directly or, in a power brake system, through the power booster.

MODULE: Electronic control unit, amplifier or igniter of solid state or integrated design which controls the current flow in the ignition primary circuit based on input from the pickup coil. When the module opens the primary circuit, the high secondary voltage is induced in the coil.

NEEDLE BEARING: A bearing which consists of a number (usually a large number) of long, thin rollers.

OHM: (Ω) The unit used to measure the resistance of conductor to electrical flow. One ohm is the amount of resistance that limits current flow to one ampere in a circuit with one volt of pressure.

OHMMETER: An instrument used for measuring the resistance, in ohms, in an electrical circuit.

OUTPUT SHAFT: The shaft which transmits torque from a device, such as a transmission.

OVERDRIVE: A gear assembly which produces more shaft revolutions than that transmitted to it.

OVERHEAD CAMSHAFT (OHC): An engine configuration in which the camshaft is mounted on top of the cylinder head and operates the valve either directly or by means of rocker arms.

OVERHEAD VALVE (OHV): An engine configuration in which all of the valves are located in the cylinder head and the camshaft is located in the cylinder block. The camshaft operates the valves via lifters and pushrods.

OXIDES OF NITROGEN (NOx): Chemical compounds of nitrogen produced as a byproduct of combustion. They combine with hydrocarbons to produce smog.

OXYGEN SENSOR: Used with the feedback system to sense the presence of oxygen in the exhaust gas and signal the computer which can reference the voltage signal to an air/fuel ratio.

PINION: The smaller of two meshing gears.

PISTON RING: An open ended ring which fits into a groove on the outer diameter of the piston. Its chief function is to form a seal between the piston and cylinder wall. Most automotive pistons have three rings: two for compression sealing; one for oil sealing.

PRELOAD: A predetermined load placed on a bearing during assembly or by adjustment.

PRIMARY CIRCUIT: Is the low voltage side of the ignition system which consists of the ignition switch, ballast resistor or resistance wire, bypass, coil, electronic control unit and pick-up coil as well as the connecting wires and harnesses.

PRESS FIT: The mating of two parts under pressure, due to the inner diameter of one being smaller than the outer diameter of the other, or vice versa; an interference fit.

RACE: The surface on the inner or outer ring of a bearing on which the balls, needles or rollers move.

REGULATOR: A device which maintains the amperage and/or voltage levels of a circuit at predetermined values.

RELAY: A switch which automatically opens and/or closes a circuit.

RESISTANCE: The opposition to the flow of current through a circuit or electrical device, and is measured in ohms. Resistance is equal to the voltage divided by the amperage.

RESISTOR: A device, usually made of wire, which offers a preset amount of resistance in an electrical circuit.

RING GEAR: The name given to a ring-shaped gear attached to a differential case, or affixed to a flywheel or as part a planetary gear set.

ROLLER BEARING: A bearing made up of hardened inner and outer races between which hardened steel rollers move.

ROTOR: 1. The disc-shaped part of a disc brake assembly, upon which the brake pads bear; also called, brake disc.
2. The device mounted atop the distributor shaft, which passes current to the distributor cap tower contacts.

SECONDARY CIRCUIT: The high voltage side of the ignition system, usually above 20,000 volts. The secondary includes the ignition coil, coil wire, distributor cap and rotor, spark plug wires and spark plugs.

SENDING UNIT: A mechanical, electrical, hydraulic or electromagnetic device which transmits information to a gauge.

SENSOR: Any device designed to measure engine operating conditions or ambient pressures and temperatures. Usually electronic in nature and designed to send a voltage signal to an on-board computer, some sensors may operate as a simple on/off switch or they may provide a variable voltage signal (like a potentiometer) as conditions or measured parameters change.

SHIM: Spacers of precise, predetermined thickness used between parts to establish a proper working relationship.

SLAVE CYLINDER: In automotive use, a device in the hydraulic clutch system which is activated by hydraulic force, disengaging the clutch.

SOLENOID: A coil used to produce a magnetic field, the effect of which is produce work.

SPARK PLUG: A device screwed into the combustion chamber of a spark ignition engine. The basic construction is a conductive core inside of a ceramic insulator, mounted in an outer conductive base. An electrical charge from the spark plug wire travels along the conductive core and jumps a preset air gap to a grounding point or points at the end of the conductive base. The resultant spark ignites the fuel/air mixture in the combustion chamber.

SPLINES: Ridges machined or cast onto the outer diameter of a shaft or inner diameter of a bore to enable parts to mate without rotation.

TACHOMETER: A device used to measure the rotary speed of an engine, shaft, gear, etc., usually in rotations per minute.

THERMOSTAT: A valve, located in the cooling system of an engine, which is closed when cold and opens gradually in response to engine heating, controlling the temperature of the coolant and rate of coolant flow.

TOP DEAD CENTER (TDC): The point at which the piston reaches the top of its travel on the compression stroke.

TORQUE: The twisting force applied to an object.

TORQUE CONVERTER: A turbine used to transmit power from a driving member to a driven member via hydraulic action, providing changes in drive ratio and torque. In automotive use, it links the driveplate at the rear of the engine to the automatic transmission.

TRANSDUCER: A device used to change a force into an electrical signal.

TRANSISTOR: A semi-conductor component which can be actuated by a small voltage to perform an electrical switching function.

TUNE-UP: A regular maintenance function, usually associated with the replacement and adjustment of parts and components in the electrical and fuel systems of a vehicle for the purpose of attaining optimum performance.

TURBOCHARGER: An exhaust driven pump which compresses intake air and forces it into the combustion chambers at higher than atmospheric pressures. The increased air pressure allows more fuel to be burned and results in increased horsepower being produced.

VACUUM ADVANCE: A device which advances the ignition timing in response to increased engine vacuum.

VACUUM GAUGE: An instrument used to measure the presence of vacuum in a chamber.

VALVE: A device which control the pressure, direction of flow or rate of flow of a liquid or gas.

VALVE CLEARANCE: The measured gap between the end of the valve stem and the rocker arm, cam lobe or follower that activates the valve.

VISCOSITY: The rating of a liquid's internal resistance to flow.

VOLTMETER: An instrument used for measuring electrical force in units called volts. Voltmeters are always connected parallel with the circuit being tested.

WHEEL CYLINDER: Found in the automotive drum brake assembly, it is a device, actuated by hydraulic pressure, which, through internal pistons, pushes the brake shoes outward against the drums.

ABBREVIATIONS AND SYMBOLS

A: Ampere

AC: Alternating current

A/C: Air conditioning

A-h: Ampere hour

AT: Automatic transmission

ATDC: After top dead center

μA: Microampere

bbl: Barrel

BDC: Bottom dead center

bhp: Brake horsepower

BTDC: Before top dead center

BTU: British thermal unit

C: Celsius (Centigrade)

CCA: Cold cranking amps

cd: Candela

cm^2: Square centimeter

cm^3, cc: Cubic centimeter

CO: Carbon monoxide

CO_2: Carbon dioxide

cu.in., in^3: Cubic inch

CV: Constant velocity

Cyl.: Cylinder

DC: Direct current

ECM: Electronic control module

EFE: Early fuel evaporation

EFI: Electronic fuel injection

EGR: Exhaust gas recirculation

Exh.: Exhaust

F: Fahrenheit

F: Farad

pF: Picofarad

μF: Microfarad

FI: Fuel injection

ft.lb., ft. lb., ft. lbs.: foot pound(s)

gal: Gallon

g: Gram

HC: Hydrocarbon

HEI: High energy ignition

HO: High output

hp: Horsepower

Hyd.: Hydraulic

Hz: Hertz

ID: Inside diameter

in.lb.; in. lb.; in. lbs: inch pound(s)

Int.: Intake

K: Kelvin

kg: Kilogram

kHz: Kilohertz

km: Kilometer

km/h: Kilometers per hour

kΩ: Kilohm

kPa: Kilopascal

kV: Kilovolt

kW: Kilowatt

l: Liter

l/s: Liters per second

m: Meter

mA: Milliampere

mg: Milligram

mHz: Megahertz

mm: Millimeter

mm^2: Square millimeter

m^3: Cubic meter

MΩ: Megohm

m/s: Meters per second

MT: Manual transmission

mV: Millivolt

μm: Micrometer

N: Newton

N-m: Newton meter

NOx: Nitrous oxide

OD: Outside diameter

OHC: Over head camshaft

OHV: Over head valve

Ω: Ohm

PCV: Positive crankcase ventilation

psi: Pounds per square inch

pts: Pints

qts: Quarts

rpm: Rotations per minute

rps: Rotations per second

R-12: A refrigerant gas (Freon)

SAE: Society of Automotive Engineers

SO$_2$: Sulfur dioxide

T: Ton

t: Megagram

TBI: Throttle Body Injection

TPS: Throttle Position Sensor

V: 1. Volt; 2. Venturi

μV: Microvolt

W: Watt

$\propto$: Infinity

$<$: Less than

$>$: Greater than

Index

U

U-joints, 142

V

Valve guides, 76
Valves, 39
  Adjustment, 39
  Service, 76
Vehicle identification, 6

W

Water pump, 91
Wheel bearings, 23, 170
Windshield wipers, 15, 123
  Arm, 123
  Blade, 123
  Linkage, 124
  Motor, 123